Wild Excursions

also by DAVID THOMSON

MOVIE MAN
A BOWL OF EGGS
HUNGRY AS HUNTERS

Wild Excursions

The Life and Fiction of
LAURENCE STERNE

DAVID THOMSON

McGRAW-HILL BOOK COMPANY
New York   St. Louis   San Francisco

for Kenneth and Julia Monkman

Could I, whilst Humour held the quill,
Could I digress with half that skill;
Could I with half that skill return,
Which we so much admire in Sterne,
Where each digression, seeming vain,
And only fit to entertain,
Is found, on better recollection,
To have a just and nice connexion,
To help the whole with wondrous art,
When it seems idly to depart;
Then should our readers ne'er accuse
These wild excursions of the Muse.

Charles Churchill, *The Ghost*, Book III, lines 967–78

Indeed Indeed Eliza! my Life will be little better
than a dream, till we approach nearer to each other
—I live scarse conscious of my existence—or as if
I wanted a vital part; & could not live above a few
hours.

Journal to Eliza, 9 July 1767

What will be my fate as a writer is very simple. My
talent for portraying my dreamlike inner life has
thrust all other matters into the background; my
life has dwindled dreadfully, nor will it cease to
dwindle. Nothing else will ever satisfy me.

Franz Kafka, *Diary,* 6 August 1914

The purpose which guided him was not impossible, though
it was supernatural. He wanted to dream a man: he wanted
to dream him with minute integrity and insert him into
reality. This magical project had exhausted the entire
content of his soul; if someone had asked him his own
name or any trait of his previous life, he would not
have been able to answer.

Jorge Luis Borges, *The Circular Ruins*

CONTENTS

ILLUSTRATIONS

The author and publishers are most grateful to the
owners for permission to reproduce the pictures.

ACKNOWLEDGEMENTS

Anyone interested in Laurence Sterne is in debt to Kenneth Monkman, Secretary of the Sterne Trust and now happily resident in the recovered and largely restored Shandy Hall in Coxwold. But for Mr. Monkman, that last real shrine for Sterne addicts would have been lost. As it is, few authors can have a better caretaker, guide and friend. I have benefited from being entertained by the Monkmans in Coxwold and from looking at the surrounding countryside with them. In addition, Mr. Monkman has directed me to sources I might otherwise have missed and persuaded me to consider approaches that I was neglecting. He offered the wisest and most generous advice on this work in manuscript, despite not sharing my basic view of Sterne.

I should also like to thank the following individuals for their help in answering queries: Rev. F.J. Wilson of Sutton on the Forest; Rev. W. Ward of Stillington; Rev. W.M. Atkinson of St. George's, Hanover Square; Rev. F.M. Williams of Cheveley, Suffolk; Rev. H.G. Jamieson of Coolcullen, Co. Carlow; Robert Barton and Patrick Duffy of Annamoe; Dr. Philip O'Connell and W.C. Darmody of Clonmel; Timothy Tuckey of Cork; Thomas Pakenham of Tullynally, Castlepollard, Co. Westmeath; Professor Richard Harrison of the Anatomy School, Cambridge; the late Mrs. Jack Egerton of Coxwold; Ruari McLean; and Lady Mersey for her kindness in allowing me to see and reproduce in this book the Reynolds portrait of Sterne.

I am very grateful for the assistance given by Patrick Henchy of the National Library of Ireland; Miss Geraldine Willis, librarian to the Representative Body of the Church of Ireland; W.P. Smith, county librarian of Westmeath; Miss E.R. Talbot Rice of the National Army Museum; H.M.G. Baillie of the Royal Commission on Historical Manuscripts; O.S. Tomlinson of York City Library; Mrs. N.K.M. Gurney and A.N. Webb of the Borthwick Institute of

Historical Research; Bernard Barr and Canon Reginald Cant of York Minster Library; and the staff of the British Museum Reading Room, the London Library, the Public Record Office and Chichester and Hove public libraries.

I am especially grateful for research in Ireland carried out by Kieran Hickey and for editorial advice from Julia Hornak and Tony Godwin. I hardly dare thank my wife since she now looks on the project in much the way that Mrs. Sterne might have regarded her husband. Her typing, however, can be acclaimed without reservation; as she said herself, it was a pity the book had to be printed.

Prologue: Touched by Sterne

The biographer should not approach Sterne too earnestly or too sure of the value of documentary records. Sterne's best jokes are played on the pompous and his life tends to shrivel under scrutiny. In the same way, the reader of *Tristram Shandy* is quickly made aware of what a complex and perilous process reading is. Sterne's greatest liberty with literary form is paradoxically a product of his own doubts about himself, and the biographer needs to see how chronically the ground before him is undermined. It is almost as if Sterne had deliberately left his own life as shimmering and intangible as the actual career of Yorick, his *alter ego*. Was it partly as a warning to onlookers, but also as a way of avoiding thorough introspection, that Sterne has Yorick make this pronouncement in *A Sentimental Journey?*

There is not a more perplexing affair in life to me, than to set about telling any one who I am—for there is scarce any body I cannot give a better account of than of myself; and I have often wish'd I could do it in a single word—and have an end of it. It was the only time and occasion in my life, I could accomplish this to any purpose—for Shakespear lying upon the table, and recollecting I was in his books, I took up Hamlet, and turning immediately to the grave-diggers scene in the fifth act, I lay'd my finger upon YORICK, and advancing the book to the Count, with my finger all the way over the name—*Me Voici!* said I.[1]

Sterne wrote nine volumes on the life and opinions of Tristram Shandy and, although the book is told in the first person, Tristram remains an obscure, unfinished character. He is sharp only in the crystal-clear description of the accidents that befall him and in the masterful direction of disorder throughout the book. That voice is as misleadingly precise as Kafka's. Regarded as a participant, Tristram stays the silent victim of the domestic chaos of the household into which he is born, where both feeling and intellect have become so distorted that they are unreliable and dangerous.

How can you write the biography of someone so suspicious of facts and so unconvinced by conventional activity? Sterne's answer was that 'it is not actions, but opinions concerning actions, which disturb men.'[2] While actions bring men inescapably together, opinion keeps them resolutely apart; thus understanding is possible only within one brain. It does not travel well, and arrives at another brain looking like prejudice or mistake. From this, Sterne derived a basic sense of human isolation which could make interaction deluding and comic, but which gives his pursuit of feelings an immense poignancy. Sterne has been reproached both for surrendering to feeling and for manipulating his own emotions – in other words, because of some pathological gulf between his head and his heart. But his is a subtler case than that and, despite undoubted failings as a companion, his view of the obstacles to human feelings is profound.

The real nature of Sterne as the man of sensibility is that he could never lose or fulfil himself in his own emotions. Feeling is only thought, and for that reason we can never be sure that overwhelming sensation has been communicated to others faithfully. Nor can we ever fully believe in an emotion so long as our mind remains observant of it. For all we know, that pity we see in ourselves may be sham, that love for another no more than self-love. Thus, it is through our analysis of our feelings that we attempt to discover who and what we are. Sterne's exploration of feeling is seldom out of control, no matter how much it plays with the prospect of disarray. In fact, it is a daring and tormented inquiry into identity. Here, for instance, is Yorick offering comfort to Maria of Moulines, but really speaking to himself:

I sat down close by her; and Maria let me wipe them away as they fell with my handkerchief.—I then steep'd it in my own—and then in hers—and then in mine—and then I wip'd hers again—and as I did it, I felt such undescribable emotions within me, as I am sure could not be accounted for from any combinations of matter and motion.

I am positive I have a soul; nor can all the books with which materialists have pester'd the world ever convince me of the contrary.[3]

***

Sterne's apparently calculated delving into disorder fascinated his contemporaries, but it also made many think that he was a flash-in-the-pan. Dr. Johnson predicted of Sterne: 'Nothing odd will do long. "Tristram Shandy" did not last',[4] but allowed Boswell to be the meticulous recorder of all his own eccentricities, humours and prejudices. And if Dr. Johnson comes down to us as one of the most beguilingly independent, rounded and humane of Englishmen, is it not partly because he himself believed in such a character and worked his way into it?

Sterne took no such care of his life – which may have been a reaction to the harsh way it first dealt with him. He had a family, a wife and a career that all proved unsatisfactory. The immediate realities of his life were such that he could hardly look them in the face. We cannot survey the succession of biographical problems and lacunae in his life without concluding that some of the vagueness came from Sterne as a disguise for inadequacy. Is it because Sterne was not satisfied with or convinced by his own life that a biographer has so often to make a scenario where there is very little reliable evidence? We feel we know Sterne, as if he were a character from fiction; for he put great store by intimacy of tone and rhythm. That feeling of charm is sometimes enough to bridge large gaps in the factual record. It may be that significant events occurred in those gaps of which we are unaware. I think it is possible, however, that very little happened but that Sterne could not admit to emptiness. Many people look back on their own lives and notice only the absence of incident. And for all the activity at certain periods of Sterne's life, it is not always easy to see him participating, so much as hurrying through them. The crucial involvement is imaginary, as if he found it easier to invent a life than experience it.

The feeling of life noticed, overheard and touched in Sterne's work is still absorbing, largely because it is casual and unconventional, giving significance to objects and sights that most writers would not have seen. Sterne is especially attentive to distractions, spontaneity and apparent diversions from a book's path. Significance is an aura he can bestow with a glance; thus he glorifies women, moments of hesitation, chance effects and mundane conversations as if they were the mainstream of life. It is worth emphasizing that in the eighteenth century that was extraordinary originality. Because more writers in this century have abandoned rigid systems of plot and character for a much wider and more fragmentary experience, Sterne seems more in key with the substance and tone of modern fiction than Dr. Johnson would ever have thought possible.

Opinion – or the deduction we make from the sense data we receive – makes Sterne a curiously detached source of emotional excitement. Thus, although he is the most feeling of writers, he has no real commitments. Nor did he in life, as far as I can see. His response is always on the point of overflowing. We might call it high spirits, joy or good humour. But Sterne's attitude is not tranquil or reassuring. It is built on fragile nervous energy and his own craving for intimacy is really the desire for a listener whose attention will convince Sterne of his own existence. For this reason, I do not find Sterne's a comfortable voice. Whatever the ostensible cheerfulness, it is his insecurity that is affecting and penetrating. Perhaps that is why, despite all his efforts to be liked, he has, over the years, earned a barrage of solemn disapproval.

If we think of Sterne as an atmospheric writer – one who attempts to capture readers with the rhetoric of his suspended story-telling and the delicacy of his emotional evocations – then it is remarkable how many notable readers have insisted on being offended. We shall see how many accusations of immodesty, tediousness and nonsense were levelled against him while he was alive. But succeeding generations attacked him principally as a charlatan, a manipulator of bogus feelings. Vicesimus Knox picked out this supposedly corrupting element in Sterne which convinced many people that he was so depraving an author that gentle women should not be allowed to read his books:

That softness, that affected and excessive sympathy at first sight, that sentimental affection, which is but lust in disguise, have been the ruin of thousands of our countrymen and countrywomen, who fancied, that while they were breaking the laws of God and man, they were activated by the fine feelings of *sentimental affections*. How much are divorces multiplied since Sterne appeared![5]

Coleridge, too, claimed that the 'sentimental philosophy' of Sterne and his imitators had allowed 'The vilest appetites and the most remorceless inconsistancy towards their objects' to acquire 'the titles of the *heart*, the *irresistible feelings, the too tender sensibility*'.[6] The urgency of these fears now seems ridiculous, but Thackeray's attack is more interesting because it is made by a man who had thought himself further than most into Sterne's skin:

> I suppose Sterne had this artistical sensibility; he used to blubber perpetually in his study, and finding his tears infectious, and that they brought him a great popularity he exercised the lucrative gift of weeping, he utilised it, and cried on every occasion. I own that I don't value or respect much the cheap dribble of those fountains. He fatigues me with his perpetual disquiet and his uneasy appeals to my risible or sentimental faculties. He is always looking in my face, watching his effect, uncertain whether I think him an impostor or not; posture-making, coaxing and imploring me.[7]

We shall see that Sterne was sometimes so hard-pressed financially that he may have pursued one vein or another in the hope that the public would pay him for it. Nor is there any question but that some of his effects – either jokes or attempts to move us – are disastrous. But most shrewd of all is Thackeray's image of an anxious author watching to see his effect upon us, to see whether we think him an impostor. I would take that image one step farther and say that Sterne was himself anxious to know whether he was genuine or not. If we picture a deliberate fraud we will not come to grips with Sterne.

His uneasiness is essential and that is one reason why rebukes levelled at him so often move from his writing to his life and why several critics have been alarmed by what they take for his pernicious influence on society at large. Thus, when Graham Greene speaks of Sterne's writing being like 'the day-dream conversation of a man with a stutter in a world of his imagination',[8] he is implying how great a compensation fiction was for

Sterne's unhappy life. Leavis's dismissal of 'irresponsible (and nasty) trifling'[9] eliminates Sterne from the Great Tradition on grounds that Sterne himself simply did not credit. If he had been more able to believe in family or in what his Church expected him to teach, or if he had been convinced by either Walter Shandy's busy brain or Toby's soft heart, then he would not have been the writer we know.

That does not mean that his fiction was just an evasion. In many ways, it is more adventurous than anything else written in his age. Fiction, he seems to say, is not just a story for the reader to enjoy vicariously, with moral refinement added to taste, but a means of experimenting with his whole sense of identity; not an escape from reality but something that reproduces the infinite texture of reality as experienced in life. For fiction ultimately is itself the universal form of experience; it is the significance that each person gives to the mass of impressions from the outside world. When we look at another person, we render them a part of our own fictional interpretation of the world. We cannot observe ourselves in any other way than by describing what we do – in the hope that that will clarify us to ourselves. This real height of Sterne's daring is neither cheerful nor playful. It touches instead on a bleak solipsism in its belief that reality for any individual is only a matter of his own consciousness.

Sterne's persistently amused pondering over his own reality is closer to the philosophy than to the fiction of his age. Bishop Berkeley had declared that 'the various sensations or ideas imprinted on the sense, however blended or combined together (that is, whatever objects they compose), cannot exist otherwise than *in* a mind perceiving them.'[10] To exist is to be perceived. But that aphorism can lead to a daunting view of our own powerlessness and perhaps Sterne consoled himself by taking one more step than Berkeley, saying that anything he perceived existed; in other words, to think of a thing is to make it real.

If this flexibility liberated Sterne's fiction and lightened his own view of life, it cannot have made him an easy son, husband or father. Sterne's life seems to me a frightening spectacle of solitude unaffected by company. This makes an extra problem for the biographer: for clearly his life and fiction are complementary, but, equally, the speculativeness that enlivens his fiction is matched by a diffuseness in his life that is sometimes impenetrable.

All too often, the apparent 'facts' of Sterne's life are unrewarding. Every contemporary report of him is a mixture of rumour and knowledge, as if Sterne had been a man about whom people were ready to believe any story. We gain very little from his letters in the way of information. He seldom recounts incidents in which he has been involved. But he lavishly describes the state of his own fluctuating mind. Consciousness, or opinion, was all his life. This passage from Hume's *Treatise of Human Nature* shows how close Sterne's sense of existence in the balance was to those pestering materialist books:

> For my part, when I enter most intimately into what I call *myself*, I always stumble on some particular perception or other, of heat or cold, light or shade, love or hatred, pain or pleasure. I never can catch *myself* at any time without a perception, and never can observe any thing but the perception. When my perceptions are remov'd for any time, as by sound-sleep; so long am I insensible of *myself*, and may truly be said not to exist. And were all my perceptions remov'd by death, and cou'd I neither think, nor feel, nor see, nor live, nor hate after the dissolution of my body, nor do I conceive what is farther requisite to make me a perfect non-entity.[11]

> Indeed Indeed Eliza! my Life will be little better than a dream, till we approach nearer to each other—I live scarse conscious of my existence—or as if I wanted a vital part; & could not live above a few hours.[12]

That is Sterne, writing to Eliza Draper, in July 1767 – when he had only months to live. It is a passage that exactly catches the quality of Sterne's intimacy. It is breathless with the revelation of a confessional brought on by the prospect of extinction; and yet, as soon as Sterne has invoked a listener, he begins to talk to himself. He stares with intense animation into another person's face and uses it as a mirror to reflect his own turmoil. In other words, his attempt to discover an intimate mode that is uniquely his own frustrates the real purpose of intimacy. It remains a style, unable actually to bring human beings together.

We are fortunate in having the portrait of Sterne by Reynolds. It seems to demonstrate just how exceptional and disconcerting Sterne was in the flesh, preoccupied with this impression of intimacy he made on others. His is an actor's face that has studied itself but remains anxious about the spectacle it is making. So demanding a face 'invents' spectators. In the same way, Sterne's literary method insists on the presence of readers and has a variety of tricks that try to take them by the hand:

—Here—pray, Sir, take hold of my cap,—nay, take the bell along with it, and my pantoufles too.—

Now, Sir, they are all at your service; and I freely make you a present of 'em, on condition, you give me all your attention to this chapter.[13]

The portrait was painted by Reynolds in March and April 1760, at the height of Sterne's fame. He had arrived in London that spring with the first two volumes of *Tristram Shandy*. It was an irresistible double act: the country clergyman and the author of the most startling and inventive book anyone had ever read. Sterne was invited all over town and sat for Reynolds when he could spare time between salons, dinners and the pleasure gardens. In view of his suspect health, it is not surprising that several commentators have judged that, wearied by London, Sterne is propping himself up. But the painting conveys no sense of Sterne's head being slumped upon his hand. Instead, the sprightly framing of the upright finger directs us point-blank into those consuming eyes.

A masterly portrait, but an exceptionally vivid face, by turns sly and amiable. In an age of photography we have learnt of the subtle ways in which a sitter may influence a portrait. And Sterne, who was an amateur painter and believed that the eye had 'the quickest commerce with the soul'[14] may have provided some of those details that are attributed to Reynolds. Admirers of the painter have remarked on how the slight displacement of the wig gives the effect of disturbance. But Sterne, too, had experimented with wigs. Tristram tells us that having thrown the wrong sheet of paper into the fire, 'Instantly I snatch'd off my wig, and threw it perpendicularly, with all imaginable violence, up to the top of the room—indeed I caught it as it fell.'[15] Even the pose in which Reynolds had shown him was one that Sterne later advertised for himself, writing to Eliza Draper that he had 'leand the whole day with my head upon My hand; sitting most dejectedly at the Table with my Eliza's Picture before me—sympathizing & soothing me'.[16]

Sterne died eight years after Reynolds had painted his portrait, with his hand outstretched. The witness of his death recorded, 'He put up his hand as if to stop a blow, and died in a minute.'[17] It was an oddly appropriate gesture. His fictional farewell, made only three weeks before his death, had caught Yorick's hand suspended in a sentimental void just short of enjoying the fille de chambre's *

Touching for Sterne was an erotic sensation, but much more than that. He feels his way out of darkness and uncertainty, touching ideas into life. *A Sentimental Journey* is a catalogue of touch as Yorick encounters one responsive woman after another. Its trembling excitement often comes close to prurience, and Sterne's life suggests that his contacts with women were often bluntly practical. But the touching in *A Sentimental Journey* is the action of a dreamer, inventing for himself skins of impossible texture and gentleness, and conjuring up unalloyed sympathetic mingling such as he had never found in reality. The touch is a metaphor for his whole use of fiction. *A Sentimental Journey* is thus a travelogue through a man's own sensibility, perhaps the first journey into interior monologue. It contains the finest examples of Sterne's masquerade as a real person.

Yorick's first sentimental encounter is at Calais with a lady who 'had a black pair of silk gloves open only at the thumb and two fore-fingers'.[18] Immediately touch becomes the primary sense. They fall into conversation and he 'continued holding her hand almost without knowing it'. Their flirtation proceeds, and when she mocks his English habit of allowing his heart to rule his head, 'she disengaged her hand with a look which I thought a sufficient commentary upon the text.'[19] Yorick is 'mortified with the loss of her hand'; but in a few seconds it re-alights on the

---

* It would be wrong to end the sentence with a full stop – even the asterisk must keep a respectful distance. The last sentence of *A Sentimental Journey* is: 'So that when I stretch'd out my hand, I caught hold of the Fille de Chambre's' The reader will recollect that Yorick was in the dark and must imagine that last touch. Sterne knew best when not to go on.

cuff of his coat and 'God knows how' they touch again. When the lady gives way to melancholy, touch is indistinguishable from feeling:

The pulsations of the arteries along my fingers pressing across hers, told her what was passing within me: she looked down—a silence of some moments followed.

I fear, in this interval, I must have made some slight efforts towards a closer compression of her hand, from a subtle sensation I felt in the palm of my own—not as if she was going to withdraw hers—but, as if she thought about it—and I had infallibly lost it a second time, had not instinct more than reason directed me to the last resource in these dangers—to hold it loosely, and in a manner as if I was every moment going to release it, of myself.[20]

This instinctive brinkmanship of sensibility may be a small skill, but Sterne is master of it. In Paris he calls at a glove shop to ask the way. The girl in the shop gives him instructions, but he is too entranced with her to listen to the directions. Only in the street does he realize that he has not taken in a word she said. He therefore returns to the shop to wait for the company of a messenger who has an errand in that part of town.

—He will be ready, Monsieur, said she, in a moment—And in that moment, replied I, most willingly would I say something very civil to you for all these courtesies. Any one may do a casual act of good nature, but a continuation of them shews it is a part of the temperature; and certainly, added I, if it is the same blood which comes from the heart, which descends to the extremes (touching her wrist) I am sure you must have one of the best pulses of any woman in the world—Feel it, said she, holding out her arm. So laying down my hat, I took hold of her fingers in one hand, and applied the two fore-fingers of my other to the artery—[21]

While they are testing each other's pulse, it occurs to Yorick that he might buy a pair of gloves. What follows takes touch into Sterne's favourite innuendo – of whim, seriousness and nonsense:

The beautiful Grisset rose up when I said this, and going behind the counter, reach'd down a parcel and untied it: I advanced to the side over-against her: they were all too large. The beautiful Grisset measured them one by one across my hand—It would not alter the dimensions—She begg'd I would try a single pair, which seemed to be the least—She held it open—my hand slipp'd into it at once—It will not do, said I, shaking my head a little—No, said she, doing the same thing.

There are certain combined looks of simple subtlety—where whim, and sense, and seriousness, and nonsense, are so blended, that all the languages of Babel set loose together could not express them—they are communicated and caught so instantaneously, that you can scarce say which party is the infecter. I leave it to your men of words to swell pages about it—it is enough in the present to say again, the gloves would not do; so folding our hands within our arms, we both loll'd upon the counter—it was narrow, and there was just room for the parcel to lay between us.

The beautiful Grisset look'd sometimes at the gloves, then sideways to the window, then at the gloves—and then at me. I was not disposed to break silence—I follow'd her example: so I look'd at the gloves, then to the window, then at the gloves, and then at her—and so on alternately.

I found I lost considerably in every attack—she had a quick black eye, and shot through two such long and silken eye-lashes with such penetration, that she look'd into my very heart and reins—It may seem strange, but I could actually feel she did—[22]

That last insistent sentence is not affectation but the sign of Sterne's preference for imaginative reality. Living so much within himself, his only way of avoiding the effect of self-preoccupation was so to dramatize himself that he could believe other people were able to look into him and see his 'soul stark naked'. For it is not merely a metaphor by which Sterne talks of someone looking into his heart. Indeed, he played with the thought that the interior might be visible. Part of the claustrophobia of Shandy Hall comes from the variety of images that refer to the innards of the human body. At one point in *Tristram Shandy* he speculates on the consequences of a window being placed in every human breast:

. . . had the said glass been there set up, nothing more would have been wanting, in order to have taken a man's character, but to have taken a chair and gone softly, as you would to a dioptrical bee-hive, and look'd in,—view'd the soul stark naked;—observ'd all her motions,—her machinations;—traced all her maggots from their first engendering to their crawling forth;—watched her loose in her frisks, her gambols, her capricios; and after some notice of her more solemn

deportment, consequent upon such frisks, &c.—then taken your pen
and ink and set down nothing but what you had seen, and could
have sworn to . . .[23]

In so many ways, that is an account of Sterne's own fictional
method. He is truly an interior writer, largely dispensing with
exterior reality and uniquely conveying the impression made by
events on nerves and brain.

No wonder Reynolds depicted Sterne with hand to head.
Which writer has fretted so pathologically about the actual
contents of his skull? 'Such a head!' he exclaims in *Tristram
Shandy*, '. . . would to heaven! my enemies only saw the inside of
it!'[24] Ideas to Sterne are not abstractions but animate things
'floating' in the brain. He describes whimsical notions – 'such
guests who, after a free and undisturbed entrance, for some
years, into our brains,—at length claim a kind of settlement
there'.[25] Another thought 'floated only in Dr *Slop*'s mind,
without sail or ballast to it, as a simple proposition; millions of
which, as your worship knows, are every day swimming quietly
in the middle of the thin juice of a man's understanding'.[26] It is
not always easy to decide how comic Sterne's learned descriptions of the brain are. Undoubtedly he had read widely if
sketchily on human physiology and could be persuaded into
mapping out the understanding as neatly as Toby might have
planned a siege:

> What, therefore, seem'd the least liable to objections of any, was,
> that the chief sensorium, or head-quarters of the soul, and to which
> place all intelligences were referred, and from whence all her man-
> dates were issued,—was in, or near, the cerebellum,—or rather
> some-where about the *medulla oblongata*, wherein it was generally
> agreed by *Dutch* anatomists, that all the minute nerves from all the
> organs of the seven senses concentered, like streets and winding alleys,
> into a square.[27]

With Sterne's eye, we look into the human frame and see one
of those fearsomely literal and functioning machines that Bosch
stripped away skin to reveal. Sterne, too, characterizes the parts
of the body and sometimes speaks of it as if it were some
immense underground factory. Ideas, in their abundance and
fragility, are like spermatozoa. While there is comic alarm

attached to Tristram's account of his conception, yet the language suggests the animism that was mixed in Sterne's view of human nature. Thus, Tristram describes what occurred at the moment of his own conception when his mother interjected the 'unseasonable question' about the clock: '... it scattered and dispersed the animal spirits, whose business it was to have escorted and gone hand-in-hand with the *HOMUN-CULUS*, and conducted him safe to the place destined for his reception.'[28]

Here is a paradox in Sterne: that he sensed advanced mechanical interpretations of the human body and understanding, but did so in such terms that he sometimes sounds like a medievalist composing the humours of the personality. The more one reads Sterne, the less satisfactory it seems to place him on a time scale. His intuition reaches backwards and forwards from his own age and never manages to allay those doubts he had about his own security. Although he laughs at his internal preoccupation, he also dwelt neurotically upon the minute functioning of himself.

Tristram confesses that, 'of all things in the world, I understand the least of mechanism',[29] but he also says that 'our family was certainly a simple machine, as it consisted of a few wheels; yet there was thus much to be said for it, that these wheels were set in motion by so many different springs, and acted one upon the other from such a variety of strange principles and impulses,—that though it was a simple machine, it had all the honour and advantages of a complex one.'[30] The book itself is often mentioned in terms of mechanical imagery. Thus, the impulsive digressionary instinct is explained – 'I have constructed the main work and the adventitious parts of it with such intersections, and have so complicated and involved the digressive and progressive movements, one wheel within another, that the whole machine, in general, has been kept a-going.'[31]

But for every picture of cogged wheels, Sterne has a recipe for the animal spirits or humours of the body. Yorick, Sterne's portrait of himself, 'instead of that cold phlegm and exact regularity of sense and humours, you would have look'd for, in one so extracted;—he was, on the contrary, as mercurial and sublimated a composition'.[32] On another occasion, Sterne prescribes for the reader:

> ... that the great gifts and endowments both of wit and judgment, with every thing which usually goes along with them,—such as memory, fancy, genius, eloquence, quick parts, and what not, may this precious moment without stint or measure, let or hinderance, be poured down warm as each of us could bear it,—scum and sediment an' all (for I would not have a drop lost) into the several receptacles, cells, cellules, domiciles, dormitories, refectories, and spare places of our brains,—in such sort, that they might continue to be injected and tunn'd into, according to the true intent and meaning of my wish, until every vessel of them, both great and small, be so replenished, saturated and fill'd up therewith, that no more, would it save a man's life, could possibly be got either in or out.[33]

It might be said that this characteristic preoccupation with inner workings is a part of Sterne's philosophy of saying whatever comes into his head. But that only shows how closely calculation and spontaneity accompany one another in his work.

***

As the first reviewers took pleasure in pointing out, Sterne had written two volumes of *Tristram Shandy* without his narrator even being born. But it is not only the first two volumes that have a 'uterine' narrative. For apart from the sudden trip to France in Volume VII, and the affair between Widow Wadman and Uncle Toby, Tristram records the Shandy household, mute, helpless and vulnerable. So far does he participate only as a victim that the house itself serves as an extension of his mother's womb and an image of a dark uncontrollable world in which the individual is never freed from a sense of mystery. A great part of the book fulfils the worst fears expressed in Volume I, Chapter II, when Tristram is considering the ordeal of the unborn homunculus:

> ... what if any accident had befallen him in his way alone?—or that, thro' terror of it, natural to so young a traveller, my little gentleman had got to his journey's end miserably spent;—his muscular strength and virility worn down to a thread;—his own animal spirits ruffled beyond description,—and that in this sad disorder'd state of nerves, he had laid down a prey to sudden starts,

or a series of melancholy dreams and fancies for nine long, long months together.—I tremble to think what a foundation had been laid for a thousand weaknesses both of body and mind, which no skill of the physician or the philosopher could ever afterwards have set thoroughly to rights.[34]

Many critics have thought it whimsical and sportive of Sterne to begin with Tristram before birth. Certainly the passage just quoted, in its context, is gay with mock alarm. But gaiety rarely goes deep with Sterne. Isolate the passage and it becomes immensely disturbing, not only because of the real dangers it lists, but because of the process of exaggeration at work in the writer's mind. Sterne is pathologically alarmed by his own awareness of the vulnerability of the human organism. As we shall see, he had ample reason to feel emotionally insecure and his health preyed upon him for most of his adult life. The reader must judge whether these are sufficient explanation for his rabid originality and tortuous self-consciousness.

At present, let us look at some of his fears of disintegration. That head seemed in constant danger. Not only was Sterne accident prone in life, but in his writings we may find 'pudding headed', 'muddleheaded', 'harebrained', 'doddypole', 'jolt head', 'ninnyhammer', 'crack-brained' and, of course, 'shandy-headed'.* In a letter of 1760, Sterne talks of a man's brains being 'as dry as a squeez'd Orange'.[35] When the Shandys are discussing the effect of Dr. Slop's calipers on Tristram's head, 'I maintain it, said my uncle *Toby*, it would have broke the cerebellum (unless indeed the skull had been as hard as a granado), and turned it all into a perfect posset. Pshaw! replied Dr. *Slop*, a child's head is naturally as soft as the pap of an apple.'[36] Later on, when Walter Shandy is proposing a scheme of education whereby every word in the dictionary 'is converted into a thesis or an hypothesis', every hypothesis into propositions, every proposition to consequences and conclusions, all of which lead on to 'fresh tracks of enquiries and doubtings', there is an exchange that hints at the physical manifestations of confusion in Sterne's mind:

---

* 'Shandy' is a Yorkshire dialect word – now out of use – meaning crack-brained, odd or unconventional.

'The force of this engine, added my father, is incredible, in opening a child's head.—'Tis enough, brother *Shandy*, cried my uncle *Toby*, to burst it into a thousand splinters.'[37]

But although Tristram is the victim of so many of his father's opinions, it is notable that Sterne and Walter Shandy share some attitudes towards the sensitive but fragile mechanism of the brain. Once again mock alarm is involved, but who can doubt that there is real anguish in Walter Shandy's lament upon the fate of a head when it is thrust through from the womb at the moment of birth:

Good God! cried my father, what havock and destruction must this make in the infinitely fine and tender texture of the cerebellum! —Or if there is such a juice as *Borri* pretends,—is it not enough to make the clearest liquor in the world both feculent and mothery? But how great was his apprehension, when he further understood, that this force, acting upon the very vertex of the head, not only injured the brain itself or cerebrum,—but that it necessarily squeez'd and propell'd the cerebrum towards the cerebellum, which was the immediate seat of the understanding.—Angels and Ministers of grace defend us! cried my father,—can any soul withstand this shock?—No wonder the intellectual web is so rent and tatter'd as we see it; and that so many of our best heads are no better than a puzzled skein of silk,—all perplexity,—all confusion within side.[38]

Just as Sterne is most conscious of the capacity for derangement in what is generally recognized as a self-balancing mechanism, so the body in his work is a source of confusion, embarrassment and distress. Sterne not only conveys a sense of powerlessness over his own limbs but he persuades himself that such precarious self-control as he has is vulnerable to every suggestion, every possibility. He asks us to witness that he is out of control and that sense takes second place to sensibility:

But mark, madam, we live amongst riddles and mysteries— the most obvious things, which come in our way, have dark sides, which the quickest sight cannot penetrate into; and even the clearest and most exalted understandings amongst us find ourselves puzzled and at a loss in almost every cranny of nature's works; so that this, like a thousand other things, falls out for us in a way, which tho' we cannot reason upon it,—yet we find the good of it, may it please your reverences and your worships—and that's enough for us.[39]

Not all of Sterne's contemporaries would have accepted that 'we cannot reason upon it.' For all the curiosity with which he unravelled the fine workings of human beings, it seems sometimes to have left him incapable of acting or deciding. He was so weighed on by the nervous detail of life that he could not always recognize an outer reality that he might share with other people. He had seen the absurdity of sequence, and so there is no plot in his books. Instead there is a motion, or travelling, that neurotic flicker of activity that keeps melancholy at bay. When Walter Shandy hears that the nose of his infant son has been crushed 'as flat as a pancake to his face', he is led, distraught, to his room so that he may collapse on his bed. That fall is described in immense, obsessive detail so that simultaneously we are struck by the comedy of regret and overpowered by the giant bodily presence that conveys it:

The moment my father got up into his chamber, he threw himself prostrate across his bed in the wildest disorder imaginable, but at the same time, in the most lamentable attitude of a man borne down with sorrows, that ever the eye of pity dropp'd a tear for.—The palm of his right hand, as he fell upon the bed, receiving his forehead, and covering the greatest part of both his eyes, gently sunk down with his head (his elbow giving way backwards) till his nose touch'd the quilt;—his left arm hung insensible over the side of the bed, his knuckles reclining upon the handle of the chamber pot, which peep'd out beyond the valance,—his right leg (his left being drawn up towards his body) hung half over the side of the bed, the edge of it pressing upon his shin-bone.[40]

He is left in this posture for several chapters. When we return to him, he lies there apparently unaltered; but, in fact, boredom has infiltrated disaster:

My father lay stretched across the bed as still as if the hand of death had pushed him down, for a full hour and a half, before he began to play upon the floor with the toe of that foot which hung over the bed-side.[41]

It is as if in a body stilled by doubt there was an irresistible current of motion – of electrical activity, of cellular growth, of nervous tremble – that persuaded inertia into movement. We have seen how consistently Sterne thought of the mobility of the tiny parts of the body, whether cogs or tadpole-like ideas. We shall see that his childhood was harrowingly restless and that, after a period of subdued pastoral retreat, he began a period of travelling between Yorkshire, London and the continent that only stopped with his death. The effect of motion at either end of his life is all the greater because of the central immobility.

But even in those middle years there is evidence of the soothing influence of motion on Sterne. Yorick liked to ride about the country on his horse, in which occupation he could spend his time 'to as much account as in his study'. The only difference the rural scene made was that, instead of the haste Sterne adopted later in life, Yorick liked to amble since 'brisk trotting and slow argumentation, like wit and judgment, were two incompatible movements.—But that upon his steed—he could unite and reconcile every thing,—he could compose his sermon,—he could compose his cough.'[42]

So composed a tread, as in some other parts of Yorick's life, may have been a daydream of Sterne's. Those interior forces often threatened to get out of hand, like the coaches in which Sterne seemed always on the point of accident. Enthusiasm in Sterne all too quickly became headlong. Hurry and dawdle might sometimes be confused. Sterne's nervy appetite for motion frequently made him incapable of an objective judgement of it. Or if it is not a matter of nervous dissatisfaction, then it is the result of a perverse unwillingness to be calm. In *A Sentimental Journey*, Yorick's animal spirits oscillate wildly as he rides in a coach through France. At first the postillion lashes the horses so that they 'set off clattering like a thousand devils'. Yorick is made miserable by the gallop – 'he'll go on tearing my nerves to pieces till he has worked me into a foolish passion, and then he'll go slow, that I may enjoy the sweets of it.' But by the time the postillion has slowed down, Yorick has been so put out of temper that slowness is inappropriate – 'a good rattling gallop would have been of real service to me.'[43]

At the beginning of Volume V of *Tristram Shandy*, the reader is addressed directly – though whether by Tristram or Sterne is not clear: that sort of ambiguity is typical of the man in that it

Laurence Sterne, painted by Reynolds, 1760

The millstream at Annamoe, County Wicklow, as photographed in the 1880s by Robert French for the William Lawrence collection

enabled him to feel free of any identity. The narrator is once more in a coach in a delirium of speed: 'He flew like lightning—there was a slope of three miles and a half—we scarce touched the ground—the motion was most rapid—most impetuous—'twas communicated to my brain—my heart partook of it.' He is so aghast at the empty hurry that he makes a vow: 'I will lock up my study door the moment I get home, and throw the key of it ninety feet below the surface of the earth, into the draw-well at the back of my house.'[44]

But once fame and money had set Sterne free, he never stayed long in one place. One of the hardest tasks for his biographer is to gauge the seriousness and nature of his illness. It was for reasons of health, ostensibly, that Sterne left England for the continent where he might best indulge that rootless detachment so characteristic of his own travelling. As in a dream, motion itself seems to have comforted him. And although in *Tristram Shandy* he depicts his flight to France as being prompted by the appearance of Death, the actual escape was so energetic as to risk life and limb:

> . . . then by heaven! I will lead him a dance he little thinks of—for I will gallop, quoth I, without looking once behind me, to the banks of the *Garonne*; and if I hear him clattering at my heels—I'll scamper away to mount *Vesuvius*—from thence to *Joppa*, and from *Joppa* to the world's end, where, if he follows me, I pray God he may break his neck—
> . . . *Allons!* said I; the post boy gave a crack with his whip—off I went like a cannon, and in half a dozen bounds got into *Dover*.[45]

For all the description of his own ill health, no crisis is more affecting than that on the boat to France. The intensity of this giddiness is extraordinary, and yet there is a sense of the victim enjoying it. Indeed, he talks of its effects upon him as a man might wonder whether hallucinogens enhanced his insight. As so often, we see how closely Sterne associated the pattern of brainstorm with his own literary style:

> Pray captain, quoth I, as I was going down into the cabin, is a man never overtaken by *Death* in this passage?
> Why, there is not time for a man to be sick in it, replied he—What a cursed lyar! for I am sick as a horse, quoth I, already—what a

B

brain!—upside down!—hey dey! the cells are broke loose one into another, and the blood, and the lymph, and the nervous juices, with the fix'd and volatile salts, are all jumbled into one mass—good g—! every thing turns round in it like a thousand whirlpools—I'd give a shilling to know if I shan't write the clearer for it.[46]

***

I have begun with a consideration of the imagery and pace of Sterne's language because so much depends on our reaction to the pulse of his style. Even today it is not possible to think of a writer who so successfully asserts that he may write what he choose, that the transforming effect of his pen upon words is sufficient to hold a reader's attention. Sterne saw that fiction was less a story than whatever author, publisher and printer composed to present within covers under the name of a book.

It is a part of this intrigue that Sterne played with spontaneity, for he was intelligent enough to know how rarely a man surprises himself no matter how frequently he makes the crowd gasp. Although, as we have seen, he willingly entered into his own haste and impulsiveness, so that he sometimes whirled himself off his feet into some weird suspension of real being, he was constantly self-conscious. This literary style, that inimitable transcript of breathlessness and hey-go-mad, is also corrected, polished, measured and nurtured. To run very fast demands strict training.

No amount of training, however, can make a sprinter out of a trotter. For all that we need to be sceptical of Sterne's admission that *Tristram Shandy* was published 'hot as it came from my Brain, without one Correction'[47] or that writing, 'when properly managed . . . is but a different name for conversation',[48] we cannot dismiss his insistence – 'Ask my pen,—it governs me,— I govern not it.'[49] That belief is to be found in both *Tristram Shandy* and the letters; doubtless Sterne cultivated it as a defence. It must have been a suitably cryptic answer to the questions showered on him at fashionable salons. Psychologically, it had the added attraction of seeming to excuse the author himself, and of allowing him to think he had escaped the ordinary.

We must be careful of Sterne's own descriptions of himself as a writer. They are conflicting; but perhaps it is the contradiction that especially characterizes Sterne. In matters of travel, as we have seen, he alternated between an amble and a rush. So, in style, he liked sometimes to think himself careful, but otherwise was enchanted with his own surrender to heady spontaneity.

'I begin with writing the first sentence,' he wrote, '—and trusting to Almighty God for the second.'[50] There are enough places where that trust seems to have been betrayed for us to believe that he often wrote out of sheer openness to whim, some momentary intrusion or the unmanageable tremor of his brain. But there may have been more motive for the irregularity than this allows. To be unconventional was perhaps the role Sterne had adopted for himself, the one area in which he might be preeminent. Is that why he delights so much in challenging the reader? Was surprise a psychological necessity, as much as a literary device or a ploy to keep tedium at bay?

What these perplexities of my uncle *Toby* were,—'tis impossible for you to guess;—if you could,—I should blush; not as a relation,—not as a man,—nor even as a woman,—but I should blush as an author; inasmuch as I set no small store by myself upon this very account, that my reader has never yet been able to guess at any thing. And in this, Sir, I am of so nice and singular a humour, that if I thought you was able to form the least judgment or probable conjecture to yourself, of what was to come in the next page,—I would tear it out of my book.[51]

But although there are chasms in *Tristram Shandy*, and although Sterne is a master of suggestion by omission, we can hardly argue that rigorous self-criticism accounted for his small output. For even allowing that he wrote for publication for only nine years, he produced but two books, and one of those a slim volume. Not that an inspection of his life encourages the idea that he wrote slowly. Whenever he overcame all other temptations and sat himself down to write, he produced quickly. Sterne once spoke of what he wrote as 'a copy of the present train running cross my brain',[52] and described his customary method of working thus: '—dropping thy pen,—spurting thy ink about thy table and thy books,—as if thy pen and thy ink, thy books and thy furniture cost thee nothing'.[53]

From the manuscripts that survive, it is not easy to decide

how far quickness excluded carefulness or the sense of nicety in words that Sterne sometimes advocated. His vocabulary – like his whole method – is as striking because of its arbitrariness and strangeness as because of its finesse. The flavour of the style is, indeed, conversational rather than literary, but the conversation of an eccentric. A great part of the persuasiveness of Sterne's work is that the reader begins to mutter and breathe with the style, constrained and propelled by the punctuation. Sterne's punctuation is entirely personal, less grammatically useful than a tic that occupies a quick pen. Full stops, dashes and dots mark the page like skid marks and places where he has had to brake or accelerate. Again, this is an attempt by Sterne to impress intimacy upon us until we sometimes believe we hear the scrape of his pen. Not every reader can tolerate such disturbance and there are passages in his work that are as nervously exhausting to read as they must have been stimulating to the author. Time and again the dots and dashes make a nervous join for sentences which do not work grammatically. The sense of being shown the flux of Sterne's brain is sometimes eerie – most of all when he draws the lines by which he suggests the first four volumes of *Tristram Shandy* have moved:

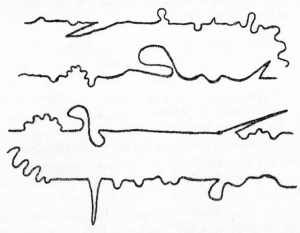

How near those lines are to the unwinding trails of an encephalograph. I do not mean to suggest that Sterne cannot be enjoyed or understood without his manuscript being electronically scanned. But it can hardly be denied that Sterne had an exceptional intuition of what went on inside a brain.

One of the most impressive instances of this is contained in a piece that was casual even by Sterne's standards. In 1762 his Yorkshire friend, John Hall-Stevenson, published a volume of *Crazy Tales*, which purported to be a collection of anecdotes from the circle that used to gather at Hall-Stevenson's home, Skelton Castle. Sterne was a member of that circle and his own contribution contains this fascinating confession, which is as deliberately revealing as anything by Rousseau:

> For to this day, when with much pain,
> I try to think strait on, and clever,
> I sidle out again, and strike
> Into the beautiful oblique.
>
> Therefore, I have no one notion,
> That is not form'd, like the designing
> Of the peristaltick motion;
> Vermicular; twisting and twining;
>   Going to work
> Just like a bottle-skrew upon a cork.[54]

We need look no further for a demonstration of this than to that flourish Trim made with his stick in praise of a man's freedom to remain celibate:

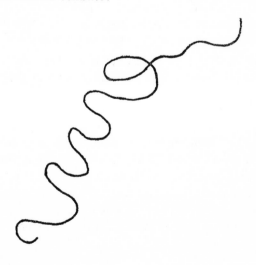

The nervous pitch of his writing cannot be dismissed. Indeed, it is one of the reasons why Sterne can be read today with so few of the allowances that one has to make for other eighteenth-century writers. It is no answer to the problem in a man's work to say that he is modern. In many ways Sterne is deliberately archaic, and must have seemed so in 1760. What is important is that, unlike his contemporaries, he believed that what went on in his own head was the most important thing in the world.

***

In view of the great personal attention Sterne attracted during his lifetime it is remarkable that no proper biography was written until almost a hundred years after his death. By then so much had been forgotten, destroyed or allowed to escape that we will never have a life of Sterne that is complete or which can avoid being built around the qualitative change in his pace and outlook after the publication of *Tristram Shandy*.

The circumstances that led to so long a delay seem genuine enough, but one cannot escape the feeling that Sterne himself had confused his life to confound a diligent recorder. There was a taste for disguise in Sterne that he may have carried with him all his life. Part of this attitude was his disparagement of fact – thus Tristram could declare in Chapter XIV of Volume I, 'I have been at it these six weeks, making all the speed I possibly could,—and am not yet born.' And Sterne himself may have used this facile enigma:

—My good friend, quoth I—as sure as I am I—and you are you— And who are you? said he.——Don't puzzle me; said I.[55]

One can hear Sterne charming a literary salon with that diffidence, and thereby only provoking every gossip-monger in town to fill in the details for him. There is every reason for thinking that Sterne discreetly fostered his own scandalous reputation, just as he took great care to keep his early life secret. The first account of Sterne's life appeared in May 1760 in the *Royal Female Magazine* on the principle that 'the chit chat of the day is the most agreeable of all histories.' It was a ragbag of stories and half-truths. Sterne disliked the article and the explanation it involved him in; but there were some who said that he had himself been involved in its production.

Sterne died eight years later – years that contain the major part of what we now think of as his 'life', and yet which are strangely empty of concrete incident and still contain some of those languors that overtook him in the country. I do not simply mean that he kept no diary and squandered records, but that he did not take himself with the necessary seriousness that is so essential to English biography. He took very little interest in events outside himself and hardly passes an opinion on the actual social, religious and political issues of his time. He did not live in the conventional order from day to day, but grew strong or weak like the wind. So much so that he seldom bothered to note – or even noticed – the external stimuli working on him. Nothing shows as well how artifice occupied him at the expense of real life than that passage in *Tristram Shandy* when he attempts to reconcile his incessant digression and the fact that time is advancing faster than he is getting on with his life:

... instead of advancing, as a common writer, in my work with what I have been doing at it—on the contrary, I am just thrown so many volumes back—was every day of my life to be as busy a day as this—And why not?—and the transactions and opinions of it to take up as much description—And for what reason should they be cut short? as at this rate I should just live 364 times faster than I should write.[56]

Thus the effect of speed and the remarkable failure ever to arrive. There is the same imbalance in his letters, which are so essential to the life. We have barely two hundred and fifty Sterne letters – a fraction of what he must have written. But it is no exaggeration to say that those letters, including the *Journal to Eliza*, are as valuable as *Tristram Shandy* or *A Sentimental Journey*. It is not only Sterne's trick of making certain passages serve in both his correspondence and his fiction that makes us remark on the similarity of tone and excited self-observation. In both, Sterne talked to himself – to persuade himself that he really existed and to attach some character to his recklessly itinerant mind.

After his death, mystery, rumour and deception added to Sterne's reputation and prevented a reliable account of his life. His widow and daughter were left impoverished so that every

project they had for exploiting Sterne's papers was prompted by
the income it might earn. They proposed a biography of Sterne,
not in any spirit of objective truth, but to make a publishing
coup. John Wilkes, a passing companion of the writer, and at
that time idle in prison, had suggested that he might write a life
of Sterne. When Sterne's Yorkshire crony, John Hall-Stevenson, published a fraudulent conclusion to *A Sentimental Journey*,
purportedly based on Sterne's own notes and remarks, this
initiative qualified him as a fellow-biographer for Wilkes. A
collection of letters was to accompany this, illustrated with
several drawings by Sterne's daughter, Lydia.

Although the project was not scholarly, we can only regret
that it failed to materialize. For two years Lydia wrote beseech-
ing letters to the two men complaining of the straitened circumstances of her mother and herself. But Hall-Stevenson was
'somewhat lazy' and Wilkes busy at the centre of one of the
major controversies of the age.

By February 1770, Lydia made a last effort and wrote to
Hall-Stevenson:

> 'tis at least six months since I wrote to you on an interesting subject
> to us namely to put you in mind of a kind promise you made me of
> assisting Mr Wilk's in the scheme he had form'd for our benefit of
> writing the life of Mr Sterne. I wrote also to him. but you have
> neither of you favour'd me with an answer. if you ever felt what
> hope defer'd occasions, you would not have put us under that
> painful situation. – from whom the neglect arises I know not but
> surely a line from you dear S^r would not have cost you much
> trouble – tax me not with boldness for using the word neglect. as
> you both promised out of the benevolence of your hearts to Write
> my Father's life for the benefit of his Widow & Daughter and as I
> myself look upon a promise as sacred & I Doubt not but you do
> think as I do. in that case the word is not improper – in short dear
> S^r I ask but this of you to tell me by a very short letter whether we may
> depend on your's & Mr Wilks's promise. – or if we must renounce
> the pleasing expectation – but dear S^r consider that the fulfilling
> of it may put 400 £ into our pockets & that the declining it would be
> unkind after having made us hope & depend upon that kindness.[57]

One obstacle may have been that the would-be authors
could not find much to say about Sterne's life. There was not

only a shortage of material, but family inhibition about some of the existing evidence. The first member of the family to examine Sterne's papers after his death had been Mrs. Sterne's brother-in-law, the Rev. John Botham. He read every paper in Sterne's last lodgings in Old Bond Street and 'burnt what he did not think proper to communicate to us [Lydia and Mrs. Sterne]'.[58] The reactions of daughter and widow to such domineering solicitousness were very mixed, as Lydia confessed:

it was not mama's intention that any one shou'd read my Father's papers. well knowing that there was some amongst them which ought not to have been seen no not even by his Daughter nor shᵈ I have wish'd to see one of them! mama is very much chagrin'd at this for notwithstanding she can perhaps rely on Mʳ Botham's secrecy yet it grieves that even he should be so well acquainted with certain anecdotes. but to burn any paper was very wrong I hope he will cease so doing, & leave that care to Mama.[59]

Perhaps Lydia would have been content to publish such letters so long as she was not called upon to look at them herself. She continued to treat them ambiguously. In 1769 she spoke of her father's letters to Wilkes and said that, though they might be dangled in front of a publisher if he was cool about the biography, 'entre nous we neither of us wish to publish those letters but if we cannot do otherwise we will & prefix the life to them.'[60] But when that life failed, Lydia was driven back upon a collection of letters and again, in 1775, wrote to Wilkes for those he had from her father. It is a sign of the thoroughness with which Wilkes had cut himself off from the project that he had by then destroyed the letters. Undaunted, Lydia wrote back asking Wilkes to be 'so good as to write a few letters in imitation of her father's style'[61] so that she could use them in the collection.

In October 1775, Lydia duly published 117 letters by her father as well as *Memoirs of the Life and Family of the late Rev. Mr. Laurence Sterne*. This last, some 1,700 words long, is the single most valuable item for the biographer of Sterne. It is not without curiosity and, even though one cannot do anything but use it, it is only proper to state a few doubts. Lydia's editorship is perhaps the chief cause for concern. Wilbur Cross said of the

1775 publication of letters that, 'It would . . . be difficult to find in the entire range of literary biography a more shiftless piece of work.'[62] The letters were often misdated and in several cases had been seriously tampered with in a clumsy effort to preserve the family reputation. As to the Memoir, no manuscript of it survives and one wonders that so indigent and enterprising a daughter should have waited seven years to publish it if it had been in her possession all that time. The Memoir appears to have been written late in 1767 'for my Lydia, in case hereafter she might have a curiosity, or kinder motive to know'[63] the facts of her father's life. It contains nothing scandalous and is largely borne out by the otherwise verifiable details of Sterne's career. But it is remarkably concentrated on Sterne's early years, giving a minute account of his childhood but gradually declining in exactness so that the period from 1760 until his death is covered in twelve lines. The language of the Memoir is certainly vivid and might easily be Sterne. But the piece is too short to be conclusive. The early detail is more than Sterne could have known and suggests a prior memorandum – from his father perhaps – that he had merely copied out. But against that, we have the one obtrusive error in the Memoir: that Sterne's father, Roger, is given the wrong rank in the wrong regiment. It is typical of things touching upon Sterne that these flaws do not dislodge confidence, but merely introduce doubt.

For all that Sterne's writings flourished after his death, and although he was not short of avid admirers, no biography appeared that might have been based on first-hand knowledge of the man, his environment and his acquaintances. It was only much later, when Sterne came under the exaggerated reproof of Thackeray, that defence took a biographical form. Thackeray's onslaught had appeared in 1851, as part of the *Lectures on the English Humourists*. Three years later, in the *Quarterly Review*, the Rev. Whitwell Elwin published an essay attempting restoration. It was this essay that inspired the publication in 1864 of Percy Fitzgerald's *Life of Laurence Sterne*. Fitzgerald did a great amount of work, if not always very cautiously. It was none the less, as Cross admitted, 'a pioneer work'. Some of its enthusiasm was corrected in an 1896 edition and then more fully in 1904 in an edition edited by Wilbur Cross of Yale University. In 1909,

Cross produced his own *Life and Times of Laurence Sterne*, sub-sequently revised in 1925 and 1929.

This is still the standard biography, even though it has too many errors and is a slow, listless book that seems to me deficient in both enjoyment and understanding of Sterne. Other biographies have appeared, most of which are markedly inferior to Cross's book. Nothing, though, has been anywhere near as thorough, informative and stimulating as the Oxford edition of *Sterne's Letters*, edited by Lewis Curtis and first published in 1935. In recent years, as Cross's book has passed out of print, the wealth of footnotes in Curtis's Letters has served as the best life of Sterne.

A major new biography is in progress by another American, Professor Arthur Cash. That book promises to be devoted to every recess of Sterne's life. Inevitably, it will involve the reader in an exhaustive and perhaps not always rewarding exploration of the gaps in the record of Sterne's life. Furthermore, Cash's book will not be in one volume. There seemed to me room for a one-volume account that was concerned equally with Sterne's life and fiction and that tried to make his rather uncertain place among English classics both credible and immediate. For although Sterne has been surrounded by academic analysis, this study has not reclaimed him for the general reader. I believe that the desire to rehabilitate Sterne may even have made him less accessible as a writer. If I present him as an equivocal, unreliable, evasive and unappetizing man it is not out of moral censoriousness. I believe, however, that his unique use of fiction, comedy and pathos cannot be separated from his shortcomings as a man. I hope that this book is biographically accurate and useful, but it springs primarily from an interest in the nature of fiction and admiration of the way Sterne cut it to fit his flexible soul.

PART ONE

'All unhing'd...'
1713–38

'When They Begot Me'

There is no memorial to the event in the town, but we gather from his own Memoir that Laurence Sterne was born in Clonmel, Tipperary, on 24 November 1713. That is precise enough to encourage hopes of reliable family history; but there is no neat beginning. On the contrary, there is a deal of confusion which is the inevitable outcome when parents take insufficient trouble over a birth. Posterity in industrious societies relies on sensible documentary investments from an early age. The English *Who's Who?* is largely inhabited by people whose parents 'put them down' for inclusion with proper foresight. This omission by Sterne's parents was symptomatic of a childhood so unofficial and hazardous that the subject of it may have had early encouragement to re-invent a life for himself that was gentler and safer.

The quality of life among the other members of the Sterne family was very close to the mainstream of provincial success; they certainly took themselves too seriously to approve of a birth as casual as Laurence's. But Sterne's father, Roger, fits uneasily with what we know of his ancestors. An unsuccessful ensign in the Flanders war can hardly have satisfied the expectations of a family of Yorkshire gentry that included a notable archbishop and that passed estates, property, capital and reputation down from one generation to the next.

The archbishop, Richard Sterne, was born in about 1596, the son of Simon Sterne, who lived at Mansfield in Nottinghamshire. Simon's father, William, came from Cropwell Butler, a village some fifteen miles south-east of Mansfield. Before that, the Sternes seem to have been a Cambridgeshire family. Sundry Sternes are mentioned in *Alumni Cantabrigienses* as coming in the middle of the sixteenth century from Kirtling and Stow-cum-Quy, villages between Cambridge and the Suffolk border. In addition to that branch of the family that went to Mansfield, another, of which more later, appeared in Ireland.

Professor Cross was prepared to believe that the Sterne family was the product of some presumably medieval Danish settlement in East Anglia, and tells us that 'the more learned of the family evidently associated their name with the old English word *stearn*, dialectical *starn* to this day, signifying a starling.'[1] At all events, some Sternes were Stearnes, and the starling sings plaintively in *A Sentimental Journey.** I doubt that Sterne ever took the trouble to trace his origins through the hinterland of East England. The thought of Danishness would have been sufficient for him to be affected by it. It would only have amused him to think of his Danish roots going back to the court of King Horwendillus; at the same time, Yorick, the Danish jester, may only have occurred to him as a disguise from overhearing the Sternes speculating about their own genealogy.

Simon Sterne, the great-great-grandfather of Laurence Sterne, married Margery Cartwright. (This event would have taken place at approximately the time of the Armada.) Of their children, Richard Sterne was by far the most notable. He is, indeed, a figure from English history and there can be little doubt that his memory persisted among the Sternes, and could never be separated from the family's standing in York during Laurence's lifetime. For Richard died only in 1683, at the probable age of eighty-seven. A student of Trinity College, Cambridge, and a Fellow at Corpus Christi, in 1634 he was appointed Master of Jesus College. He was an active developer of the college and had an organ put in the chapel.

Richard Sterne was a High Church royalist and chaplain to Archbishop Laud. On the outbreak of the Civil War, when Charles I appealed to the universities for money and valuables, Sterne ordered plate to be provided for the king's funds.[2] For this boldness, he was arrested by Cromwell and taken first to the Tower, and then to be confined below decks on a ship lying at Wapping. It was originally intended that he be transported; but in the event mercy was shown, and Sterne was allowed the sad

---

* Sterne's own seal also employed the figure of a starling.

honour and example of attending his patron Laud at the archbishop's execution in 1645.

Under the Protectorate he lived unobtrusively in Stevenage, supporting himself with pupils. But at the Restoration he was reinstated as Master of Jesus and made Bishop of Carlisle. Then, in 1664, he was promoted to be Archbishop of York, where he disappointed aspirants by living for a further nineteen years. He was buried at York Minster on 22 June 1683 after a funeral procession of thirty-four coaches, which was much more ceremony than his great-grandson received.[3]

Richard's wife, Elizabeth Dickenson of Farnborough, Hampshire, had died nine years earlier, but not before bearing her husband thirteen children. However, Richard's will divided his estate between three surviving sons, William, Richard and Simon.

Richard, who lived at Kilvington, near Thirsk, was a Commissioner of Exchequer, a J.P. and also Member of Parliament for Ripon from 1678–85. He married Mary Loveland but died without issue and was buried at the Minster on 29 January 1715.

Simon Sterne – whose debts were written off in his father's will – married an heiress, Mary Jaques. Mary was the granddaughter of Sir Roger Jaques, Lord Mayor of York in 1639, and of Mary Rawdon. She brought to the marriage an estate at Elvington, five miles south-east of York. With his own and his wife's resources, Simon Sterne bought an estate at Woodhouse, south-east of Halifax, for £1,800. Like his brother, Simon was a J.P.; he also governed a charity in Halifax. He died suddenly in April 1703 'having undergone a severe salivation for cancer in his mouth'.[4]

Simon of Woodhouse had three sons – Richard, Roger and Jaques. Richard, the eldest, inherited the estates at Elvington and Woodhouse. Jaques, the youngest, took his B.A. at Jesus College, Cambridge, in 1714/15 and entered the Church. Richard married Dorothy, the widow of Samuel Lister of Shibden Hall. Jaques also married sensibly, in January 1720. His wife, Catherine, the daughter of Sir John Goodricke of Ribston, was sixteen years older than he, but she too was an heiress.

I have compressed the details of Sterne affairs as much as possible. But the pattern is relevant for the way it highlights the wayward career of Roger Sterne, the brother between Richard and Jaques. Lewis Curtis rather dismisses Roger's choice of the army as the result of 'quixotic disposition'.[5] This is akin to Uncle Toby's reluctance to understand his own martial inclinations. It is an intriguing moment in *Tristram Shandy* when Toby (and Tristram's narrative) rejects Walter Shandy's 'motive-mongering' and asks the reader to respond to this appeal: 'If, when I was a school-boy, I could not hear a drum beat, but my heart beat with it—was it my fault?—Did I plant the propensity there?—did I sound the alarm within, or Nature?'[6] 'Was it my fault?' would have been a good motto for Sterne himself: it is the gist of so many of his self-defences. Like Toby – and perhaps like his own father – he interpreted his own refusal to deny instinct as an excuse for what sometimes looked like frivolity, capriciousness or thoughtlessness. There is something very modern in this adherence to being true to one's inner imperatives, and it is the cultivated ideal that has made Sterne the prophet of feeling. But it seems to me to have been much more of a device than a spontaneous response, a way of dodging through introspection and of holding himself at a distance.

The events of Roger's service illustrated only too well what a hard and thankless life the army was. The persistent lowliness of his rank seems to indicate either that his family disapproved of his enlistment and refused to sponsor him or that he made enemies where a more ambitious man sought friends. As far as can be gathered, no other Sterne in living memory had taken up arms as a livelihood.* This point is essential: Laurence Sterne was the son of the black sheep of the family. 'Quixotic disposition' is hardly sufficient explanation for Roger stepping so far outside the family traditions. It is sure now that we will never know what prompted his enlistment. But we can be equally certain

---

* It is true that one of Roger Sterne's sisters, Mary Elizabeth (1686–1719), had married a soldier, Walter Palliser. But Palliser was a colonel – owner rather than employee. Palliser came from North Deighton, a few miles away from York, and it is possible that he was Roger's inspiration. But Roger's static rank only shows that Palliser took no step to encourage the young man. Another member of Roger's regiment (as captain, in 1722) was Hugh Palliser, Walter's brother.

that it established his son as an outsider, as someone conceived and brought up outside polite and respectable society.

Roger Sterne was born probably in 1692, twelve years younger than his brother Richard and three or four years older than Jaques. He was thus eleven when his father died in 1703 and sixteen when his mother, Mary Jaques, died in 1708. Mary was buried at Elvington on 22 August.[7] We do not know her age reliably, nor whether her death was sudden; so that we are not bound to wonder that her adolescent son should, at the time of her funeral, have been encamped on the Isle of Wight, about to embark for Ostend and the continental war. It is not likely that the Sternes would have deliberately deprived a boy of eleven, nor even one of sixteen, so that we can hardly blame Roger's enlistment on lack of domestic support.

Marlborough's success was at that time enough for any recruiting sergeant to boast of. There were the great victories of Blenheim in 1704 and Ramillies in 1706; the surrender of Brussels, Antwerp, Bruges and Ostend; and, immediately, on 11 July 1708, the victory at Oudenarde, where only night saved the French from slaughter. There was no way of knowing that most of the glory had been exhausted and that the remainder of the war would be, as the first part had been for most participants, miserable, lethal and unrewarding.

The 34th Regiment of Foot had had its share of glory. Raised early in 1702, it had, under Lieutenant-Colonel Hans Hamilton, been active at the siege of Barcelona, where it withstood fierce French attacks. In the autumn of 1707, the regiment returned to England to replace its dead. But in the spring of 1708 there was an alarm of invasion from Scotland, whose inhabitants were uncomfortable under the Act of Union of the previous year. The 34th moved north as a safeguard, but only got as far as Leeds.[8] The danger then abated and the regiment took the opportunity to recruit (Yorkshire was not its original catchment area; it had first been drawn from East Anglia and based at Norwich and Colchester). Whether or not Roger's East Anglian blood was stirred, his enthusiasm had the better of him. Although there were other ways of being recruited. Some men were taken to join Marlborough handcuffed or with their trouser buttons removed. Farquhar's Serjeant Kite* promised that he would neither coax nor wheedle recruits but admitted that 'canting, lying, impudence, pimping, bullying, swearing, whoring, drinking, and a halberd, you will find the sum total will amount to a recruiting sergeant.'[9]

It is difficult to convey the nature of military service in 1708 more cogently than Sergeant Kite does. No one would now question how appalling conditions were; and yet Marlborough's army was the best and most humanely organized England had ever fielded. It was also campaigning with an adventure and success that the English army matched only under Wellington, who fought mainly defensive actions.

Even Wellington was under no illusion that his troops were anything but wild creatures who had to be controlled in every detail of their service. The army had for so long treated its men like animals that it is no wonder they came to resemble them. One reason why the English disapproved of standing armies is because they were so consistently made the resort of rowdies and criminals. This stigma must have been emphasized by the surprising smallness of the army. Even at the height of the Flanders campaign, the 'prodigious' forces recollected by Uncle Toby numbered no more than 25,000 English troops.[10] Major Scouller, the historian of that army, describes how self-sufficient and mercenary the regimental units were:

A regiment could fairly be described as a property owned by an unlimited company of which the Commanding Officer was managing director, and the officers partners or sole shareholders. . . . Once on the rungs of the ladder, an officer had to pay for every promotion, whether by seniority or merit. If he had no money, then he got no promotion, unless he were fortunate enough to be promoted to a vacancy caused by death.[11]

As it was, an ensign received three shillings (15p) a day, with

* The first part played, in an amateur performance, by David Garrick. In view of the later association between Garrick and Sterne, it is interesting to note that Garrick was the son of a recruiting officer and one of ten children (three of whom did not survive infancy). Furthermore, in 1732, only a little more than a year after Roger Sterne had left the Rock, Garrick's father took a posting to Gibraltar. David Garrick had even contemplated joining the army as a young man and he may have been the more drawn to Sterne because of these parallels. (Carola Oman, *David Garrick* [London, 1958], p. 6.)

eightpence for a servant, if he had one. Out of that he had to feed himself as best he could. His uniform was provided, though no more reliably than his pay: it consisted of a 'good full-bodied cloth coat', a waistcoat, a pair of Karsey breeches, a pair of stockings, a pair of shoes, two shirts and neck-cloths and a 'good strong hat, well laced'. Even so, at Oudenarde, 'the greater part of the Welch Fusiliers marched without shoes.'[12]

Roger Sterne was not made an ensign until 1 July 1710.[13] As a new recruit, he would have gone to the Isle of Wight, where the 34th was reviewed on 19 July 1708 before sailing to the continent under Sir George Byng and arriving at Ostend on 21 September. The regiment 'being composed of young soldiers was employed on garrison duty during the year 1709'.[14]

This may have been as well for literature, for at the battle of Malplaquet that year Marlborough suffered his heaviest losses. French morale was restored, England was tired of the war and Marlborough's unpopularity increased. Roger Sterne came to service in a war not of open battles, but of sieges, such as Uncle Toby had enjoyed in the armies of King William. In 1710, at the siege of Douay, conducted by Marlborough himself, the 34th lost over eighty men and had 130 wounded.[15] A confirmed ensign, Roger Sterne proceeded to the sieges of Bethune, Aire, and St. Venant and, in 1711, to that of Bouchaine, which was taken by capitulation in the middle of September.[16] It was probably at Bouchaine, while the English were restoring the defences they had razed, that Roger Sterne married Agnes Hebert. There, or on the way to winter-quarters.

Laurence Sterne's mother has passed into history, hung round her son's neck as a rebuke. Byron adapted Horace Walpole* when he boasted, 'I am as bad as that dog Sterne, who preferred whining over "a dead ass to relieving a living mother"',[17] and no biographer has been comfortable in dealing with the way Sterne seemed to flinch from his indigent mother once he was

---

* Walpole wrote: 'One would imagine that Sterne had been a man of very tender heart – yet I know, from indubitable authority, that his mother, who kept a school, having run in debt, on account of an extravagant daughter, would have rotted in jail, if the parents of her scholars had not raised a subscription for her. Her son had too much sentiment to have any feeling. A dead ass was more important to him than a living mother.' (*Walpoliana*, ed. John Pinkerton [London, 1799], pp. 133–4.)

settled in Yorkshire. A fuller account of that confrontation and the subsequent recrimination can wait for its proper place. But probably neither the disowning nor the unease would have occurred had Agnes Sterne not been even less acceptable in the eyes of the Sternes than Roger, her husband, was.

One reason why it has been difficult for biographers to take sides over Agnes Sterne is that they do not know who she was. Her son's Memoir – perhaps forgetful, perhaps calculating – is the source of the trouble:

> Roger Sterne . . . Lieutenant in Handaside's regiment,* was married to Agnes Hebert, widow of a captain of a good family: her family name was (I believe) Nuttle — though, upon recollection, that was the name of her father-in-law, who was a noted sutler in Flanders, in Queen Ann's wars, where my father married his wife's daughter (N.B. he was in debt to him) which was in September 25, 1711, Old Stile.[18]

Roger would have been nineteen at his marriage, and since she had been married once already, Agnes was probably older. With seniority and the knowledge that she had been married off to absolve a debt both weighing on her, it would be easy to expect sullen reproach in Agnes Sterne. But the union bore fruit quickly. At Lille, on 10 July 1712, a daughter was born and named Mary.†

The young family was soon moved on by the demands of war. In December 1711, the enemies of Marlborough had succeeded in having him replaced as commander-in-chief by the Duke of Ormonde.‡ England had lost heart for the inconclusive war and

---

* There is no good explanation of why Sterne should have misreported both his father's rank and his regiment.

† Mary was one of the three children of Roger Sterne who survived infancy. But she too was 'most unfortunate'. She married 'one Weemans in Dublin —who used her most unmercifully—spent his substance, became a bankrupt, and left my poor sister to shift for herself,—which she was able to do but for a few months, for she went to a friend's house in the country, and died of a broken heart. She was a most beautiful woman—of a fine figure, and deserved a better fate.' (*Letters*, Memoir, p. 1.)

‡ James Butler, 2nd Duke of Ormonde (1665–1745), grandson of the 1st Duke. He never returned to England again after his ineffectual part on the Jacobite side in the 1715 uprising. Corporal Trim, Uncle Toby's Sancho-like batman, is also named James Butler. Sterne insists that he does not intend the connection to be made, but the insistence comes soon after the assertion of the importance of names provoked by Tristram's mis-Christening.

Ormonde kept to his camp 'playing the devil' while Prince Eugene, his ally, was defeated by the French at the battle of Derain in July 1712. The protracted negotiations towards the Peace of Utrecht began with Louis XIV handing over Dunkirk as a token of sincerity. On 4 August, babe in arms, Roger Sterne and the 34th entered that port as part of the occupying force.[19]

It was a bitter sincerity that had Dunkirk for its proof. It had been a base for privateers with elaborate defences, to both land and sea, that the English now set about destroying. The military establishment at Dunkirk had risen to over eight thousand by the first half of 1713. The idle soldiers crowded together with predictable results. 'There was a notorious sickness, known as Dunkirk fever, which may have been a species of malaria, and records show that, in the early days of the occupation, at least 2,400 men were sick at one time, and the cost of medicines between 1 August 1712 and 5 April 1714 was nearly £12,000.'[20]

In sickness or health, Roger and Agnes Sterne there set in motion the homunculus essential to this book – the only man of English letters, perhaps, conceived under canvas. The parents cannot have wished to have the birth performed on a ground-sheet by surgeons trained on pox and amputations; but war itself was by now a declining trade. As the peace negotiations inched on, and the regiments seemed less promising investments, the 34th changed hands. On 30 November 1712 Lieutenant-Colonel Thomas Chudleigh was appointed colonel in place of Hans Hamilton.[21] By the end of the year thirteen regiments of dragoons and twenty-one of foot had already been broken and sent home.

The discarding of the remainder waited only on the signing of the peace. When this was announced by the queen in Parliament on 9 April 1713 there were the traditional rejoicings: bonfires in the streets, the churchbells ringing, and the surviving veterans stripped down to half-pay or worse. Not that the peace had much bearing on ordinary people. Indeed, it hardly amounted to more than the various rulers of Europe swapping a few small principalities and agreeing to recognize one another. The king of Spain was to stay as he was and relinquish claim to the French throne, the Emperor Charles VI remained emperor, and the rest of the world acknowledged the Hanoverian succession in England. England had the best pickings: Gibraltar, Minorca and a thirty-year licence to the *asiento*, the right to provide the civilized world with Negro slaves.

The 34th, or Chudleigh's, as marching orders henceforward refer to it, was not broken it seems until the very day of the infant's birth – 24 November 1713.[22] Coincidence, then, was the only auspicious indication of our hero's birth.

Sterne's Memoir puts the crucial events of his birth in this order: arrival at Clonmel, the announcement that the regiment was broken, his own delivery – all within the space of a week at the most. There is no record that the regiment, as well as the Sterne family, came to Clonmel. It would seem an unnecessarily long and expensive journey for a regiment due to be scattered. The men had only to be tipped ashore at some channel port. Nor can the breaking have come as any surprise: Chudleigh's regiment was preserved longer than most. Since there is every suggestion that Agnes had connections in or about Clonmel, it is probable that, so advanced in pregnancy, she anticipated Roger's breaking and headed for a friendly roof. Otherwise we must suppose a double coincidence: that a regiment was broken at a time and place to suit one ensign.

Clonmel is pleasantly situated on the north bank of the river Suir – in which there are a few islands – and in a valley between the Knockmealdown and Comeragh mountains in the south and the peak of Slievenamon to the north-east. Frank O'Connor called it 'a picturesque wreck of a hole',[23] but the biographer who travels across Ireland to it will be surprised how much sense of what it once was Clonmel retains. Compared with most other Irish towns of the same size, it has preserved an unusual number of eighteenth-century buildings. For in the time of Sterne's birth it was, by Irish standards, a town of some note.

Clonmel's wool trade was well known in Yorkshire; nowhere else was it contested and hindered so strenuously, with the unconsidering exploitation that the English have always reserved for the Irish. Later in life, during his involvement in York politics, Laurence Sterne himself was prepared to be indignant about the unfair advantages obtained by Irish wool merchants who sold directly to France. Outside the town, however, the land was what Swift called 'a bare face of nature, without houses or plantations; filthy cabins, miserable, tattered, half-starved creatures, scarce in human shape'.[24] He thought the parish of Clonmel 'one of the largest and poorest in the entire kingdom'. In 1700 a working man in Clonmel earned five (old) pence a day and depended on the potato for sustenance. Shortly before Laurence Sterne's birth, in 1707 and 1709, there were severe famines when that staple crop failed.

War, too, had left its mark on the town. Cromwell had lost some two thousand men and spent five weeks in taking Clonmel in 1659. After the Stuart Restoration, the 1st Duke of Ormonde* took the town in hand. He ordered the building of the Main Guard, in about 1665, which still stands, very handsome. Two years later, he invited five hundred Walloon families from Canterbury to establish a textile industry at Clonmel; 'pendant plusieurs années, la colonie de Clonmel fabrique des bas, des lainages, et du drap'.[25] Therefore, Clonmel in 1713 probably had a flourishing community of Flemish weavers, including several Huguenots.

It would not be worth saying so much about Clonmel if Sterne had not insisted on his mother's connection with the town. In 1751, he was so embarrassed by the presence of his mother in England that he wrote a long, vindicatory letter to his uncle Jaques in which he talks repeatedly of his mother having lived 'with her own relations in Ireland',[26] supporting herself with an embroidery school. And in his Memoir, written probably in 1767, although claiming little knowledge of his mother's family, Sterne says that any of them left alive would be in Clonmel. In Clonmel, itself, the tradition holds that Agnes Sterne had family in the town. The Rev. William Burke's *History of Clonmel*, published in 1907, recounts:

A tradition recorded by Mr William Clarke of the *Clonmel Chronicle* . . . that Sterne was born in a house in Mary's Street, a few doors from O'Connell Street corner, right side going towards the church. Sterne's mother was a native of the town, and at the date of his birth . . . her family the Tuttles (or Tothalls) occupied a prominent position. That year Thomas Tothall was mayor of the town.[27]

---

* James Butler (1610–88) had earlier organised Charles I's support in Ireland.

There is nothing else to connect Agnes Sterne with the Tuttles or to clear the vagueness attached to her. In 1967, after very extensive research, Professor Arthur Cash[28] concluded that we hardly knew more than was implied in her son's cryptic note, except that Agnes might have been the step-daughter of Captain Christopher Nuttall, who was almost certainly an Irishman. Otherwise, we can only wonder whether Agnes was Irish by birth, or perhaps a French or Flemish Huguenot.* The most crucial thing about her, however, is the distaste with which her son responded to her when he was an adult. If mystery does surround her, perhaps it is partly because Sterne himself disliked to think, let alone talk, about his mother.

Clonmel remains mute, empty of documentary evidence. On the site prescribed by tradition there is a ruined building. Perhaps Laurence Sterne was born there and passed his first few months there or in the barracks in the town. It is more to the point that, from the moment of birth, Sterne should have been a transient creature. The most significant fixed locations of his life are in his books: those claustrophobic interiors in which my father, my uncle Toby and Corporal Trim sat endlessly passing the time, monuments of static lugubriousness, are the dream of a man who never felt at home.

Birth was only one of the profound human experiences that fascinated Sterne. It is tempting to guess at the emotional effects of the circumstances of his birth, largely because of the extraordinary avidity with which Sterne himself liked to imagine the interior of the body and personality. Thus Tristram rebukes his parents for the way they upset his own animal spirits – for 'nine parts in ten of a man's sense or his nonsense, his successes and miscarriages in this world depend upon their motions and activity, and the different tracks and trains you put them into, so that when they are once set a-going, whether right or wrong, 'tis not a halfpenny matter,—away they go cluttering like hey-go-mad.'[29] What is most characteristic of Sterne in that passage is the way comedy and mockery are used to disguise seriousness.

* In 1910, R.M. Hutchinson-Low reported finding a Church of England prayer book in Halifax, printed in French with the name 'Agnes Sterne'. (*Notes & Queries*, Vol. II, 1910, p. 329.)

'Hey-go-mad'

At the time of Sterne's childhood, travelling beyond an immediate vicinity was arduous, slow and dangerous. By far the most
detailed section of his Memoir is concerned with the hectic
back-and-forth of his early years. Such an emphasis supposes
some earlier note – from either Roger or Agnes – which regarded
the itinerary as remarkable. It does not need a child psycho-
logist to relate Sterne's later preoccupation with motion and
restlessness to the alarming jerkiness of his early life. Nor is it
fanciful to see there the origins of the insecurity and detachment
from roots and reality that are characteristic of the man and
author.

Whatever ties Agnes Sterne may have had in Clonmel, and
however much she had hurried there for the birth of Laurence,
the family was soon enough on the move. Now on half-pay –
1s 6d (7½p) a day – Roger took his wife, his daughter Mary
(some eighteen months old) and the new baby, 'as soon as I was
able to be carried' – probably in the spring of 1714 – and made
the journey from Clonmel to the Sterne house at Elvington in
Yorkshire.

Roger's reappearance at Elvington must have aroused great
interest. The Sternes had not, as far as we know, seen him since
he enlisted in 1708. Now he was back, only twenty-two or so,
but with a wife, two children and the stains of camp life.
Elvington was by now the property of Roger's brother, Richard,
who was aged thirty-four. His first wife dead, at or about the
time of Roger's arrival, on 9 September 1714, Richard married
again, to Esther Booth, a Halifax girl. Richard's second marriage
was not the only family event during Roger's visit. For in
January 1715, the erstwhile member for Ripon, Uncle Richard,

died, and was buried in York Minster. Almost certainly, Roger would have attended that funeral. But, although childless himself, Richard's will made no bequest to Roger, however deserving a spectacle his nephew's family may have presented.

By midsummer, 1715, Roger Sterne was recalled to the drum by renewed threats of invasion from Scotland. The 34th was re-established by a needy government, 'as if [it] had not been broke notwithstanding any former Order, Direction or Instruction to the Contrary'.[1] However much the Sternes may have disapproved of Roger's military career, his return to the family seat had not persuaded him to abandon a service that was so vulnerable to the whim and necessity of the country. Nor was Roger promoted at the re-establishment, although two ensigns junior to him were made lieutenants in the 34th.

At the re-establishment, rather than leave his family at Elvington or return them to Clonmel, Roger and his 'household decamped with bag and baggage for Dublin'.[2] Less than a month later, the Memoir continues, 'my father left us, being ordered to Exeter, where, in a sad winter, my mother and her two children followed him, travelling from Liverpool by land to Plymouth.'[3] It was at Plymouth that a third child, Joram, was born. Sterne says that Agnes and the three children returned to Dublin twelve months after arriving at Plymouth, in other words late in 1716. The regiment, however, did not follow them until 1 June 1717.

Travelling on their own, Agnes and the children 'had a narrow escape from being cast away by a leak springing up in the vessel.—At length, after many perils, and struggles, we got to Dublin'.[4] Does this mean that they were actually ship-wrecked, or at least had to abandon ship? In those days, of course, sea travel was very hazardous. Swift never went farther than the Irish Sea but in *Gulliver's Travels* he describes very credibly the perils of storm. *Robinson Crusoe*, similarly, depends upon the foundering of a ship. Thomas Gent, a York contemporary of Sterne, had several unpleasant experiences at sea. On one occasion he set out from Holyhead for Dublin but was driven helplessly north and had to put in at the Isle of Man and wait eleven days until the storm abated. And in 1725, on an undermanned ship in sight of Howth Head, a storm came up so that Gent had to do 'such hard labour at the pump, that I was in a lather with sweat, and frequently nigh covered with the waves'.[5]

But fate had a different, if equally unpleasant, fate in mind for Roger Sterne. For the moment, he arrived safely in Dublin and there 'took a large house, furnished it, and in a year and a half's time spent a great deal of money'.[6] It is far from clear what money Roger had to spend or what he and his family did in Dublin. Perhaps the Yorkshire Sternes had given him a present as he left them again, either to make his service more comfortable or to let their consciences lie quiet. But perhaps another branch of the Sterne family came to the aid of the ensign and his family in Dublin.

For Roger Sterne had ample and potent relatives in Ireland, where the Sterne family had achieved a rather more varied eminence than it had in Yorkshire. The common Irish form of the name is Stearne, which is a more accurate spelling of the way that the name is frequently pronounced in Ireland, even today.

The family first appears in Ireland in the person of John Stearne, once of Stapleford in Cambridgeshire, but who subsequently settled at Greenan in County Wicklow. He held some position in the retinue of Theophilus Buckworth, the bishop of Dromore, and married Mabel Bermingham. John and Mabel Stearne had three sons: John, James and Robert. Of these, John was the most celebrated. Born in 1624 at Ardbraccan, John Stearne had to leave his studies at Trinity College, Dublin, at the time of Cromwell. Nevertheless, he managed to continue his studies at Cambridge, even though his relative Richard Sterne had been expelled from there. After the Restoration, he was appointed Senior Fellow at Trinity College, Dublin, and, rather exceptionally, practised law and medicine while studying Hebrew. But it was in medicine that he was pre-eminent. He was President of the College of Surgeons in Dublin and acknowledged head of the Irish medical profession. He died in Dublin in 1669.

By his marriage to Dorothy Ryves, he had one son and three daughters. The son, another John, born in 1660, attended Trinity College, Dublin, and was ordained a deacon in 1682. In

1688 he was made vicar of Trim and later became, in turn, dean of St. Patrick's Cathedral, Dublin, bishop of Dromore in 1713, bishop of Clogher in 1717 and vice-chancellor of Dublin University in 1721. He did not die until 1745, at the age of eighty-five.*

Bishop Stearne was the friend and contemporary of Swift. Indeed, it was largely at Swift's instigation that Stearne was made dean of St. Patrick's, a post which Swift himself occupied after Stearne, although he thought it was a poor reward for his services at Queen Anne's court. The two men had met when they were vicars of neighbouring parishes: Swift at Laracor, Stearne at Trim, both in County Meath. Stearne was famous for his large library and for his hospitality. In 1707 Swift wrote to Stearne comparing the dean's generosity very favourably with what he was then receiving in London: 'I must here tell you, that the Dean of *St. Patrick's* lives better than any man of quality I know.'[7]

Although Bishop Stearne is supposed never to have married, Lady Mary Wortley Montagu's letters tell a story that suggests he was not immune to the female sex. For all that the known facts argue against the central part of the story, it is too much in a Shandean character to be omitted. 'Mr. Sterne, the titular Bishop,' wrote Lady Mary in 1713, 'was last week marry'd to a very pritty Woman, Mrs. Bateman, whom he fell in Love with for falling backward from her Horse, Leaping a ditch, where she display'd all her Charms, which he found irresistible.'[8]

It is difficult to believe that Roger Sterne would not have met this leading figure in Dublin society. The 'large house' in which the Sternes lived may have been recommended by the Dean; so generous a relative may even have helped the ensign with the rent. Dublin at this time was a most active city. The building of Trinity College Library, designed by Colonel Thomas Burgh, was in progress and the Royal Hospital had recently been completed. In 1719 the plans were drawn up for Dr. Steevens's Hospital, the institution that was to benefit from Swift's will. Around Swift himself there was a lively social group that included Bishop Stearne, Patrick Delany, Patrick Grattan and

---

* That death was recorded in the *York Courant*, but without mention of the Yorkshire–Irish connection.

Richard Helsham, Swift's physician and husband to Bishop Stearne's niece.

But the Sterne family never rested long enough to secure themselves. The Memoir resumes its travels: 'In the year one thousand seven hundred and nineteen, all unhing'd again; the regiment was ordered, with many others, to the Isle of Wight, in order to embark for Spain in the Vigo expedition.'[9] Agnes and the children accompanied Roger on his return to England. The Memoir says that, driven in to Milford Haven, they landed at Bristol and then proceeded by way of Plymouth to the Isle of Wight. According to marching orders, on 22 April 1719, Chudleigh's regiment was ordered from Bath to Bristol and, on 21 July from 'Froom' to Portsmouth, there to embark for the Isle of Wight.[10] Whether or not the Sternes went by the round-about way of Plymouth, it was on the way from Bristol to Portsmouth – a route that went by daily stages through Warminster, Amesbury, Stockbridge and Waltham – that the infant Joram died, 'a pretty boy, four years old, of the small-pox'.*[11] Within two months, on 23 September, this loss was made good by the birth of another daughter, Anne.

The family remained on the island while Roger played his part in the Drake-like expedition against Vigo. This renewed fighting was on behalf of Stanhope's Quadruple Alliance, flung together in August 1718, between England, France, the Emperor and the Netherlands. The Alliance was designed to make Spain surrender its possessions in Italy and to gain Sicily for the Emperor.† England, for her part, was anxious to prevent Spanish aid to any renewed Jacobite rebellion. A large Spanish fleet was dispatched to Sicily and it was this fleet that encountered Byng off Cape Passaro. Cardinal Alberoni, the chief minister of Spain, had raised another fleet to invade England

---

* Inoculation against smallpox was introduced only in 1720 by Lady Mary Wortley Montagu, who had discovered it in Constantinople. But for many years it was a mistrusted precaution. Apart from the many deaths from smallpox, survivors were invariably badly scarred. Such a victim was Dick Turpin. In 1739, a man named 'Palmer' was held at York. Suspicions that he was Turpin were confirmed by the marks of smallpox that the highwayman was known to carry. (The Turpin execution was the public spectacle of Sterne's first full year at York.) (*York Courant*, 27 February, 10 April 1739.)

† It was these hostilities that persuaded Uncle Toby to order Trim to make an Italian drawbridge for his bowling-green fortifications. (*TS*, Vol. III, Ch. XXV.)

and offered its command to the Duke of Ormonde, now in Jacobite exile. Ensign Sterne may have marvelled that he should be the enemy of his former commander-in-chief. But the two men did not come to blows. Ormonde* wisely mistrusted the weather and a French army and English fleet made a mild plunder of northern Spain. The attack on Vigo sailed from Spithead in September with four thousand troops under Lord Cobham. It was intended originally as an attack on Corunna where Ormonde's putative fleet had been mustered.†

Roger survived the Vigo expedition but the 34th was ordered to Wicklow, from where he sent for his family, uncertain how many they numbered. Agnes gathered up the children and ventured forth again: 'We embarked for Dublin, and had all been cast away by a most violent storm; but through the intercessions of my mother, the captain was prevailed upon to turn back into Wales, where we stayed a month, and at length got into Dublin, and travelled by land to Wicklow, where my father had for some Weeks given us over for lost.'[12]

But just as Sterne's childhood seems so much at the mercy of arbitrary movement, there now occurs another of those brief interludes of rest. The family remained in barracks at Wicklow for a year, and while there another son, Devijeher, was born. This child was probably named after a colleague in Roger's regiment, Abraham Devischer. Significantly, Devischer had been made an ensign only in 1711 – a year later than Roger. But by 1714 he was a captain and in April 1720 – about when Devijeher was born – he was appointed lieutenant-colonel.[13] Roger was an ensign still.

* Ormonde subsequently retired to the French provinces and when Tristram toured through France he was delayed at Avignon only by the house where Ormonde had lived. (*TS*, Vol. III, Ch. XLI.)

† Carlyle believed that Roger's participation was the only thing that made the Vigo expedition memorable. But for Sterne and the other young soldiers it may have held a greater resonance. For in 1702 there had been a previous expedition to Vigo, which was in fact diverted to Cadiz. Ironically, Ormonde had been captain-general of that mission. Henry Esmond was also involved; the only blood he spilt was that of a fellow-Englishman who was about to attack a nun in the course of the plunder that replaced any serious military action. On their way back, the expedition seized the treasure fleet at Vigo. Thus Sterne may have had hopes of pickings, since Vigo was known as a source of plunder. 'Indeed, Hounslow or Vigo – which matters much?' asked Thackeray.

Sterne at Ranelagh watching the trade in his own Sermons with Mrs. Vesey, perhaps, at his side.

Hogarth's view of Trim reading the sermon to Dr. Slop and the Shandy brothers

A portrait of Sterne by an unknown artist, painted at some time during the 1760s. It is possible that the head is by Hogarth

Soon after the birth of Devijeher, the Sternes were invited to Annamoe to stay with the clergyman there, Mr. Fetherston – 'a relation of my mother's'.[14] Thomas Fetherston had been married to Mary, a daughter of Christopher Nuttall. He had been born in 1684, the son of Thomas and grandson of Cuthbert Fetherston, who was a native of Durham but settled in Philips-town in 1651. From this date we may deduce that he had been a soldier in Cromwell's army. Certainly his son, Thomas, was a soldier and had carried the Enniskillens' standard at the battle of the Boyne.

Thomas Fetherston was appointed curate of Derrylossory in Wicklow on 5 February 1717.[15] He was by that time married to his second wife, Parnella Parry. Derrylossory is a few miles north of Annamoe and the church there is on an exposed hillside. Both villages are in the same steep valley in a wild but very beautiful part of the Wicklow mountains. Not that such dramatic landscape was without its dangers. The elder son of Thomas Fetherston, in fact, was later murdered by a marauding gang in the Wicklow mountains. No one who has followed the old military road out of Dublin and over those mountains can have failed to sense the potential for menace in the area.

Laurence Sterne nearly met his death in the valley itself, within sight and call of the rectory at Annamoe. 'It was in this parish, during our stay, that I had that wonderful escape in falling through a mill-race whilst the mill was going, and of being taken up unhurt—the story is incredible, but known for truth in all that part of Ireland—where hundreds of the common people flocked to see me.'[16]

Some writers have doubted this story, believing Sterne stole it from the childhood of his great-grandfather, the archbishop. Ralph Thoresby records this incident from the childhood of the archbishop in his diary: 'playing near a mill, he fell within the clow; there was but one board or bucket wanting in the whole wheel, but a gracious Providence so ordered it, that the void place came down at that moment, else he had been inevitably crushed to death.'[17] It is a coincidence that the same accident should have befallen Laurence, but surely not beyond explanation. The story was probably well-known among the Sternes and

c

would have been told many times to Laurence.* No wonder
then that, on seeing the mill, the boy should have approached it
to discover exactly how momentous an adventure it must have
been for his famous ancestor. A little closer and Laurence was
re-enacting the drama.

I can vouch for the likelihood of this sequence of events since
I almost fell in the water myself in 1969. Not that there is any
danger now. Only a slow and shallow stream passes the shattered wheel. The river, still fast, is some yards away. It was
delightful to discover what seemed a true relic at Annamoe.
Since Sir Walter Scott reported in the 1820s that the mill had
been recently destroyed,[18]† few people can have bothered to
explore Annamoe. Not that the wheel there now, suitably
wrecked as it is, can have been the one Sterne survived: only a
clever imitation of it to taunt biographers. Mr. Robert Barton
of Annamoe has a photograph of the mill taken in 1875 which
shows it in full working order. The wheel in this picture is
clearly sound and fairly new. At some time between 1825 and
1875 it must have been restored. According to Mr. Barton – who
was alive then to observe it – the millwheel has not been
worked since 1900. The mill now is unused and unoccupied.
However, there is no doubt that the mill itself is original,
though that, too, is dilapidated. It is of the same construction as
the stables of the rectory at Annamoe.

From Annamoe the Sternes moved on to the barracks at
Dublin, no longer able to afford a house of their own. They
stayed there a year, during which Anne died – that 'pretty
blossom . . . she was, as I well remember, of a fine delicate
frame, not made to last long, as were most of my father's
babies'.[19] It was also at this time, Sterne tells us, that he learned
to write. The Royal Barracks, now Collins Barracks, had only
been built in 1704 to the design of Burgh. It was on the north
bank of the Liffey, near to Phoenix Park. We need not be too
fanciful to think of young Laurence exploring that huge park,
larger than all the parks in London put together, or watching

* Archbishop Sterne was, indeed, accident prone. On another occasion he went
birdnesting on a church steeple and fell to the ground without damage. (*Diary of
Ralph Thoresby*, ed. Joseph Hunter [London, 1830], Vol. II, p. 15.)

† Scott stayed at Glendalough near by in July 1825.

the brutal battles on the quays between the immigrant Huguenot 'Liberty-Boys' and the Catholic butchers.

In 1722, the regiment was ordered to Carrickfergus: 'we all
decamped, but got no further than Drogheda, thence ordered to
Mullengar, forty miles west, where by Providence we stumbled
upon a kind relation, a collateral descendant from Archbishop
Sterne, who took us all to his castle and kindly entreated us for
a year—and sent us to the regiment at Carrickfergus, loaded
with kindnesses.'[20]

This kind relative I take to be Robert Stearne, the cousin of
Bishop John Stearne of Dromore and Clogher. Robert Stearne
was a career soldier and a devoted follower of William III,
whom he had served in Ireland and on the continent. It is
especially interesting that, like Uncle Toby, he was present at
both the siege of Limerick in 1691 and the taking of Namur in
1695, where Toby had suffered his embarrassing wound. Indeed,
it was for his conduct at Namur that Robert Stearne was raised
to the rank of lieutenant-colonel and that his regiment, originally
the 18th Irish, was designated the Royal Regiment of Ireland
by the king himself. Like Toby, Robert Stearne was personally
engaged in a desperate assault at Namur, in which his regiment
had twenty-six officers and over 380 men killed or wounded.[21]

Subsequently, under Marlborough and the despised
Ormonde, Stearne served throughout the Flanders campaigns.
He fought at Blenheim, Ramillies, Oudenarde and Malplaquet
and in 1712 – not before time, in his opinion – he was made
colonel of the Royal Irish. He was also present at the sieges of
Bethune, Aire and Bouchaine, engagements that figure in the
service record of Ensign Roger Sterne. Despite the gulf in rank
(Robert had first served as an ensign in 1678), it is possible that
Sterne met Stearne, compared spellings and formed an acquain-
tance that encouraged hopes of hospitality in a career ensign.

Robert Stearne's journal of the Flanders campaign is full of
bantering and belligerent irony, such as suggests a robust and
hospitable man. There are vivid phrases: he speaks of 'shuffling
old Louis' and says of a ship he was in that it 'was old but not
quite so soft as a rotten pear'.[22] Sometimes irony and a curious
animation of language are not too far from the voice of Laurence
Sterne: 'Our King was the active verb and as he made no

motion the French passives remained as usual quiescent, contented with peaceably enjoying during the summer their strawberries and cream and other *bon bons* which they prefer to fighting, though they are a gallant set of fellows on a pinch as we found at Namur.'[23]

Uncle Toby and Robert Stearne seem to have been equally unhappy at the prospect of peace. The very mention of Utrecht was enough to make Toby sigh and prompted him to his apologetical oration on behalf of war and the odd conclusion that it is only 'the getting together of quiet and harmless people, with their swords in their hands, to keep the ambitious and the turbulent within bounds'.[24] Beguiling as Toby is, perhaps Robert Stearne's acid comments on Ormonde's reluctance to press the war home are more characteristic of the army: 'The Duke shewed *great skill* in the encampment of his army under the cannon of this town [Bruges], his right being secured by the canal to Bruges his left to Dumgen Cloysters and a strong morass, and his front might be easily secured by an entrenchment which could be thrown up in a trice in case Prince Eugene, Villars or the Emperor of China should dare to attack him.'[25]

In 1717, Robert Stearne retired from service to live at Tullynally, near Castlepollard in County Westmeath, only some ten miles from Mullengar. It is tempting to see Robert Stearne as an original of Uncle Toby* but legitimate only if we acknowledge how lightly Sterne related real-life models to invented characters. A year in the veteran's company may have made a lasting impression on the boy's view of the military, and the closeness of the two careers makes it doubtful that Sterne simply based Toby's life on reference to a history book, as Theodore Baird has suggested.[26] However amused Robert Stearne's voice, it is much more confident than Toby's. Toby is a portrait of diffidence and failure, of which his wound is the most telling detail. But Robert Stearne had been through twenty-one campaigns, seven battles, fifteen sieges, seven 'grand attacks on counterscarps and breaches', not to mention 'two remarkable retreats' and never

---

* One of Robert Stearne's sisters, Mabel, had married Richard or Robert Tighe, and they lived – as far as I can establish – within visiting distance of Tullynally, at Mitchelstown. Suppose that Robert Stearne shared Uncle Toby's predilection for *Lillabullero*, and its first line may have had an extra relevance for the two brothers-in-law: 'Ho, broder Teague, dost hear de decree . . .'

lost a drop of blood.[27] Even if Sterne remembered some traces of Robert Stearne in Toby, he did not allow one cheerful and unscathed veteran to alter his imaginative view of melancholy military pipe-dream.

Regretfully, the Sternes moved on to Carrickfergus. 'Devijeher here died, he was three years old—He had been left behind at nurse at a farmhouse near Wicklow, but was fetch'd to us by my father the summer after—another child sent to fill his place, Susan; this babe too left us behind in this weary journey.'[28]

It was shortly after this double tragedy that Roger Sterne took Laurence back to England and put him in a school. But before talking about the school or pursuing Roger in his melancholy campaigns, it is proper to take stock. It is almost certain that after being put in school at the age of ten, Laurence never saw his father again. It is equally likely that he did not re-encounter his mother for nearly ten years, and then only fleetingly.

The subsequent rift between Laurence and his mother makes it easy to suppose that the antipathy began even while he was a child. But Agnes Sterne can hardly be criticized for her conduct during her son's childhood. Whether or not she was of low birth, no matter how intransigent a personality she may have been, she followed her husband through hardship and tragedy with a persistence and hardiness that can only be admired. She had little enough to gain from it. Sixteen years after his enlistment, her husband was still an ensign, vulnerable to the caprice of the military authorities.* When Laurence, in later life, rebuked his mother for demanding more than she deserved, this record should be borne in mind. Agnes may have failed to nurture the capacity for mature affection in him, perhaps she had hastened the recklessness in his nature, but she had at least kept him alive.

As well as being parted now from his mother and family, Sterne left Ireland, never to return. This is the right place to ask how far we should think of him as an Irish writer? The Irish today do very little to encourage that. For all their eagerness to see the rage of Irish patriotism in Swift, they are happy to resign

---

* It is worth noting that Henry Fielding's father was a poor lieutenant at the time of his son's birth in 1707, but eventually rose to the rank of lieutenant-colonel. He thus had means enough to send his son to Eton.

so shifty a creature as Sterne to the English. Clonmel and Annamoe are blandly indifferent to their connection with Sterne and the official attitude is summed up by his absence from the Irish National Biography.

But there are a few links. Large parts of Fitzgerald's life of Sterne appeared first in the *Dublin University Magazine* in 1862–3. In 1814, the *Dublin Literary Repository* went so far as to call Tristram 'an O'Shandy of the county of Tipperary',[29] while at the end of the nineteenth century the Clonmel newspapers had several references to Sterne as a 'worthy' of the town.

The influence of Ireland on the young Sterne may have been very substantial. As we have seen, he had travelled widely in the country and may have come into contact with some of Ireland's leading citizens. If, later in life, it seemed a vague, uneasy emotional landscape, that is no more than the reaction of many who have lived there all their lives. Samuel Smiles, in his study of Huguenot settlements in Ireland, reported that a M. Le Fevre, a schoolmaster at Portarlington (less than thirty miles from Mullengar), who died in 1718, was 'said to have been the father of Sterne's "poor sick lieutenant"' Le Fever.[30] We have already noted the possible influence of Robert Stearne. It is not always appreciated that *Lillabullero*, Toby's theme, is a specifically Irish tune originating in the upheavals James II* had brought about in Ireland and of which no Irishman has ever needed reminding. It was a Protestant battle song from a conflict that had involved Sterne's Irish relatives, particularly Robert Stearne, who had first to flee the country and then returned with William of Orange for the Boyne campaign.

But the most important Irish influence on Sterne is in the matters of voice, humour and personality. On those grounds alone, it is hardly possible to forget that he learned to talk and read in Ireland and that some of his basic notions of human beings were formed there. But even when Sterne's Irishness has been recognized, it has usually been as a contributory defect.

---

* Bishop Burnet reported that the song 'made an impression on the army, that cannot be well imagined by those who saw it not. The whole army, and at last all people both in city and country, were singing it perpetually. And perhaps never had so slight a thing so great an effect.' (Burnet, *History of His Own Times* [1833 edn], Vol. III, p. 336.)

V.S. Pritchett has called Sterne the man something of a bore because, 'That Irish loquacity which he got from his mother and his early years in Tipperary had deluded him. He has that terrible, professional, non-stop streak of the Irish. One feels, sometimes, that one has been cornered by some brilliant Irish drunk, one whose mind is incurably suggestible.'[31] Certainly Sterne was constantly experimenting with suggestion and possibility; but very seldom did he surrender to them. And though he may have been talkative, it was not the chatter of intoxication. Indeed, his words were often measured exactly and few Irishmen know as well as Sterne what to leave out. His finest use of suggestion is in passing it on to the reader.

That picture of the Irish drunk – so close to Blarney – tells us as much about the English as about the Irish. The English tend to think all Irish frivolous, whether or not they have been drinking. What seems to me more authentically Irish in Sterne's voice is the belligerent cheerfulness and the guile that makes a comic performance out of inadequacy. We know that Joyce responded to the liberty Sterne had revealed in fiction.* But the voice nearest to Sterne's is the bold-as-brass mock seriousness of Bernard Shaw that is a device to overcome emotional detachment and stop the comedian laughing at his own joke. This sort of vivacity is always holding desperation at bay. It revels in fictional reality as an escape from a life that hardly seems credible to the participant himself. Although it describes a much later and dominantly Roman Catholic Ireland, this passage from Shaw's *John Bull's Other Island* is illuminating of Sterne's debt to the country:

Oh, the dreaming! the dreaming! the torturing, heart-scalding, never satisfying dreaming, dreaming, dreaming, dreaming! No

---

* Here, for instance, is Joyce talking about *Finnegans Wake*: 'I might easily have written this story in the traditional manner. Every novelist knows the recipe. It is not very difficult to follow a simple, chronological scheme which the critics will understand. But I, after all, am trying to tell the story of this Chapelizod family in a new way. Time and the river and the mountain are the real heroes of my book. Yet the elements are exactly what every novelist might use: man and woman, birth, childhood, night, sleep, marriage, prayer, death. Only I am trying to build many planes of narrative with a single aesthetic purpose. Did you ever read Laurence Sterne?' (Eugene Jolas, 'My Friend James Joyce', *James Joyce: Two Decades of Criticism*, ed. Seon Givens [New York, 1948], pp. 11–12.)

debauchery that ever coarsened and brutalized an Englishman can take the worth and usefulness out of him like that dreaming. An Irishman's imagination never lets him alone, never convinces him, never satisfies him; but it makes him that he can't face reality, nor deal with it, nor handle it, nor conquer it: he can only sneer at them that do, and be 'agreeable to strangers' like a good-for-nothing woman on the streets. It's all dreaming, all imagination.[32]

'A Boy of Genius'?

As with so many things, Sterne the writer was ambivalent about learning – mocking its worst excesses of arid scholarship in those ancient authorities ushered in and out of *Tristram Shandy*. And as always with Sterne, the mockery is based on impenetrably mixed feelings. He had clearly an affection for old and otherwise neglected libraries. (In July 1761, he bought seven hundred books 'at a purchase dog cheap—and many good'.[1] But men who haunt second-hand bookshops often fail to read what they buy.) Sterne's display of recondite learning – even if sometimes it ventured into the spurious – may have been a disguise for shortcomings in more basic education. I do not mean to put a slur on Sterne, rather to suggest that in all his bantering with language, as in his flirting with women, it is possible to detect an essential insecurity. In that respect, as in many others, Sterne's credentials were never quite straight.

Even if barrack-life taught the young Sterne 'to write, &c.', it is no surprise that Roger Sterne decided 'to fix me at school'.[2] The seasoned ensign can have had few illusions left at this time, however Micawberish a figure we suppose him to have been, and he may have sensed how crucial a decision this was for the boy's life. Otherwise, in a few more years, he might have been sucked into the army. Roger perhaps saw sufficient individuality and promise in his son to settle any doubts. That the girl, Mary, was not put to school is hardly surprising. Girls then were left to their mothers, though some said they learned more than their brothers did at the institutions that passed for schools.

Laurence's school was 'near Halifax, with an able master; with whom I staid some time'.[3] Although he remained there until the end of 1731, that is until he was eighteen, his Memoir

relates only one detail of his time there. The anecdote concerns
Sterne, his schoolmaster and a ceiling: 'He had the cieling of
the school-room new white-washed—the ladder remained there
—I one unlucky day mounted it, and wrote with a brush in
large capital letters, LAU. STERNE, for which the usher
severely whipped me. My master was very much hurt at this, and
said, before me, that never should that name be effaced, for I was
a boy of genius, and he was sure I should come to preferment—
this expression made me forget the stripes I had received.'[4]

Though the scene is vivid, there remains doubt as to whether
Sterne's school was at Heath or Hipperholme, two villages
near Halifax. If Roger Sterne chose Heath – a particularly
badly run establishment – it is likely that the boy's uncle,
Richard Sterne, took it upon himself to remove the unfortunate
Sterne to Hipperholme. His own son, Richard, was only six
years older than Laurence and may well have attended Hipperholme. Uncle Richard knew the defects of Heath and its
teachers. He also had family connections with the master at
Hipperholme.

The educational system that Sterne would have known seems
to us so narrow and strict that it is hard to say whether a diligent
or lax master would have been most beneficial. The summer
programme at Heath, for instance, called for lessons from six in
the morning until eleven and then from one until five. In winter,
between October and March, the start was at eight and the day
ended at four. Such hours were general and applied to children
of seven and upwards.

Nor was the whipping that Sterne claims to have had at all
unusual. Thrashing was a normal part of school life, criticized
only rarely by such sceptics as Locke. Tom Jones, for instance,
had as his tutor Mr. Thwackum, who 'had a great reputation for
learning, religion and sobriety of manners' but 'whose media-
tions were full of birch'.[5] It was not unusual for Tom to suffer
'so severe a whipping, that it possibly fell little short of the
torture with which confessions are in some countries extorted
from criminals'.[6]

Such discipline may have been demanded by lessons that
were intended to instil little more than religious learning and
the rules and systems of archaic languages. The charter of Heath

set down the task of 'bringing up teaching and instructing of children and youth in Grammar and other good learning'.[7] Grammar meant Latin and Greek, essential for any pupil intending to go on to university. Beyond that, a child was taught the catechism, reading, writing and – if he showed aptitude – arithmetic. But Latin was the principal concern, to the exclusion of the pupil's native and spoken language. Locke had been alarmed that 'young men are forced to learn the grammars of foreign and dead languages, and are never once told of the grammar of their own tongues: they do not so much as know there is any such thing, much less is it made their business to be instructed in it.'[8]

It was while Sterne was at school that *Gulliver's Travels* was published with its satires upon crazily learned academies, all in a prose more succinct, vigorous and simple than the eighteenth-century academy aspired to. Although narrative was not his prime intention, Swift's was strong and flexible prose, more able to sustain interest in a story than Defoe's. The elements of realism in the first novels are inseparable from a prose style that would be widely accessible and which would persuade readers to follow an extended narrative. It is no surprise therefore that at this period people should have become conscious of the deficiencies in teaching of the English language. Sterne's English is unique, but perhaps it is also distorted by the conflict between old rules and new feelings.

Sterne's language darts restlessly away from sustained sequence, from slowness and order. While no one could doubt that this was a mark of his flighty, fickle nature, it is true that many of the ellipses and breathless dashes join up his sentences in the absence of an intrinsic grammatical ease. A child, like Tristram or Laurence, was subjected to systems of faith and convention which had endured for centuries but which by about 1730 had come very close to colliding with a felt reality of experience, reason and naturalism. Berkeley, for instance, at the beginning of his *Principles of Human Knowledge*, noted that for all philosophy's search for truth and serenity, it was the ordinary man of common sense who was most easy with the world. We can see something of the self-induced confusion of Walter Shandy in Berkeley's view that 'Upon the whole I am inclined to think that the far greater part, if not all, of those difficulties which have hitherto amused philosophers, and blocked up the way to knowledge, are entirely owing to ourselves. That we have first raised a dust, and then complain we cannot see.'[9]

Not that we can detect in Sterne anything resembling proposals for the reform of education. Like Swift and Locke, Sterne was a sceptic. But while Swift was distraught and Locke inquiring, Sterne's tone is one of affectionate bewilderment. His subjectivity is so great that he does not realize that man might take steps to improve and regulate his affairs. Instead, he assumes that his state of whimsical confusion is shared by everyone else. It is from fear of, or unease with, conventional learning and the discipline involved, that Sterne seems to endorse Walter Shandy's faith in some vague, instinctive path to understanding – 'there is a North-west passage to the intellectual world; and . . . the soul of man has shorter ways of going to work, in furnishing itself with knowledge and instruction, than we generally take with it.'[10]

This sort of romantic notion of the secret springs of knowledge barely conceals obscurantism and a sense of intellectual inferiority. It emphasizes how much Tristram is the victim of the Shandy household, just as Sterne himself had been encouraged to see himself as the plaything of an arbitrary destiny. And just as the voice of Sterne is most alive in his puzzled, if apologetic, disruptions of the stately debates between the Shandy brothers – in the diversions from the 'story' of the book – so John Traugott is surely right in claiming that 'Sterne's capacity for doubt is his capacity for expression.'[11]

Doubt also promotes an unrestricted sense of possibility: if nothing is certain, then, equally, nothing is impossible. Herein lies so much of the speculative detachment that must have made Sterne so exasperating to many contemporaries, but which also provides a note of real existential wonder in his work. Nothing illustrates this so well as Walter Shandy's consideration of the 'auxiliary verbs'. He defines them as '*am*; *was*; *have*; *had*; *do*; *did*; *make*; *made*; *suffer*; *shall*; *should*; *will*; *would*; *can*; *could*; *owe*; *ought*; *used*'. There is such a wealth of possibility contained in these instruments, that 'by the right use and application of these, continued my father, in which a child's memory should be exercised, there is no one idea can enter his brain how barren soever, but a magazine of conceptions and conclusions may be drawn forth from it.'[12]

But this means to open-mindedness also serves to explain Sterne's own great attention to fantasy. For if the mind is so stimulated by ideas, what need does it have of reality? Walter Shandy demonstrates his thesis by asking Trim to consider a white bear. But he has never seen one, reasons Toby. Walter is unabashed: the properly agile mind requires no manifestation: 'If I never have, can, must or shall see a white bear alive; have I ever seen the skin of one? Did I ever see one painted?— described? Have I never dreamed of one?'[13] For all that Sterne seems to be aware of the eccentricity of Walter Shandy's theory, he never freed himself from its implication that dreaming was sufficient power for a sensitive man.

This is to advance a good way beyond the schoolboy, but I think it is reasonable to believe that, from its beginning, Sterne's education was a negative process, working against his nature. It may not be so strange that our one item from his schooling is an instance of his breaking the rules in an extravagant attempt to assert his own identity. As if in an environment in which nonsense and rote learning might be drummed into his skull, he stood up and insisted for protection and assurance: 'I am Laurence Sterne.'

For although he was at a proper school and tended by his uncle, Sterne was still essentially on his own. He may have missed his parents very much, been bewildered by the new standards expected of him and suddenly aware that few of his fellow-pupils had observed as many of the unwholesome realities of life as he had in the camps and barracks. The boy must have found it hard to believe in school and realized, like Pope, that he would have to educate himself. But Pope's invalid self-education was also the sybaritic retreat of a bookworm that produced a man of wide and deep knowledge. Sterne's pursuit was private in a much more radical way; he needed to know things and to have assets that no one else possessed. But for all that he cultivated uniqueness, Sterne never sounds conceited or boastful. A cult of originality may only indicate failure in traditional pursuits. Sterne seems to insist on himself partly to convince himself of his existence and partly because he frequently needed the inspiration of someone else's writing to stimulate his own novelty.*

It is paradoxical that so assertively inventive a writer should have so frequently needed models and originals to draw upon. Sometimes his copying has been considered part of his fraudulence sufficient to damn him. Mrs. Thrale, for instance, fell with glee upon *The Life and Memoirs of Mr. Ephraim Tristram Bates, commonly called Corporal Bates, a broken-hearted Soldier*, published in 1756, and 'found it to be the very Novel from which Sterne took his first Idea: the Character of Uncle Toby, the Behaviour of Corporal Trim, even the name of Tristram itself seems to be borrowed from this stupid History of Corporal Bates forsooth'.[14]

No one would deny that Sterne had noticed that book or that details from it had stuck in his mind. It is only one of innumerable small debts that go largely unacknowledged in Sterne's writing. The tracking down of these sources will always be a good game for scholars. But the successful huntsmen should beware of attaching too great a significance to what they find. Theodore Baird discovered, beyond doubt, that Sterne had had *The History of England*, by Rapin de Thoyras, to hand while relating Uncle Toby's military career. But this *coup* drove him on to attempt to prove that in *Tristram Shandy* 'there is a carefully planned and executed framework of calendar time in what is usually considered a chaos of whimsicalities and indecencies.'[15] All he really establishes, though, is that when someone takes the trouble to unravel the family affairs in *Tristram Shandy* they do appear largely consistent and plausible. To say that there is a 'time-scheme' in *Shandy* and to explain it on the grounds that 'Sterne learned from Locke the secret of why time moves slowly or rapidly in the consciousness of an individual: namely, that its speed depends upon the rapidity of the succession of ideas'[16] is diligently to map a blind alley.

A more interesting question is whether or not Sterne thought his nine-volume *Tristram Shandy* a completed work. The leading

---

* In *A Sentimental Journey*, Yorick needs to write a letter to a lady. But his mood is not right. He throws down his pen and La Fleur, his servant, offers a letter of his own. Yorick 'took the cream gently off it, and whipping it up in my own way' sends it off to the lady forthwith. (*SJ*, Vol. I, The Letters.)

exponent of the view that 'the book he had completed re-
presented the completion of a plan, however rough, which was
present in his mind from the beginning'[17] has been Wayne
Booth. He admits that there is very little conclusive external
evidence of Sterne's attitude to Volume IX of *Tristram Shandy*
and relies upon internal resonances from the text itself. In that
sense, Volume IX does appear to have a rather weary winding-
up. It tells the story of Uncle Toby's *amour*, the most persistently
promised event in the earlier volumes; it ends with the assembled
characters and with the cock-and-bull, which can be taken as a
verdict on the whole work. There is also a strong hint of resignation on the author's part. Thus, in Chapter XXIV of Volume
IX, he proposes to the reader that 'the story' be dropped: 'for
though I have all along been hastening towards this part of it,
with so much earnest desire, as well knowing it to be the
choicest morsel of what I had to offer to the world, yet now that
I am got to it, any one is welcome to take my pen, and go on
with the story for me that will.'[18]

But there is a crucial difference between believing that in
Volume IX Sterne was deliberately coming to a halt and that
all along he had had the design of *Tristram Shandy* in mind. One
has only to read *Tristram Shandy* to realize how often Sterne was
at a loss for what to do next. Because succeeding volumes do not,
very often, contradict one another is not proof that Sterne had a
plan for nine volumes from the start or that there are subtle
systems at work within these volumes, no matter how improvisa-
tional they seem when read.

The note of conclusion is no more significant than the last,
prize joke with which a comedian might walk off the stage or
the graceful footlight speech with which an actor might yield to
retirement. Comedians are back again next night and few actors
have abided by their own description of the pleasures of rest and
retirement. To take Volume IX as proof of a larger formal
awareness only exposes Sterne to the inescapable criticism that
many other parts of *Tristram Shandy* are formally disastrous. It is
surely a serious underestimate of Sterne to think that, if life had
allowed, he could not have picked Tristram up again with
much the same combination of brilliance and slackness. It is
just as misleading to suppose that he entertained serious

preoccupation on the design of *Tristram Shandy* over a period of years. And yet that was Professor Booth's aim; the purpose of his article 'Did Sterne Complete *Tristram Shandy*?' was to ensure that 'Questions about the form of this "formless work" . . . can now for the first time receive adequate consideration.'[19] I believe it is a disservice to Sterne to omit the element of opportunism in his life and fiction. Sterne's genius is elemental but passive: like liquid it takes the shape of whatever vessel it is poured into. If he ever envisaged any formal receptacle, it was the mind of a reader. His 'plan' is not to create a literary shape, but to implant his work in human curiosity, amusement, protest and surprise. He had such an intimate feel for these recesses that he may be said to have invented the reader.

No matter how hopefully Sterne advertised his nearness to Locke's *Essay on Human Understanding*, it is surely fanciful to think of him doggedly embarking on a fictional demonstration of Locke's philosophical inquiry. Egotism made Sterne independent of mentors just as it kept him from close personal relationships in life. When Sterne looked at Locke he saw what he chose to see. Reacting against the sober generalization of human communication, Sterne loved to find a mundane, garish incident from the clutter of domestic life that illustrated Locke's theory of the association of ideas: for when Obadiah reports 'My young master in *London* is dead!' what should this bring into Susannah's head but 'a green sattin night-gown of my mother's – Well might *Locke* write a chapter upon the imperfections of words.'[20] He felt warmly towards Locke because he reacted towards argument not intellectually but quickly and sentimentally.* If we suppose that Sterne read with the swiftness that he claimed he wrote, then it is impossible to see Sterne doing more than skip through Locke, sensing but not understanding that here was a composed argument tending towards a conclusion that Sterne knew instinctively – that human intercourse was not the classical means to enlightenment, but simply the opportunity for self-expression. In other words, a man spoke

---

* 'I wish you saw me half starting out of my chair, with what confidence, as I grasp the elbow of it, I look up—catching the idea, even sometimes before it half way reaches me—

'I believe in my conscience I intercept many a thought which heaven intended for another man.' (*TS*, Vol. VIII, Ch. II.)

so that he might understand himself. Thus John Traugott says of the empathy between Locke and Sterne:

Locke's is a rational system for comparing ideas and determining language. Sterne's is something else, but by developing the possibilities of confusion or absurdity in Locke's rational system Sterne has created a dramatic engine which controls situation and character. The characters are so made that, operating on Locke's premises, they completely foil his rational method for communication. And in the consequent isolation of personalities the vitality of situations is maintained by the comic gropings of those personalities for some sort of concourse. The excitement of *Tristram Shandy* lies not in its whimsical view of man's nature, but in its rhetorical demonstration that what is easily called odd, whimsical, and eccentric *must* know the difficulty not only in communication with foreign minds but also in discovering his own.[21]

Sterne in the library, therefore, is not the measured, conscientious student, neither a learned man nor a clever thief, but a heightened fictional consciousness, intellectually deferring but instinctively penetrating. In the first serious survey of his plagiarism, *Illustrations of Sterne*, John Ferriar made it clear that, 'If some instances of copying be proved against him, they will detract nothing from his genius, and will only lessen that imposing appearance he sometimes assumed, of erudition which he really wanted.' Although Sterne steals – and there are probably still undetected robberies in his works – the theft is not so much for gain as an exposure of the confused nature of literary property. Time and again he elaborates on something he has borrowed or even playfully hints at where it has come from. The most audacious instance of this was noticed by Ferriar. When Sterne apostrophized the endless reworking of materials in books – 'Shall we for ever make new books, as apothecaries make new mixtures, by pouring only out of one vessel into another?

'Are we for ever to be twisting and untwisting the same rope? for ever in the same track—for ever at the same pace?'[22] – he is in fact employing the argument and imagery of Burton's *Anatomy of Melancholy*, one of his favourite books. This sort of joke is also a very shrewd comment on literary identity and seems to predict that extraordinary story by Jorge Luis Borges,

Pierre Menard, Author of the 'Quixote', which recounts a word-by-word rewriting of parts of *Don Quixote* (another of Sterne's bedside books) and establishes that the second version is in fact superior to Cervantes.*

The wish to appear acquainted with other men's books was like Sterne's later desire to hobnob with the distinguished, high and low, in London. In both cases he made no real connection. By 1765, when Volume VIII of *Tristram Shandy* was published, Sterne had come to this conclusion: 'For my own part, I am resolved never to read any book but my own, as long as I live.'[23] No other writer could seriously affect him if only because Sterne dared not risk his insecure intellectual identity.

It was without vanity and scarcely thinking of the actual quality of his own prose that he was confident he could do whatever he wanted in *Tristram Shandy.* The combination of artifice and credulity involved in writing and reading a book entranced him and allowed him to address a reader with an unequalled authority. He did not write to tell stories; indeed, his treatment of narrative is often deliberately disruptive, provoking interruption and even leaving stories to the aroused interest of the reader. His whole concern is to capture that interest and Sterne felt it as acutely as, say, Garrick must have treasured the attentive hush of an audience in the theatre.

Is it not particularly remarkable that so native a writer should wait so long to exercise his command? Only one thing explains the delay: the extreme personal diffidence, the lack of confidence and the abstracting shyness that allowed him to live for so long in his own head.

* *Pierre Menard* is a very serious joke. It manages simultaneously to satirize literary pretension and to expand fictional potential. That these effects do not cancel one another out is the best tribute to the theory Borges attributes to 'Menard': 'Thinking, analysing, inventing (he also wrote me) are not anomalous acts; they are the normal respiration of the intelligence. To glorify the occasional performance of that function, to hoard ancient and alien thoughts, to recall with incredulous stupor what the *doctor universalis* thought, is to confess our laziness or our barbarity. Every man should be capable of all ideas and I understand that in the future this will be the case.' (Jorge Luis Borges, 'Pierre Menard', *Labyrinths* [New York, 1964].)

The Story of Roger Sterne, Concluded

In the year of Laurence's departure to school at Halifax, the 34th changed hands. Thomas Chudleigh retired and the regiment was purchased in February 1723 by Robert Hayes, who had been an officer in the 34th since 1715 and had risen to the rank of lieutenant-colonel.[1] The change in proprietorship did nothing to alter Roger Sterne's status, but must have underlined the hopelessness of his position at the foot of the hierarchy of officers. Whatever hopes he had had on enlisting, we must conclude that neither his own nor his wife's family had offered the funds which were generally able to obtain promotion.

The regiment was removed to Londonderry in 1723 and there another child was born, Catherine, who lived to trouble her brother. Although Roger Sterne and his family seem to have remained at Londonderry for four years, we know nothing of their life there. If they corresponded with their son, no letters remain. Nor is there any hint of a visit between them.

In 1727 the 34th was sent to relieve the garrison at Gibraltar. Gibraltar had been taken in 1704 and retained by the Peace of Utrecht, but was already as vulnerable as it was useful. By February 1727, a Spanish army of 20,000 was laying siege to the Rock. Reinforcements, including the 34th, were quickly dispatched, bringing the garrison up to some 5,500. But the threatened action was little more than an exchange of artillery barrages. By the end of June the Spaniards agreed to settle. It had been a mild encounter: seventy-four men and officers killed on the British side, and 361 on the Spanish.[2]

For our purposes, the most intriguing action was domestic. It was while at Gibraltar that Roger Sterne 'was run through the body by Captain Phillips, in a duel (the quarrel begun about a goose), with much difficulty he survived—tho' with an impaired constitution'.[3] Geese are quarrelsome creatures – Sterne himself had a hectic adventure with some – but not many men would put their lives at risk on their behalf. Whatever provocation the goose caused, the duel is supposed to have taken place indoors. Roger was not only run through, but pinned to a plaster wall. Despite his wound, the ensign was alert enough to ask his successful opponent to clean the tip of his rapier before withdrawing it.

Roger survived, but might have wished that the rapier had been more accurate. His next posting was capable of killing the healthiest soldier. Indeed, it was known as the graveyard of the army: a place of heat, jungle, fever and wild natives.

Early in 1731, the 34th and 39th were dispatched from Gibraltar to Jamaica where the English colonists were troubled by the guerrilla activities of some five hundred Maroon Negroes who lived in the mountains. Barracks had been erected in the mountains, Indian trackers hired from the Mosquito coast and packs of dogs procured, all to subdue the Maroons. But to no avail.

The voyage across the Atlantic was surprisingly trouble-free. Colonel Hayes reported from Port Royale on 14 February 1731 that the 34th 'had very Good weather all the way & brought these Regiments here in very Good health'.[4] But on shore the men quickly deteriorated. Regiments in Jamaica were expected to fend for themselves and make whatever bargain they could for provisions and accommodation with the local authorities. The regiment was allowed 20s (£1.00) a week for officers and 5s (25p) for the men. On their arrival, the regimental quartermaster judged the accommodation provided by the Governor and Assembly of Jamaica as inadequate. The soldiers stayed on the ships, but began to sicken there and were put ashore so that the transports could be discharged.[5]

The 34th never encountered the Maroons. Sickness and the hardships of the island overwhelmed them. Colonel Hayes reported, 'No Oven sure was ever so Hot, I find it Affects my Eyes very much & stile have the Gravel very Much, & my legs swell.'[6] For lack of proper quarters, the regiments were dispersed about the island. Hayes thought the Maroons were a sham; no one had heard or seen them. He also lamented how unprofitable it was to have a regiment in the West Indies and complained that he had no more allowance than an ensign. In a letter of 11 March Hayes anticipated his regiment being cut by half within three months and expected 'very soon to hear a Miserable Account... whenever any of them fall sick there's no helping of them for there's no such thing as a surgeon going from Quarter to Quarter here'.[7]

But by 17 March Colonel Hayes himself was dead, and there were vacancies for three captains. Governor Hunter recommended promotions and, at last, the thirty-nine-year old Roger Sterne was raised to the rank of lieutenant.[8] Ironically, he enjoyed the privilege for only four months. He died at Port Antonio, on 31 July 1731, 'by the country fever, which took away his senses first, and made a child of him, and then, in a month or two, walking about continually without complaining, till the moment he sat down in an arm chair, and breathed his last'.[9]

This news would have reached Laurence at about the time he finished school, when he was nearly eighteen. What can he have thought of this wretched soldier, beset by feverish motion and dying as soon as he came to rest? Compared with all his denigration of Agnes, Laurence's requiem for Roger Sterne is tender and nostalgic:

My father was a little smart man—active to the last degree, in all exercises—most patient of fatigue and disappointments, of which it pleased God to give him full measure—he was in his temper somewhat rapid, and hasty—but of a kindly, sweet disposition, void of all design; and so innocent in his own intentions, that he suspected no one; so that you might have cheated him ten times in a day, if nine had not been sufficient for your purpose.*[10]

It is a brilliant sketch, lightning but penetrating, of a character not far from one Sterne often put on for himself: guileless,

---

* '... so naked and defenceless did he stand before you, (when a siege was out of his head) that you might have stood behind any one of your serpentine walks, and shot my uncle *Toby* ten times in a day, through his liver, if nine times in a day, Madam, had not served your purpose.' (*TS*, Vol. VI, Ch. XXIX.)

impulsive and unlucky. But it probably served as an example to avoid rather than emulate.

The only other picture we have of Roger Sterne the soldier is that invented by Thackeray in *Henry Esmond*. It is an affectionate portrait that suggests how compelling a fascination Sterne held for Thackeray. In *Esmond*, as in Sterne's Memoir, Roger is a member of Handyside's regiment 'and as brave a little soul as ever wore a sword' who talks 'in his wild way, in which there was sense as well as absurdity'.[11] But Thackeray has Roger enter the fiercest action of Malplaquet in an attempt to escape the daughter of the sutler to whom he is in debt. But 'he rushed so desperately on the French lines' that he was promoted. 'To run out of the reach of bill and marriage,' writes Thackeray in a Shandean aside, 'he ran on the enemy's pikes; and as these did not kill him he was thrown back upon t'other horn of his dilemma.'[12]

For all the exhaustive period detail of *Henry Esmond*, Thackeray allows his hero a nineteenth-century awareness of the horrors of Marlborough's war that would hardly have been articulated at the time:

Mr Esmond beheld another part of military duty; our troops entering the enemy's territory, and putting all around them to fire and sword; burning farms, wasted fields, shrieking women, slaughtered sons and fathers, and drunken soldiery, cursing and carousing in the midst of tears, terror, and murder. Why does the stately Muse of History, that delights in describing the valour of heroes and the grandeur of conquest, leave out these scenes, so brutal, mean, and degrading, that yet form by far the greater part of the drama of war?[13]

That question is much nearer to the aroused sensibilities of the Crimean War and to Mathew Brady's photographs of the American Civil War. It would have bemused Uncle Toby; despite his tenderness towards individual suffering he remains a connoisseur of the bloodthirsty and never guesses that war might be anything more or less controllable than climate. Even in his 'apologetical oration' – that strange defence of martial spirit – he sees the evils of war as being visited only upon soldiers:

—'Tis one thing, brother *Shandy*, for a soldier to hazard his own life—to leap first down into the trench, where he is sure to be cut in pieces:—'Tis one thing, from public spirit and a thirst of glory, to enter the breach the first man,—to stand in the foremost rank, and march bravely on with drums and trumpets, and colours flying about his ears:—'Tis one thing, I say, brother *Shandy*, to do this— and 'tis another thing to reflect on the miseries of war;—to view the desolations of whole countries, and consider the intolerable fatigues and hardships which the soldier himself, the instrument who works them, is forced (for six-pence a day, if he can get it) to undergo.[14]

Neither Walter nor Toby Shandy can really be a version of Roger Sterne, no matter how busy and ineffectual Walter is nor Toby preoccupied with military charades. It is more to the point that both the Shandys survived into middle age to sit day after day with little to do but smoke a sociable pipe and wrangle in a comfortable house, and compose and inhabit their rambling theories as an alternative to real life. Roger never knew such relaxation. And although Laurence left the barracks at ten he probably had learned enough to distinguish between a real and an armchair soldier. Uncle Toby and Trim are not just sur- vivors but emotional refugees from the army, oblivious of its imperfections and so loyal to the dream of its romance that they believe some insurmountable necessity in their own nature made them soldiers. The military reality was too harsh for fic- tion. It barely features in the English novel, even in the twen- tieth century.* Even as a child, Sterne could have seen how badly so uncompromisingly faithful a soldier as Uncle Toby would have fared. But military preoccupation was a perfect spectacle of comedy; it is all the more remarkable that one of the few English writers who knew the reality should yet be able to transcend it. Uncle Toby is the original of an enormous regi- ment of literary veterans, chatting away their retirement with dinner-table or bowling-green reconstructions – pepper-pots for cannon, oranges for cavalry, flower-beds for fortifications – and he has still not been equalled for the stoic melancholy that speaks of abused simplicity. Like Falstaff, Toby is both comic relief and a central, tragic figure. It may contribute to our pic- ture of Sterne if we recognize that one implication of Toby's life is Sterne's view of the frustration of straightforward, honest virtues.

* Even so, Evelyn Waugh's Apthorpe is perhaps Toby's most suitable com- panion-in-arms.

'In Such a Gloom'

Sterne's Memoir claims that he finished school towards the end of 1731 and went up to Jesus College, Cambridge, the next year. But the records of the college make it clear that he was not admitted until July 1733. There is thus an ellipsis – neither the first nor the last in his life – of eighteen months in which we do not know what happened to Sterne.

The youth may have roamed round Halifax, a place remarked upon by the industrious Defoe for the way it prefigured the transformation from rural settlement to industrial urbanization that was to have so profound an effect on the north of England in the next hundred years. Halifax, said Defoe, 'with all its dependencies, . . . is not to be equalled in England'. The parish was 'a monster' and Defoe was told that it had 100,000 communicants, and had provided 12,000 troops for Queen Elizabeth.[1]

Trade does not seem to have interested Sterne, no matter that his uncle may have extolled it. Indeed, Laurence was to be more honest about money: he appreciated it simply for itself and did not need the justification of industry or service. What, then, was to be done with him? If only because the same period was eventful for the Sterne family it is likely that judgement on Laurence's future hung in the balance.

Not only was news of Roger's death brought to the family in the summer of 1731. In October 1732, Richard Sterne – Laurence's effective guardian – died, aged fifty-two. Like his father, Simon, Richard was buried at Halifax, where he had lived most of his life. His will indicated the prosperity of the Sternes. He left to Richard, his son by his first marriage, his estates at Elvington, Kexby, Ovenden, Halifax, Hipperholme,

Sowerby and Norland. We may judge the value of this legacy by the fact that Richard instructed his son to pay £2,000 each to his sisters, Mary and Anne. To Timothy, his son by his second marriage to Esther Booth, he left his estates at Skircoat and Otley. Timothy was expected to provide for his two sisters, Dorothy and Frances, to the tune of £1,000 each.[2]

There were sundry other bequests. To Mrs. Elizabeth Haigh, perhaps a housekeeper, he left the rents of his estates at Midgley for as long as she remained unmarried; he also allowed her to live rent-free for one year in Lower Woodhouse Hall. Mary, his daughter, was left all the furniture in a house he owned in North Street, York, while Mary and Anne had divided between them all their father's gold and silver plate. Richard, Mary and Anne shared their father's holding 'in the Mine adventures' and Timothy inherited fifteen shares in the Hamstead Waterworks. Richard was to collect anything else his father might have forgotten.[3] Laurence Sterne was not mentioned in the will.

Richard, Timothy and Laurence Sterne were approximate contemporaries: in 1732 Richard was twenty-five, Laurence eighteen and Timothy twelve. They were far enough apart in age not to have been playmates, but they must have shared much at Woodhouse and no doubt the Yorkshire cousins were eager to hear whatever stories Laurence could recall or invent about soldiers. At home, as at school, his background must have given him a raffish, unconventional appeal. It was exactly this mixed effect that Sterne so enjoyed making in later life. Even so, he would have been very conscious of the way their father's will had smoothed the future for his cousins' lives. If he dined on the unrespectable, he doubtless envied the inheritance of an unflawed pedigree. A hundred years later, a writer in Sterne's position might have turned social satirist. But Sterne is never bitter about his misfortunes, just as when he prospered he was never complacent or grasping of the rewards.

Whatever the relationship between Laurence and his cousins, Sterne was later to admit how much his career had depended on the patronage and goodwill of his cousin Richard. The senior surviving Sterne, Uncle Jaques, 'absolutely refused giving me any aid' and it was Richard 'to whose Protection *then*, I cheifly owe What I now am ... without *his* [aid], I should have been driven out naked into the World, Young as I was, to have shifted for myself as well as I could.'[4]

Jaques at this moment seems to have been unwilling to involve himself in any of the affairs of his brother's family. He denied both Laurence and his mother, Agnes. Roger's will can have passed on very little except a few military mementoes. Letters of administration for these relics had been granted to Agnes by the Irish Courts on 18 August 1732. But according to her son, Agnes

> upon the first news of his [Roger's] Death came over to England; She was then in some difficulties about her Pension, & her Business was with You [Jaques] to Sollicit your Interest to procure it for her upon the English Establishment.

> But I well remember she was forced to return back, without having so much Interest as to obtain the favor of being admitted to Your Presence. (not being sufferd even to reach York).[5]

In fact, it was not until February 1736 that Agnes received her pension of £20 a year. If she met Laurence on that earlier visit, there was nothing she could have done to help her son. She may already have thought of him as given over to the influence of the uncharitable Yorkshire Sternes. Perhaps the youthful Laurence, embarrassed by the reappearance of his mother, was offhand with her. His father's death, and her appearance in Yorkshire, can only have reminded the respectable Sternes of Laurence's disreputable origins.

The apparent delay between Sterne's schooling and his moving on to the university may be explained by the fact that his cousin, flush with an inheritance, was rather more amenable than Uncle Richard. Once the idea of a university education had been accepted, there could be little doubt that a Sterne should proceed to Jesus College, Cambridge. Not only had the archbishop been one of its most distinguished masters; his son Simon had been there, although without graduating. Jaques Sterne had taken his B.A. at Jesus and Cousin Richard had been admitted there as a pensioner as recently as June 1725. Two years later, he had obtained a scholarship but, like Simon his grandfather, he had not taken a degree. Jesus, naturally, was also the Shandys' college.

When Tristram Shandy went up to Jesus to be entered there, his father went with him, but Laurence had only a cousin as sponsor. More than that, he was late for the university: Gibbon, for instance, matriculated at Magdalen College, Oxford, before he was fifteen; David Hume attended Edinburgh University in 1723, when only twelve; even Sterne's cousin Richard had been eighteen on arriving at Jesus. Sterne was only four months short of twenty when on 6 July 1733 he was admitted as a sizar.

The college register asserts that the admission was in the absence of Sterne himself and *cum consensu Magistri & Sociorum*. As a rule, sizars had first to be examined and approved, and the exception of this entry shows to what extent family influence was working for him. Even so, Laurence was a sizar, the lowest rank of undergraduate, and it was not until July 1734 that he was elected to one of the scholarships that his great-grandfather had laid down at the college. This foundation was intended for natives of Yorkshire or Nottinghamshire so that, once again, a rule was twisted a little in Sterne's favour.

Sterne's first year at Cambridge cannot have been comfortable. Sizars were usually the sons of poor clergymen and small farmers, sometimes even of tradesmen or artisans; if they no longer had to feed themselves from the leavings of the Fellows' table, they were still expected to act as servants on several occasions. Their finances could be a constant anxiety. Charles Churchill, the clergyman and poet, had to abandon his studies at Cambridge for lack of funds. Sterne himself was pressed into borrowing: in his letter of 1751 to Uncle Jaques, he revealed that, whatever aid he had had from the Sternes, it was all recorded and subsequently presented as owing: 'the whole Debt of My School Education, Cloathing &c for nine Years together, which came upon me, the Moment I was able to pay it.—To this, a great Part of the Expence of my Education at the University, too Scantily defray'd by my Cosin Sterne wth only 30p^ds a Year, & the last Year not pay'd'.[6]

But for all the financial hardship, we may wonder at the value of Sterne's education at Cambridge. In fact, the universities were in their period of greatest stagnation. Hogarth in 1737 depicted *Scholars at a Lecture* in which the undergraduates are vacant, fuddled or asleep. Gibbon spoke of his months at

university as 'the most idle and unprofitable of my whole life'.[7]
Gray compared Cambridge with Babylon and complained that
there was nothing but smoking and drinking.[8] Even Parson
Woodforde filled his diary with accounts of drunkenness at
Oxford and records a bet that one man could not drink three
pints of wine in three hours and then write out verses from the
Bible. He drank the wine 'but could not write right for his
Life'.[9] The *History of Jesus College* admits that 'Scarcely even in
the dark days of Edward VI and Mary, when learning was
discounted and bankruptcy imminent, had the College des-
cended to so low a position in numbers and perhaps in reputation.'[10] The numbers of admissions and degrees fell alarmingly
at Jesus, as throughout Cambridge, from 1660 onwards. In the
late 1740s, Jesus obtained no more than an annual average of
fourteen B.A.s; the other students settled for the college testimonial which was apparently given without discrimination.

As at school, Latin was of the utmost importance, and the
student was expected to be able to carry on precise moral and
philosophical arguments in that language. History, science,
mathematics and English language were barely touched upon.
Many Fellows never lectured, but sat snug in their colleges,
provided for and no longer likely to be put to the test of doctrinal issues. Trevelyan called them as helpless as fifteenth-
century monks.[11] To take their degree, students had to perform
the statutory two acts and two opponencies and to have been in
residence for the greater part of ten terms.* To keep an act the
undergraduate selected three propositions which he was prepared to defend and then, on the appointed day, read a Latin
essay upon one of them and engaged in arguments on it. Thus
the essence of this education was in formal learning and
articulation.

There were tutorials, but they were not meant to trouble
either tutors or students. Many of the dons were unversed in the
subjects they proposed to teach, but quite content with the
comforts of the fellowships they held in perpetuity. Gibbon
attended tutorials faithfully during his first weeks at Oxford,

---

* 'Four years at his *probations* and his *negations*—the fine statue still lying in the
middle of the marble block,—and nothing done, but his tools sharpened to hew it
out!—'Tis a piteous delay!' (*TS*, Vol. V, Ch. XLII.)

'but as they appeared equally devoid of profit and pleasure, I was once tempted to try the experiment of a formal apology. The apology was accepted with a smile: I repeated the offence with less ceremony, the excuse was admitted with the same indulgence: the slightest motive of lazyness or indisposition, the most trifling avocation at home or abroad was allowed as a worthy impediment nor did my tutor appear conscious of my absence or neglect.'[12]

It is probable that the Sternes had already indicated the advisability of a career in the Church. In which case, according to Daniel Waterland's *Advice to a Young Student*, Sterne would have begun by abridging and copying out sermons – a task that his own sermons suggest he carried out faithfully. Then he would have studied philosophy, classics and divinity. In his fourth year he was expected to 'get a general view of the several controversies on foot' by reading Church histories and such works as Pearson on the Creed and Barnet on the Articles. The prescribed reading for students in moral philosophy and metaphysics included Berkeley's *Dialogues and the Treatise on the Principles of Human Knowledge*, Hobbes's *Leviathan*, the works of Locke – particularly *An Essay concerning Human Understanding* – Newton on *Opticks*, Puffendorf's *Law of Nature* and Tillotson's *Sermons*.[13]

If an undergraduate spent his time in reading he might profit, but the organization of studies, when it was not impossibly arid, was slack. The Master of Jesus during Sterne's attendance was Dr. Charles Ashton, a patristic theologian and High Church Tory. His tutors at Jesus were first Charles Cannon, who died in 1735, and then Lynford Caryl. But although on 14 January 1737 Sterne took his B.A., it is fair to remark how little significant impression the university had made on him, except that it stimulated his sense of the ridiculous in grave learning. Some twenty-five years later, Sterne gave a hint of the dullness he had endured at Jesus in a verse commentary on the effects of the great walnut tree that grew in the college quadrangle:

> It overshadow'd ev'ry room,
> And consequently, more or less,
> Forc'd ev'ry brain, in such a gloom,
> To grope its way, and go by guess.[14]

It is more to the point that at Cambridge Sterne may have read Locke, Swift, Berkeley, Rabelais and Cervantes – finding out for himself voices that contained some of the ingredients of his own style and tone. This sort of development may have been enhanced by the opportunities he had to mix with other mettlesome but bored young men. The picture of Sterne at Jesus, as presented in *Crazy Tales*, has him and his friend, John Hall, sitting beneath the 'scientifick shade' of the walnut tree and swapping jokes from Rabelais. Since, in later life, Sterne contrived to function so often outside the rules and conduct of his profession, it is likely that at Jesus he took most pleasure in extra-mural activities. John Hall, five years younger but substantially wealthier than Sterne, might have been his most effective tutor. He was the son of the heiress to Skelton Castle, in Yorkshire; it is possible that he and Sterne had heard vaguely of one another before meeting at Cambridge. It appears that, from an early age, Hall was rich enough to be as idle and playful as he wished. That he is known to history as Sterne's best friend only illustrates how solitary a figure Sterne was.

There was no sport at Cambridge other than fishing and shooting, talking in coffee houses and what the undergraduates could find for themselves. Girls were sometimes kept in college, although few could afford that luxury. Prostitutes found Cambridge a very remunerative market and later in the century the town was 'much pestered with lewd women who swarm as much in our streets as they do in Fleet Street or Ludgate Hill'.[15]

***

His lack of means left Laurence Sterne with no other career than the Church. The army would no longer have tempted him; he had no capital to make himself welcome in business. In retrospect, the theatre might have suited him but in 1737 that would have seemed so fanciful that the Sternes would hardly have needed to disapprove of it. At this period, Laurence must have been very much under their influence. The family were his benefactors, he owed them money, and during the adolescence spent with them he must have been as attracted to their comfort and assurance as much as he was made aware of the unruly edges of his own character. The Church had probably been decided on before Laurence was sent up to Jesus: otherwise such an investment would have been wasteful. A quiet living near by would settle the young man and make him available in whatever local interests the Sternes might pursue. The Church was as useful a source of support in provincial patronage as it was a heaven-sent means of placing deserving but impoverished young men.

Less than two months after taking his B.A., on 6 March 1737, Sterne was ordained a deacon by Richard Reynolds, bishop of Lincoln.[16] The ceremony took place in the chapel of Buckden Palace, in Huntingdonshire, and Sterne's first Church appointment was to the curacy of St. Ives, only a few miles away. We have no word from Sterne about the ordination and his year at St. Ives. But whatever befell him there, he was never far from the main road to London and York and he was doubtless kept up to date with news. He was probably also eager to hear of further preferment for himself. From what follows, we can assume that his uncle Jaques was now interested in the young cleric and was only waiting for a suitable position for his nephew in the vicinity of York. Obligation and service were bound together in the Church as in politics: it was part of the reasonableness on which the eighteenth century prided itself. We may look down upon it today, when the convention orders that patronage and corruption are underground forces, but in 1738 they were thought proper and sensible. It had always been a natural means of getting on and the eighteenth century liked to encourage nature.

On 18 February 1738, Sterne went to York to be licensed to serve as assistant curate at Catton, seven miles south-east of the city and very close to Elvington. On 20 August 1738 he was ordained a priest by the bishop of Chester at Chester Cathedral[17] and four days later he was appointed vicar of Sutton on the Forest, some eight miles north of York. This appointment was to serve Sterne for over twenty years – the proper subject of the next part of this book.

PART TWO

'In a bye corner ...'
1738–59

When, belatedly, in 1760, Laurence Sterne launched himself at the world, he spoke of having come from 'a bye corner of the kingdom',[1] as if to charm sophisticated London with the hayseed in his ear. But the life he led between 1738 and 1759 was far from uneventful. He had time to acquire at least a local reputation for oddity, wit and insouciance. Indeed, he was justified in anticipating in 1759 that his local reputation would provide an avid market for *Tristram Shandy* in York. He seems less active during the 1750s perhaps because his various ploys for fame, office and income had been disappointed, and perhaps because of some deeper crisis of which we remain ignorant. I do not doubt that as a young man Sterne took his career in the Church seriously and hopefully. But, a few months before the publication of *Tristram Shandy*, he answered advice to be cautious with his outspoken book thus: 'But suppose preferment is long acoming (& for aught I know I may not be preferr'd till the Resurrection of the Just) and am all that time in labour—how must I bear my Pains?'[2]

Sterne complained of 'a bye corner' because he believed himself too mettlesome for a country pasture. Although this central period of his life seems to see Sterne coerced into becoming a recognizable member of a traditional English community, this is a picture in his own hand. Let loose on London and Europe itself, he was to be no more assured, no less out of his element. But it was only the oppressiveness of provincial decay during the 1750s that persuaded him to make a career out of his unique vivacity and thus dispel the doldrums of pastoral life.

Let there be no doubt: he was a strange cleric, the more so for the glee with which he exploited his own outrageousness. The estrangement of the English country clergyman from the realities of life begins in the eighteenth century. As the intensity of doctrinal disputes became diluted, so the clergyman grew into a symbol in middle-class dreams. He was regarded as a totem of conservatism, even if he often lacked the means or had too many scruples really to participate in that self-righteous society. What could be more reassuring than that good, charitable and self-effacing man in the midst of single-minded self-interest? Even Pope managed to think of the country parson in terms of sham idyll – a contented creature with his conserve-making wife, a horse, 'October store', tobacco, tithes and a 'mortuary Guinea':

> He that has these, may pass his life,
> Drink with the 'Squire, and kiss his wife;
> On Sundays preach, and eat his fill;
> And fast on Fridays – if he will.[3]

The reality sometimes presented a more uncomfortable picture: private, neglected or inadequate men occupied some of the rural parishes on very lean incomes. In 1760, the *Gentleman's Magazine* contained a report of a clergyman who had a wife and nine children to support on £11 a year.[4] This was exceptional, but Charles Churchill was driven to abandon his career in the Church because it offered him nothing more than 'To pray, and starve, on forty pounds a year'.[5]

Rural society was often an embarrassment for such a man, in that he might be stranded between the poverty of his parishioners and the solidity and blandness of the local gentry. In 1819, Keats saw a predicament for the parson which would undoubtedly have weighed on Sterne's high spirits:

A Parson is a Lamb in a drawing room and a lion in a Vestry – The notions of Society will not permit a Parson to give way to his temper in any shape. . . . He is continually acting – His mind is against every Man and every Mans mind is against him – He is an Hippocrite to the Believer and a Coward to the unbeliever – He must be either a Knave or an Ideot.[6]

For a man without means, the Church was as much a backwater as the army. But for a presentable candidate, with some money, influential friends and eyes cast upwards, it was a profession full of handholds, all the more accessible to tact and moderation, as witness this confession from William Warburton,* bishop of Gloucester and a famous figure in Sterne's later life:

> I do the best I can, and should, I think, do the same if I were a mere pagan to make life passable. To be always lamenting the miseries of it, or always seeking after the pleasures of it, equally take us off from the work of our salvation. And though I be extremely cautious what sect I follow in religion, yet any in philosophy will serve my turn, and honest Sancho Panca's is as good as any; who on his return from an important commission, when asked by his master, whether they should mark the day with a *black* or a *white* stone; replied 'Faith, Sir, if you will be ruled by me, with neither, but with good *brown Ochre*.'[7]

When Sterne went up to London, his smart black coat was remarked on; perhaps he had found drab ochre irksome and compromising. But Sterne had been given a good start in the Church and, had he been temperamentally inclined to compromise, might have taken more advantage of it. Although he followed in the family tradition of plurality, liked to mix with local gentry and was a frequent visitor at York, he could never convincingly maintain the dutiful gravity of a conscientious place-seeker. However, he was plainly among the better-off clerics, for all that he complained of the money he had to spend on the parsonage at Sutton, and about the extent to which his mother was milking him. The true picture of clerical poverty is to be seen in the curate that Sterne engaged after 1760 to take care of his parishioners at Stillington and Sutton for a fraction of his own income. In terms of standard of living, a priest of Sterne's resources and preferments was on a level that the squire and the successful farmer could accept. The ordinary parishioner – essentially agricultural labourers – endured poverty so great that he had no option but to attribute the discrepancy to the mysterious ways of God.

* Warburton (1698–1779) studied for the law before changing course to the Church. He collected fat livings in Nottinghamshire and Lincolnshire and, in 1736, published the *Alliance between Church and State* and, between 1737–41, the *Divine Legation of Moses*. He was chaplain to the Prince of Wales and in 1755 was made a prebend of Durham. He moved on to the bishopric of Gloucester late in 1759.

Just as some philanthropists recommended education only to a certain depth in the social hierarchy, so most parsons were very practical about the usefulness of salvation. Jane Austen's Mr. Collins was not unusual in depending upon a patroness, and when he announced his duty 'to promote and establish the blessing of peace in all families within the reach of my influence',[8] we are left in no doubt about what sort of families he aimed at.

It was in such spirit that Laurence Sterne accepted the parish of Sutton on the Forest but stayed close to the man who had put it in his way, his uncle Jaques, who lived near enough to York Minster to hear every bell strike and every rumour circulate.

York was hardly more than eight miles south of Sutton and while the Forest of Galtres to the north of York was then still dense in parts and the flat plain frequently marshy, it was not too great a hardship for Sterne to live in York and ride out to Sutton to take service on Sunday mornings. Even so, in 1740 he licensed a curate, Richard Wilkinson, to supervise everyday parish matters and to permit him to spend more time near the fountainhead of preferment. Wilkinson, in fact, kept the Sutton register during 1739 and 1740. Ironically, he was to leapfrog over Sterne in the game of preferment. By 1743 he had moved on to an assistant position at Kilburn, a mile and a half north of Coxwold. While there, he so impressed Lord Fauconberg,* the local landowner, that he was recommended to the curacy of Coxwold in 1753 and thus preceded Sterne there. For the meanwhile, Wilkinson remained at Sutton, tending the parish and planting several elm trees in the garden and churchyard, that had been presented by Philip Harland.† If they were meant as a gift to the new vicar, Sterne's preference for York may have begun the uneasy relations with the squire of Sutton, whose handsome house was immediately opposite the church.

During the first half of the eighteenth century York had a population of some 12,000. It was only after 1760 that this figure began to rise, and reached more than 16,000 by the end

---

* Thomas Belasyse (1699–1774), 4th Viscount Fauconberg, created Earl Fauconberg of Newburgh in 1756. He lived at Newburgh Priory, near Coxwold. The manor of Newburgh extended at that time as far as Sutton.

† Philip Harland (1708–66), the son of Richard, who died in 1751. Tory squirearchy, the Harlands were not likely to be at ease with parson Sterne.

of the century. From this it would be easy to deduce that York conformed to the pattern of expansion in north-country towns during the eighteenth century. But, in attitude, it stood apart from the industrial concentration in the south-west corner of Yorkshire. It preferred to look towards Harrogate, Scarborough and the moors that begin some twenty miles to the north, rather than to Sheffield, Halifax and Bradford, all of which were considerably larger than York in Sterne's day. In terms of society, York was proud of being the capital of the north and worked hard to be a centre of leisure and provincial civilization. The knowing and witty gossip of its narrow streets features very little in Sterne's works, but events demonstrated how easily the impressionable young man adapted to his new centre of activities.

The period of Sterne's arrival in York was busy with improvements and adornments to the city. In 1732, work had begun on the New Walk, a genteel and avenued promenade along the bank of the Ouse. We may gauge some of the propriety of York from the fact that, by 1742, as this Walk had become fashionable, the affront of naked bathing in the river was forbidden. The Mansion House was built between 1725 and 1730 and in 1731 work was begun on Burlington's design for the Assembly Rooms. A few years later, in 1736, a new theatre was built in Mint Yard and the Minster pavement, badly damaged by Roundheads, was replaced with a new one designed by Kent and Burlington. In 1745 the County Hospital was begun, and, in 1754, William Carr designed a grandstand for the new racecourse made out of specially drained land on Knavesmire. Racing was one of York's passions and the week's meeting in August provided a setpiece for York society with a ball every night at the Assembly Rooms.

Clearly a great deal of the city's resources and ingenuity were devoted to making it a more pleasant place to live in. Although crowded with merchants, tradesmen and shopkeepers, York had no industries of its own and was opposed to any foreign manufacturers in the city.[9] This xenophobia was recent. Robinson Crusoe's father – a Bremen merchant – had settled in York some time before 1632 and flourished there, although his son had found it politic to abridge his name from Kreutznaer to Crusoe.

Defoe noted that York had 'no trade indeed, except such as depends upon the confluence of the gentry'.[10] The shops in the city would have been stocked to appeal to the wealthy families who had town houses in York, and throughout the eighteenth century the city corporation had to battle against the encroachment on to the narrow streets of these properties in the form of bow windows, porches, steps and railings. Defoe disapproved of the irresponsibility that accompanied York's social ostentation:

> there is abundance of good company here, and abundance of good families live here, for the sake of the good company and cheap living; a man converses here with all the world as effectually as at London; the keeping up assemblies among the younger gentry was first set up here, a thing other writers recommend mightily as the character of a good country, and of a pleasant place; but which I look upon with a different view, and esteem it as a plan laid for the ruin of the nation's morals, and which, in time, threatens us with too much success that way.[11]

In such an environment, the Church tended to be manned by smooth and accomplished clerics, many of whom lived in the handsome houses – 'little palaces' Defoe called them – that ringed the Minster. So smooth was Lancelot Blackburne that he had overcome the rumour of having been chaplain on a privateer to become Bishop of Exeter and then, in 1724, Archbishop of York. Blackburne neglected his diocese, rarely spending more than three months a year at York, and conducted himself in a wanton manner. Almost certainly, it was Blackburne's indolence that left Sterne's ordination to be performed by the Bishop of Chester. Blackburne did not even like to confirm, but on one occasion when he was left without choice he caused a scandal by ordering tobacco and drink to refresh himself during the unaccustomed labour.

Blackburne died in 1743 and was succeeded by Thomas Herring, a graduate of Jesus College, Cambridge. Herring was precocious: he had been made chaplain to George II at the age of thirty-three and after only four years at York moved on to Canterbury. His successor at York was Matthew Hutton, another student at Sterne's college. Hutton followed Herring from Jesus in and out of the sees of Bangor, York and Canterbury in an unrivalled progress of patronage. Herring was an active man and in his brief stay at York did much to atone for Blackburne's neglect, but the description of his promotion to York by Edmund Pyle speaks for his professionalism: 'I am just going ... to see ... the Bishop of Bangor kiss the King's hand for the archbishoprick of York, which prize in the lottery of the church has, as everything else has done, fallen into his lap.'[12] As for Hutton, when he died in 1758 he left some £50,000, 'which he had saved out of the Church in twelve years, and not one penny to any good use or public charity'.[13]

It cannot have hurt Laurence Sterne that his Church bosses during this period had shared his college. But both Herring and Hutton regarded York as a stepping stone, albeit a distinguished, profitable and enjoyable one. Sterne relied much more on the goodwill of his uncle. In addition to having married an heiress, Catherine Goodricke, whose family owned the Trinity Gardens, one of York's most pleasant open spaces, Jaques Sterne had the livings of Rise and Hornsea-cum-Riston, two small parishes on the east coast between Bridlington and Hull. He was also prebend at York Minster for Ulskelf and at Southwell for South Muskham. In 1735, he resigned Ulskelf to become precentor of York and archdeacon of Cleveland. In 1742, he bought the larger part of the Great House in Minster Yard which he subsequently sold in 1757 for £2,000. His annual income was about £800. But that did not prevent him hunting further preferment from the Duke of Newcastle, who contrived to have a guiding hand in the distribution of both political and ecclesiastical patronage. In 1749, Jaques Sterne wrote to Newcastle asking for the prebendaryship at Westminster relinquished by Thomas Hayter on his becoming Bishop of Norwich: 'There is no doubt but Your Grace will have many applications for this Prebend, But if Your Grace is inclind to honour me with your notice at this time, there can't long be wanting an opportunity, from D[r] Manningham's* ill State of Health, of distinguishing any other person whom Your Grace is pleased to think of also.'[14]

Newcastle did not oblige and in 1752 Jaques Sterne was again importuning in a curious mixture of whine and bluster that his nephew may have found it all too tempting to ridicule:

* Another prebend at Westminster who died next year.

I hope Your Grace finds that it is not in my nature to be trouble-some in my Solicitations; and indeed I am the less so, as I had the Honour of being taken in so kind a manner under Your immediate Protection. But hearing of the Bishop of Glocester's Death, in my Passage thro' this Town to Bath, I am willing to hope that I shall not be thought impertinent in acquainting Your Grace that a Prebend in the Church of Durham, where there are two Vacant, as it lies near my other Preferments, will be equally agreeable to me, as either Westminster, Windsor, or Canterbury; But I submit it intirely to Your Grace's Judgment & Pleasure, only begging Leave to hope that as I have spent now upwards of Thirty five Years in a faithful Service of the Crown, at an Expense that I believe no Clergyman else has done, that I shall, thro' Your Grace's Friendship & Good-ness, receive a Mark of the King's Favour at this time, when there are so many Stalls vacant in different Churches.[15]

Eventually Jaques Sterne gained the stall at Durham, which brought him another £550 per annum. It is easy to criticize his pluralism; for Laurence Sterne, such blatant, belligerent and humourless hypocrisy may have been an irresistible target. But he waited first for whatever pickings there were to be had from so powerful a local benefactor.

It may even have been Jaques Sterne who introduced Laurence to his future wife. Certainly the clergy of York did not exclude themselves from affairs of the heart. Jaques himself had the reputation of being '*bon-vivant*'[16] and seems to have found many ways of compensating for a wife sixteen years his senior. There was a story of an exchange between Jaques Sterne and Richard Warneford, a York clergyman. Warneford had apparently been absent from several services in the Minster and Sterne called him to account. Warneford answered: 'Mr. Precentor, I went to Acomb where my wife was very ill, my *own* wife, Mr. Precentor.'[17]

Edmund Pyle, who was at York in Herring's retinue, later described the emotional temptations that confronted a young man in a prominent place in the Minster: 'I had like to have lost my heart at York. It is a terrible thing to have such a place in the church as I have; – nothing but ladies by dozens (& very pretty ones) on the right hand or the left, or in front of my stall. But, through mercy, having the service to read, I was forced to look, at least, as much upon the rubrick of the book as upon that of their cheeks!'*[18]

Either in or near to the Minster, Laurence Sterne's eye had fallen on Elizabeth Lumley. A year younger than Sterne,† she was the daughter of Robert Lumley, the vicar of Bedale, one of the richest parishes in Yorkshire, and of Lydia Kirke. Lydia Kirke's mother, Elizabeth Clarke, had been married twice; first to Anthony Light, Lydia's father, and second to Thomas Robinson, the son of Sir Leonard Robinson, and grandfather of Elizabeth Robinson‡ who married Edward Montagu, a grandson of the first Earl of Sandwich. This cousin, Elizabeth Montagu, the 'Bluestocking' and leading London hostess, was thus a cousin to Elizabeth Lumley, although she proved a more sympathetic friend to Laurence Sterne than ever she was to his wife.

Sterne's marriage proved a failure; but although its consequences may often have depressed him, it is not clear whether it seriously changed him. Marital unreliability may only have been the sign of a more profoundly unsettled nature. Nor for that matter do we know what he expected of marriage. It may have been a more substantial prize for Elizabeth Lumley. For, although she was a moderate heiress, both her parents were dead and her younger sister already married, to John Botham, the son of the vicar of Clifton-Campville in Staffordshire. Furthermore, if we are to judge by the opinions of her held by her cousin Elizabeth Montagu, Elizabeth Lumley was not the most eligible of young women.

---

* Sterne may have known this temptation, too. In 1760, Boswell celebrated Sterne the country parson in a poem thus:

> Let me attempt Sue's count'nance sweet,
> The little Gipsey drest in blue,
> Who to the Pulpit sits next Pew,
> Whose tender-smiling, starlike eyes
> Make mine half wander from the skies.

(Frederick A. Pottle, 'Bozzy and Yorick', *Blackwood's Magazine*, Vol. CCXVII, 1925, p. 305.)

† Years later, in 1767, Sterne told Eliza Draper that his wife had deceived him about her age, that she was ten years older than he had thought, i.e. 'on the edge of sixty'. Elizabeth Lumley may have stolen a few years, but Sterne's surprise was more for Eliza's benefit than his own. (*Letters, JE*, 1 November 1767, p. 399.)

‡ Elizabeth Montagu (*née* Robinson) (1720-1800).

This crucial emphasis in a young woman's life as to whether and how she would marry is of great significance in the subject matter of the early novel. *Pamela*, written when Sterne was probably courting Elizabeth Lumley, is a sustained work of suspense on the theme: 'I should be a sad wicked creature, if, for the sake of riches or favour, I should forfeit my good name',[19] as voiced by a shrewd young woman determined on marrying her master. It seems certain that one of the main reasons for the success of *Pamela* was the insinuation that sex was a social weapon just as suspense and identification were literary measures.

If, in subtler ways, this preoccupation with the moral implications of marriage and sex characterize the classical English novel from Jane Austen to Henry James, Sterne virtually ignores it and, in *A Sentimental Journey*, provides the first of the few English works that celebrate sexual irresponsibility. Equally, however, he is one of the few authors to look seriously at the interior of a marriage – that stonewall duologue between Walter and Elizabeth Shandy. Whereas Jane Austen concludes with marriage and a discreet but spinsterly confidence that everyone will live happily ever after, Sterne actually explores the aftermath. Not that he discovers the vague, crushing despair that Henry James can hardly bring himself to spell out between, say, Isabel and Osmond in *The Portrait of a Lady*. On the contrary, the English marriage in Sterne is ludicrous: two private views marooned within conversational distance of each other, a premonition of those couples in Beckett and Pinter made listless by their own company.

But Elizabeth Lumley, in 1740, may have felt a keen identity with Pamela. As Ian Watt argues in relating the changing status of women to Richardson's novel:

> . . . the transition to an individualist social and economic order brought with it a crisis in marriage which bore particularly hard upon the feminine part of the population. Their future depended much more completely than before on their being able to marry and on the kind of marriage they made, while at the same time it was more and more difficult for them to find a husband.[20]

But how would Sterne have anticipated marriage? Like his

wife, he was effectively an orphan who may have hoped for some stability in making a family for himself. He was, in 1740, twenty-six years old, the age at which, he later tells us, Yorick 'knew just about as well how to steer his course in it [the world], as a romping, unsuspicious girl of thirteen'.[21]

There is striking evidence of this immaturity which suggests how far Sterne may have married on the rebound from another blighted affair. For in November 1739 he wrote to the Rev. John Dealtry, a friend, from Skelton where he was staying with John Hall:

> ... you have now received a Letter from one of the most miserable and Discontented Creatures upon Earth; Since I writ last to you, I have drawn Miss C— into a Correspondence: in the Course of which together with her Consistency in acting towards me, since the beginning of this affair; I am convinced she is fixed in a resolution never to marry, and as the whole summ of happiness I ever proposed was staked upon that single Point, I see nothing left for me at present but a dreadfull Scene of uneasiness & Heartachs.[22]

We do not know who this Miss C— was, but the conclusion is unavoidable that Sterne was making love to her at much the same time that he was courting Elizabeth Lumley. For, as he later told his daughter, Sterne had courted his wife for two years – 'she owned she liked me, but thought herself not rich enough, or me too poor, to be joined together—she went to her sister's in S [Staffordshire], and I wrote to her often.'[23]

Four of these letters have survived, but one is notorious for the way it seems to mimic a passage from the *Journal to Eliza*, the feverish rhapsody on consumptive love that Sterne wrote to Eliza Draper in 1767. Sterne's early commentators thought that, whatever their warmth, he had been cold-blooded enough to keep the early letters and re-employ them in his epistolary love-making. There was enough of the plagiarist in Sterne for this, initially, to seem plausible. But it is the very exactness of comparison that is most suspicious. When Sterne borrowed from other masters in composing his sermons, he usually took the trouble to make a rudimentary disguise of his debt. He was not by nature a copyist. Even allowing that while writing the *Journal to Eliza* he was not overwhelmed by the sense of his own spontaneity, I do not think that Sterne had the patience to leave sentences more than twenty-five years old unchanged. The *Journal* is molten and any original would have been reshaped and reworked before appearing in it.

The style of this first letter is, in fact, much closer to that of the *Journal* than to its three supposed companions. The other three are more in keeping with traditional romantic posture, with their references to the conventional symbols of love:

My L.!—thou art surrounded by all the melancholy gloom of winter; wert thou alone, the retirement would be agreeable.— Disappointed ambition might envy such a retreat, and disappointed love would seek it out.—Crouded towns, and busy societies, may delight the unthinking, and the gay—but solitude is the best nurse of wisdom.—Methinks I see my contemplative girl now in the garden, watching the gradual approaches of spring.—Do'st not thou mark with delight the first vernal buds? the snow-drop, and primrose, these early and welcome visitors, spring beneath thy feet.—Flora and Pomona already consider thee as their handmaid; and in a little time will load thee with their sweetest blessing.—The feathered race are all thy own, and with them, untaught harmony will soon begin to cheer thy morning and evening walks.—Sweet as this may be, return— return—the birds of Yorkshire will tune their pipes, and sing as melodiously as those of Staffordshire.[24]

Such tuneful creatures usually reside in Arcadia, along with 'melancholy gloom', 'the first vernal buds', Flora, Pomona and 'untaught harmony'. However, this letter does at least call into being the picture of the beloved, even if she seems rather more idyllic than Elizabeth Lumley appeared once she had changed her name to Sterne. The disputed letter, on the other hand, is singular not only for its more deft revelling in unhappiness but because it focuses on the distraught Sterne rather than his absent love:

The hour you left D'Estella I took to my bed.—I was worn out with fevers of all kinds, but most by that fever of the heart with which thou knowest well I have been wasting these two years. . . . She [a mutual friend] made me stay an hour with her, and in that short space I burst into tears a dozen different times—and in such affectionate gusts of passion that she was constrained to leave the room, and sympathize in her dressing room. . . . Fanny [a maid?] had prepared me a supper—she is all attention to me—but I sat over it with tears; a bitter sauce my L. [Elizabeth Lumley] but I could eat it with no other—for the moment she began to spread my little table, my heart fainted within me.—One solitary plate, one knife, one fork, one glass!—I gave a thousand pensive, penetrating looks at the chair thou hadst so often graced, in those quiet, and sentimental repasts— then laid down my knife, and fork, and took out my handkerchief, and clapped it across my face, and wept like a child.—I do so this very moment, my L. for as I take up my pen my poor pulse quickens, my pale face glows, and tears are trickling down upon the paper, as I trace the word L—.[25]

A damp patch might mark the spot, the tumescent, lachrymose and consumptive strains inextricably mixed.* However tearful, this author is not distraught. As he admits, his pulse quickens at the feel of a pen; rather than a woman, he is in love with literary creation – which may prove a more lasting devotion. What begins as an attempt to move a woman, works most affectingly on the author himself. All those domestic details of furniture, crocks and cutlery make one great throb of romantic disappointment. Sterne inflamed himself so often that we must conclude by believing the trick was a means to convince himself of his own sincerity and feelings.

Professor Curtis has also pointed out that the use of the word 'sentimental' counts against an early date for this letter. In 1749, he recalls, Lady Bradshaigh found the word unintelligible, even though it was 'so much in vogue among the polite'.[26] Although we cannot be certain about the date or origin of this letter, I agree with Curtis that it was probably copied by Sterne's daughter, Lydia, and added to the trio to Miss Lumley. As we have seen, Lydia was not above the thought of inventing some letters to fatten her father's collection. There are problems confronting this solution: we are not sure that Lydia had access to the *Journal*, and it is still not clear why she should have wanted to produce only one artificial Sterne letter. But I do not believe Sterne could cast his own nervous passion so fine as early as 1740. His real love letters are conventional in their eagerness

* Trim's tears could be distinguished: 'The Corporal blush'd down to his fingers ends—a tear of sentimental bashfulness—another of gratitude to my uncle *Toby*— and a tear of sorrow for his brother's misfortunes started into his eye and ran sweetly down his cheek together.' (*TS*, Vol. IX, Ch. V.)

and in their author's wholehearted conviction. Second-hand imagery in a writer like Sterne is a mark of earnestness.

Sterne later told his daughter that he thought the love letters had been unnecessary:

I believe then she was partly determined to have me, but would not say so—at her return [to York] she fell into a consumption—and one evening that I was sitting by her with an almost broken heart to see her so ill, she said, 'my dear Lawrey, I can never be yours, for I verily believe I have not long to live—but I have left you every shilling of my fortune;'—upon that she shewed me her will—this generosity overpowered me.—It pleased God that she recovered, and I married her in the year 1741.[27]

This willingness to be seen submitting to self-interest is rather like Crusoe's confession of frailty when confronted with money.* At any event, if the recovery pleased God it is likely that in later years Laurence Sterne might have preferred to have done with the inheritance. He and Elizabeth Lumley married eventually with the impression of haste. They were talking together in the Assembly Rooms† one day when 'she asked him the question herself and they went off directly from the Rooms and were married.'[28] It is plausible that so eloquent a suitor as Sterne had finally to be nudged into action. Whatever his enthusiasm, the couple were married in the Minster on 30 March 1741 (Easter Monday) by Richard Osbaldeston,‡ dean of York.§

---

* While scouring the wreck for useful objects, Crusoe discovers some money: '"O drug!" said I aloud, "what are thou good for? Thou art not worth to me, no not the taking off of the ground; one of these knives is worth all this heap; I have no manner of use for thee, e'en remain where thou art, and go to the bottom as a creature whose life is not worth saving." However, upon second thoughts, I took it away . . .' (*Robinson Crusoe* [1719], Penguin edn [Harmondsworth, 1965], p. 75.)

† One of the stories told by John Croft in *Scrapeana* talks of a famous 'Love-Corner' at the Assembly Rooms. (*Scrapeana*, 2nd edn [York, 1792], p. 6.)

‡ Osbaldeston (1690/91–1764) was a Cambridge graduate who went on to be Bishop of Carlisle (1747) and of London (1762). He and Sterne remained on good terms, Osbaldeston calling on the newly famous author at Coxwold in June 1760. (*Letters*, p. 116.)

§ Rumour had it that at Sutton, on the first Sunday after his marriage, Sterne climbed into the pulpit and began: 'We have toiled all night and have taken nothing.' Curtis thought this story 'shocking' but could not bear to omit it. Why does it seem credible? I think because we believe Sterne had the comedian's willingness to sacrifice honour and dignity for a laugh. Possibly this story from *Scrapeana* is fruit from the same bush: 'Mr S— meeting a Lady in the street the day

News of the marriage spread and, in its reception, gives us valuable neutral accounts of the bride and groom. In April 1741 Matthew Robinson wrote from Bath to his sister Elizabeth with the news that

> our cousin Betty Lumley is married to a Parson who once delighted in debauchery, who is possessed of about £100 a year in preferment, and has a good prospect of more. What hopes our relation may have of settling the affections of a light and fickle man I know not, but I imagine she will set about it not by means of the beauty but of the arm of flesh. In other respects I see no fault in the match; no woman ought to venture upon the state of Old Maiden without a consciousness of an inexhaustible fund of good nature.[29]

This last, disparaging aside forebodes Sterne's later disharmony with his wife. But, as with every relation of Sterne's, it is not easy to characterize Elizabeth Sterne. The Robinsons do not appear to have had much time for the Lumleys. Elizabeth Robinson had written to her father in August 1740: 'Lady Andover told me in a letter I received from her last post, that Mrs. Botham [Lydia Lumley] was grown very grave, and a great workwoman and an excellent housewife; if that is the case, Mr. Botham preaches to those of his household as well as those of his parish.'[30] It may have been because Laurence Sterne hardly preached in his own home that Elizabeth Robinson later enjoyed his company.

She seems to have had an enthusiastic letter from the new Mrs. Sterne for she wrote to her sister Sarah in a gaily malicious mood:

> I never saw a more comical letter than my sweet cousin's, with her heart and head full of matrimony, pray do matrimonial thoughts come upon *your recovery?* . . . Mr. Sterne has a hundred a year living, with a good prospect of better preferment. He was a great rake, but being japanned and married, has varnished his character. I do not comprehend what my cousin means by their little desires, if she had said little stomachs, it had been some help to their economy, but when people have not enough for the necessities of life, what avails

after he was married; she wished him joy. On which S. replied, "I thank you kindly, Madam, but I have had quite enough." (John Seward, *The Spirit of Anecdote and Wit* [London, 1823], Vol. IV, pp. 239–40; *Scrapeana*, p. 32.)

it that they can do without the superfluities and pomps of it? Does she mean that she won't keep a coach and six, and four footmen? What a wonderful occupation she made of courtship that it left her no leisure nor inclination to think of anything else. I wish they may live well together.[31]

John Croft, in 1795, recollected that Mrs. Sterne had as a girl 'lived in stile, from whence she derived a superior education. Tho' she was but a homely woman, still she had many Admirers, as she was reported to have a Fortune, and she possessed a first rate understanding.'[32] The 'Fortune' may have been more in reputation than fact. In 1741, Elizabeth and her sister had inherited property in Leeds worth £60 a year. That would have brought £30 to the marriage in addition to whatever remained of Elizabeth's inheritance from her father. This may have been substantial since, before her marriage, Elizabeth lived in Little Alice Lane, close to the Minster, with a maid.

Sterne by now was moderately well set up, largely through the good offices of his uncle Jaques. In January 1741, an encouraging two months before his marriage, Sterne was installed in the Chapter House at York as prebend for Givendale. This position carried with it £66 a year, so that at this period Sterne would have had an annual income of about £150, with the prospect of more.

His hopes depended upon continual close relations with Jaques Sterne; but within a year of his marriage those relations had been seriously upset. Unluckily for Sterne, there was an election in 1741–2 which caused a furore in York and put a limit on his own ambition for preferment. Not that Sterne fell foul of events, so much as his own fickleness. It is almost as if he resented having to depend on his uncle and went out of any sensible way to offend him.

The election of 1741 was decisive for the country in that it signalled the fall of Walpole, who had managed government for nineteen years. As to whether Walpole acted in the interests of Whig ideas, the Court Party or simply himself is to place oneself in the maze of eighteenth-century politics. Whiggery is supposed to have stood for the Hanoverian succession in opposition to Stuart restoration, for no wars, few taxes and the increase of personal and national prosperity. But Dr. Johnson, a Tory, described *Whig* as 'the name of a faction' and a *Tory* as 'one who adheres to the ancient constitution of the state, and the apostolical hierarchy of the church of England, opposed to a whig'.[33] The importance of Walpole is that, following broadly Whig policies, he occupied power for so long that he served both to define and to discredit it. Not only was he the first 'prime minister' but, with Newcastle, he laid down a national apparatus of patronage and jobbery, all the more worthwhile in that most of its members had similar opinions, all the more effective in that they depended on Walpole for their fortune.

Anyone at the head of such a hierarchy for as long as Walpole must ultimately come to believe in the status quo, and little else. He had reached that stage some time before 1741. Taxes had been growing, Spanish privateers had been taking increasing advantage of his diplomatic inertia and his majority had been waning. Worst of all, in 1737, his balance of the royal household had been irrevocably disturbed. Queen Caroline, his greatest ally, had died and Frederick, the Prince of Wales, had set up a separate establishment at Leicester House as a gathering place for opposition. The physically ponderous Walpole must have been very tired.

But that did not prevent fevered mobilization of the Whigs in 1741. Nowhere were they more active than in York, where the Minster was almost entirely Whig in attitude and obligation. The situation in York was made perilous when Cholmley Turner, the sitting Whig knight of the shire, announced in April that he preferred not to stand again in the election to be held in May. Yorkshire provided two knights of the shire and, by mutual arrangement, the Whig and Tory interests usually put up a candidate each. But if the Whigs found no suitable replacement for Turner, then the Tories would not hesitate to put up another man of their own. The sitting Tory, or Country Party member, Sir Miles Stapylton, had already agreed to stand again. Turner's place was now taken by Viscount Morpeth, and he and Stapylton were duly and unanimously elected in May. However, by 9 August, Morpeth was dead of tuberculosis and the election was open again.

The Country Interest put up George Fox, a Leeds landowner, but with Irish origins. On 29 August the Whig gentlemen, clergy and freeholders met at the George Inn to choose a candidate. Their leading spirit was Jaques Sterne who had already played an organizing part in the election of 1734. As his yes-man, he had his nephew, Laurence Sterne. When no one could be found to accept their nomination, the gathering fell back on the absent and unwilling Cholmley Turner. This nomination was immediately published as if to present Turner with a *fait accompli*. Whatever the persuasion, within a few days Turner had grudgingly accepted.[34]

But with a less than enthusiastic candidate, and the prospect of a close poll, the Whigs were the more concerned that York's newspaper, the *Courant*, should have been in the hands of a Tory, Caesar Ward.* Jaques Sterne had thus begun a paper of his own, the *Gazetteer*. This rival paper intended to provide not only 'the fullest and most disinterested Accounts of *Foreign* and *Domestic* Affairs', but also 'to correct the Weekly Poison of the York-Courant'.[35] It expected the encouragement of all those who favoured liberty and Protestantism, the Whig banners. Its leading propagandist was Laurence Sterne.

In his Memoir, Sterne attributes his later quarrel with Jaques to the fact that 'I would not write paragraphs in the newspapers—though he was a party-man, I was not, and detested such dirty work: thinking it beneath me.'[36] It is clear that Sterne was never a committed party man. Apart from this brief involvement, he scarcely passed a serious political opinion in the rest of his life, nor looked on politics as anything more than a sightseer. It may be that he found politicians too solemn or that political issues seemed too mundane to deserve his attention. It may also be that, after 1741, he preferred to let it be thought that he was too rarefied for such matters. But the facts of the 1741 election in York show that he was initially willing to dirty his hands and that, when the affair was over, his uncle may have had some reason for being angry with his nephew. Another reason for Sterne's distaste could be that he received something of a drubbing in these polemical exchanges.

Once candidates had been adopted, a campaign was begun to abuse and discredit the rivals. The first sign of this dispute is

---

* Caesar Ward, born in 1711, was to die only a few months before *Tristram Shandy* went to his press, to be supervised by his widow.

a letter in the *Courant* on 8 September indignant at handbills being circulated to the effect that Fox was untrustworthy because he was Irish. Fox's Irishness could be made to suggest not only a Papist tinge to his Tory colours, but a willingness to promote the Irish woollen industry in opposition to that of Yorkshire. The letter defending Fox was signed J.S. If Sterne was not the author of the bills complained of, he must have been involved in their production. It is also likely that he was the source of several violent letters to the *Courant*, signed J. Wainman, abusing the mysterious J.S. Caesar Ward published a notice on 29 September that he did not intend 'to be impos'd upon by counterfeited Letters' until the real author 'thinks fit to subscribe *his own Name*'.[37]

However, a month later, on 20 October, an increasingly confident Ward published simultaneously an article by J.S. that attacked Turner and the assurance that he was 'willing to preserve that Impartiality, he has constantly observ'd' by opening his paper to a reply from the Whigs on condition that 'it is wrote with Decency and good Manners.'[38]

Such a challenge could not be resisted and on 27 October the *Courant* carried a lengthy reply to J.S., unsigned but in fact by Sterne. At a later stage of the campaign, in December, Ward revealed Sterne's authorship in recounting the manner in which the letters had been submitted to the *Courant* by a go-between:

... there were some Passages I made Objections to, whereupon the Messenger went away, and return'd again with those obnoxious Passages expunged, and I agreed to insert it in the next Paper: But the same Evening the abovementioned Mr *Sterne* came to me, and said, He *had made some Mistakes in the Letter which* He *had sent that Evening, and particularly by inserting the word* Not *superfluously*; whereupon I gave him his Letter, and he made some few Alterations in it.[39]

It is fascinating to see the anxious and hurried author abandoning secrecy by nursing his work through the press; but the letter itself hardly justifies the trouble. No more than sketchy rhetoric, it makes an uninspired defence of Turner and concludes with an attack on Fox's Irish connections that could be relied upon to appeal to the already over-protected Yorkshire woollen industry: '*Query*, 17. Whether Mr. Fox did not actually

Vote in Favour of the Irish Manufacture, in the Bill for import-
ing Irish Yarn into ENGLAND, to the Ruin of the Combers,
Spinners, &c. of this Country?'*[40]

On 3 November, J.S. retaliated rather more bitingly by
adapting some lines from Pope's *Epistle to Dr. Arbuthnot* at
Sterne's expense. The contest now was one of only personal
abuse, but J.S. seems to have known his victim well:

> Let L—y *Scribble – what? that Thing of Silk,*
> L—y *that mere white Curd of Ass's Milk?*
> *Satire or Sense, alas! can* L—y *feel?*
> *Who breaks a* Butterfly *upon a Wheel?*[41]

A week later, Sterne admitted that it was 'with some Difficulty
that I have prevailed with myself to take Pen in Hand to make
a *serious* Reply to one of the most scurrilous and uncharitable
Letters that ever appear'd in a civiliz'd and Christian Country'.[42]
Yet again, Sterne lauded Turner and berated Fox. He was
plainly stung by the Popean assault and replied with a blast
more in the manner of Swift:

As J.S. in your last Courant has shown some Marks of Fear and
Penitence in denying his Name, and promising never to offend again,
it would be almost an Act of Cruelty to pursue the Man any farther;
however since he has left the Field with ill Language in his Mouth, I
shall send one Shot after him, which, I am confident, is too well
founded to miss him.

A certain nasty Animal in *Egypt*, which, I think, *Herodotus* takes
notice of, when he finds he cannot possibly defend himself, and prey
any longer, partly out of Malice, partly out of Policy, he lets fly
backward full against his adversary, and thereby covers his Retreat
with the Fumes of his own Filth and Excrement.

As this Creature is naturally very *impotent*, and its chief Safety
depends on a plentiful Discharge on such Occasions, the Naturalists
affirm, that Self-preservation directs it to a certain Vegitable on the
Banks of the River *Nile*, which constantly arms it with a proper Habit
of Body against all Emergencies. I am,

Yours, L.S.[43]

---

* This letter was published separately as a pamphlet, *Query upon Query.* C.
Collyer has shown that the publication was the work of Jaques Sterne, who made
certain editorial changes which may have offended the young author. (Collyer,
'Laurence Sterne and Yorkshire Politics: Some New Evidence', *Proceedings of the
Leeds Philosophical and Literary Society*, Vol. VII, 1952, pp. 83–7.)

This was the first time Sterne had owned up to his part in the correspondence. After J.S.'s verse sally he had no option but to acknowledge the familiar form of his name. Sterne may have been at a disadvantage in not knowing for certain the identity of J.S. He seems to have accused James Scott* in the *Gazetteer*, but on 24 November Scott wrote a solemn denial.

This squabble of identities and personal insult had by now put the election itself in the shade. On 15 December J.S. spoke up again, Pope in hand:

> *Mr* Pope *against* L.S. *once more*
> A Wight, who reads not, and but scans and spells;
> A Word-Catcher that lives on Syllables.
> Who shames this Scribbler? break one Cobweb thro,
> He spins the slight self-pleasing Thread a-new:
> Destroy his Fib, or Sophistry, in vain,
> The Creature's at his dirty Work again,
> Thron'd in the Centre of his thin Designs,
> Proud of a vast Extent of flimzy Lines.
> *From his humble Servant,*
>
> J.S.[44]

Sterne's web was now shaking perilously with the buffeting. On 15 December the *Gazetteer* carried a letter from its printer John Jackson saying that all the other side were liars, which indicated the proximity of the poll. Two days before Christmas the Speaker of the Commons issued a warrant for the election. It was in this last, festive drumming up of support that fortune did much to soothe Sterne's hurts. On 26 December, Robert Hitch, the prebendary of North Newbald, while campaigning for the Whigs, 'over-heated himself at the Strife ... that threw him into a mortal Fever'.[45] Hitch died and on 5 January Sterne was rewarded with the stall for North Newbald.

On the same day, the *Courant* noted his good luck in verse that owes nothing to Pope but catches the mocking tone of J.S.'s pastiches:

---

* James Scott (1700–82), vicar of Bardsey, three miles north-east of Leeds. Collyer argues, very reasonably, that it was Jaques Sterne who suggested Scott as the culprit. That mistake would have added to Sterne's grievance. (*Op. cit.*)

A New Year's Gift *for* L—y
Grave Legends tell, nor is it yet deny'd,
That old St. Lawrence on a Grid-Iron fry'd;
Our young St. Lawrence is so wond'rous dry,
I'll wager, that he'd sooner *burn than fry.*
And, try to *roast* him – he's so lean and *sallow,*
'Tis Ten to One he drops *more T—d than Tallow.*[46]

Votes were registered throughout January as freeholders
travelled to York despite the severe winter. The campaign had
needed to be warm because of the exceptional weather. Snow
fell in September and October and then from 1–22 December
so that the Ouse froze over and the bridge across it was in danger
of breaking up.

More than 15,000 votes were eventually polled and on 21
January Cholmley Turner was declared elected by nearly a
thousand votes' majority.* It is an interesting sidelight that of
eighteen freeholders from Sutton, nine voted for Turner and
nine for Fox, the candidate supported by Philip Harland, the
squire of Sutton.

But although the Whigs had triumphed in York, in London
they were finished. On 3 February 1742 Walpole resigned, thus
ending an era of Whig dominance. In July, Edward Thompson,
the Whig member for the City of York, died and the detested
George Fox was returned in his place.

In the end, therefore, Sterne had prospered amid a party
defeat. He had gathered North Newbald for his efforts and he
was hardly the man to shrink from the notoriety he had earned
for himself in York. He perhaps felt it tactful to make friends
with the new power in the city. He may have been itching to
snub his overbearing uncle once he had gained North Newbald.
Or was it simply that irrepressible bias towards self-destruction
that instability had bred in Sterne and which he chose to call
'unwary pleasantry' when it betrayed Yorick? It may have been
a pathological weakness in Sterne that he teased the serious until
they turned on him. It need not have prevented the caprice that,
like Yorick, Sterne knew that "tis no extravagant arithmetic to

* By then, Sterne had tracked down 'J.S.' In *The York Gazetteer* for 19 January,
there is a mock epitaph for John Stanhope, an attorney–sportsman, 'Devoid of
sense and eke of Strife, Who in a Fox-Chace lost his Life'. (*The Winged Skull,* pp.
283–4.

say, that for every ten jokes,—thou hast got a hundred enemies; and till thou hast gone on, and raised a swarm of wasps about thy ears, and art half stung to death by them, thou wilt never be convinced it is so.'[47]

Whatever the case, it does not appear to have been strictly necessary for Sterne to write to the *Courant* on 27 July 1742:

> Sir,
> I find by some late Preferments, that it may not be improper to change Sides; therefore I beg the Favour of you to inform the Publick, that I sincerely beg Pardon for the abusive Gazetteers I wrote during the late contested Election for the County of York, and that I heartily wish Mr Fox Joy of his Election for the City.
> *Tempora Mutantur, & nos mutemur in illis.*
> *I am, Sir, your Penitent Friend and Servant.*
>
> L.S.[48]

***

Whether penitent, apprehensive or merely flustered by the election, Laurence Sterne was probably persuaded by its aftermath to spend more time at Sutton. The register of baptisms at Sutton for the year 1740 'is defective' Sterne's hand admits, 'by the Negligence of The Gentleman who was Curate'. Richard Wilkinson may not have survived this shortcoming; by 1743, Sterne had no curate and attended to parish business himself. Furthermore, he never seems to have attended to York as closely as he did during his first four years as a young cleric.

But the offence to his uncle was not to be forgotten. John Croft believed that, in addition to the nephew's frivolous attitude to politics, the two Sternes

> fell out about a favourite Mistress of the Precentors, who proved with child by Laury and the cause of their breach is now [1795] living. The Lady is said to resemble Sterne very much, tho' at the time of their rupture, he gave out as a reason in the publick Coffee House, that it arose from that he wou'd not continue to write periodicall papers for his Uncle. However the Quarrell remained abroach and his Uncle was never afterwards reconciled.[49]

The *York Courant* contains one titbit of gossip that alludes to Jaques Sterne's love life. In November 1744, a W. Charnley asked to have this 'epigram' inserted in the paper:

Ad Prae—em quendam,
Phillida amas: Bacchis sobolens convicia jactat,
Ne spera ambabus posse placere diu.
Ah! Bacchis nondum didicit spectare lacunar:
Sed dudum hanc artem vir suus edidicit.[50]

By 4 December, Thomas English of Northallerton had volun-
teered a translation:

Molly he loves: But jealous *Sarah* growls;
'Tis hard for one to please two am'rous Souls.
Ah *Sarah*! learn to look and not to see;
Thy Husband long has known that Mystery.[51]

The same issue of the *Courant* contained this 'answer' to the
original Latin:

Your *Epigram* is quite too keen,
To touch the Fair's Mistakes;
For if it smells not all obscene,
I never smelled a *Jaques*.[52]

That pun is too obvious for us to attribute it confidently to
Sterne; at the same time, it shows the fatal and unavoidable
flaw in the image of a man who sought as much respect as
Jaques Sterne. The 'Sarah' in question is probably Sarah
Benson, the precentor's housekeeper. Jaques Sterne's wife had
died in January 1742 and there is every indication that he
eventually settled to a *modus vivendi* with Sarah. When he died,
in 1759, it was she who inherited all his real and personal estate
by a will drawn up as early as November 1746.

The exchange of verse in the *Courant* is all the more interesting
because it is so exceptional. The three verses were in fact
reprinted three more times – on 16 April, 30 April and 7 May
1745 – so that from a reading of Sterne's life one might suspect
that the *Courant* was always filled with the innuendo and insult
of local squabbles. But the only personal and private battles to
appear in the *Courant* between 1738 and 1760 concern the
Sternes. Whether or not Laurence took a hand in this doggerel
crossfire, we can see what outstanding figures of provincial
controversy the Sternes were. Jaques cannot have enjoyed being
made fun of, but his nephew may have relished the role of local

clown.* It is by no means the last appearance of Sterne as self-appointed jester.

But this exchange looks ahead. For the moment, Sterne had more pressing problems than his uncle. Soon after his marriage in 1741, Agnes Sterne had arrived in England from Ireland with her teenage daughter, Catherine. The events that followed come to us largely through a letter Sterne wrote to his uncle in 1751 to justify his treatment of his mother. Sterne apologizes for that letter being 'long & hasty wrote',[53] but in fact it is composed with all the close care of an attempt at whitewash and shows that, when need pressed, he could be practical, sequential and lucid in writing.

Agnes Sterne, according to her son, had hurried over to England as soon as she heard of his marriage to Elizabeth Lumley, 'a Woman of Fortune'. Although she may have arrived during the campaign for the election, 'The very Hour I received Notice of her Landing at Leverpool, I took Post to prevent her coming nearer Me, —stay'd three Days with her,—used all the Arguments I could fairly, to engage her to return to Ireland & end her Days with her Own Relations.'[54]

Sterne told Agnes that, apart from his wife's income, he had barely £100 a year, out of which he had to pay for Wilkinson's curacy at Sutton. In addition, Sterne was now incurring considerable expense in making the 'large ruinous House' at Sutton inhabitable for newly-weds. There is a note in Sterne's own hand in the Sutton register that shows the extent of these repairs:

Laid out in Sashing the House	£12	0	0
In Stukoing and Bricking the Hall	4	16	0
In Building the Chair House	5	0	0
In Building the Parl^r Chimney	3	0	0
Little House	2	3	0
Spent in Shapeing the Rooms, Plastering, Underdrawing & Jobbery – God knows what –[55]			

* It is likely that, even at this stage, Sterne was a character odd stories clung to. The 'facts' of his life are all too inextricably confused with unsubstantiated gossip. John Croft's *Scrapeana*, for instance, contains several anecdotes of Sterne or 'Mr S—', such as one about Sterne seeing a lady in the Assembly Rooms. He asks her name: Hobson, she says. I've heard of Hobson's Choice, he retorts, but never seen it before. (*Scrapeana*, p. 25.)

In that one year he seems to have spent at least £30 on his house, £10 more than the pension he assured his mother was sufficient for her in 'a Cheap Country' like Ireland. The protesting son 'concluded with representing to her, the Inhumanity of a Mother *able* to Maintain herself, thus forcing herself as a Burden upon a Son who was scarce able to Support himself without breaking in upon the future Support of another Person whom she might imagine, was much dearer to me'.[56]

Not a gracious answer to a mother, yet Sterne is so earnest he seems to have convinced himself. Even so, he made his mother a gift of twenty guineas, 'Which with a Present of Cloaths &c— which I had given her the Day before, I doubted not, Would have the Effect I wanted'.[57] But if so many outsiders thought Laurence Sterne marked down for further preferment, it may not have been difficult for the mother to see the light of ambition in her son's eye. Indeed, the prebendal stall of North Newbald, which had come to Sterne within a year of his marriage and for which he resigned Givendale, carried with it £158 a year. With this, Sutton, his wife's income and the fees due to him for preaching at York Minster, Sterne's annual income cannot have fallen far short of £250.

But Agnes was not tractable:

She told me with an Air of the utmost Insolence
'That as for going back to live in Ireland; She was determined to Shew me no such Sport—That she found, I had married a Wife who had brought me a Fortune—& she was resolved to enjoy her Share of it, & live the Rest of her Days at her ease either at York or Chester'.[58]

This put Sterne in a huff and he answered bleakly that 'I should not forget I was a Son, Tho she had forgot she was a *Mother*.'[59] Agnes duly moved from Liverpool to Chester with her daughter Catherine. Although he is not specific, Sterne claims to have helped support them there:

we were kind to her above our power & common Justice to ourselves, and tho it went hard enough down with us, to reflect We were supporting both her and my Sister in the Pleasures and Advantages of a Town Life, which for prudent Reasons we denyed ourselves;

Yet Still we were Weak enough to do it for five Years together, tho'
I own, not without continual Remonstrances on my Side, as well as
perpetual Clamours on theirs.[60]

The picture of Sterne's rural self-denial is offset only by the
thought that at about this time in York he may have been
enjoying the 'Pleasures and Advantages' of Sarah Benson, his
uncle's mistress. As well as that, in February 1744, the living of
Stillington, a mile and a half north of Sutton, fell vacant by the
death of Richard Musgrave. It was a convenient addition to
Sterne's living; from his garden he could see his way across the
fields to Stillington. Sterne could not have counted on his uncle's
support for this living, but he did not need to: 'By my wife's
means I got the living of Stillington—a friend* of her's in the
south had promised her, that if she married a clergyman in
Yorkshire, when the living became vacant, he would make her
a compliment of it.'[61] On 25 February, three of his clerical
acquaintances, William Dodsworth, William Berdmore and
Thomas Harrison, all signed testimonials to the effect that
Sterne possessed both 'good life and conversations' and on 14
March he was inducted to the living. Stillington increased his
annual income by £40 so that it must by now have been some
ten times the sum his mother depended on.

Perhaps hearing of this new preferment, Agnes sent her
daughter Catherine to York, 'That she might make her Complaints to You [Jaques Sterne] and engage You to Second them
in these unreasonable Claims upon us'.[62] This may have been a
shrewd move by Agnes since once before, after the death of
Roger Sterne, she had herself been denied an audience by
Jaques Sterne. Indeed, Sterne recalled that his uncle had then
remarked upon the 'Clamourous & rapacious Temper'[63] of his
Irish sister-in-law. Catherine seems to have been much more
appealing. She was no more than twenty at this time and
Richard Greenwood, a servant in Laurence Sterne's household
at Sutton, thought her 'one of the finest women ever seen'.[64]

Although plotting against her brother, Catherine stayed with
Laurence Sterne during her visit to York, and 'was received by
us with all Kindness'.[65] When she returned to Chester, it was at
Sterne's expense, with five guineas in her pocket and 'a Six &

* Apparently, Lord Thomas Fairfax.

thirty Piece which my Wife put into her Hand as she took Horse'. Sterne and his wife even attempted to persuade Catherine to take up a more suitable and rewarding career:

as the truest Mark of our Friendship in Such a Situation, My Wife & self took no Small Pains, the time she was with us, to turn her Thoughts to some way of depending upon her own Industry, In which we offer'd her all imaginable Assistance. 1st By proposing to her, that if She would set herself to learn the Business of a Mantua-Maker, as soon as she could get Insight enough into it, to make a Gown & set up for herself,—'*That* we would give her 30.pounds to begin the World & Support her till Business fell in.—Or if she Would go into a Milliners Shop in London, My Wife engaged not only to get her into a Shop where she should have Ten pounds a Year Wages, But to equip her with Cloaths &c: properly for the Place: or lastly if she liked it better, As my Wife had then an Opportunity of recommending her to the family of one of the first of our Nobility—She undertook to get her a creditable place in it where she would receive no less than 8 or 10pds a Year Wages with other Advantages.—My Sister shew'd no seeming opposition to either of the two last proposals, till my Wife had wrote & got a favourable Answer to the one—& an immediate offer of the Other.—It will Astonish you, Sir, when I tell You, She rejected them with the Utmost Scorn;—telling me, I might send my own Children to Service when I had any

But for her part, As she was the Daughter of a Gentleman, *she would not Disgrace* herself, but would Live as Such.[66]

So spirited a reply to such lordly recommendations is not quite as astonishing as Sterne pretends. Catherine, after all, was Laurence Sterne's full sister and if he had attained the life of a gentleman, why should she not hope to do the same? It is revealing of eighteenth-century social climbing that Laurence Sterne should choose to represent his sister as the daughter of an Irish tradeswoman, and himself as a member of a Yorkshire gentry family. The brutality in this distinction may be remembered when viewing those pictures Sterne liked to offer in which he mixed as easily with lords as beggars.

But if Sterne's treatment of his Irish family seems hypocritical, he came to suffer the most dreaded fate of the hypocrite – public exposure. And he can hardly have been surprised that a discarded mother and a betrayed uncle should conspire to spread uncomplimentary opinions of him. In 1747, Agnes finally gained access to Jaques Sterne. According to Sterne, his mother chose not to mention the several gifts and allowances he had made her. He had also agreed to let her have £8 a year for as long as she lived, but Agnes, on Jaques's advice, insisted on making this sum binding on Sterne's wife.* Sterne was adamant that he could not exploit his wife so:

I feel I have *no Power* in Equity or in Conscience to do so; & I will add in her behalf, considering how much she has merited at my hands, as the best of Wives, That was I capable of being worried into so cruel a Measure as to give away hers & her Child's Bread upon the clamour which you and my Mother have raised—That I should not only be the Weakest, But the *Worst Man* that ever Woman trusted with all She had.[67]

As we shall see, Sarah Benson is not the only reason for murmurs at this last sentiment. By this stage, indeed, Elizabeth Sterne cannot have retained too many illusions about her husband. Richard Greenwood believed that it was Sterne's wife who prevented him from helping his mother and sister, and the several references to his duty to his wife in the letter of 1751 argue for such pressure. By whatever means, Agnes and Jaques Sterne seem to have raised a clamour. And it is largely in terms of rumour that the story of Sterne and his mother survives. Some years after the deaths of all the interested parties, in 1776, Daniel Watson, the vicar of Leake in Yorkshire, told this story to George Whateley, treasurer of the Foundling Hospital in London: 'Shall I tell you what York scandal says? viz. that Sterne, when possessed of preferment of 300£ a year, would not pay 10£ to release his mother out of Ousebridge prison, when poverty was her only fault, and her character so good, that two of her neighbours clubbed to set her at liberty, to gain a livelihood . . . by taking in washing.'[68] John Croft claimed that Agnes was never released: 'Sterne's Mother died in the common Goal at York in a wretched condition, or soon after she was released. It was held unpardonable in him not to relieve her, when he had the means of doing it, as a subscription was

* This may be a hint that Sterne's health was already considered to be unreliable.

set on foot for the purpose. . . . Never anyone dwelt more upon
Humanity in Theory but it does not appear that he putt so
much of it in practice.'[69]

We do not know whether Sterne's mother was put in prison,
nor whether she died there. The son's Memoir is very reserved
about his mother, but the rigmarole of explanation in the 1751
letter was clearly provoked by some major event. The feverish
self-defence of that letter speaks for a man who has been jabbed
in some sensitive, inner part:

> . . . being told of late by some of My Friends, That this Clamour
> has been kept up against me, & by as Singular a Stroke of Ill-Design
> as could be levell'd against a Defenceless Man Who Lives retired in
> the Country & has few Opportunities of Disabusing the World, That
> my Mother has moreover been fix'd in that Very place where a hard
> report might do me (as a Clergyman) the most real Disservice,—I
> was roused by the advice of my Friends to think of some way of
> defending myself; which I own I should have set about immediately
> by telling my Story publickly to the World,—But for the following
> Inconvenience, That I could not do myself Justice this Way, without
> doing myself an Injury at the same time by laying Open the Naked-
> ness of my Circumstances, which for ought I knew was likely to make
> me Suffer more in the Opinion of one Half of the World, than I
> could possibly gain from the other part of it by the clearest defence
> that could be made.[70]

There is a startling callousness and calculation in that passage
that seems to me characteristic of Sterne. Feeling here is something invoked but not experienced and the frantic contortions
to influence opinion show a truly unstable personality. Most
remarkable of all, this letter was addressed to an enemy quite
capable of broadcasting Sterne's confessions. It is as if Sterne
hardly realized how damaging they were. The combination of
ingenuousness and calculation can only be explained by the
social journey Sterne had made in nearly forty years. This letter
is more unhinged than its author ever realized.

How did the story end? In September 1758, Sterne wrote
cryptically to John Blake, a friend, 'I hope my mothers Affair is
by this Time ended, to $\frac{our}{my}$ Comfort & I trust her's.'[71] In December of the same year he speaks of having to visit his mother on a

trip to York. Agnes by now would have been over sixty. The year 1758 was the last in which she drew her widow's military pension of £20, and on 5 May 1759 a 'Mrs. Sterne' was buried at the church of St. Michael le Belfrey, opposite the Minster. As for Catherine, his sister, John Croft said she married a publican in London. In his Memoir, Sterne said she was still alive but otherwise hardly mentions her again. It is the case, therefore, that before presenting himself to the world he had dislodged his sister and buried his mother.

***

If mother, sister and uncle all fell out with Laurence Sterne, what did his wife make of him?

Although Sterne liked to dream of 'that tender and delicious sentiment, which ever mixes in friendship, where there is a difference of sex',[72] he winced at the word *wife* – ''Tis a shrill, penetrating sound of itself.'[73] Mrs. Walter Shandy is the only wife in Sterne's fiction, and it would be no exaggeration to call her the butt of *Tristram Shandy* if we were not told that 'she knew no more than her backside what my father meant.'[74] She is bland to 'that little subacid soreness of humour' in her husband and, as for his most elaborate and systematic arguments – such as when and how a lad should be put into breeches – she was 'indifferent whether it was done this way or that,—provided it was but done at all'.[75] Her greatest fault is to have no interest in style and to be possessed by an obdurately mundane common sense. Mrs. Shandy is as indifferent to her husband's fanciful notions as Margaret Dumont always was of Groucho's innuendo. Yet much of the Shandy comedy turns on my mother's imperturbable vacuousness. It is the sort of portrait of a wife that might emerge from years of inconsequential misunderstanding, and perhaps the gulf of Sterne's married life is remembered in the ruminating voice that interrupts the swelter of passion – '*Pray, my dear, have you not forgot to wind up the clock?*'[76]

If Elizabeth Sterne – Mrs. Shandy's maiden name was Elizabeth Mollineux – ever thought to recognize herself in her husband's book she might have been upset by the comic disasters at the birth of Tristram. She was not herself the luckiest woman in matters of childbirth; nor for that matter can many parsons' wives have counted on such unruly husbands.

E

Mrs. Shandy's earlier hysterical pregnancy had doomed Tristram to the exigencies of a village birth, but as far as we know Mrs. Sterne did not enjoy a treaty with her husband whereby she might be confined in London, or even at York. Elizabeth Sterne became pregnant early in 1745. Did she then mention a fashionable midwife, or did Sterne, like Walter Shandy, 'as they lay chatting gravely in bed afterwards, talking over what was to come',[77] tell her that she must have the child at Sutton? A daughter was born, and baptized Lydia, on 1 October and buried on the next day.

This sad event is recorded in the parish registers of both Sutton and Stillington, as though Sterne wished to impress his disappointment on both his parishes. However relaxed a cleric Sterne sometimes seems, scepticism about his essential religious awe should be tempered with that instant baptism of the dying (or even dead) Lydia. Christening is still the hardiest survivor of Anglican practices and W. Henderson recalls, in *Folklore of the Northern Counties*, 'I have heard old people say of sickly infants, Ah, there will be a change when he has been taken to church; children never thrive till they have been christened.'[78]

We have no details of Lydia's death and it is unremarkable that such a child should die so young. On the day Lydia died, another baby was buried in Stillington only one day her senior, while at Sutton, in 1738, twins had died three days old. It was around mid-century that the population of Britain began steadily to rise. Only in the late 1750s did the annual baptisms in York start to exceed the total of burials. Not only were epidemics prevalent in the first half of the century, but bad winters and harvests could equally affect the figures. In the years of Sterne's incumbency at Sutton for which reliable records survive, 1738–56, baptisms exceed burials by less than ten per cent (241 to 220). In eight of those years there were more burials than baptisms. Average life expectancy was considerably lower than it is today, but we have already encountered several people who lived into their eighties. At Sutton, in 1749, two men died aged eighty-six and ninety-five, while in 1760, at Stillington, a William Walker died claiming to be 112: old enough to have seen Cromwell.[79] It was not so hard for the well-to-do to live a full term once they had survived childhood. Average expectancy was held down by the dreadful vulnerability of the poorer people in infancy and in times of economic crisis.

The Sternes, during the 1740s, were especially vulnerable. In addition to Sterne's short-lived daughter, his cousin Richard died in 1744, aged thirty-seven, Richard's daughter, Mary, in 1745, aged ten, and Sterne's other cousin, Timothy, in 1746, aged twenty-five.[80] Roger's brood had been very frail. Two of Sterne's children died at or soon after birth* and his surviving daughter, Lydia, was an asthmatic who barely lived past thirty. Even so, another cousin, Frances, lived to be eighty-six, only dying in 1801, and Sterne himself, a conscientious invalid, reached as far as fifty-four.†

As it happens, one of the several English doctors gradually improving the practice of medicine was living in York at this time. But John Burton was no friend of Sterne. One story of an encounter between the two of them in the Minster Yard shows how easily Burton's belligerent seriousness and Sterne's counter-punching drollery quarrelled. Burton hoped to settle an argument that arose by, 'Sir, I never give way to a fool!', but Sterne only answered, 'But I always do, Sir', and waved the doctor through.[81] The culmination of this hostility was Sterne's use of Burton in *Tristram Shandy* as the model for Dr. Slop‡ – 'a little, squat, uncourtly figure . . . about four feet and a half perpendicular height, with a breadth of back, and a sesquipedality of belly, which might have done honour to a serjeant in the horse guards'.[82]

Burton was certainly a swollen figure, but not invited to

* Richard Greenwood, Sterne's servant during the early 1740s, was reported as saying that Elizabeth gave birth to 'several children', Lydia alone surviving. He added that one other was a boy, who died after three weeks so that 'Sterne was inconsolable on his death, took to his chamber, and would not leave it of a week.' No other evidence supports this and it does seem unlikely that Sterne would have failed to note the birth in the Sutton register. (Kuist, *op. cit.*, p. 549.)

† Although Sterne proclaimed and was duly known for his illness, it is worth noting that, among contemporary men of letters, Smollett, Goldsmith and Fielding all died younger than he did, while Boswell and Gibbon were only a few years older.

‡ Arthur Cash has shown how closely the account of Tristram's birth mocks Burton's obstetrical writings. Burton had, indeed, come off worse in a battle of books with Dr. William Smellie, author of a *Treatise on the Theory and Practice of Midwifery*. (Cash, 'The Birth of Tristram Shandy: Sterne and Dr Burton', *Studies in the Eighteenth Century*, ed. R. F. Brissenden [Canberra, 1968], pp. 149–50.)

attend Mrs. Sterne's labour. Dr. Slop was the most recognizable of the caricatures in *Tristram Shandy*, not least because the animosity between Burton and the Sternes had been well known for several years. Yet Slop is an unfair disguise to be foisted upon Burton. He was, in fact, a notable doctor who published in 1751 – the year in which Elizabeth Sterne suffered a miscarriage – *An Essay towards a complete new system of midwifery*.* More than that, he had played a leading part in the foundation at York of the County Hospital for the Poor.

Burton was a Tory, and some said a Papist; but his benevolent activities show the professed liberalism of Yorkshire Whigs in a bad light. 'When I came to *York*,' wrote Burton, 'I daily saw the Misery, that the poorer Sort of People underwent, and that numbers frequently died, not only for want of Advice and Medicines, but also for want of common Necessaries; I therefore projected the building an Infirmary.'[83] Thanks to a bequest of £500 from Lady Elizabeth Hastings† the Hospital was set up in 1742 with Burton as one of its physicians. The success of the institution is shown in the fact that in its first three years it recorded 1,335 cures and only fifty-two deaths.

The only Sterne who subscribed to this hospital was Richard, Laurence's cousin. Both Jaques and Laurence were ingrained political enemies of Burton and of any project he touched. Burton and Jaques Sterne had crossed swords during the election of 1734 when the Tory made it his business to guard one of the voting booths and 'prevented several from being poll'd in an

---

* Burton (1710–71) was born at Colchester, the son of a London merchant. He went up to St. John's College, Cambridge, in 1727, and later studied under Boerhaeve at Leyden. In 1758, Burton published the first volume of *Monasticon Eboracense*, the failure of which prohibited the second volume he had promised.

† Lady Elizabeth Hastings (1682–1739) was an outstanding charitable *grande dame* who also made bequests of £1,000 each to Trinity Church, Leeds, and the Society for Propagating Christian Knowledge. Equally, she was sufficiently professional at distributing her own wealth to threaten to withdraw her donation to the Hospital at York when the project loitered. She died in December 1739 and the *York Courant* noted that 'about six Hours before her Death, she order'd all her Servants to be call'd into her Chamber, and in the most affecting Manner gave a charge to each of them for the future Conduct of their Life – An Example as rare, as worthy of Imitation.' Richardson may have thought just this. The opening of *Pamela* – written between November 1739 and January 1740 – has a very similar scene in which Lady B recommends Pamela to her son – a suggestion he responds to eagerly. (*York Courant*, 1 January 1740.)

unfair Manner'.[84] But in 1741 Burton trespassed even further on
Jaques Sterne's systems of interest when he exposed the precentor's plan to pack the church wardens with amenable Whigs
as a means to diverting the sacrament monies to political uses.
Burton even managed to have the story printed in the *London
Evening Post* and felt sure that no honest man could any longer
support the Whigs. Indignation may only be a style, and
Burton seems to have been a truculent man. None the less, his
anger at Walpolean Whiggery is typical of Tory outrage, and
not without substance: 'Can these People call themselves
Whigs, and Defenders of Liberty? Are such People proper to be
trusted in any Shape, let their Pretence be what it will? View
them thoroughly, and you'll always find that their own Interest
is at the Bottom; and provided they get but their own Ends
served, they don't care if all the Rest of their Neighbours were
sent a begging.'[85]

Jaques Sterne had his revenge on Burton at the time of the
1745 risings, an event which put all of York in great excitement
and consternation. The Church at York was solidly Whig, and
the election of 1741 had shown an appreciable Whig bias in the
area; but York had once had the reputation of being particularly tolerant towards Roman Catholics. News of the Jacobite
rising caused great alarm in York – indeed, the Highland army
was to reach as far as Derby, fifty miles south of York, so that
the fears were not unjustified. Superstition might have remarked
on the fact that in July 1745 a thunderstorm had split a pinnacle
on the Minster.[86] Within a month news came south that the
Highlanders had some four thousand men in the field and were
laying siege to Fort Augustus.

Sir John Cope had been sent out against them but had been
defeated at Prestonpans. On hearing this news, Archbishop
Herring had delivered a rousing sermon of warning and called
for a volunteer force. Contemporary prints offer alternative
interpretations for this action: in some, Herring exclaims
'Religion! Liberty! My Country', but in others, 'My Mitre, my
Lands, My Gold, Church'.[87] By September the Pretender was
boasting of being in London for Christmas. An Association for
the Defence of York was formed, troops arrived in the York area
as reinforcements and a letter appeared in the *Courant* urging the

defence of 'the best Constitution and the purest Religion under Heaven'.[88] More practically, as the Highlanders entered Carlisle, a verse was circulated rhyming Cope and rope.

Laurence Sterne seems to have been detained at Sutton during this alarm attending to his wife's recovery from childbirth, but he attempted to persuade his servant, Richard Greenwood, to enlist in a regiment of cavalry raised against the rebellion. There is no evidence of Sterne having played any part in his uncle's subsequent persecution of Burton,* although Cross believes that Sterne was still writing political articles at this time.[89]

Burton was in a dilemma. He was not a Catholic, but he was spiritually loyal to the Stuarts and must have listened to reports of the approaching Highlanders with mixed feelings. On 22 November, news arrived at York that the Highland army was at Kendal. Everything depended on whether they would decide to come down the west or east side of the Pennines. Burton had some land, in Birkwith and South House, to the west of York and he asked permission from the Recorder of York to go there immediately to safeguard his property. It was a clever compromise: if the Highlanders seemed strong he might join them, but if not he had established an alibi.

The Recorder hedged – 'it was so nice a Case, he could scarce tell how to direct me'[90] – but Burton set out. He was delayed by bad weather and at Settle heard that the Highlanders were proceeding through Lancashire. He went to Hornby, some fifteen miles south-east of Kendal, and was sitting in a barber's chair when a party of rebels appeared. According to Burton, nothing took place that might have disturbed the lather on his chin. But 'one B—rb—k of Settle (who abounded more with the evil Spirit and Malice, than Meekness and Truth)'[91] sent news to York that Burton had been fraternizing.

---

* However, Kenneth Monkman has recently reported one letter (in the *Protestant York Courant*, 1 July 1746), arguably by Sterne, attacking 'the Hand of Popery'. Mr. Monkman also reported another letter (*Protestant York Courant*, 3 November 1747), probably by Sterne, which contains fascinating glimpses of a man grasping his own character: 'I'll be so sincere as to confess to you, I have some oddities. . . . However my Friends allow them to be very pardonable, as in my most violent Moods I never go beyond the snapping of a Pipe, or the skimming of my Hat and Wig across the Room.'

When Burton returned to York, Jaques Sterne had him seized as 'a suspicious Person to his Majesty's Government'. 'Burton's guilt seems unquestionable,' rejoiced Sterne to Lord Irwin, Lord-Lieutenant of the East Riding.[92] He was imprisoned in York Castle while the fickle *London Evening Post* carried reports of his downfall, furnished undoubtedly by Jaques Sterne. In fact, the complete absence of evidence against Burton preserved him, but not before he had been sent to London and held there for a year. But Crusoe-like, Burton did not waste this time. He talked with several Jacobites who were imprisoned with him and subsequently published *A Genuine and True Journal of the Most Miraculous Escape of the Young Chevalier.*

It seems a foolish story of blind malice. But the fears in York had not been hysterical, and not all the retribution dissipated. Two rebels, James Mayne and William Connolly, were executed and their heads posted on Micklegate Bar for over eight years before a tailor took them down and buried them one night in 1754. By that time, Jacobitism was a relinquished cause. In the same year, the restored Burton was offered the freedom of the city.* He declined this honour but lived on till 1771, pointed out probably as the original of Dr. Slop, indelibly marked by the Sternes.

All of which is something of a diversion from Laurence Sterne's married life, but no book on Sterne can omit John Burton, and diversions are the 'sunshine of reading'.

Sterne's only surviving child by marriage was born at Sutton on 1 December 1747. It was another daughter, and, unheeding their initial bad luck, the parents called her Lydia.

Elizabeth Sterne had at least one further miscarriage. Some time in 1751, Sterne wrote to Theophilus Garencieres, a York apothecary: 'My Wife is troubled with the Piles to a great degree, wch in her Condition will be very dangerous, unless removed immediately, before her Delivery, wch is expected every Hour.'[93] Whatever medicine Garencieres supplied, a few days later Sterne reported a failure: 'Mrs Sterne was last

* Ironically, in December 1746, Jaques Sterne offered 200 guineas and a portrait of the Duke of Cumberland for the freedom of York. The *York Courant* observed that, since no one supported 'this Generous and Disinterested Proposal', it was not taken up. (*Letters*, Jaques Sterne to the Lord Mayor of York, 2 December 1746, p. 425; *York Courant*, 16 December 1746.)

Night deliverd of a dead Child; She is very weak & I think wants some comforting Liquid or other to take of, every 2 or 3 hours.'[94]

This stillbirth may have marked an end in the marital relations: in May 1767 Sterne declared, 'I have had no commerce whatever with the sex, not even with my wife . . . these fifteen years.'[95] Since this defence was provoked by an attack of what the doctors insisted on calling venereal disease, it may be that the remark referred accurately only to his wife.

Sterne's language with women was always suggestive – sometimes crudely so, but more characteristically it had an overwhelming sentimental pressure. The stories about Sterne's extra-marital life reveal a very practical lecher. Elizabeth Montagu, it may be remembered, had heard of him as coming to marriage already debauched. His quarrel with his uncle had been sharpened by the nephew's usurpation of Jaques's mistress. John Croft implied that Sterne's instinctive pursuit of the female quickly upset his marriage: 'Afterwards they did not live on the best terms and harmony together, chiefly owing to his infidelity, to the Marriage Bed. . . . As an instance of his infidelity, his wife once caught him with the maid, when she pulled him out of bed on the Floor.'[96] This too easily resembles a situation from Feydeau in which the wronged wife is passed off as a figure of fun. But Sterne's own servant, Richard Greenwood, portrayed him as a devouring lecher:

He used to accompany his master whenever Sterne came to York, & when there he rarely spent a night without a girl or two which Richard used to procure for him. He promised Richard to reward him for keeping these private amours of his secret, particularly from Mrs. Sterne. Richard says he was as good as his promise & that for his part he never mentioned these things concerning his master. Sterne too was continually after his female servants.[97]

That Sterne had so many women may mean one of two things: either he was insatiable or few women could tolerate him in more than sips. It would seem that the separate lives he and his wife led for so much of the time after the first publication of *Tristram Shandy* had had their origins long before it. Croft says that her husband's infidelities drove Elizabeth Sterne out of her senses. But that is an extreme resort and if she was anything like Mrs. Shandy she would have been doomed to remain injured rather than insane. Croft paints an almost Gothic picture in which a deluded Mrs. Sterne fancied herself the Queen of Bohemia and the amused Sterne played the fool to humour her:

> Tristram, her husband, to amuse and induce her to take the air, proposed coursing, in the way practised in Bohemia; for that purpose he procured bladders, and filled them with beans, and tied them to the wheels of a single horse chair. When he drove madam into a stubble field, with the motion of the carriage and the bladders, rattle bladder, rattle; it alarmed the hares, and the greyhounds were ready to take them.[98]

Whatever this game did for Mrs. Sterne's illusions, the nervous sensibility of her husband may have been soothed by so hectic and noisy a motion. As for Bohemia, that name is still applied to land immediately to the south of Sutton, so that Mrs. Sterne's regal pretensions may not have been quite as audacious as they have been presented.

Elizabeth Sterne does not seem the sort of woman to have surrendered her sense to sorrow. She may have been especially uncongenial to her husband because, like Mrs. Shandy, 'A temperate current of blood ran orderly through her veins in all months of the year, and in all critical moments both of the day and night alike.'[99] There are hints that Mrs. Sterne evolved a resigned and practical way of dealing with Sterne that put him a little in awe of her. After all, she survived his absence, proved able to look after herself and her daughter in France, and could produce this realization in her husband. 'As to matrimony, I should be a beast to rail at it, for my wife is easy—but the world is not—and had I staid from her a second longer it would have been a burning shame—else she declares herself happier without me—but not in anger is this declaration made—but in pure sober good-sense, built on sound experience.'[100]

It may have been simply good-sense that Laurence Sterne could not bear to be confined with. Certainly, as the 1750s proceed, Sterne and his wife seem to act singly. In 1758, in

letters to John Blake,* Sterne talks of himself and his wife
coming to York together, but as if strangers, hardly talking to
each other on the journey: 'My wife I told you is engaged & as
I come alone I take pot luck',[101] or 'I will be with You & my
friend by eleven on Saturday—my wife talks of taking a wheel
to York the same Day—But if she does twill be of no Consequence to the Affair.'[102] On another occasion, Sterne told
Blake he had 'tore off the Bottom of Y^{rs} before I let my Wife
see it, to save a Lye',[103] only for her to notice the ragged edge—
as if it had been a clue arranged to tease her.

All the evidence suggests they were opposites, unlikely to
'*gee* well together'.[104] Sterne loved to be liked and expected to
have his foibles overlooked, if only because in his eyes they were
as trivial as everything else in his life. But Elizabeth Sterne, as
Elizabeth Montagu knew, was 'certainly very ill temperd',[105]
and Sterne himself once confided in Latin to his friend Hall-
Stevenson, 'sed sum fatigatus & aegrotus de mea uxore plus
quam unquam.'[106] In a letter to Elizabeth Montagu, Sterne's
wife spoke of being 'Cruelly Seperated from all my Friends',
only two weeks before her sister, Lydia Botham, was to die. Not
that the sisters had been close correspondents. Indeed, Elizabeth Sterne complained that she knew no more than the sex and
names of her sister's children and lamented 'the want of a more
intimate Acquaintance with her Kindred'.[107]

The predicament of Elizabeth Sterne is a reminder of the
vulnerability of women of her time. The little direct evidence
we have of her suggests a plain, sharp-tempered but perceptive
woman. But so little of her life remains that our picture of her is
largely influenced by the view we take of her husband. Accept
him as a gay, good-natured fellow and she quickly becomes a
scold. But suppose Sterne to have behaved with half the randi-
ness of his love-making prose and she seems in turn a stoic.

We have a few glimpses of how persistently sexual notoriety
attached itself to Sterne and in what ordeals of face-saving this
must have involved his wife. One letter, recently discovered,

---

* John Blake (1723–84) was one of Sterne's closer friends. A graduate of Oxford,
Blake was appointed, in 1756, to be rector of Catton, the parish that Sterne had
been briefly licensed to in 1738. In 1757, Blake followed his father, Zachary, as
Master of the Royal Grammar School in York.

from Sterne to a Sutton parishioner, written in March 1758, is
an indignant rebuttal of allegations that Sterne has been accus-
ing a Mrs. Sturdy of adultery. Sterne, in fact, had married the
Sturdys in 1755. Two and a half years later, a 'Scandalous
Report' is put about that Sterne has accused Mrs. Sturdy of
adultery. Sterne then writes to the alleged cuckold since he
'thought it necessary for me to write you a Letter, as well to
vindicate the Honor & Character of You & Mrs Sturdy, as my
own, wch of the three, I think is most injured'.[108] He traces the
rumour to a man named Young, an agent of Lord Fauconberg,
who claimed to have heard the story from 'a Company of idle
Dykers'. Sterne immediately took Young before witnesses,
charged him and extracted a full confession:

I do hereby certify & attest, That the Report of Mr Sterne's
having hinted words to the Dishonor of Mrs Sturdy, is an absolute
Falshood. . . . I do moreover solemnly declare, That whatever has
been spread of that Kind I Believe has been done by malicious people
with no End but to create Disturbance betwixt Mr Sterne & M^r
Sturdy. This I willingly attest & subscribe at the Desire of M^r
Sterne, & in Justification of his Character wch has been vily abused &
injured by the above Calumny.[109]

This, again, is Sterne diligently marshalling his own defence,
just as he had for his uncle. So diligently, that we see how per-
vasive his insecurity is. For as soon as it has accomplished his
purpose, Sterne's self-righteousness slips askew:

I must not conclude before I tell you that the Counterpart of the
same Report, was propagated at the same Time, with the same
wicked View That this was. namly, That In consideration of a favor
shown by me in procuring a Farm for an poor Farmer here,—I had
lay'[d with] his Wife, wth Circumstances of time & [place]—This
Calumny was charitably bro[ught to] Mrs Sterne, who only made
merry as did the Supposed Cuckold, kn[owing what] Forge it came
from. . . .[110]

That merriment may have been forced. It is of interest that
there were 'malicious people' in or around Sutton intent on
blackening Sterne's character. But it is remarkable that the man
himself should crush one rumour and release another in the
same letter. The effect of this insouciance would have been all

the more striking in a rural community. If one is to believe Richard Greenwood's account of his master's recreation in York, then Sterne might be the father of every parish bastard.*

Later in 1758 there is another curiosity that seems to involve Sterne in intrigue. We have already seen him asking John Blake's complicity in deceiving Mrs. Sterne. It now appears that the complexities of the Sterne household had an extra dimension. At about the same time, Mrs. Sterne was also corresponding secretly with Blake and relying upon his tact and silence. The cause is not clear. Nor do we know the exact date of this letter from Elizabeth Sterne to Blake, but it seems to fit somewhere in that time when Blake himself was looking to the Sternes for support in his unsuccessful wooing of a young lady in York. Mrs. Sterne's letter discloses a hotbed of conspiracy to which we have no plan:

A Thousand Blessings on your Heart for your kindness to me; You sent my Husband home to me in a disposition which promises me better Days, therefore not one word of our Conversation to T—r, or any one Soul, for that might Blast all my hopes. I likewise find he has not told Mr T.r the worst of his Circumstances, but as he has Comply'd with all that can reasonably be expected to mend 'em, I cou'd wish he might not be further press'd. therefore if you have told Mr Taylor give him a little Caution lest 'tis suspected from whence the Intelligence came. I trust I shall e'er long tell you by word of mouth how truely Thankfull I am to you, had I opportunity at present I cou'd not my head & Heart are so distirb'd by the extravagance of his Repentance.[111]

What issue has provoked such disturbing contrition from Sterne, and what are we to make of this tactful wife who hopes that her husband 'might not be further press'd'? In Sterne's case, there is always the chance that his own philandering has been found out. In one of his letters to Blake, in the summer of 1758, there is this postscript – perhaps genuine, but perhaps the outburst of a man who cannot resist shedding his own secrets: 'I beg pardon for detain y^r stockings wch was the Maid's

* Such there were. During Sterne's incumbency of Stillington, Jane Harbottle had at least two bastards. In 1753, she was ordered to do a formal penance. Robert Jepson, the alleged father of one of her children, was also ordered to do penance. He refused and Sterne excommunicated him.

forgetfulness but she has a sweetheart in her head, wch puts all other things out, this I'm sure you'l excuse.'[112]

But would Mrs. Sterne have resorted to the confidence of another man in a matter of husband's infidelity? Her letter to Blake seems to refer to some business in York. Messrs. T—r, T.r and Taylor – if they are all one – might be John Taylor of York, about whom all too little is known. The talk of 'the worst of his Circumstances', of not being further pressed and of complying with all that might be expected of him suggests some monetary negotiation. We know that, in 1758, Blake was handling some financial affair for Sterne at York, although there is no evidence of its nature. Indeed, this passage from a letter from Sterne to Blake omits concrete reference with a care that can hardly be fortuitous:

> It was very kindly done in You to send me the Letter to Sutton, & I thank You for y^r & all other friendly Offices—But for the future You shall not be at such a trouble unless something *extraordinary* makes it adviseable, Because as You will always first peruse the Acc^{ts}, I am perfectly easy ab^t what is in y^{rs}, knowing You will do for me as for Y^{r}self.—You percieve, That he will write from time to time to give us a proper Preparation in Case the Event sh^d happen, Upon wch preparation given by him, it will be time enough for us to plann somethin more particular than what is done already, & it will be time enough, When he writes me Word That He grows worse, to settle the Matter of the Express with him in my answer to that Acc^t . . .[113]

We can only speculate about the subject of this letter. Is Blake acting as go-between for Sterne with his mother or with some other unknown person to whom Sterne was financially obliged? What is 'the Event' that Sterne and Blake are taking trouble to prepare for, and who is keeping them informed of its progress? It might concern Jaques Sterne who had only a year to live and may have been involved with Sterne in some financial provision for Agnes Sterne. (Jaques had sold his part of the Great House in 1757, an unlikely sacrifice unless he had need of cash.) But what has Taylor to do with the matter, and what is the immediate cause for such repentance in Sterne? I would guess that it involves money rather than sex. There is some support for the theory that Sterne had incurred a serious debt in his efforts, in December 1758, to 'clear my hands & head of all country Entanglements'.[114] If he was seriously embarrassed late in 1758 then the need for ready cash may have played a large part in the origins of *Tristram Shandy*. Once we adopt this hypothesis, a pleasant irony emerges in that between the writing and publication of the book, both Jaques and Agnes Sterne – the most likely drains on his resources – had died.

Apart from references to Lydia being 'very much out of all Sorts',[115] we hear little from Sterne about his daughter during those years at Sutton. Lydia was twelve when *Tristram Shandy* was published, and, if frail, still with some of her father's idiosyncrasy, as events were soon to show. But Sterne's humour may not have been the sort to entertain a child. No child appears in *Tristram Shandy* other than the speechless and defenceless infant. That young Tristram's misfortunes are told to us by Tristram senior certainly allows them to be more comic. But there is sometimes a disturbing dislocation between the detached voice and the child bandied about in that inept household. A century later, a Dickens could not have left that gap. A whole novel might have sprung from it. All we can say of Sterne's use of his childhood is that there are times when *Tristram Shandy* seems to be working strenuously to ignore the deficit.

Not one human relationship in Sterne's life seems mature, lasting or to have been experienced mutually. Just as Tristram's own narrative merely relates the disasters of his life, so Sterne may have felt that his own daughter was beyond his help. The peculiar intensity of Sterne's imagination was all devoted to himself. Our one story of Lydia's childhood is that her parents had a money box in which they kept funds for her education, until Mrs. Sterne caught her husband at it one day recovering their donations.[116]

***

It was not only family that failed to touch or discover an inner Sterne. Politics had already disappointed him. All the conventional pursuits of the country priest proved similarly unfulfilling, and I think it is legitimate to see his years at Sutton being increasingly occupied by boredom and a menacing sense of inertia. Immobility must have fretted his nerves.

His earliest country activity was farming. The clergy were

traditionally involved in agriculture, both in the collecting of tithes and in the farming of the glebe that adjoined so many livings. Not that this extra interest was to emphasize the pastoral duties of the clergyman. Instead, the farms often took up a disproportionate amount of time, money and interest. Parson Trulliber, for instance, in *Joseph Andrews* was 'a parson on Sundays, but all the other six days might more properly be called a farmer. He occupied a small piece of land of his own, besides which he rented a considerable deal more. His wife milked his cows, managed his dairy, and followed the markets with butter and eggs. The hogs fell chiefly to his care, which he carefully waited on at home, and attended to fairs; on which occasion he was liable to many jokes, his own size being with much ale rendered little inferior to that of the beasts he sold.'[117]

Sterne began cautiously in the garden at Sutton and in 1742–3 planted cherry trees, espalier apples, nectarines and peaches, pear and plum trees and an orchard of apples. Nectarines and peaches cannot have flourished in the Sutton climate and in May 1745 Sterne recorded a hail storm – 'the Stones measured six Inches in Circumference. It broke almost all the South & West Windows, both of this House and my Vicarage at Stillington.'[118] Hail of that size would certainly have accounted for blossom or immature fruit, just as it would have dashed out the brains of most creatures.

In 1744, Sterne bought a farm to the north of Sutton from William Dawson and kept seven cows there. But, according to John Croft, the Sternes 'allways sold their Butter cheaper than their Neighbours, as they had not the least idea of œconomy, [so] that they were allways behindhand and in arrears with Fortune'.[119] But later in 1744, Sterne bought more land from Richard Harland, the squire of Sutton.

The picture of Sterne as farmer is not convincing, particularly in an England undergoing a major revolution in agricultural methods. Jethro Tull had begun an entire reappraisal of land husbandry that was continued in mid-century by 'Turnip' Townshend and Thomas Coke of Norfolk. They recognized that land could be helped, improved and better organized just as Robert Bakewell had set about experimenting with the various strains of sheep and cattle to produce more profitable animals. More land was made cultivable and the number of sheep doubled during the course of the century. Most important of all, agriculture became a business and not just a means of providing for those who owned and rented the soil. Two vastly important social changes sprang from this: fewer men were occupied on the land, and fewer men owned larger portions of it.

One instrument of these changes was enclosure. In the first decade of the eighteenth century there was one Enclosure Act, and in the first decade of the next century over 900. But this acceleration only really began after 1750: in the 1740s there were 38 acts, in the 1750s 156 and in the 1760s 424.[120] It probably reflects Sterne's own disposition towards the land that by the 1750s he was abandoning some of his own holdings and engaging with fellow-gentry in the entrepreneurial activity of enclosure. In 1756, with Lord Fauconberg of Newburgh Priory and Philip Harland – the largest landowners in the area – Sterne combined to obtain an Act of Enclosure for various pieces of land around Sutton.[121]

Sterne's farming may have begun with all Walter Shandy's optimism for system and only later grown tedious with the detail of daily labour and the risk of weather and profit. Paper farming could be very beguiling:

for whenever my father took pen and ink in hand, and set about calculating the simple expence of paring and burning, and fencing in the *Ox-moor*,* &c. &c.—with the certain profit it would bring him in return—the latter turned out so prodigiously in his way of working the account, that you would have sworn the *Ox-moor* would have carried all before it. For it was plain he should reap a hundred lasts of rape, at twenty pounds a last, the very first year—besides an excellent crop of wheat the year following—and the year after that, to speak within bounds, a hundred—but, in all likelihood, a hundred and fifty—if not two hundred quarters of pease and beans—besides potatoes without end—But then, to think he was all this while breeding up my brother like a hog to eat them—knocked all on the head again, and generally left the old gentleman in such a state of suspence—that, as he often declared to my uncle *Toby*—he knew no more than his heels what to do.[122]

---

* There is still land known as Ox Moor in the vicinity, to the south of the road between Stillington and Easingwold. It is now a nine-hole golf course and retains an essential intractability.

That is Shandean indecision, but it is in the spirit of someone who has been gullible about projects but dismayed by real fields. In 1767, Sterne confessed to a friend that he had been a failure as a farmer and that he had emerged £200 out of pocket.[123] He was engaged at farming until a year before the publication of *Tristram Shandy* and regretted all through the summer of 1758 that having to supervise the barley harvest prevented him from visiting York. In December 1758 he was mortified with intransigent threshers and half distracted by the glut of business in a mind bent on pleasure. 'I thank God however,' he wrote to John Blake, 'I have settled most of my Affairs—Let my freehold to a promising Tenent—have likewise this Week let him the most considerable part of my Tyths & shall clear my hands & head of all country Entanglements, having at present only ten p^{ds} [a] year in land & 7p^{ds} a year in Corn Tyth left undisposed of, wch shall be quitted with all provident Speed: This will bring me & mine into a narrow Compass—& make us, I hope both rich & happy.'[124]

For all that Sterne hardly enjoyed farming, he undoubtedly managed to feed his family comfortably. When he was flush from selling *Tristram Shandy*, his Sermons and from the curacy of Coxwold, he nevertheless looked back on the preceding years and admitted, 'I was quiet, for I was below Envy—& yet above Want; & indeed so very far above it, that the idea of it never once enterd my head, in writing.'[125] That is Sterne once more dazzled by the green of discarded fields, choosing to be nostalgic over rural quiet. However, it does suggest that his years at Sutton were comfortable and solvent.

The thirty years before the publication of *Tristram Shandy* were remarkable for the stability of prices, particularly in view of the increase in the quality and variety of so many goods. The average price for a quarter of wheat at York market in 1760, for instance, was 24s compared with 30s in 1730. There are sudden peaks in between, 51s in 1740 – a year of severe winter – and 50s in 1757; but the overall average for the period stayed at only a little over 30s. And yet the wheat was better and was produced in such quantity that white bread would have entirely replaced rye bread at Sterne's table.

Beef and mutton could be had for 3d a pound and fresh

butter for 5d a pound. Strong ale was 4d a quart, potatoes 4d a peck, best cheese 3d a pound. Port* was sold in York for 5s 6d a gallon. Diet was also being expanded: tea and coffee became increasingly common, and tropical fruit arrived in England from the various pickings of war.[126]

We may judge Sterne's standard of living by the fact that he had an income ten times as great as that of most agricultural labourers who still lived well enough to astound visiting foreigners. But there were more and more things for a family like Sterne's to spend its money on. Furniture, clothes, wallpaper and books all catered for bourgeois tastes.

Jethro Tull's *Horse-Hoeing Husbandry* sold at 6s, Johnson's *Dictionary of the English Language* for £4 10s. The *York Courant* was 2d per weekly issue, increasingly occupied during Sterne's life in Yorkshire with advertisements for livestock, furniture, property and the wares of York shops.

The entertainment at York would have been well within Sterne's pocket. Subscription to the Monday assemblies and the musical and theatrical evenings amounted, in 1736, to £4 10s a year. There was no question of value not being given in the theatre. In 1751, for instance, a benefit performance of *Othello* had singing between the acts and a farce to take away the taste in the mouth. Another concert offered *The Way of the World* as a diversion during the interval. And if anyone in York thought of visiting London, the trip could sometimes be done in two days if the weather allowed at between 2d and 3d a mile, or £5 for the return trip.

In several matters of eighteenth-century enjoyment Sterne appears to have been an abstemious man. He rarely mentions drinking in books or letters, and in all the descriptions of him as light-headed, there is no hint of drunkenness. One of his servants reported that Sterne 'never drank to excess—he usually after Dinner took one glass of wine, of which he drank half, & filled his glass with water for the rest'.†[127] Such spirits as his, perhaps,

---

* The Croft family had a large wine business in Portugal and Sterne may have had the offer of best port at a friend's price.

† Boswell later guessed how little Sterne depended upon artificial stimulants:

> Sometimes our Priest with limbs so taper
> Before his glass would cut a caper,
> Indulging each suggestion airy,

could become sufficiently intoxicated with their own humours. As to smoking, Sterne claimed that his brain would not tolerate tobacco, 'inasmuch as the fumes thereof do concoct my conceits too fast so that they would be all done to rags before they could be well served up'.[128] The Shandy brothers, of course, are pipe-smokers and pipe-dreamers. Indeed, when Trim finally convinces Toby of the true motives of the Widow Wadman, the pipe becomes a beautiful symbol of his disappointed dream of kindness:

'My uncle Toby laid down his pipe as gently upon the fender as if it had been spun from the unravellings of a spider's web—'[129]

But in a book largely confined to domestic interiors, it is noticeable that the Shandys hardly eat, a delight of the period so great that it excused extraordinary grossness and premature heart failure. Parson Woodforde, for instance, sat down to dinner – essentially a midday meal, but penetrating the afternoon as the century progressed – one day in 1770 with five guests:

I gave them ... a dish of fine Tench which I caught out of my brother's Pond in Pond Close this morning, Ham, and 3 Fowls boiled, a Plumb pudding; a couple of Ducks roasted, a roasted neck of Pork, a Plumb Tart and an Apple Tart, Pears, Apples and Nutts after dinner; White Wine and red, Beer and Cyder. Coffee and Tea in the evening at six o'clock. Hashed Fowl and Duck and Eggs and Potatoes etc. for supper. We did not dine till four o'clock – nor supped till ten.[130]

Francis Drake said that 'Feasting to excess with one another is strongly in use at *York*. . . . It is for this reason and their constantly living upon solid meat that few of the inhabitants are Long lived in *York*; there are not many instances of people living to an extreme old age in it.'[131] This may explain Sterne's moderation as well as his dislike for smoking. For although his

---

Each whim and innocent vagary.
The heliconian stream he'd quaff
And by himself transported laugh.
In short, without the help of Sherry,
He ever Hearty was and merry.

(Pottle, *op. cit.*, p. 307.)

years in Yorkshire contain few references to illness, it is likely that he was constantly expecting to be overtaken by it.

Sterne's health is a subject of some importance, if only because of the traditional association of pulmonary illness with nervous instability. But Sterne has left all too few clues about the nature of his illness and consumption can take a variety of forms. We know none of Sterne's doctors and have few reports on his health except those provided by the patient himself. As with so many parts of Sterne's life, we have to deal with the emotional expression of invalidism rather than the clinical evidence of it. The most circumstantial account of his consumption comes in a letter Sterne wrote to Hall-Stevenson from Toulouse in 1762 and which described a recent repetition of a crisis Sterne had suffered some twenty-five years earlier at Cambridge:

> ... of breaking a vessel in my lungs. It happen'd in the night, and I bled the bed full, and finding in the morning I was likely to bleed to death, I sent immediately for a surgeon to bleed me at both arms—this saved me, and with lying speechless three days I recovered upon my back in bed.[132]

That bed full of blood may at first sound like Sterne's hyperbole, particularly when he lived so long afterwards. But consumption has not always advanced as hungrily as it did on Keats, carrying him off within a year of his first serious haemorrhage. Nor was so much blood fatal, although it may have stunned the spirit. Chekhov's consumption lasted him most of his adult life, and he noticed two heavy flows of blood every year. Chekhov had the additional burden of being a doctor himself and his self-diagnosis had to comfort relatives. Although the flow of blood alarmed him – 'just as sinister as the red glow of a fire' – he claimed that it was not necessarily lethal.

> By itself a discharge of blood from the lungs is not serious: blood sometimes flows from the lungs for a whole day, it simply pours out, the patient and the family are terrified, but it all ends in the patient's recovery – more often than not, at any rate. ... If my haemorrhage in the district court had been a symptom of incipient consumption, I should have been dead long ago – that is my reasoning.[133]

Chekhov had such regular symptoms that he needed to

reassure himself. In Sterne's case, however, we have no mention of haemorrhage between the Cambridge attack of, say, 1736 and the crisis in Paris in 1762. It is possible that, although always subject to bronchial ailments, Sterne did enjoy so long an interval. George Orwell was another example of the consumptive who has a lesion that gives no trouble for many years. In Orwell's case the interval was only ten years and his hardships in Catalonia (like Sterne's unaccustomed exertions in the world of fashion) seem to have been enough to open the wound.

But we cannot tie too much significance to Sterne's medical record and it is more useful and more interesting when reading Sterne the invalid to bear in mind the matter-of-fact resolution of this letter from Orwell written within a year of his death:

I asked the doctor recently whether she thought I would survive, & she wouldn't go further than saying she didn't know. If the 'prognosis' after the photo [X-Ray] is bad, I shall get a second opinion. . . . They can't *do* anything, as I am not a case for operation, but I would like an expert opinion on how long I am likely to stay alive. I do hope people won't now start chasing me to make me go to Switzerland, which is supposed to have magical qualities. I don't believe it makes any difference where you are, & a journey would be the death of me. The one chance of surviving, I imagine, is to keep quiet.[134]

Like Orwell, Sterne in his last years was recommended to travel abroad. But as to his part of Yorkshire, according to Drake, 'though the flatness of the city and country about it, may make the air to be suspected for unwholesome, yet, it is well known, we have no distempers, which the physicians call *endemick*, attend our climate; but on the contrary even diseased people, especially *consumptive*, are known to be much supported by the mildness of it.'[135] In later years, however, Sterne was to remark on the unhealthiness of the area as a reason for escaping to the south of France. In the event he found Toulouse and Montpellier equally debilitating, but despite attacks managed to travel back and forth and Shandy it with the best. Sterne had suspect lungs, but he cannot have been as weak as he sometimes claimed. Perhaps he was impressionable in advance of true pulmonary decline and perhaps his illness was as much a symptom of insecurity as of physical disease.

Resorting to doctors and pharmacists may only have convinced Sterne that he was ill. It seems perverse to bleed a patient who has already burst a blood vessel. And some of the available patent medicines must have tested the hardiest. The *York Courant* advertised 'The most Incomparable and Never-Failing CHYMICAL DROPS' which took care of coughs, colds, asthma, wheezing, shortness of breath, consumptions and catarrhs, 'for they gently open the Breast, and immediately give Liberty of Breathing, without any Danger of taking Cold. . . . Price One Shilling the Bottle'. Daffey's Elixir – 'the greatest Preserver of Mankind' – might taste of ink in York since the printer Caesar Ward had the licence to sell it at 1s 3d for a quarter-pint bottle. Better perhaps to settle for a nourishing concoction advocated by Joseph Spence in 1758 for a cold working into the lungs: 'two handfulls of bran boiled in two quarts of water till the bran is all sunk, put into it a pound of raisins and half a pound of figs, and sweeten it with sugar-candy'.[136]

Sterne said that 'Our Operator' in Sutton was 'a very penetrating Man'[137] but he was prepared to call in a York doctor for his daughter's asthma. As for himself, he had only 'not good health' and stayed in during the winter because of the bad roads and weather: 'I know you could not possibly expect us on so terrible a day as this . . . the day grows worse and worse upon our heads, and the sky gathering in on all sides leaves no prospect of any but a most dismal going and coming. . . . What remains, but that we undress ourselves.'[138] It was on such a 'very rainy day' as this – 26 March 1759 – that Sterne recorded himself writing Chapter XXI of Volume I of *Tristram Shandy*.

Sterne even noted that 'this strange irregularity in our climate, producing so strange an irregularity in our characters, —doth thereby, in some sort, make us amends, by giving us somewhat to make us merry with when the weather will not suffer us to go out of doors.'[139] *Tristram Shandy* is an escape from the nerve-wracked idleness of a man confined indoors during dismal Yorkshire winters: dark by four in the afternoon and until eight next morning; sixteen hours of darkness and winter daylight opaque with mist and cloud that seemed to isolate every man from the rest of the world.

When the weather was better, Sterne followed traditional country pursuits. He would walk across the flat fields with a gun and a dog. In summer, it is delightful country with the many trees serving to disrupt the levelness of the ground and give the effect of local charm and privacy. Between the thickets one might go unnoticed. In Sterne's day the woods would have been much more dense, so much so that after dark lanterns were put on the towers and steeples of York as a guide to late travellers feeling their way through the trees.[140] On one occasion, according to Croft, Sterne 'was going over the Fields on a sunday to preach at Stillington it happened that his Pointer Dog* sprung a Covey of Partridges, when he went directly home for his Gun and left his Flock that was waiting for him in the Church, in the lurch'.[141]

Since Sutton and Stillington were both somewhat out of the way, and in an area that tended to be marshy, the condition of the roads would have been a perpetual concern of Sterne's. The origin of the name Sutton is 'sut', meaning boggy. The country around the Shandys' house was of such deep clay that one mile was equal to two and thus Dr. Slop could reach Shandy Hall in 'all the majesty of mud'. Even the road from Sutton to York could be made impassable and, in June 1757, Sterne, Stephen Croft, Francis Cholmley and Philip Harland complained to the Overseers of Highways that 'if you don't directly sett about Effectually repairing the Horse Fair or the Lane to yᵣ Town from the Forrest & also make Sufficient bridges for Carriage's Over the Several Letches on the Forest (now that the Weather is good) you may depend upon being Indicted the next Assize.'[142]

At times like this, the isolation of Sutton must have seemed all the greater so that Sterne could write as a country mouse to John Blake in York, 'If you have 3 or 4 of the last York's Courants, pray Send 'em us, for We are as much Strangers to all that has pass'd amongst You, as if we were in a Mine in Siberia.'[143] Indoors, Sterne tried his hand at painting and music

---

* *Scrapeana* has a story of a 'Rev. Mr.—' who had a pointer called Sancho. When out in the fields one day he unfortunately shot the dog's tail off and thereafter called it *San-cu*. The joke and the allusion to one of Sterne's favourite authors suggests that he may be the subject of this story. (*Scrapeana*, p. 90.)

and undoubtedly wrote many more letters than have survived.
Just as letters pass between the inhabitants of the Shandy household, so, according to Croft, Sterne and his wife were forever
writing love letters to one another to repair quarrels, soften
hurts and break silences.

There was not too much local company. But at Stillington,
he was always a welcome guest at Stephen Croft's house, even if
he was on cooler terms with the Harlands at Sutton. Another
friend was John Hall-Stevenson, Sterne's contemporary at
Jesus. The then John Hall had extended his name in February
1740 when Sterne married him to Anne Stevenson, the daughter
and heiress* of Ambrose Stevenson, from Lanchester, near
Durham. The Hall-Stevensons lived at Skelton Castle, a hard
thirty-five miles north of Sutton across the desolate North York
Moors and farther still on the road that skirted the moors.
Hall-Stevenson seems to have encouraged decay and oddness in
his house, just as Gothic revivalism stimulated a spurious anti-
quity and nostalgia. In *Crazy Tales*, he pictured the castle as a
home fit for Macbeth, where:

> Myriads of rooks rise up and fly,
>   Like legions of damn'd souls,
>   As black as coals,
> That foul and darken all the sky.[144]

But he could also persuade himself to take a picturesque view of
its decline:

> A turrit also you may note,
>   Its glory vanish'd like a dream,
> Transform'd, into a pigeon-coat,
>   Nodding beside the sleepy stream.[145]

Sterne and Hall-Stevenson, said Croft, were 'elemented
together', so that after being fellow-students, they 'continued
one and indivisible thro' Life'.[146] Hall-Stevenson was a coarse
and dull version of Sterne, useful to any book on Sterne for the
way he illustrates that extra quality of gay and nervous genius
in Sterne. His appearance in *Tristram Shandy* as the Eugenius
who advised Yorick to be more circumspect is as misleading as

* According to the *York Courant* she had a fortune of £25,000.

all the associations between characters in Sterne's life and their cousins in books. Stevenson was rich enough to be able to ignore caution. At Skelton, 'he kept a full-spread board, and wore down the steps of his cellar. His open heart filled his dining room with choice company.'[147] He announced himself in *Crazy Tales* in these optimistic terms:

> Neither a fisher, nor a shooter,
> No man's, but any woman's vassal,
> If he could find a way to suit her.[148]

The entertaining and impulsive parson from over the moors must have been a welcome addition to Hall-Stevenson's company, whenever he could make the journey. Sterne unquestionably stimulated Stevenson, who spewed out several ribald publications after Sterne's success and was briefly interested in writing a biography of Sterne. It is much more doubtful how profound an impression Stevenson made on Sterne. Skelton offered Sterne company and diversion from the squared circle of life at Sutton. But Sterne was marked by none of his acquaintances; no bond in his life seems to have had the mutual enrichment of friendship which existed between, say, Boswell and Johnson, or Horace Walpole and Gray. Although the effect is more marked in his dealings with women, Sterne seems to have needed a host of companions, all to be held at a distance.

However, some biographers of Sterne have put the influence of Skelton and its circle on Sterne very high. This is all the more tempting because of the deliberately rakish life Stevenson organized at Skelton, or 'Crazy Castle' as he liked to call it. According to Cross, 'The master of Skelton formed his merry Yorkshire friends into a convivial club, called the Demoniacs, in imitation of the Rabelaisian Monks of Medmenham Abbey, who were then creating great scandal in southern England.'[149] But what sort of depravity is it that needs to imitate?

Medmenham was the resort of Sir Francis Dashwood, Chancellor of the Exchequer under Bute, who held assemblies for his friends in the old abbey under a motto taken from Rabelais' Abbey of Theleme: '*Fay ce que vouldras*', subsequently adopted by that 'great beast' Aleister Crowley. It is a slogan that has often been misunderstood, especially by those who wear it on their sleeves. It was once thought that Dashwood's profane brotherhood – which included Sir William Stanhope, Lord Melcombe and John Wilkes – was a band of debauchery, but more recently Betty Kemp has restored their reputation and substituted a slightly more ridiculous but credible picture of grown men dressing up as monks. As for Skelton,

> Some fell to fiddling, some to fluting,
>   Some to shooting, some to fishing,
> Others to pishing and disputing,
>   Or to computing by wishing.[150]

Certainly there are few more depressing spectacles than that of frustrated men banding together to be outrageous. Nor is it in Yorkshire's character to mimic southern scandals. There must, at this time, have been all too many comfortable and intelligent men with time, wit, money and boredom to squander. Sterne was a member of the group, although less regularly than most of the others. As well as Stevenson, there was his younger brother, Charles Lawson Hall, Charles Lee, a captain of the army, and the Rev. Robert Lascelles, a gamekeeper-parson, who later published *Angling, Shooting, and Coursing*.

In 1762, Hall-Stevenson published *Crazy Tales*, supposedly a collection of verse stories from the Skelton circle. It hardly makes one envious of their company. Sterne may not have found it difficult to be the centre of interest there, but without feeling any more settled. His most vivid memory of Skelton in later life, when he thought of Hall-Stevenson 'as a bank-note in a corner drawr of my bureau—I know it is there (I wish I did)—and its value, tho' I seldome take a peep at it',[151] was of racing chariots on the beach with one wheel in the surf. On seeing the book of *Crazy Tales*, Sterne wrote to its author from Toulouse about the charm of 'our parental seat' and said he gazed ten times a day at a picture of Skelton 'with a *quando te aspiciam?*'.[152] But Sterne was always distracted by the unattainable and disappointed by possession. The best story of Sterne at Skelton has him rigging the weathervane to deceive Stevenson, who was such a hypochondriac that he would not get out of bed if the wind was in the wrong quarter.[153] It is a trick the Shandy brothers might have played as boys.

As John Croft said, Sterne 'was not steady to his Pastimes, or Recreations.* At one time he wou'd take up the Gun and follow shooting till he became a good shott, then he wou'd take up the Pencil and paint Pictures. He chiefly copied Portraits. He had a good Idea of Drawing, but not the least of mixing his colours.'[154]

R.F. Brissenden has argued for the influence of painting on Sterne's literary themes, traced his use of such theoretical works as Hogarth's *Analysis of Beauty* and Leonardo's *A Treatise of Painting* and even described Sterne as an exponent of the rococo, 'striking into "the beautiful oblique"'.[155] This seems a very fruitful argument, especially to the extent that it coincides with the nervous, Romantic disarray in Sterne's writing. But it is an incomplete label for Sterne; his pathological individualism deliberately goes out of the way of categorization. It is more useful to consider how exactly Sterne employs the visual in his fiction.

It is true that he frequently drops into the terminology of painting, that he draws upon the current theory of painting and often seems to be conjuring up a picture. There are stunning images to fill the reader's eye, none more delightful than this moment from *A Sentimental Journey*:

It was a fine still evening in the latter end of the month of May—the crimson window curtains (which were of the same colour as those of the bed) were drawn close—the sun was setting and reflected through them so warm a tint into the fair *fille de chambre*'s face—I thought she blush'd—the idea of it made me blush myself—we were quite alone; and that super-induced a second blush before the first could get off.[156]

This is entirely a matter of super-inducement – the offering of a real view is only a subterfuge so that Sterne may concentrate upon the subtlety and human tenderness to confuse the suffusion of crimson light with a blush. It is also comic that this fake blush should set off real ones. But the crucial omission is that the *fille de chambre* remains uninvolved in the illuminations.

---

* Tristram also followed variable pursuits: 'for happening, at certain intervals and changes of the Moon, to be both fiddler and painter, according as the fly stings'. (*TS*, Vol. I, Ch. VIII.)

She never grasps the complexity of the moment, but simply obtrudes her cheek in the right place at the right moment to trigger off the super-inducing lover. The most fanciful element of all is the suggestion that Yorick is deceived by the trick of the light. He is detached enough to see it for what it is, but sufficiently tender to his own imagination still to use it as a pretext.

The 'blush' is the prelude to one of the most brilliant pieces of titillation in all of Sterne's work – the pliant girl plays her part to perfection, stimulating Yorick's nerves deliciously. His conscience tugs this way and that. They hold hands: he cannot free himself – 'I felt my legs and every limb about me tremble at the idea.'[157] 'Every limb about me' shows how sly Sterne can be at the pitch of excitement. In this nervous ecstasy they both sink down on the bed. The innocent girl then shows him her purse 'to hold your crown'. *The fille de chambre* notices a broken stitch in his stock and begins to sew it up; as her hand passes back and forth 'I felt the laurels shake which fancy had wreathed about my head.' The girl's shoe needs repair. Yorick lifts her feet to attend to this – only for her to fall back on to the bed . . . 'and then'?[158]

Why, then, Sterne recollects himself and asks why 'clay-cold heads and luke-warm hearts' should get the better of passions. But he only gives the girl a peck on the cheek and sends her away. As always, Yorick and Sterne do not eventually penetrate the willing female flesh: it is yet another, if the most skilfully prevaricated, *coitus interruptus*. And Sterne has already predicted this: 'the idea of it made me blush' and was enough for him.

It is typical of Sterne's fiction that the visual is never an organic element, but scenery in his mind. The idea of illustration is apparent in *Tristram Shandy*, but in such an unreal and disembodied way as to make it remarkable that so many subsequent editions of Sterne have been accompanied by insipid *genre* scenes. More than any of his contemporaries in fiction, Sterne ridicules the idea that an imaginary but 'real' world is being made for the reader to inhabit.

One reason why Sterne has sometimes been thought strange is because of the bodiless, unseen nature of his characters, for all that they assume a vast proportion in our minds and enjoy an immensely heightened fleshly surface. It is as if Sterne's world existed in darkness and presence was apprehended simply by the sound of breathing, the heavy sighs of effort of people attempting to sustain themselves and the contact of skin. Here, for instance, is what Sterne pretends is clear and helpful instruction for an illustrator of Corporal Trim as he delivers the sermon found in the volume of Stevinus:

He stood,—for I repeat it, to take the picture of him in at one view, with his body sway'd, and somewhat bent forwards,—his right-leg firm under him, sustaining seven-eighths of his whole weight,—the foot of his left-leg, the defect of which was no disadvantage to his attitude, advanced a little,—not laterally, not forwards, but in a line betwixt them;—his knee bent, but that not violently,—but so as to fall within the limits of the line of beauty;*—and I add, of the line of science too;—for consider, it had one eighth part of his body to bear up;—so that in this case the position of the leg is determined,—because the foot could be no further advanced, or the knee more bent, than what would allow him mechanically, to receive an eighth part of his whole weight under it,—and to carry it too.

☞ This I recommend to painters:—need I add,—to orators? —I think not; for, unless they practise it,—they must fall upon their noses.[159]

But anyone who tried to stand according to this definition might equally be undermined. It is a peculiar penetration of mechanical detail so thorough as to reduce it to deadlock, like that moment when Porthos, escaping from a bomb, considered how it was that he was able to put one foot in front of another and was so entranced by the conundrum that he never moved again and was killed by the explosion. The description, for all its apparent elucidation, only makes uncertainty more grotesque. Hogarth in fact illustrated this scene for the second edition, but in a cursory and anecdotal way. Rather than attempt to portray the towering unlikelihood of Trim's posture, he concentrates on the effect of an observed domestic interior. The eye goes straight to the sunken attention of Dr. Slop and the Shandy brothers and Trim stands with his back to us. Sterne could never have achieved so objective and appealing an effect himself. His notes towards a picture of Trim show why.

* A reference to Hogarth's concept of an elongated S-slope on the basis of beauty.

The idea of standing itself, not to mention illustration, becomes ridiculous under the obsessive dismantling of his inspection. There is little suggestion of Trim's character in this description; rather, a profound dissatisfaction with all forms of physical manifestation. It is, in part, the idea of stillness that appals Sterne; he can hardly think of it without conveying paralysis. To read this study of Trim's attitude is to ache for the contortions of the corporal's body. Motion shatters the idea of illustration and the hectic speed of the pen had hurried Sterne to this intimation. When he besought '*Howgarth's* witty Chissel'[160] for the second edition of the first two volumes of *Tristram Shandy* it was only to satisfy his desire for accredited fame. To inhabit Sterne's world is to make Hogarth seem a rather naïve artist.

No authenticated drawing by Sterne survives, as if he could not be bothered to keep them. What then should such a man without perseverance or application, with a sense of line but none of harmony, a man rummaging for his own talent and identity in a drawer, what should he do in the methodical life of the Church? Parson Woodforde's diary indicates how placid a man the eighteenth-century parson needed to be if he was to accommodate himself to the low state of some of his flock and to the dullness of so much of his own life. No wonder that some parsons pursued private interests: thus Gilbert White observed with infinite patience the natural history of Selbourne. Woodforde sometimes played fives against the church wall, just as Sterne might forget a congregation while he stalked partridge.

***

We have some formal knowledge of Sterne's pastoral life in the answers he gave to Archbishop Herring's visitational questionnaire in 1743. Sterne then had about 120 families at Sutton, five of whom were Quaker. He performed two services on Sundays and gave the sacrament five times a year. He catechized 'every Sunday in my Church during Lent, But explain our Religion to the Children and Servants of my Parishioners in my own House every Sunday Night during Lent, from six o'clock till nine. I mention the Length of Time as my reason for not doing it in Church.'[161]

These simple facts can be put into perspective thanks to the analysis of the 1743 returns performed by Canon S.L. Ollard. Of 836 returns, 393 had non-resident parsons and 266 had no school or secular education, though at Sutton Sterne could report two schools where about forty children were taught. Of 711 clergy, 335 were pluralists: 453 churches failed to have two services every Sunday and 208 had less than four communion services in a year.[162] In other words, Sterne's activities were a little better than average. But the figures as a whole only indicate the relaxation of the Church. Herring's inquiry was in itself something of a novelty. Blackburne, his predecessor, had only 'visited' his diocese twice in nineteen years, once personally and once through the bishop of Gloucester.

Clearly, the demoralization of the Church worked from the top downwards, but it is remarkable how quickly cynicism spread after all the fierce adherence of the seventeenth century. It is around the middle of the eighteenth century that the acknowledged hollowness of religious observance passes into English life as a treasured inconsistency. Boswell recorded this exchange with Johnson in 1772:

I mentioned the petition for removing the subscription to the Thirty-nine Articles. Said he, 'It was soon thrown out. Sir, they talk of not making boys at the University subscribe to what they do not understand. But they ought to consider that our universities were founded to bring up members of the Church of England and we must not supply our enemies with arms from our arsenal. No, Sir, the meaning of subscribing is not that they fully understand all the articles but that they will adhere to the Church of England.[163]

This from a man who was a devout member of that Church – and who dismissed Sterne's sermons as 'merely the froth from the surface'[164] of the cup of salvation. But Johnson's complacent irony about the Articles could be digested by the accused body because of its mildness. In *Joseph Andrews*, Mr. Adams engages in a debate about church-going with an innkeeper who, typically of eighteenth-century observance, thought that heaven and hell should only be talked about in a church. Adams asked why the man went to church: 'to say my prayers and behave godly' comes the answer. '"And dost not thou then tremble," cries Adams, "at the thought of eternal punishment?"

– "As for that, master," said he, "I never once thought about it; but what signifies talking about matters so far off? The mug is out, shall I draw another?"'[165]

No wonder in a world that so distinguished between the far and near that Sterne should talk about Shandeism as his fortieth article. Consistently, Sterne's enemies have attacked him all the more solemnly because he was a clergyman, for which profession a place has always been reserved in England in sensational Sunday papers. But this response may only illustrate the particular sensibility Sterne calculated on affronting in the years when he was a cleric about town. There is no reason to doubt the comparative dutifulness indicated in Sterne's answers to Herring's questionnaire, and sufficient evidence of pluralism and non-residence in the Church for his years at Sutton to deserve some credit.

The larger fault lies in the declining reality of the Church as an institution. We need not agree with Bagehot's verdict on *Tristram Shandy*, but he makes a valid point about Sterne and his Church: 'If a clergyman publishes his sermons *because* he has written an indecent novel – a novel which is purely pagan – which is outside the ideas of Christianity, whose author can scarcely have been inside of them, – if a man so made and so circumstanced is *as such* to publish Christian sermons, surely Christianity is a joke and a dream.'[166]

As complacency and hypocrisy stilled the Church, so the observation of conventional proprieties became more important. Under such circumstances it is not surprising that some of Sterne's parishioners thought him 'crazy' or 'crackbrained'; though it is likely that such charges came from the privileged or from social climbers. There would have been many in Sterne's flock who could hardly see the oddity in a cleric once they had learned to accept their own condition as part of the wisdom of God.

For such as these, it is probable that Sterne was of more practical than spiritual comfort. At the very least, he must have made them laugh out loud. Richard Greenwood said that Sterne loved to take cases to the Quarter Sessions on behalf of poorer people and there 'talk down the Lawyer'. But obviously this action would have made as many enemies as friends.

Greenwood also describes the way Sterne supported a local tradesman against Squire Harland – '& he never spoke to the Harlands after.'[167]

It is too easy to call Sterne's faith hollow, even if it is absurdly sanguine to believe, all in all, that 'he was content to refer to, rather than expound, the great truths of Christianity; but his acceptance of those truths is clear.'[168] On the contrary, Sterne was a misfit in a compromising institution. His whole tone of voice is to suspect truths and demolish cant. Few anxious souls can have found doctrinal comfort in so sceptical a teacher. But he elaborates on human nature in a way that is much more heartwarming. Sterne's cheerfulness – and that is as far as he fully coincides with the message of Christianity – is all the more admirable for the obvious difficulties he had in sustaining it.

To discover a sense of pastoral mission, we have to look to the Methodists and to a man as humourless as William Grimshaw of Haworth, a contemporary of Sterne's and 'the herald of the Evangelical Revival in the north of England'.[169] Grimshaw came to Haworth in 1742 and, finding the church there too small, preached in the churchyard until the money could be raised for extension. In addition, he walked his parish once a month and gave extempore services in cottages to a few families at a time. But Grimshaw did not confine himself to his own parish or locality. He toured round the West Riding, preaching twenty times a week to swell the new Wesleyan movement. But what separates Grimshaw and Sterne most tellingly is, again, the tone of voice. Here is Grimshaw, lashing himself for idleness: 'To Day I have trifled. I have loitered it away doing little, or I fear but little to GOD's Glory. Let it not come into the Number of my Months. Be ashamed, O my Soul, before ye LORD, for so embezzling thy golden Moments'.[170]

It is because so many moments of Sterne's ministry were lead to his quicksilver that he wrote *Tristram Shandy*. We can only criticize his slackness if we would be prepared to do without the book. The sort of conviction that Grimshaw radiated is intense but very narrow; it is not possible to notice such absurdity in man as Sterne did and still be as convinced as Grimshaw. Sterne doubted every step he took in a way that made it impossible for him to embark on an apostolic journey.

F

We should instead think of Sterne as one of the earliest examples of a particular type in the Anglican Church: the restless spirit bemused by the slowness of the body. Even so, the Church started Sterne writing; and if he inserted one of his sermons in the second volume of *Tristram Shandy*, he could not deny himself the honesty of admitting that it served to advertise 'that there are now in the possession of the *Shandy* family, as many as will make a handsome volume, at the world's service'.[171]

The writing, reading and publishing of sermons was a very serious trade in the eighteenth century. They were not only bought by other clerics, just as Sterne himself had a large library of printed sermons to draw on, but occupied a secure position on the reading lists of young people. In 1767, for instance, Fanny Burney consulted Lady Sarah Pennington's *An Unfortunate Mother's Advice to Her Absent Daughters*, which recommended the sermons of Hoadley, Seed, Sherlock, Fordyce and Sterne.[172] But despite this distinction and the favourable contemporary opinion of men like Gray, who thought his sermons showed 'a very strong imagination and a sensible heart',[173] Sterne has frequently been attacked for the way he appeared to trifle with the form. The *Monthly Review* was appalled by the sleight of hand with which Sterne had published 'Yorick's' sermons:

... we think it becomes us to make some animadversions on the manner of their publication, which we consider as the greatest outrage against Sense and Decency, that has been offered since the first establishment of Christianity – an outrage which would scarce have been tolerated in the days of paganism.

Had these Discourses been sent into the world, as the Sermons of Mr. *Yorick*, pursuant to the *first* title-page, every serious and sober Reader must have been offended at the indecency of such an assumed character. For who is this *Yorick*? We have read of a *Yorick* likewise, in an obscene Romance. – But are the solemn dictates of religion fit to be conveyed from the mouths of Buffoons, and ludicrous Romancers? Would any man believe that a Preacher was in earnest, who should mount the pulpit in a *Harlequin's coat*?[174]

If Sterne never dressed up quite so colourfully in Sutton or Stillington church, he may still have exploited the theatrical potential of the pulpit. The description of 'dramatick' for his sermons was one he chose himself.[175] There are conflicting accounts of Sterne's manner as a preacher, but they do suggest that in this, as in so many other things, he was beyond the ordinary. It is worth pursuing since the sermons have been unreasonably deplored by so many writers on Sterne and because the oratorical situation contributes so much to the voice and direction of Sterne's fiction.

The general nineteenth-century opinion of Sterne's sermons was, at best, Bagehot's view of 'well-expressed, vigorous, moral essays',[176] and, at worst, H.D. Traill's unseeing condemnation – 'of the most commonplace character; platitudinous with the platitudes of a thousand pulpits, and insipid with the *crambe repetita* of a hundred thousand homilies'.[177] There are torpid passages in the sermons – just as there are in *Tristram Shandy* – but they are infinitely richer and more revealing than these verdicts allow.

John Croft claimed that, 'When it was Sterne's turn to preach at the Minster half of the Congregation usually went out of Church as soon as he mounted the Pulpit, as his Delivery and Voice were so very disagreeable.'[178] Richard Greenwood, on the other hand, said that

> when he preached, the audience were quite delighted with him, & he never preached at Sutton but half the [congregation] were in tears – The Minster was crowded whenever it was known that he was to preach – he used often to preach nearly extempore. He had engaged to preach . . . a few miles from Sutton, & when there found he had forgot his sermon – he only [asked] for a bible, & composed a most excellent sermon which he delivered from a scrap of paper no bigger than his hand.[179]

This seems more likely since we know that Sterne frequently preached at the Minster, not only in his own right but as a deputy for Francis Blackburne, archdeacon of Cleveland, and his uncle. There was a fee of £1 for each sermon at the Minster and Sterne solicited 'Vacant Turns' and performed as often as twenty times a year. He had even had two of his sermons published, in 1747 and 1750, one at the express request of Sir William Pennyman, the Sheriff of Yorkshire, and the Grand Jury of the County of York. These found 'neither purchasers nor readers', but would have made Sterne one of the better known preachers before the beguiling young ladies Edmund Pyle had had to look away from. In the Minster, wit and sentiment would have been admired and Sterne may even have been treasured there for the feeling Gray detected in him of 'tottering on the verge of laughter, & ready to throw his periwig in the face of his audience'.[180] But too great a play on the emotions of his congregation perhaps gave offence in a country parish. Religious enthusiasm was disapproved of, particularly from the pulpit. Methodism was above all condemned for its enthusiasm. A letter to the *York Courant* in November 1739 took great offence at the rapidity with which Methodists set the labouring poor quoting from the Bible and asked whether 'those *Feelings* and *violent Emotions* which the *Methodists* pretend to, be the *Spirit of God* or the *Spirit of Delusions?*'.[181]

Sterne's sermons were at least shorter than those of most of his contemporaries,* which must have increased enthusiasm in the audience. He wrote to George Whateley who invited him to preach at the London Foundling Hospital in 1761:

> sure as the day comes, and as sure as the Foundling Hospital stands, will I—(that is, in case I stand myself) discharge my conscience of my promise in giving you, not a half hour (not a poor half hour), for I never could preach so long without fatiguing both myself and my flock to death—but I will give you a short sermon, and *flap* you in my turn:—preaching (you must know) is a theologic flap upon the heart, as the dunning for a promise is a political flap upon the memory.[182]

This aiming at the heart is borne out by the attitude of Yorick who, rather than 'preach, to shew the extent of our reading, or the subtleties of our wit—to parade it in the eyes of the vulgar with the beggarly accounts of a little learning, tinseled over with a few words which glitter, but convey little light and less warmth', preferred to 'direct five words point blank to the heart'.[183]

It is exactly this intimate knowledge of ordinary human motivation that is so striking in Sterne's sermons. For many

---

* Hammond compares Sterne's sermons (average length 3,160 words) with eighteenth-century norms that include Blackall (11,850), Stillingfleet (9,500), Tillotson (5,600) and Swift (3,750). (Hammond, *op. cit.*, pp. 101–2 n.)

years these sermons were largely dismissed as plagiarism and
denied their proper consideration as preliminaries to Sterne's
fiction. Lansing van der Heyden Hammond's meticulous study
of Sterne's borrowings from the available libraries of sermons
reveals two things: that the sermon has no equal as a crossbred
form, and that Sterne's 'imitations', borrowings and thefts do
not detract from his originality.

In the Preface to his first two volumes of sermons, Sterne
advised that 'the reader, upon old and beaten subjects, must
not look for many new thoughts—'tis well if he has new
language.'[184] One might therefore expect deliberately original
sermons, but in fact their language is noticeably more tranquil,
musical and modulated than that of the fiction. It is the quality
of their didacticism that makes them so interesting.*

Sterne thought his sermons turned 'chiefly upon philan-
thropy, and those kindred virtues to it, upon which hang all
the Law and the Prophets, I trust they will be no less felt, or
worse received, for the evidence they bear, of proceeding more
from the heart than the head'.[185] In terms of doctrinal purity
and religious inspiration, the sermons are almost apologetic.
They often depart from the traditional form of the sermon, but
as expositions of the way the human mind approaches its own
moral problems they are subtle, tender and penetrating, with
all the beneficial effects Sterne attributed to true Shandeism.

There are few more idiosyncratic than the Sermon on the
Prodigal Son, a stock character wonderfully refreshed in Sterne's
treatment. Sterne cannot resist the feeling that the Bible has
hardly done the story justice: 'The account is short: the interesting and pathetic passages with which such a transaction
would be necessarily connected, are left to be supplied by the
heart.' The moral of the fable, of course, 'is so clear from the
occasion of it, that it will not be necessary to perplex it with any
tedious explanations'. Instead, Sterne supplies some of the
scenes that scripture has omitted. 'No doubt,' argues Sterne,
'many a tender expostulation, would fall from the father's
lips . . . upon this occasion.'[186] And so he proceeds, with all the
gusto of that other biblical popularizer, Cecil B. De Mille:

* Of course, Sterne may not have kept to his own text always. He would not have
been the man to resist any new path that came into his head.

He would dissuade his son upon the folly of so rash an enterprise, by showing him the dangers of the journey,—the inexperience of his age,—the hazards his life, his fortune, his virtue would run, without a guide, without a friend: he would tell him of the many snares and temptations which he had to avoid, or encounter at every step,—the pleasures which would solicit him in every luxurious court,—the little knowledge he could gain—except that of evil: he would speak of the seduction of women,—their charms—their poisons . . .

I see the picture of his departure . . .—the prodigal son standing on the foreground, with a forced sedateness, struggling against the fluttering movement of joy, upon his deliverance from restraint . . .[187]

How appropriate that Sterne should notice the urge for liberation in a body stilled by politeness. Far from dwelling on the Crusoe-like recklessness of the son, or the magnanimity of the father, Sterne hurries off on a less beaten track but one nearer to his own heart: 'that fatal passion which led him,—and so many thousands after the example, *to gather all he had together, and take his journey into a far country*'.[188] In a moment Sterne is praising 'the love of variety, or curiosity of seeing new things',[189] and is soon as far as the towns of Europe and 'every stage from Calais to Rome'.[190] Although this sermon was only published posthumously, it is likely to have featured in Sterne's repertoire for many years. If the published version contains the details of journeys he had made, an earlier form – before Sterne had actually travelled* – may have been all the more encouraging in prospect, as if Sterne looked forward to trying on the part of the prodigal son for himself.

Although the 'Prodigal Son' is exceptional in its originality, the essence of these sermons is to be brief with their message and to expand in diagnosis and narrative. Thus, the conclusion to 'Inquiry after Happiness' is perfunctory – 'to fear God and keep his commandments'.[191] But the body of the sermon consists of

---

* Was 1762 Sterne's first trip to the continent? In Vol. I, Ch. XI of *Tristram Shandy* we hear of 'my travels through Denmark' and 'most parts of Europe' in 1741 with 'Mr. Noddy's eldest son'. There are enough gaps in Sterne's life for him to have toured Europe, but 1741 hardly seems the likeliest time. Not only was he married in March but for most of the autumn he was busy with the election. Mr. Noddy's son may have been the young Earl of Aboyne. The *Dictionary of National Biography* and Cross suggest that he accompanied the young nobleman on a tour in summer 1741. When Sterne came to accept the living of Stillington he was described as 'chaplain' to the earl. (Cross, p. 57 n.)

brilliant sketches of the contradictory definitions of happiness proposed by a miser, an epicure and a philosopher. What catches Sterne's interest is the elusive nature of happiness in such a whirl of different opinions: 'Upon summing up the account, all is found to be seated merely in the imagination.— The faster he has pursued, the faster the phantom flies before him;—and to use the satirist's comparison of the chariot-wheels,—haste as they will, they must for ever keep the same distance.'[192] We do not have to recall Sterne's racing on the beach with Hall-Stevenson to hear in this a philosophical disenchantment with actual satisfaction and an amused preoccupation with the tantalizing idea of pleasure.

But it is in the sermon on 'Self-Knowledge' that Sterne's sense of human isolation is most clearly related to the philosophy of knowledge. In this passage, we can see not only that revelation of the machinery of understanding but the limit of any comfort that Sterne could ever have offered from the pulpit. If Sterne has been castigated for being an irreverent clergyman, I think nevertheless that it was in preparing himself to preach that he came to intellectual seriousness:

We have a chain of thoughts, desires, engagements, and idlenesses, which perpetually return upon us in their proper time and order—let us, I beseech you, assign and set apart some small portion of the day for this purpose,—of retiring into ourselves, and searching into the dark corners and recesses of the heart, and taking notice of what is passing there. If a man can bring himself to do this task with a curious and impartial eye, he will quickly find the fruits of it will more than recompense his time and labour. He will see several irregularities and unsuspected passions within him which he never was aware of:—he will discover in his progress many secret turnings and windings in his heart to which he was a stranger, which now gradually open and disclose themselves to him upon a nearer view; in these labyrinths he will trace out such hidden springs and motives for many of his most applauded actions, as will make him rather sorry and ashamed of himself, than proud.*[193]

* As Hammond has made clear, this passage is an example of Sterne's re-working of other people's material in his sermons. In this case, it is a sermon of Swift's, 'The Difficulty of Knowing One's-Self'. Comparison of the two texts is fascinating for the way it shows the importance of Sterne's own selection and adaptation. For instance, Sterne has surely expanded Swift's 'severe and impartial eye' through the very

Striking as that passage is, it may have sounded introspective in a crowded church. Sterne is really talking to himself, and that may sometimes have made him an unconvincing preacher. The social implication of Sterne's meditation is contrary to the idea of a sermon, whereby a congregation is spoken to in mass. The realization of intellectual loneliness, of the isolating capacity of the intelligent faculties, makes Sterne's natural mode either fiction or soliloquy. The vicar is expected to engage himself with his flock, and yet here is Sterne explaining the great obstacles that confront true sympathy. Many of Sterne's sermons dwell upon this view of human understanding and predict the unique interest in *Tristram Shandy* in the workings of the book itself.

There is one other work – hardly more than a fragment – which shows Sterne's literary experiments before *Tristram Shandy*. It is called *A Dream* and describes how the author wandered out at night into just such a plum orchard as Sterne had planted at Sutton. While there, he gazes at the stars and philosophizes on the relativity of such a spectacle:

The inhabitants of ye most inconsiderable Planet that revolves round ye most inconsiderable Star I can pick out of this vast number, look upon *their world*, I'll warrant you, as ye only one y^t [that] exists. They believe it the center of ye universe, and suppose y^t ye whole system of ye Heavens turns round them, and was made, and moves purely for *their sakes*.[194]

It is not surprising that a man with so fallible a sense of himself should wander into dream, as though it were only a matter of making a minor adjustment of consciousness. In his dream, the author travels in space and returns to earth. His reports are

characteristic substitution of 'curious' for 'severe'. In Swift's treatment of the idea there is a matter-of-fact rationality – 'Thus, let every man look with a severe and impartial eye into all the distinct regions of the heart; and no doubt, several deformities and irregularities, that he never thought of, will open and disclose themselves upon so near a view.' That is cool and observing. But Sterne's version is participatory and the prose itself seems to unwind the reader's caution – 'he will discover in his progress many secret turnings and windings in his heart to which he was a stranger, which now gradually open and disclose themselves to him upon a nearer view; in the labyrinths he will trace out such hidden springs and motives for many of his most applauded actions . . .' (Hammond, *op. cit.*, pp. 153–4.)

laughed at but 'At this time began to be heard all over the world a huge noise and fragor in ye skys, as if all nature was approaching to her dissolution.'[195] The world becomes alarmed – 'no less was expected than an universal wreck of nature. What ensu'd I know not. All of a sudden, I knew not how, I found myself in bed, as just waking from a sound sleep.'[196]

The description that follows of the author's uncertainty about the worlds of dream and reality is worthy of Borges. And in its hallucinatory quality, it affords us an insight of Sterne's own view of his 'real' life at Sutton.

I recollected ye bed, ye hangings, ye room, my last night's thoughts, ye whole series of my former life. All this wou'd seem to persuade me that I had been in a dream. On ye other hand, my whole existence in the present state appear'd so small and so inconsiderable, and there appear'd so much of soli[dity and regulari]ty in the other state, wherein I had spent thousands of years, that I could not be persuaded but I was at present in a dream.[197]

Perhaps it was by persuading himself that he lived on the edges of dream that Sterne was able to introduce Yorick as a benign double. In the first volume of *Tristram Shandy*, Sterne assured his readers that in 'several sallies about his parish ... the parson, so appointed, would both hear and see enough to keep his philosophy from rusting'.[198] But Yorick is a ghostly figure who dies in that first volume to absolve the failures of Sterne's own clerical life. Yorick is a portrait kept by its subject in his own mind – a picture of what he might have been, an excuse for what he has to be and, not least, someone to talk to. If Sterne himself had no choice but to be a very practical womanizer, then it is Yorick, in *A Sentimental Journey*, who can invent a delicate, roving flirtation appealing to the bourgeois. And if Sterne withered in a country retreat, was harrowed by his own domestic failure and watched sadly the unnourishing effect of Christianity, then Yorick was a figure on whom failure sat gracefully, excused by oddity:

instead of that cold phlegm and exact regularity of sense and humours, you would have look'd for, in one so extracted,—he was, on the contrary, as mercurial and sublimated a composition,—as heteroclite a creature in all his declensions,—with as much life and whim, and *gaieté de coeur* about him, as the kindliest climate could have engendered and put together.[199]

But true eccentricity is an effect noticed by spectators, not an ingredient deliberately mixed. Sterne was compelled to invent Yorick as a diversion – for others and for himself – philosophical where he was distracted, whimsical when he was despairing. Yorick was a jester in holy orders, a character who might allow Sterne to get away with miscalculated jokes and unwarranted familiarity. And Tristram says of Yorick – 'I have the highest idea of the spiritual and refined sentiments of this reverend gentleman'[200] – as if there was a calm in that dream figure that Sterne envied. No wonder Yorick dies 'worn out at length' because of a mysterious conspiracy of the hostile elements in Church and village. The vagueness of that malice and of Yorick's actual symptoms seems to show a certain paranoia in Sterne. It may also conceal some as yet undiscovered crisis in his life late in the 1750s:

> The whole plan of the attack, just as *Eugenius* had foreboded, was put in execution all at once,—with so little mercy on the side of the allies,—and so little suspicion in *Yorick,* of what was carrying on against him,—that when he thought, good easy man! full surely preferment was o' ripening,—they had smote his root, and then he fell, as many a worthy man had fallen before him.[201]

'Alas, poor Yorick', the first great sentimental appeal in Sterne's work, is therefore a requiem for a part of himself. These first tears watered a new, liberated character, one that would appear spruce and glittering in the Reynolds portrait and revive Yorick, in London and on the continent, as a philandering, emotional confessor adept at comforting young feminine skin.

Yorick dies to escape winters in the marshy Sutton fields and that 'dirty village' that gossiped about him. Although we do not know the exact nature of the hiatus in Sterne's life in the 1750s, there are various indications of it: the predicament hinted at in the letters to Blake, the physical and emotional insecurity of his family, the virtual abandonment of the parish register at Sutton after 1756* and the lapsing

---

* The decline in detail begins in 1754. Entries stop after 1756 and do not begin again until 1760, when Sutton had a curate. At Stillington, from 1756, marriages were performed by Thomas Donnyson, the curate of Crayke.

of Sterne's subscription to the York Assembly for the years 1750–56.*

Grant that Sterne was chronically insecure, bored as easily as he breathed, and 'so small and inconsiderable' a life is enough to urge him into dream. His fiction then becomes the sublimation of an unsatisfactory and insufficiently apprehended life. For all his faults as a man, husband, father and clergyman, Sterne possessed 'a curious and impartial eye', far in advance of his time. He had seen in fiction not just an entertainment, but a fertile model and a means by which man might talk to himself. The sermon on 'The Prodigal Son' begins:

> ... lessons of wisdom have never such a power over us, as when they are wrought into the heart, through the ground-work of a story which engages the passions: Is it that we are like iron, and must first be heated before we can be wrought upon? or, Is the heart so in love with deceit, that where a true report will not reach it, we must cheat it with a fable, in order to come at truth?[202]

It was in seeing that there was a truth in dream and deceit that Sterne seized upon fiction and made other men's use of it appear timid. For, unlike Fielding or Richardson, Sterne committed his reputation, emotions and identity entirely to fiction. Not only did it rescue him from a petty existence, but it allowed him the opportunity of reinventing himself in Yorick, that parson 'utterly unpractised in the world'. In the first volume of *Tristram Shandy*, Sterne presented an immortal and exquisite view of Yorick and his village. Sterne can never have really resembled Yorick, except in his own eyes, but the passage none the less conveys all his frustration with twenty years as a country priest. While it is the village that suspends animation as Yorick passes by, all that immobility seems to press remorselessly on the obsessive mobility of Sterne's spirits and action. Sterne is here performer and spectator at the same time:

> To speak the truth, he never could enter a village, but he caught the attention of both old and young.—Labour stood still as he pass'd, —the bucket hung suspended in the middle of the well,—the

---

* These years are not necessarily the only ones in which Sterne absented himself from the focus of the social year at York. Lists of subscribers were printed in the *York Courant* and only these years can be vouched for.

spinning-wheel forgot its round,—even chuck-farthing and shuffle-cap themselves stood gaping till he had got out of sight; and as his movement was not of the quickest, he had generally time enough upon his hands to make his observations,—to hear the groans of the serious,—and the laughter of the light-hearted;—all which he bore with excellent tranquility.—His character was,—he loved a jest in his heart—and as he saw himself in the true point of ridicule, he would say, he could not be angry with others for seeing him in a light, in which he so strongly saw himself.[203]

That is the floating creation of daydream. The real Sterne had sometimes aroused different reactions in his parishioners. One winter he was skating on Stillington pond when the ice broke. No one came forward to assist the floundering parson. On another occasion, some village geese gathered in the church-yard at Sutton and Sterne would have impounded them for himself had not the villagers been 'ready to riot and mob Laurie'.[204] Parson Sterne was accomplished enough to be able to look guileless when the need arose. And Parson Yorick was a disguise that would carry him to London, Paris, into the carriages of gently palpitating ladies and, eventually, into history itself. And like a man with luggage in both hands, he travelled perilously, not always in balance.

***

1759 was a more momentous year than even proud Englishmen realized at the time. All over the known world, British interests proved victorious in the Seven Years' War. 'Our bells are worn threadbare with ringing for victories,' wrote Horace Walpole.[205] In August, Boscawen defeated a French fleet off Lagos and Ferdinand of Brunswick won the battle of Minden. Next month, Wolfe scaled the Heights of Abraham to defeat Montcalm. In November, Hawke thrashed another French fleet in Quiberon Bay. In India, Clive cleared Bengal of the French. It was the apogee of a straggling continental and colonial war in which the success of Pitt's strategy made England, if a little unwittingly, master of an empire. 1759 was also, by a few days, the year of publication of *The Life and Opinions of Tristram Shandy*.

'Now for your desire of knowing the reason of my turning author?' Sterne wrote to an acquaintance in November 1759, 'why truly I am tired of employing my brains for other people's advantage.'[206] We can hardly expect a more thoughtful answer from so deliberately instinctive a man as Sterne. And 1759 certainly marks Sterne's transition from a private and provincial author – of sermons, letters and pamphlets in local politics – to one bent on being famous in the wide world.

If any single event nudged Sterne into looking for a larger public, it was the circumstances surrounding his last contribution to diocesan quarrels, *A Political Romance*. The relevant quarrel was between two notable figures in York society: Dr. Francis Topham and Dean John Fountayne. Topham, the same age as Sterne and a Cambridge graduate, was a lawyer and friend of Jaques Sterne. Like Jaques, Topham collected every possible office and, among many others, he was Commissary and Keeper-General of the Exchequer and Prerogative Court of York. Fountayne was a year younger than Sterne and another Cambridge graduate who had come to York in 1747 as dean.

It seems that, as Sterne fell out with his uncle, he did what he could to make an alliance with the new dean. Sterne sometimes preached for the dean at the Minster and when, in 1751, Fountayne was awarded a D.D. degree it was Sterne who wrote a *Concio ad Clerum* address that he could deliver in thanks. Curtis[207] has made it clear that, only after Fountayne's arrival in York, did Sterne re-enter Church affairs with any hopes of further preferment. And in August 1751 he was rewarded with the Commissaryship of the Peculiar Court of Pickering and Pocklington. Financially this was unrewarding, but it was a position of considerable local power and a recognized and honoured stage in the hierarchy of preferment.

Sterne's major rival for this office had been Francis Topham, who claimed to have had Fountayne's promise of the perk. A little later, at a Sessions dinner in York, Fountayne and Sterne confronted Topham and, to their own satisfaction, routed him. The quarrel lay fallow for a few years but reasserted itself in 1758. Topham laid himself open to attack by attempting to persuade the new archbishop, John Gilbert, into extending the patent of Topham's Commissaryship of the Exchequer and Prerogative Courts so that his son might have it after he died.

The matter soon became common knowledge and Sterne hoped to court Fountayne's favour by composing *A Political Romance*, a thinly disguised parody of the incident. The piece itself is minor, but amusing and ingenious once it is keyed in to the events and personalities of York. It is a stroke of some cunning by which Sterne transposes a cathedral quarrel into a small village bickering and renders the desirable office both concrete and ridiculous, in the form of a good warm watchcoat. Fountayne appears in the romance as *John* – 'he rather did honour to his office, than that his office did honour to him'[208]– Topham as *Trim* – 'a little dirty, pimping, pettyfogging, ambidextrous fellow'[209]– and Sterne himself as *Lorry Slim*, 'an unlucky wight'.[210]

At the time, the *Romance* must indeed have 'set the mob a laughing, and sent every man home in perfect good humour, except *Trim*, who waddled very slowly off with that kind of inflexible gravity only to be equalled by one animal in the creation, and surpassed by none'.[211] But cautious voices advised Sterne against the publication and, though it was printed early in 1759, it is uncertain how many copies saw the light of day. Most of the five hundred copies were burned. More to the point, Dean Fountayne, perhaps embarrassed by his supporter's comedy, did nothing to improve Sterne's position. Disappointed in two patrons, Sterne naturally thought to exercise his brain henceforward in his own interest. The episode had produced an essential realization, for 'till he had finished his Watchcoat, he says, he hardly knew that he could write at all, much less with Humour, so as to make his Reader laugh.'[212]

But how could laughter be capitalized? If Sterne was to write for a general public, what sort of book was he capable of? We cannot hope to discover what we think of it today unless we ask what sort of book *Tristram Shandy* was when it first appeared. Is *Tristram Shandy* a novel, that must take its place in the history of the novel, or is it rather a work of fiction?

In his Dictionary, published in 1755, Johnson defined the novel, as 'a small tale, generally of love'. If we ignore the disparagement in that definition, it still serves quite well. A majority of those works published as novels do deal with love, they are small – in terms of ambition and length – and they are tales, that is to say, books that depend upon their narrative content.

Tristram Shandy, by that criterion, is far from a novel, and it would be equally careless to apply the description to, say, *Robinson Crusoe*, *Tom Jones* or *Clarissa Harlowe*. One of the most interesting things about the success of these books when they appeared is the uncertainty with which their readers regarded the new form. The gaiety, the life-like people and the overall 'entertainment' were all thought suspect in some quarters, not to mention the bawdiness. Not only *Tristram Shandy* was criticized for its subversiveness. Johnson regretted that a young lady should have read that model of robust health, *Tom Jones* – 'I scarcely know a more corrupt work.'[213] Lady Mary Wortley Montagu revealed how much the new form could divide sensibility when she said: 'This Richardson is a strange fellow. I heartily despise him and eagerly read him, nay, sob over his works in a most scandalous manner. The 2 first Tomes of Clarissa touch'd me as being a very resembling to my Maiden Days. I find in the pictures of Sir Thomas Grandison and his Lady what I have heard of my Mother and seen of my Father.'[214]

This sense of seeing life accurately described in fiction was one of the most common reactions and allows us to appreciate the effect of 'realism' in eighteenth-century fiction. In 1750, in *The Rambler*, Johnson spoke of this effect: 'The works of fiction, with which the present generation seems more particularly delighted, are such as exhibit life in its true state, diversified only by accidents that daily happen in the world, and influenced by passions and qualities which are really to be found in conversing with mankind.'[215]

Johnson, as we have seen, hardly approved of these books. He thought that they were 'written chiefly to the young, the ignorant, and the idle, to whom they serve as lectures of conduct, and introductions into life. They are the entertainment of minds unfurnished with ideas, and therefore easily susceptible of impressions.'[216] Johnson's own *History of Rasselas*, published in 1759, was not for those 'unfurnished with ideas' and it did not purport to mirror the lives of its readers. It is, in fact, a work of philosophical fiction, employing mythical settings and exotic and representative characters like Rasselas himself, a prince of Abyssinia. *Rasselas* is in a classical tradition, being essentially a discourse on – rather than a demonstration of – human nature. It is a narrative only to the extent that *Gulliver's Travels* is a fictional account of extraordinary adventures. *Robinson Crusoe*, although coarsely written and ponderous with its message of puritan self-sufficiency, none the less enthralled readers because of its seeming actuality. And Defoe, already contorted by a career in business and espionage, seems to have needed to persuade himself he was telling a 'real' story, even though *Crusoe* was written for ready cash.

It is the particularity and the ambivalent invocation of reality that makes *Robinson Crusoe* so important a landmark. But even in 1759, Johnson could still hope that he who

writes upon general principles, or delivers universal truths, may hope to be read long, because his work will be equally useful at all times and in every country, but he cannot expect it to be received with eagerness, or to spread with rapidity, because desire can have no particular stimulation; that which is to be loved long must be loved with reason rather than with passion. He that lays out his labours upon temporary subjects easily finds readers, and quickly loses them; for what should make the book valued when its subject is no more?[217]

There is a paradoxical contrast between Johnson and Sterne. For although the ostensible meaning of *Rasselas* is 'that none are happy but by the anticipation of change: the change itself is nothing; when we have made it, the next wish is to change again'[218] his language remains measured, lapidary and contented. Sterne, on the other hand, makes his protestations of cheerfulness and optimism in a nerve-racked and perpetually incomplete style. Johnson's writing is exposed as being limited by Sterne's simply because it does not countenance the anxiety or uncertainty that dogged Sterne. There is an episode in which Rasselas encounters a sage; at first he is drawn to his calm reason, but on a second visit disappointed to find the wise man's wholeness shattered by the sudden death of his daughter. But Johnson only states that emotional blow; he does not convey it. The implication of the language is that the wise man's original, unflawed intelligence was closer to Johnson's ideal:

'I have found,' said the prince at his return to Imlac, 'a man who can teach all that is necessary to be known, who, from the unshaken throne of rational fortitude, looks down on the scenes of life changing beneath him. He speaks, and attention watches his lips. He reasons, and conviction closes his periods. This man shall be my future guide: I will learn his doctrines, and imitate his life.'[219]

From this throne, it is not surprising that Johnson found *Tristram Shandy* strange. But when Sterne asked Robert Dodsley,* the London publisher, to take on his book, he suggested that the production should resemble that of *Rasselas*. I doubt if he was simply concerned with imitating the appearance of that book. The generalizing influence on Sterne of Locke and Swift is very strong in *Tristram Shandy*, for all that the naturalness of the scenes between the Shandy brothers is so intense. I do not think it is possible to know what Sterne intended; unlike Johnson, he could not make a running commentary on the method and purpose of what he wrote. The difference is crucial, for Johnson's detachment enabled him to think and speak of such things as the 'true state' of life. Sterne is the first writer of fiction to believe that there is no such happy thing as objective and universal reality. Instead, he knows intuitively that reality is no more than a projection in his own head – and we know what he thought of that head. The true subject of *Tristram Shandy* is therefore fiction itself, or the imaginative potential in the relationship between writer and reader.

***

As if to pinch himself to be sure that he was really awake, twice in the first volume of *Tristram Shandy* Sterne records the date on which he is writing: 9 and 26 March 1759. In the previous December he had done what he could to simplify his varied commitments and he probably worked steadily at *Tristram Shandy* during the winter and early spring of 1759. It is difficult not to think of Sterne as a hurrying, preoccupied

---

* Dodsley (1703–64) provides a good example of how social barriers could be overcome. At one time a footman, he had considerable success as a dramatist before becoming London's most notable publisher. He virtually retired in 1759, after having handled *Rasselas*, and passed the business on to his younger brother James.

writer who 'when [composing] would often pull down his [wig] over one eye, & remove it from side to side'.[220]

This agitation was profound. It was probably some time during the winter of 1759 that Sterne dined with Stephen Croft at Stillington and, after the meal, read aloud a few passages from his manuscript. But the company 'fell asleep at which Sterne was so nettled that he threw the Manuscript into the fire, and had not luckily M͏ʳ Croft rescued the scorched papers from the flames, the work wou'd have been consigned to oblivion'.[221]

Sterne would never have better cause for nervousness and his own peculiar mixture of exhilaration and foreboding. It was a combination that drove out discretion. Not only did the first draft of the book probably contain a deal of scurrilous satire on York personalities, but the author was also inserting sly references to his latest flirtation, and one all the more delightful for the way that it accompanied his composition. A philandering writer may have a special sentimental affection for those who have attended his hours of decision, and here is such an example:

Now this I like;—when we cannot get at the very thing we wish,—never to take up with the next best in degree to it;—no; that's pitiful beyond description;—it is no more than a week from this very day, in which I am now writing this book for the edification of the world, —which is *March 9, 1759,*—that my dear, dear *Jenny* observing I look'd a little grave, as she stood cheapening a silk of five-and-twenty shillings a yard,—told the mercer, she was sorry she had given him so much trouble;—and immediately went and bought herself a yard-wide stuff of tenpence a yard.[222]

This economical Jenny was almost certainly a singer of Huguenot origins, Catherine Fourmantel, who was in York with her mother to perform at the Assembly Rooms. But Jenny may have meant less to Sterne than the delicious sensation of being able to drop coy hints about her. For, a little later in the same chapter, Sterne teases the reader about her and conjures up a boisterous argument with the old lady in the reader over his own morals:

Not that I can be so vain or unreasonable, Madam, as to desire

you should therefore think, that my dear, dear *Jenny* is my kept
mistress;—no,—that would be flattering my character in the other
extream, and giving it an air of freedom, which, perhaps, it has no
kind of right to. All I contend for, is the utter impossibility for some
volumes, that you, or the most penetrating spirit upon earth, should
know how this matter really stands.—It is not impossible, but that
my dear, dear *Jenny*! tender as the appellation is, may be my child.—
Consider,—I was born in the year eighteen.—Nor is there anything
unnatural or extravagant in the supposition that my dear *Jenny* may
be my friend.—Friend!—My friend.—Surely, Madam, a friendship
between the two sexes may subsist, and be supported without—Fy!
Mr. *Shandy*:—Without any thing, Madam, but that tender and
delicious sentiment, which ever mixes in friendship, where there is a
difference of sex.[223]

By May, Sterne was offering his literary child to Robert
Dodsley. He wrote, he said, on the recommendation of John
Hinxman, once an employee of Dodsley, but now set up for
himself at York in Stonegate. Sterne spoke of his book being
about everything he found 'Laugh-at-able in my way' and
wondered whether Dodsley might take it on for, say, £50.[224]

Dodsley's immediate answer seems to have been thoroughly
conventional: that the book might not sell and that he did not
wish to saddle his brother with so uncertain a venture. He may
also have made some criticism of the book's contents, since
during the summer of 1759 Sterne appears to have taken some
second opinions of his book. He thanked one acquaintance for
comments 'which contrary to My Natural humour, set Me
upon looking gravely & thinking gravely for half a day together'.[225] To charges that some of the book was reckless,
Sterne answered, 'I will use all reasonable caution—Only with
this caution along with it, not to spoil My Book;—that is the
air and originality of it, which must resemble the Author—&
I fear 'tis a Number of these slighter touches which Mark this
resemblance & Identify it from all Others of the [same]
Stamp—Which this understrapping Virtue of Prudence would
Oblige Me to strike out.'[226]

By October, he had made up his mind. He wrote to Dodsley
saying that he planned 'to feel the pulse of the world' with a
small edition at York – 'a lean edition, in two small volumes,

of the size of Rasselas, and on the same paper and type, at my own expense'.[227] He hoped that Dodsley would carry the book in London* and perhaps answered an earlier objection when he said, 'All locality is taken out of the book—the satire general.'[228] Any doubts Sterne may have had about proceeding with provincial publication were settled by the offer of £100 from William Phillips of York towards the costs of production.[229]

That autumn was a giddy time with Sterne hurrying back and forth between the press of Mrs. Ann Ward, the widow of Caesar Ward, to admire his proofs, and the lodging of Catherine Fourmantel. He crowded her with presents – bottles of sweet Portuguese wine and pots of honey – just as he may have tormented his printer with late corrections. With Sterne and this singer to be seen in and out of York shops, it is no surprise that Mrs. Sterne went into something of a decline. We have no details. But it was said that, towards the end of the year, she 'lost her senses by a stroke of the palsy'[230] and Lydia was so upset that she had a fever. Sterne therefore let it be known that his gay book had been written 'under the greatest heaviness of heart'.

It is to the credit of Sterne's judgement of public taste that he was so confident of his book. By November, he had hired a small house in the Minster Yard for his wife and daughter. Already, he was planning to be in London next spring so as to perform with his own book and he hired Marmaduke Callis to act as his curate at Sutton and Stillington. He bubbled with the rumours that returned to him of 'an extraordinary book'[231] about to appear, and could hardly sleep for excitement. Catherine Fourmantel may have been exhausted by his consuming enthusiasm: 'If this Billet catches you in Bed,' he wrote to her, 'You are a lazy, sleepy little Slut—and I am a giddy foolish unthinking fellow for keeping You so late up.'[232]

In the last week of December,† *Tristram Shandy* appeared in

---

* In Vol. I, Ch. IX, Sterne asks the purchaser of his dedication 'to order the sum to be paid into the hands of Mr. Dodsley'; he liked always to advertise his associates, perhaps to make them his friends.

† Cross believed that the book was both printed and published by Dodsley in London and published on 1 January 1760. However, circumstantial evidence, as well as a detailed investigation by Curtis, and more recently Kenneth Monkman, of paper, type, watermarks etc., make it clear that *Tristram Shandy* was first printed

York and had 'a prodigious Run'[233] – in two days, two hundred copies were sold. Sterne at last was touching the world and with every 'electrical assimilation' he had anticipated. What a future was now made possible: Sterne could see himself publishing two volumes a year of Tristram's life – that life that would transform his own – 'which, if I am suffered to go on quietly, and can make a tolerable bargain with my bookseller, I shall continue to do as long as I live'.[234]

---

and published in York late in December 1759. External contemporary evidence is denied to us because no copies of the *York Courant* for December 1759 have survived. (Lewis P. Curtis, 'The First Printer of *Tristram Shandy*', *P.M.L.A.*, Vol. XLVII, 1932, pp. 777–89; Kenneth Monkman, 'The Bibliography of the Early Editions of *Tristram Shandy*', *Transactions of the Bibliographical Society*, March 1970, pp. 11–39.)

PART THREE
'Tristram is the fashion ...'
1760–68

1760

Sterne appears to have spent the first day of the new decade resolved to establish an image for himself. Tristram's entry into polite society was an enterprise over which he was prepared to take unusual pains, no matter that the public character he chose for himself was unruly, haphazard and fey. On 1 January 1760 he began a Letter Book, foreseeing that a literary celebrity might be wise to preserve everything that he wrote. He began by transcribing a letter of the previous summer acknowledging advice and suggestions from a friend who had read the manuscript of *Tristram Shandy*. But copying is a taxing discipline for a quick mind and Sterne now saw several ways in which the letter could be amended. It is hard to say whether that indicates literary meticulousness or simply surrender to the moment. Spontaneity believes in its own mysterious complicity with the *bon mot* and if Sterne generally wrote swiftly perhaps it was to prevent doubt from settling on any word or thought. And if there was not always a word on the tip of his pen, then a —, . . . or * : anything to maintain contact.

One passage from this letter extended in the transcription illustrates Sterne's equivocal preoccupation with his own talent. There is surely a desperate self-destroying frankness – much more raw than honesty – in the pleasure he has in exposing the mechanism of his own trick:

I know not whether I am entirely free from the fault Ovid is so justly censured for—of being *Nimium ingenij sui amator.* the hint however is right—to sport too much with a Man's own wit is surfeiting: like toying with a man's mistress, it may be delightful enough to the Inamorato but of little or no entertainment to By-standers, in general I have ever endeavour'd to avoid it, by leaving off as soon as possible whenever a point of humour or Wit was started, for fear of saying too much; and tother day a gentleman found fault with me upon that very score—but yours and my friend Fothergils* Judgment upon this head, I hold to be more truely nice and critical—and on that side, it is the safest to err.

after all, I fear Tristram Shandy must go into the world with a hundred faults—if he is so happy as to have some striking beauties, merciful & good Judges will spare it . . .[1]

So many of Sterne's attitudes are contained in that: the hope that beauties outweighed blemishes; the thought that it might be to his advantage to confess to faults; above all, the sexual metaphor for his originality. To judge by the sweet and sour mixture of swoon and chiding in his letters to Catherine Fourmantel, Sterne was quite willing to be seen toying with her in public. Miss Fourmantel sang several times at the Assembly Rooms during the winter and was no doubt escorted about York by Sterne. The girl may have been flattered by this as much as Mrs. Sterne was harrowed. But did either of them realize how much Kitty/Jenny was a prop to Sterne's moods, something to reflect his own potency?

my dear Kitty.
I have sent You a Pot of Sweetmeats, and a Pot of Honey, neither of them, half so sweet as yourself.—but don't be vain upon this,—or presume to grow Sour, upon this Character of Sweetness I give You; for if you do I shall send You a pot of Pickles, (by way of contrarys) to sweeten you up, & bring you to yourself again—whatever Changes happen to You, believe me that I am unalterably Yours, & according to y^r Motto, such a One, my dear Kitty *qui ne Changera pas, que en mourant*.[2]

But doting unalterability had a purpose. Also on 1 January Sterne drafted a letter that his mistress might send to David Garrick in London. The letter told Garrick of the 'great noise' caused in York by *Tristram Shandy* – 'If you have not seen it, pray get it & read it, because it has a great Character as a witty smart Book, and if You think it is so, your good word in Town will do the Author; I am sure great Service.'[3] Yet again, we see Sterne's unique capacity for launching rumours about himself;

* Marmaduke Fothergill (d. 1778), a surgeon, was a friend of Sterne and one of several who advised caution in proceeding with *Tristram Shandy*.

few men have counted so much on distinction coming out of shadiness. The letter to Garrick ends, '... the Graver People however say, tis not fit for young Ladies to read his Book. so perhaps you'l think it not fit for a young Lady to recommend it however the Nobility, & great Folks stand up mightily for it. & say tis a good Book tho' a little tawdry in some places.'[4]

Sterne presumably counted on some acquaintance between his Kitty and the leading figure of the London theatre. If it ever occurred to him that perhaps only that connection had made her attractive to him, he would probably have smiled all the more, for Sterne seems to have been so rapt in himself as to enjoy even his shortcomings. Here was a shy outsider feeling his way into notoriety.

But the letter may not have been necessary. For just as Sterne had sent copies of his book up to London, so one had found its way to *The Monthly Review*. It was actually reviewed in the issue for December 1759, and in terms that must have pleased Sterne, not only because of the compliments but for the way the authorship was attributed to Tristram Shandy as if he were a real person. When we recollect that Sterne's name had not appeared in the books themselves,* 'Kitty's Letter' may have been all the more useful to Garrick in that it disclosed the real identity of the author. Garrick was well known for the pleasure he took in leading society into new fashions and crazes and Sterne may have counted upon Garrick adopting the book because of the very exclusiveness of his information.

The Monthly Review approved Sterne's replacement of the normal 'Life and Adventures' with 'Life and Opinions' since opinions would 'in all probability, afford him matter enough to write about, tho' he should live to the age of Methusalem'. Digression, thought the *Review*, and Mr. Shandy's taste for 'giving his historical Readers the slip on all occasions' constituted the one weakness in the work. Although, even on this account, it was acknowledged that 'he generally carries his

---

* Sterne's name does not appear in the first four volumes of *Tristram Shandy*. But by the time later volumes appeared, he had become so embarrassed by forgeries and imitations that he signed copies personally above the first chapter. This considerable labour is not the least stroke of irony in his life. *A Sentimental Journey* was credited to 'Mr. Yorick' and only the *Sermons* had a proper half-title page with Sterne's name on it after the title '*Sermons of Mr. Yorick*'.

excuse for rambling along with him; and tho' he be not always hammering at his tale, yet he is busy enough.'[5]

The *Review* had also noticed that caressing of his own wit that Sterne had talked about: 'There prevails, indeed, a certain quaintness, and something like an affectation of being immoderately witty, throughout the whole work. But this is perhaps the Author's *manner*. Be that, however, as it will, it is generally attended with spirit and humour enough to render it entertaining.'[6] In conclusion, Mr. Tristram Shandy was recommended 'as a writer infinitely more ingenious and entertaining than any other of the present race of novelists'.[7]

Towards the end of January, Sterne heard from Dr. Henry Goddard that Garrick 'had actually spoke well of my Book'. As pleased with the success of his trick as with the praise, Sterne dashed off a letter to the actor dramatizing his own indecision: 'I had a strong Propensity when I did myself the pleasure of sending You the two Vol[s] to have accompanied them with a Letter to You:—I took up my Pen twice—hang it!—I shall write a vile insinuating Letter, the english of which will be,—to beg M[r] Garrick's good word for my Book, whether the Book deserves it no—I will not,—the Book shall go to the Devil first.'[8] It is so captivating a picture of fitful pride and shyness that it may have deceived Sterne long enough for him to forget the re-writing he had done on *Tristram* and to assure Garrick that the book had 'gone forth into the world, hot as it came from my Brain, without one Correction:—tis however a picture of myself, & so far may bid the fairer for being an Original'.[9]

Word of Garrick's approval probably decided Sterne to make his trip to London, and thus present the picture and the original side by side. Was it this contrast that finally made the book? It is clear that Sterne was the London sensation of the spring of 1760 and that wherever he went he was remarked upon as the author of 'that book'. He must have met at least a thousand of the leading figures in London society and been eagerly described to ten times that number; no one could remain immune to Sterne. Although he was inexperienced in business matters, not perhaps naturally happy in large assemblies and – as far as we know – making his first visit to London, nevertheless he manipulated the taste and opinion of the city in a way that is remarkably adroit and modern. But Sterne had no public relations men. At the nub of his performance was the essential incongruity of Sterne himself: that the author of so original and racy a book should have been a country parson.

Sterne probably left York on Monday, 3 March. On the first day of the month, the Saturday, he attended a meeting of the York Chapter, the last of his life. At the same time, he arranged for an advertisement to appear in the next *Courant*, inviting subscriptions for the forthcoming *Dramatick Sermons of Mr Yorick*.[10] The advertisement was signed by Tristram Shandy, and if the '*Dramatick*' was thought to appeal to people in York who had actually heard Sterne preach, the manœuvre itself testifies to the calculated assault Sterne was making on London.

Coaches left for London from Bluitt's Inn in Lendal every morning except Sunday and hoped to reach the capital by the second night, having stopped the first at Grantham. It is possible that the actual moment of Sterne's departure, if not the idea, was left to chance. According to John Croft, his brother Stephen, who was off to London on business, met Sterne in the street and asked if the author would go up to town with him. Croft even offered to pay Sterne's fare 'to which Sterne replied all that was very kind, but that he cou'd not leave his wife in the state that she was in, to which Mr C. answered that as he cou'd not possibly do her any good by his attendance that he had better go along with him, which was agreed upon, with this *Proviso* that Sterne was to have an hours law to go home to pack up his best breeches, which being granted they sett off together . . .'.[11]

The two men arrived on the evening of Tuesday, 4 March and lodged with Croft's son-in-law, Nathaniel Cholmley, in Chapel Street. At breakfast next morning, Sterne was nowhere to be seen. Instead, he had taken an early morning walk to Dodsley's shop in Pall Mall,* impatient to see how his book did. It seems likely that London had had all too few copies once *The Monthly Review* and Garrick had spoken up for the

---

* Now demolished, on the site of the present No. 52. The house, built in 1726–7, was known as Tully's Head, after Cicero. (*Survey of London* [London, 1960], Vol. XXIX, pp. 335–6.)

book. Sterne was delighted to be told that 'there was not such a Book to be had in London either for Love or money.'[12]

Then and there, Sterne entered into negotiations with James Dodsley and, when Croft and Cholmley rode by after breakfast, Sterne rushed out of the shop and told them

he was mortgaging his brains to Dodsley for £50, the over-plus of Six hundred pounds, that he stood out for above the Bargain of Six hundred pounds, that he offered him for the Copy of the two volumes of Tristram Shandy, and for two Volumes of Sermons which he was to compose in two months time, under the title of Yorick's Sermons, on a further condition that he was to engage to write a vol. of Tristram Shandy every year, and so to continue the work during his life and that he stood out for the odd Fifty pounds, when the Gent[n] advized him not to haggle, or bargain any longer about the matter, but to close the agreem[t] with Dodsley which he did, after which he returned to Chapell street and came skipping into the room, and said that he was the richest man in Europe.[13]

Few authors, at least, had done as well. In the previous year, Dodsley had paid Johnson £100 for *Rasselas* and £25 for the second edition. Gray remarked on the extraordinary payments Sterne received with the beginnings of an envy that marks a turning point in publishing history. Dodsley had published Gray's 'Elegy Wrote in a Country Church-yard' in 1751. It had gone through four editions in a year and made about £1,000 for its publisher. Gray himself received nothing – 'He held a Quixotic notion that it was beneath a gentleman to take money for his inventions from a bookseller.'[14]

The formal agreement between Sterne and James Dodsley was only signed on 8 March with Richard Berenger as witness and possibly with Garrick acting as Sterne's adviser – 'he has undertaken the whole Management of the Booksellers, & will procure me a great price.'[15] The price of the final agreement was very close to that of those initial unbreakfasted hagglings: Sterne was to receive £630 for the copyright of four volumes of *Tristram Shandy* and all the profits of those volumes printed in York that Dodsley had already sold. Later, in May, when Sterne's first volumes of sermons were about to appear, this agreement was amended so that Sterne received £250 for Volumes I and II, £380 for III and IV and £200 for the

Sermons – a grand total of £830, getting on for three times the annual income of Parson Sterne. It is not often appreciated that Sterne was the first *coup* of the newly independent James Dodsley. The size of the payment to Sterne may well reflect the younger brother's hope that he had a best-seller of his own in this completely new author.

Dodsley's immediate concern was to publish a second edition of the first two volumes of *Tristram*. This new edition appeared on 3 April with a frontispiece by Hogarth and a fetching dedication to Pitt. Sterne seemed shy of soliciting Hogarth himself and asked Richard Berenger, 'prithee sally out to Leicester fields, and when You have knockd at the door (for you must knock first) and art got in—begin thus "—Mr Hogarth, I have been with my friend Shandy this morning"—but go on yr own Way—as I shall do mine.'[16] As for Pitt, Sterne wrote to the Secretary of State less than a week before the second edition appeared simply as a matter of duty. Thus the dedication itself was almost certainly composed in London some two hundred miles, and much farther in spirit, from the 'bye-corner of the kingdom' and the 'retired thatched house' it invoked.

Throughout March, April and most of May *Tristram* was the fashion and its author a bizarre celebrity. If Garrick, Dodsley and Berenger were Sterne's first sponsors, no doubt he made innumerable rapid if brief impressions himself, like fingers in dough. And like dough that quickly reasserts itself against such marks, London was not permanently touched by Sterne. No more was he affected by the city. Even fame amounted to little more than a dream, and the friendships that Sterne made in London were seldom more than that sort of association that depends upon people being in each other's company. Out of sight, out of mind: only Sterne's actual presence did the trick. Once he was away from London there were rumours that he was dead. If in that first season of 1760 he was passed round with all the glamour that might attach to a novel drug, he proved strangely non-addictive in the minds of the people he met.

Thus Sterne's eyes give us very little of London or of the people he met. And when, in years to come, he had some difficulty in knowing how to occupy later volumes of *Tristram Shandy*, he rehashed his tour of France rather than give us

Tristram in London. Perhaps he felt more able to dash like a tourist through France and was nervous of offending London, just as he had been persuaded to omit identifiable pictures of citizens of York. Sterne is so persistent a traveller, partly because of a sort of provincial unease in very worldly company. His antics in London may have been all the more extravagant, his jokes especially inappropriate, because, in the words of John Croft, he 'shewed himself to most advantage in a small Company, for in a large one he was frequently at a Loss, and dumbfounded as he assumed the privilege of a Wit, he wou'd frequently come out with very silly things and expressions which if they did not meet that share of approbation from the Publick which he expected he wou'd be very angry and even affrontive'.[17]

Even so by 8 March he was writing to Catherine Fourmantel (still in York), that he was 'engaged allready to ten Noble men & men of fashion to dine'.[18] He had taken lodgings – 'the genteelest in Town' – in Pall Mall, to be near Dodsley's perhaps. Garrick had welcomed him to see Home's tragedy, *The Siege of Aquileia*, at Drury Lane Theatre, and given him the liberty of the house for the season. John Beard, the acting manager of Covent Garden, had had no option but to offer Sterne a similar privilege.

At Pall Mall, Sterne's lodgings were constantly 'full of the greatest Company'. He dined with Lord Chesterfield, 'Ld Rockingham, Ld Edgecomb—Lord Winchelsea, Lord Littleton, A Bishop—&c &c—':[19] a chess-board of dignitaries; so many he may not have remembered all their names.

To add to his excitement, by coming to London Sterne had won for himself another living in Yorkshire and one that he may have been envious of for some years. Indeed, in his Memoir, he was to call Coxwold 'a sweet retirement in comparison of Sutton'. On 12 March, Richard Wilkinson, Sterne's former curate and subsequently the incumbent of Coxwold, had died. The gift of the living was in the hands of Thomas Belasyse, the Earl of Fauconberg, who lived within a mile of Coxwold church. Fauconberg was in London for the season and was delighted to recruit Sterne as a neighbour. The living was worth about £150 a year and Sterne himself wrote out the article of his nomination, so that there should be no mistake, and took it to be signed by Fauconberg on the 28th and the next day to Archbishop Gilbert who was staying in Grosvenor Square.

Another resident of that square, unwillingly attracted by Sterne's glitter, was William Warburton, the new bishop of Gloucester. We have already seen the conventional colouring of Warburton's faith. He has traditionally figured in Sterne's life as an example of humbug exposed. But he is rather more interesting than that. Some twenty-four years older than Sterne, he had acquired a reputation for dry erudition and thoroughness. Pope, for instance, believed that 'he was the most capable of seeing through all the possibilities of things.'[20] His literary fame was based on the *Divine Legation of Moses*, published in 1738, and although his writing smacked of pomposity and arrogance, in person he was much more amenable. Warburton was probably drawn to Sterne by having known his uncle at Durham (they had been fellow-prebends). For all that Sterne made a fool of the older man, it was as much out of wantonness as wit; all of Warburton's comments on Sterne suggest that he saw accurately into the younger man's confused soul.

Warburton was initially anxious because of a rumour that Sterne intended to caricature him as Tristram's tutor in the next volume of *Shandy*. He appears to have approached Garrick to act as a go-between to scotch any such possibility. Garrick mentioned the rumour to Sterne who reacted in mock horror, just as he may originally have voiced the thought of lampooning Warburton without ever really intending to do so: 'Are we so run out of stock, that there is no one lumber-headed, muddle-headed, mortar-headed, pudding-headed *chap* amongst our doctors?—Is there no one single wight of much reading and no learning amongst the many children in my *mother's* nursery, who bid high for this charge—but I must disable my judgment by choosing a Wn?'[21]

The bishop was relieved to hear that he would be spared and 'pleased to find I have no reason to change my opinion of so agreeable and so original a writer as Mr Sterne'.[22] But when his turn came to meet the author, he brought gifts of advice, books to improve Sterne's style and a purse of guineas. Sterne reacted to advice like an unbroken horse and Warburton, a man of more than seventy, was probably sensitive to any hollowness in dutiful respect. If his approach was meant to win over Sterne, it naturally gave gossips all the more reason for mocking the bishop's fears. For the rest of that season, at least, the bishop had to suffer a variety of thinly disguised jokes at his own expense.

However uncongenial Warburton's advice may have seemed to Sterne, it came out of understanding. He was to pass on to Sterne a maxim of Richard Bentley, 'that a man was never writ out of reputation he had once fairly won, but by himself'. In later life, Warburton became fixed in his disapproval of 'that egregious Puppy', but did not attempt to conceal the misguided way that he had played into Sterne's hands. Indeed, he remained sympathetic to Sterne's self-destructive bent and, on hearing of his death, made this revealing comment on his life and the London that had acclaimed him: 'Poor Sterne . . . was the idol of the higher mob. . . . He found a strong disposition in the many to laugh away life; and as now every one *makes himself*, he chose the office of common jester to the many. But what is hard, he never will obtain the frivolous end he aimed at, the reputation of a wit, though at the expence of his character, as a man, a scholar, and a clergyman.'[23]

But although Sterne was the toast of a leading publisher, he does not seem to have appealed to other men of letters. Johnson disparaged Sterne's success as a measure of London's unthinking hospitality. Goldsmith* retorted that Sterne was 'a very dull fellow' to which Johnson merely replied, 'Why, no, Sir.'[24] We need not be surprised that Johnson† could not respond to Sterne's strangeness, nor that many writers should resent his monopoly on attention. 'Tristram Shandy is still a greater object of admiration,' wrote Gray, 'the Man as well as the Book. One is invited to dinner, where he dines, a fortnight

---

* Goldsmith (1728–74) would have been especially envious. Several years' application in London had not removed him from poverty. He was not to publish *The Vicar of Wakefield* until 1766.

† Johnson (1709–84), personally, had very little to say about Sterne. 'I was but once,' he said, 'in Sterne's company, and then his only attempt at merriment consisted in his display of a drawing too indecently gross to have delighted even in a brothel.' (Johnson, *Works* [1787], Vol. XI, p. 214.)

beforehand, his portrait is done by Reynolds.'[25] In fact, Sterne went eight times to Reynolds's house between 20 March and 21 April. Reynolds at this time was a most methodical port-raitist, satisfying over a hundred sitters a year, and while he was painting Sterne, Reynolds was also doing Garrick and Stephen Croft. An engraving of the portrait, by Ravenet, was used as a frontispiece to the Sermons when they were published on 22 May.

Part of the extraordinary splash Sterne was making was due to the actual scarcity of *Tristram Shandy* until the second edition was published early in April. There is no sensation more calculated to appeal to polite society than that in short supply. Horace Walpole seems to have been one of those kept impatient for the new edition. When it arrived, he wrote to Sir David Dalrymple on 4 April with all the irritation of disappointed suspense, and accused Sterne of spurious novelty:

At present, nothing is talked of, nothing admired, but what I cannot help calling a very insipid and tedious performance: it is a kind of novel, called *The Life and Opinions of Tristram Shandy*; the great humour of which consists in the whole narrative always going backwards. I can conceive a man saying that it would be droll to write a book in that manner, but have no notion of his persevering in executing it. It makes one smile two or three times at the begin-ning, but in recompense makes one yawn for two hours. The charac-ters are tolerably kept up, but the humour is for ever attempted and missed. The best thing in it is a sermon, oddly coupled with a good deal of bawdy, and both the composition of a clergyman. The man's head, indeed, was a little turned before, now topsy-turvy with his success and fame.[26]

Was it this spectacle of an excitable man spinning with his own success that made Sterne so entertaining? Certainly, Sterne was adopted more as a social curiosity than as a man of letters. Lord Rockingham, the Lord-Lieutenant of the North and East Ridings and owner of a property at Malton, only ten miles from Sutton on the Forest, took the newcomer to Court. On 6 May, both Rockingham and Prince Ferdinand of Bruns-wick, the victor of Minden, were installed at Windsor as knights of the Garter and Sterne may even have extended his London stay to be present in Rockingham's entourage.

Sterne 'received great notice from' and supped with Prince Edward Augustus, the Duke of York. It was on an occasion at the Court of Augusta of Saxe-Gotha, the widow of Frederick, the Prince of Wales, that Lord Bathurst introduced himself to Sterne. Bathurst was then seventy-six, 'always the protector of men of wit and genius'. He told Sterne of his former patronage of Swift and Pope and said that 'despairing ever to find their equals, it is some years since I have closed my accounts, and shut up my books, with thoughts of never opening them again: but you have kindled a desire in me of opening them once more before I die; which I now do; so go home and dine with me'.[27] Even more striking than this renewed enthusiasm for literature, a generation after its first expression, was the fact that the elderly Bathurst would outlive the new sensation.*

Court patronage introduced Sterne to another new face in London, a much younger climber, James Boswell. The Scot, only nineteen, visited Sterne at his lodgings and read to him a poem he had written at Newmarket. Sterne had reacted very favourably and pronounced Boswell a worthy heir of Matthew Prior. Oblivious to the charity of this comparison, Boswell went away conquered by Shandyism and composed a poem to the Sterne trinity: 'A Poetical Epistle to Doctor Sterne; Parson Yorick and Tristram Shandy'. For all its rattle of rhymes and mechanical pace, it gives a lively picture of Sterne at large – and is inspired by all the respect of one would-be sensation for the genuine article:

> By Fashion's hands compleatly drest,
> He's everywhere a wellcome Guest:
> He runs about from place to place,
> Now with my Lord, then with his Grace,
> And, mixing with the brilliant throng,
> He straight commences *Beau Garcon.*
> In Ranelagh's delightfull round
> Squire Tristram oft is flaunting found;
> A buzzing whisper flys about;
> Where'er he comes they point him out;

---

* Bathurst died in 1775, aged ninety-one. He lived at Cirencester Park, where Pope acted as a consultant on the arrangement of the garden. Bathurst was a confirmed voluptuary, the father of many children, legitimate and illegitimate.

Each Waiter with an eager eye
Observes him as he passes by;
'That there he is, do, Thomas! look
Who's wrote such a damn'd clever book.'[28]

The rage for Sterne entirely captivated the young Boswell, and yet there is considerable shrewdness in the recognition of three personalities that the Yorkshireman shuffled with. The longer Sterne stayed in London, the more the consequences of this trick crowded in on him. Who indeed was the real Sterne? It was hardly sufficient for the man himself to parry that question with 'Don't puzzle me.'[29] The world quickly began to provide Sterne with identities, some of which proved a great trouble to him. The literary market and newspapers were glutted with imitations of the Shandean style, impersonations of Sterne and anonymous additions to *Tristram Shandy*.

The April issue of the *Royal Female Magazine* carried as contribution to 'the chit chat of the day' an article on Sterne written by Dr. John Hill* and purporting to be based on 'anecdotes dropped from the mouths of those who knew him in the country, or have been intimate with him in town'.[30] The contents were quickly spread about town and held up against Sterne, for comparison and rebuke. Sterne tried to dismiss the article. But it is particularly interesting that so many people believed that Sterne himself had written this report. That speaks not only for mimicry but for the irresponsibility people saw in Sterne and which made him willing to slander himself. Hill's article even quoted Sterne's bravado: 'I'm an odd fellow; but if you hear any good of me, don't believe it.'[31]

As to the clutter of imitative pamphlets, Sterne declared, 'I wish they would write a hundred such.'[32] And so they swarmed about him: *Explanatory Remarks upon the Life and Opinions of*

---

* Hill (?1716–75) had been a botanist, actor, journalist and scandal-monger. A quarrelsome, apparently unscrupulous man he must have had some inner integrity, otherwise he would hardly have embarked on and completed a twenty-six-volume work on *The Vegetable System*. His account of Sterne contains much that is accurate, particularly its version of the history of the *Political Romance* of 1759. It also has this acknowledgement from Sterne of the shallowness of his fame: 'He says he is now just like a fashionable mistress, whom every body solicits, because 'tis the fashion, but who may walk the street a fortnight, and in vain solicit corporal Stare for a dinner.' (*Works*, Letters, Vol. I, p. 46.)

Tristram Shandy. Tristram Shandy's Bon Mots, Repartees, odd Adventures, and Humourous Stories. A Sermon on Lying, preached by Mr Yorick. Two Lyric Epistles by John Hall-Stevenson, one on my Cousin Shandy coming to Town, and one on the ladies of York, both of which, Gray thought, were 'absolute madness'. Shandean humour was easily picked up and not all the copies were worthless. *The Clock-Maker's Outcry against the Author of Tristram Shandy* was a genuinely merry rebuke for the damage done to clocks and their winding by the circumstances of Tristram's conception:

> Time's out of rule; no clock is now *wound up*:
> TRISTRAM the *lewd* had *knock'd* clock-making up.[33]

Little by little Sterne had become fretful with all London's activity. There were many unfavourable opinions of *Tristram Shandy*, and many people who remained uncompromising about such clerical irregularity. In May, *The Gentleman's Magazine* published a poem that ticked off most of the common grievances against Sterne:

> Tho' in fashion he's grown,
> It's very well known
>   His merit is small as it can be;
> The woman of pleasure
> And *Rochester's* treasure
>   Are brother and sister to *Shandy* . . .
> Ye ladies so fair,
> And beaus debonair,
>   Do all in your power that can be,
> The author to shame,
> And purchaser blame,
>   Who gave his six hundred for *Shandy*.[34]

Mrs. Sterne was complaining from York that she was short of money. He was obliged to take up his curacy at Coxwold as soon as possible. Kitty Fourmantel had at last arrived in London, eager to be thanked for that last letter to Garrick. In March, Sterne had urged Kitty to hurry to London. But on 1 April, although sorry that her journey was to be delayed, he admitted, 'I have scarse time to tell You how much I love You my dear Kitty.'[35] When at last she arrived in London with her mother,

her engagement to sing at Ranelagh had fallen through. Sterne perhaps hoped to repay his debt by recommending the singer to John Beard.

Kitty lodged in Soho, but Sterne had so little time now to linger. He was 'hurried off my Legs—by going to great People',[36] and had to postpone appointments with Kitty – 'I forgot I had been engaged all this week to visit a Gentleman's family, on this day. . . . I will however contrive to give my dear friend [Kitty] a Call at 4 o'Clock—tho' by the by, I think it not quite prudent —but what has prudence, my dear Girl, to do with Love? in this I have no Gover[n]ment, at least not half so much as I ought.'[37] A little later he complained of having no time to see her: 'I am as much a Prisoner as if I was in Jayl.'[38]

By the end of May Sterne rode home in a carriage he had bought for himself that might look suitably triumphant in York. He does not seem to have crossed Kitty's path again: we cannot be too sorry for her, since she does not speak for herself in Sterne's life. We have only his letters to her. Perhaps she was a dull, insensitive girl?* She might even have been a creature of his dreams, just as with sublime indifference Sterne continued to refer to 'Jenny' in *Tristram Shandy* years after he had discarded Kitty. A mistress in his mind could be taken up and put down at the author's fancy and would never reproach him for callousness or neglect.

The three months in London had changed Sterne's life. He was committed now to the world outside Yorkshire; not just to writing but to the perpetual metamorphoses of Sterne, Yorick and Tristram. Nothing indicates the change in the man so well as the gap between the charitable praise with which *The Monthly Review* welcomed *Tristram Shandy* and its disgust for the calculatingly ambiguous offering of Yorick's Sermons. *Tristram Shandy* owed its full success to the way its author had put himself on display. That action had alienated as many people as it had conquered. The friendships Sterne made in London appear to have been short-lived. Boswell was briefly overcome, but never met his hero again. Although Sterne had made men and, above

---

* Mrs. Henry Weston, who was given several of Sterne's letters to Catherine Fourmantel, said that the singer went mad and even provided the original for Maria of Moulines.

all, women laugh, it was at the cost of marking himself down for ever as frivolous. Within a month of Sterne's departure from London, Goldsmith attacked him for his offences against seriousness in the *Public Ledger*. Although envy of success undoubtedly stoked Goldsmith's fire, his attack picked out the self-preoccupation of *Tristram Shandy*: 'He must speak of himself, and his chapters, and his manner, and what he would be at, and his own importance, and his mother's importance, with the most unpitying prolixity; now and then testifying his contempt for all but himself, smiling without a jest, and without wit professing vivacity.'[39] The admirer of Sterne should not discount that opinion simply because of its hostility. It says pertinent things about Sterne: his vivacity is contrived, perhaps because, to extend Goldsmith, he had more than a little contempt for himself.

In York, Sterne was reunited with his family. His daughter, Lydia, had behaved during his absence in a way that may have amused her father but which indicates the instability of her childhood. At school, the other girls had been calling her 'Miss Tristram' and 'Miss Shandy'. In revenge, Lydia had written them love letters as if from the actors at the theatre in York, 'and when most of the Letters were interrupted, by their Parents or Guardians, severall of them were flogg^d, others shutt up in dark closetts, and severely treated as you may suppose, and it brought such a Slurr upon the Play House that the Theatre was a good deal deserted.'[40]

Sterne moved to Coxwold in about the middle of June. Little more than ten miles to the north of Sutton, Coxwold was on higher ground and yet sheltered by its position under the edge of the moors. Since there was no parsonage in the village Sterne rented a house from Lord Fauconberg for £12 a year and was soon talking of 'this Shandy-castle of mine'.[41] (This house, at the western extreme of Coxwold, still stands and has been rescued from imminent ruin by the Laurence Sterne Trust.) Already, he was embarked on the next instalments of *Tristram Shandy*. He appears to have worked quickly; but the speed may partly have owed itself to the existing material that he had cut from Volumes I and II. On 3 August he had finished one volume and wanted only 'to read it to some one who I know can taste and rellish humour—this by the way, is a little impudent in me—for I take the thing for granted, which their high Mightinesses the World have yet to determine'.[42] By 9 September, he could write to Robert Brown, an intrigued well-wisher from Geneva, that he could be found 'either pruneing, or digging or trenching, or weeding, or hacking up old roots, or wheeling away Rubbish'[43] in the garden of his new house.

For other duties, he had the house to equip, and curates to obtain for the livings he would again be deserting next year. It may only have been at Coxwold, away from the crowd, that he realized how thoroughly the pace and prospects of his life had altered. Even so, he was inconsistent in his reactions to the change.* Soon after Sterne's arrival at Coxwold, Warburton had written to him, avuncular with advice: 'You have it in your power to make that, which is an amusement to yourself and others, useful to both: at least, you should above all things, beware of its becoming hurtful to either, by any violations of decency and good manners.'[44]

Sterne reacted to this counsel in two quite distinct ways, but within the space of one letter. On the one hand, he stood up for making people laugh:

Be assured, my lord, that willingly and knowingly I will give no offence to any mortal by anything which I think can look like the least violation either of decency or good manners; and yet, with all the caution of a heart void of offence or intention of giving it, I may find it very hard, in writing such a book as 'Tristram Shandy', to mutilate everything in it down to the prudish humour of every particular. I will, however, do my best; though laugh, my lord, I will, and as loud as I can too.[45]

A few lines later, though, he confessed that the variety of stories spread about London of and in his name had proved a

* There is an unsubstantiated rumour that in this or the next summer, Sterne told a dying woman in Coxwold that he would 'inherit' her children. There may be no substance to the story: Sterne never refers to these orphans. But it is a quixotic notion, not out of character. Perhaps the legacy was quickly deposited in some safe Coxwold household: the idea would have been more appealing than the reality, and there may have been uncharitable local explanations for the curate's care of bereaved children. (*Yorkshire Notes & Queries*, June 1904, Vol. I, p. 87; see also *Works*, Letters, Vol. I, p. 46 [Hill's biographical article] which suggests the children were Richard Wilkinson's.)

great torment: 'These strokes in the Dark, with the many Kicks, Cuffs & Bastinados I openly get on all sides of me, are begining to make me sick of this foolish humour of mine of sallying forth into this wide & wicked world to redress wrongs . . .'[46]

How strange a mixture: the determination to laugh as long as he lived and, at the same time, the vulnerability to despair that could creep up on him in the space of a single sentence. He is as fluctuating as some primitive cell life seen under the microscope. It was a flimsy and evasive self-knowledge that persuaded Sterne that he was pledged to bring a little laughter into people's lives, to supply just that cheering influence of which Warburton would most have approved and least needed.* With the second instalment of *Tristram Shandy*, we can see that Sterne's freedom is itself limited, local and wasteful. Although he had liberated fiction from plot, he lacked the stamina or concentrated intelligence to go deeper into the reader's mind. Inevitably, subsequent volumes repeat innovations without turning them to use. Whereas Sterne might have been expected to be at the peak of creative confidence as he wrote Volumes III and IV, they seem to me the least assured, as though his own victory had overawed him. The excommunication and Slawkenburgius's tale, for instance, might more happily have been lost in that 'chasm of ten pages' in Volume IV.

There are even moments when Walpole's comment, that the idea of so original a book was more attractive than its execution, seems just. As it is, dull and unamusing digressions often seem a poor substitute for further conventional scenes from Shandy family life. Sterne's diffidence makes for several knowing references to the London that had celebrated him, little pinches to be sure that his memory was true: '*Reynolds* himself, as great and gracefully as he paints',[47] might have done justice to a pose of Walter Shandy's; in another place, Sterne speculated – no doubt in the real hope that the actor might pick up the hint – '*O Garrick!* what a rich scene of this would thy exquisite powers make!'[48]

One of the most interesting passages in these two volumes has

* Sterne did not omit Warburton completely. In Vol. IV, Ch. XX, he calls up an 'undertaking critick' who scolds him for 'riding like a madcap full tilt . . . your horse throws dirt; see you've splash'd a bishop'.

Sterne comparing a man's body and his mind to a jerkin and its lining. Thus, we may recognize a note of anguish, albeit representative rather than actual, in the sudden aside:

'—You Messrs. the monthly Reviewers! —how could you cut and slash my jerkin as you did?—how did you know, but you would cut my lining too?'[49]

The excitement and commotion of 1760 had been very confusing. No wonder then that so febrile a man as Sterne should late in October, as he finished Volume IV, have inserted an attempt at a definition of himself and his nature in his own book:

'—True *Shandeism*, think what you will against it, opens the heart and lungs, and like all those affections which partake of its nature, it forces the blood and other vital fluids of the body to run freely thro' its channels, and makes the wheel of life run long and chearfully round.'[50]

1761

Sterne did not set out again for London until December 1760, although he confessed to Hall-Stevenson that 'sum possessus cum diabolo qui pellet me in urbem'. That letter, in schoolboy Latin, was written in York, 'in domo coffeatariâ & plenâ sociorum strepitosorum, qui non permittent me cogitare unam cogitationem'.[1] The same letter contains Sterne's confession of being tired with his wife, and he may have resorted to Latin to heighten the effect of confiding in his crony at Skelton. Not that Hall-Stevenson could be relied on for secrecy, when he had already tried to exploit his fellow-Demoniac's new fame. Earlier in the year, Warburton had reproached Sterne for any possible association with Hall-Stevenson's *Two Lyric Epistles* – 'the author . . . appears to be a monster of impiety and lewdness'.[2] Sterne was blandly ingenuous in reply. The *Epistles* had indeed been sent to him but he never dreamed that they came from Hall-Stevenson, 'for from a nineteen years' total interruption of all correspondence with him, I had forgot his hand.'[3]

Sterne wrote frequently to Hall: his Letter Book included the note that 'Hall has rec^d hundreds, they have been wrote most of 'em in too careless a way, besides he is careless.' It is hardly credible that Hall-Stevenson played no answering part in the correspondence. And since Dodsley had published the *Two Lyric Epistles*, it is unlikely that Sterne was surprised by their appearance. Sterne told Warburton that he was sure Hall would make amends: 'He is worth reclaiming, being one of those whom nature has enabled to do much hurt or much good.'[4]

Nevertheless, Sterne was seriously worried by the imitations of his books. In September 1760, John Carr had produced a forged third volume of *Tristram Shandy* and Sterne had been forced to advertise that it was a fake and that the genuine article would come from Dodsley at the end of the year.[5]

He arrived in London early in December, in time to see the fourth edition of Volumes I and II which was published on 21 December. Two days later he dined at Bubb Dodington's with a group of politicians waiting to see what direction their fortunes might take with the new king. George II had died on 25 October and the new king was only twenty-two and 'resolv'd in myself to take the resolute part, to act the man in everything'.

But, for the moment, Sterne was in 'a continual hurry', seeing the new volumes through the press and coping with 'visiters and visitings'.[6] He was nervous of the reception of Volumes III and IV and told Stephen Croft he expected to be 'attacked and pelted, either from cellars or garrets, write what I will—and besides, must expect to have a party against me of many hundreds —who either do not—or will not laugh.—'Tis enough if I divide the world . . .'[7]

He seems to have been determined to be philosophical. The latest additions to *Tristram Shandy* were published on 28 January. By the middle of February, Sterne was reporting to Stephen Croft 'One half of the town abuse my book as bitterly, as the other half cry it up to the skies—the best is, they abuse and buy it, and at such a rate, that we are going on with a second edition, as fast as possible.'[8]

In fact, opinion was less divided than Sterne allowed. Only the *London Magazine* had welcomed 'the *real*, the inimitable Shandy . . . all the host of impotent cricks and imitators look aghast, at his superior genius. Whoever of our readers have, with true relish read his former volumes, may be assured that their perusal of the third and fourth will not be attended with less delight.'[9] *The Monthly Review*, on the other hand, had now rejected Sterne and wished to be forgiven for its earlier praise of him. Taking up his play with coats and linings, the review sneered: 'Do for shame, Mr Shandy, hide your jerkin, or at least, send the lining to the scowerer's. . . . We must tax you

with what you will dread above the most terrible of all imputa-
tions – nothing less than DULLNESS. Yes, indeed, Mr
Tristram, you are dull, *very dull*.'[10] The *Critical Review* probably
recognized the reason for Sterne's critical reverse when it said,
'The trouble has really been with the public. ... All novel
readers, from the stale maiden of quality to the snuff-taking
chambermaid, devoured the first part with a most voracious
swallow, and rejected the last with marks of loathing and
aversion.'[11]

But *The Monthly Review* jab at dullness was the worst punishment for so unconventional a writer. Individual opinions were
equally critical and again illustrate the difficulty Sterne had in
winning the respect of literary figures. Walpole became triumphant with disapproval: 'The second and third volumes of
Tristram Shandy, the dregs of nonsense, have universally met the
contempt they deserve: genius may be exhausted; – I see that
folly's invention may be so too.'[12] Meanwhile, Richard Hurd,
the bishop of Worcester, wrote to William Mason, the precentor of York, 'The 3ᵈ Vol. is insufferably dull and even stupid.
The 4ᵗʰ is full as humourous as either of the other two. But this
broad humour, even at its best, can never be endured in a work
of length.'[13]

Thomas Newton, sub-almoner to the archbishop of York,
reported that the bishops and clergy were crying shame upon
Sterne. The archbishop appears to have been particularly
embarrassed. When Sterne first arrived in London in December
1760 he had been invited to dine with Gilbert and his daughter.
Perhaps it was on that occasion that Sterne guaranteed the
sobriety of Volumes III and IV. When they were published,
however, the archbishop was 'very angry with him for having
broke his promise'. When Sterne called on Gilbert, in January,
he was turned away as a rebuke. Newton fancied that
Sterne had been so daunted by unfavourable attention that
he was deliberately lying low and 'is almost ashamed to see
us'.[14]

Richardson, now near his death, disparaged Sterne in a
letter of poker-faced finesse. Bishop Hildesley had written to
him inquiring who Yorick was. 'You cannot, I imagine have
looked into his books,' replied Richardson, 'execrable I cannot

but call them.' He saw only one extenuation for the shabby performance – 'that they are too gross to be inflaming'.[15] As if so much labour had tired him, Richardson then announced that he was handing his pen to 'My daughter' so that she could 'transcribe ... the sentiments of a young lady, as written to another lady, her friend in the country' on *Tristram Shandy*. Perhaps this was the case; but perhaps he merely dictated to his daughter, most comfortable in the character of a young lady. Certainly the daughter's critique manages to be scathing of both Sterne and the whim-swept milieu of young ladies that so attracted Richardson:

Happy are you in your retirement, where you read what books you choose, either for instruction or entertainment; but in this foolish town, we are obliged to read every foolish book that fashion renders prevalent in conversation; and I am horribly out of humour with the present taste, which makes people ashamed to own they have not read, what if fashion did not authorise, they would with more reason blush to say they had read! Perhaps some polite person from London, may have forced this piece into your hands, but give it not a place in your library; let not Tristram Shandy be ranked among the well chosen authors there. It is, indeed, a little book, and little is its merit, though great has been the writer's reward! Unaccountable wildness; whimsical digressions; comical incoherencies; uncommon indecencies; all with an air of novelty, has catched the reader's attention, and applause has flown from one to another, till it is almost singular to disapprove: even the bishops admire, and recompense his wit, though his own character as a clergyman seems much impeached by printing such gross and vulgar tales, as no decent mind can endure without extreme disgust![16]

Sterne's success had always been of the sort that stores up retribution for itself. A provincial novelty could not expect to dominate London two years running, and the town had a new hero to concern itself with. In March 1761 Charles Churchill published his poem, *The Rosciad*, a brilliant satire on actors and acting. Churchill's success was even more dramatic than Sterne's since it raised him from much greater poverty. Not only had he been doomed to miserable livings in the Church, but he had also suffered from a disastrous Fleet marriage. When no publisher was bold enough to take on *The Rosciad*, Churchill proceeded independently and with instant success. It was said that he had made over £700 from the one poem.

Although Sterne was soon claiming to be 'fourteen dinners deep engaged just now, and fear matters will be worse',[17] it is likely that he had time on his hands. Once his first sprint faltered, he was made to loiter until notoriety caught up with him. When Sterne was presented at a royal levee, the austere young king seems to have taken the opportunity of showing his distaste. Sterne was introduced, but the king only bowed slightly and moved on. Sterne told a bystander that the young king could not have heard the introduction and 'begged to be presented a second time'. His name was announced again but the king replied to the nobleman, 'My Lord, you have told me so already.'[18]

This new king was a great disturbance: youthful in his need to snub his grandfather's supporters and in forming emotional attachments with his own followers, he was, as Namier says, 'a youth who had never been allowed to be young and who had not managed to grow up'. As soon as he had arrived in London, Sterne had appreciated that eyes were concentrated on the new king who seemed 'resolved to bring all things back to their original principles, and to stop the torrent of corruption and laziness'.[19] The young George rose early and worked hard: the most alarming characteristics. Sterne may have been only a by-stander, attempting to insinuate himself into the suspense, but he saw that the king 'knows every thing, and weighs every thing and then is inflexible—this puts old stagers off their game— how it will end we are all in the dark'.[20]

George II's death had in fact been sudden – of a stroke in his own water-closet – but there had already been growing dis-satisfaction with the Pitt–Newcastle ministry. Despite the success of the colonial war, there were those like Bubb Dodington who believed that 'The ruinous expense of men and money it has brought upon us, has with use greatly sunk the value of the advantages we have gain'd, and if the account were made up in a mercantile way, I am not sure that the balance would appear in our favour . . .'[21]

The change of king was more than enough to focus these doubts and the envy of those who had been left out of office.

George himself was a grave but unstable youth, infatuated with the Earl of Bute, who had been an intimate confidant of his mother. Above all, George III was violently hostile to anyone who had supported his grandfather's administration and was a victim of the polarity in politics thereby caused by the division between Leicester House and the Court.

Thus the London Sterne came to late in 1760 was already divided between Butes and anti-Butes. Pitt, himself, had no illusions about his own prospects. Sterne had attended a debate at the Commons – 'There never was so full a house—the gallery full to the top.'[22] Pitt had been expected to make a rousing defence of his determination to continue the war with Spain but submitted to 'a political fit of the gout' and perhaps consoled himself at home with *Shandy*. Sterne reported the speech of William Beckford that peace was inevitable, just as it had been at the time of Utrecht, because 'the people behind the curtain could not both maintain the war and their places too, so were for making another sacrifice of the nation, to their own interests.'[23]

Sterne had only to recollect his own family history to realize how inopportune a moment it was to carry out a favour with which he had been charged by Stephen Croft: to obtain promotion for Croft's son, Stephen, who had recently been made cornet, although only seventeen. As Sterne explained to Croft, the court was 'turning topsy-turvy'. Bute had been given the seals of government, Sir Francis Dashwood was appointed Treasurer on 21 March, Lord Talbot was made Steward of the Household and the Earl of Halifax was appointed Viceroy of Ireland. Pitt himself resigned in October and Newcastle next year.

But Sterne was not partisan in these changes. Instead, he made what he could of his own affairs and pronounced, a little forlornly, 'I thank God . . . I have never yet made a friend, or connection I have forfeited, or done ought to forfeit—but on the contrary, my true character is better understood, and where I had one friend last year, who did me honour, I have three now.'[24] But these numbers are hard to supply with the names or signs of real affection.

As it was, Sterne seized on acquaintances, just as he believed himself in love with every woman he met. Such naked availability may have made striking first impressions, but it quickly became obvious how undiscriminating Sterne was in his attentions. Mrs. Montagu subsequently spoke of the way Sterne never employed his wit to be hurtful in company, no matter how insupportable he might be domestically.[25] Was this innate good nature or part of that unease with sophisticated society that may have been bred in Skelton rough-houses? Mrs. Montagu would have welcomed Sterne to her 'blue-stocking' *salon* in Hill Street in 1761. Another London hostess who took Sterne's eye was Mrs. Elizabeth Vesey, the wife of an Irish M.P. and landowner, who had not yet entered into full rivalry with Mrs. Montagu. Just as Richardson had been most encouraged by the new breed of intelligent woman, so it was among female society and readers that Sterne's originality made most impression. Indeed, it required a new sort of woman who could openly admire Sterne's work.

Mrs. Vesey seemed to Sterne 'surely the most penetrating of her sex'. He assured her of their fellow-feeling, no matter how brief their acquaintance, for 'intercourses of this kind are not to be dated by hours, days or months, but by the slow or rapid progress of our intimacies which can be measured only by the degrees of penetration by wch we discover Characters at first sight, or by the openess and frankness of heart w lets the by-stander into it.'[26]

Sterne's frankness consisted of making love to Mrs. Vesey by letter in one of his earliest examples of *double entendre*:

... in honest truth You are a System of harmonic Vibrations— You are the sweetest and best tuned of all Instruments—O Lord! I would give away my other Cassoc to touch you—but in giving this last rag of my Priesthood for this pleasure You perceive I should be left naked—if not quite dis-*Orderd*:—so divine a hand as y^{rs} would presently get me into Order again—but if Yo[u] suppose, this would leave me, as You found me—believe me dear Lady, You are mistaken.[27]

It is peculiarly characteristic of Sterne that this coquettish rapture should conjure up his own nakedness, rather than that of his beloved. What can Mrs. Vesey's reaction have been? One print of the day has them arm-in-arm at Ranelagh watching the sale of subscriptions for his sermons. Sterne told her that she was admirable for having a character that could be read at a glance; he had only walked ten steps beside her before recognizing 'dear Lady, that you have absolutely no inside at all'.[28] She probably tolerated his innuendo in the same spirit as Mrs. Montagu regarded Sterne: 'He is full of the milk of human kindness, harmless as a child, but often a naughty boy, and a little apt to dirty his *frock*.'[29]

For the rest, Sterne mixed with Samuel Foote, John Wilkes and Delaval. His one public engagement of the season was to preach at the Foundling Hospital on 3 May. A large audience was present, 'several of whom were persons of distinction',[30] and Sterne preached on 'The Parable of the Rich Man and Lazarus Considered' and prompted a collection of £55 9s 2d.

If the London of 1761 had not fully satisfied Sterne, he carried that discontent back with him to York and too quickly perhaps to Coxwold. He described his restlessness to Hall-Stevenson in one of his most elaborate metaphors of motion, as if he conceived of every pulse, flow and tremor in his body. One can sense unappeased nerves shivering from the exposure to a hasty journey:

... the transition from rapid motion to absolute rest was too violent.—I should have walked about the streets of York ten days, as a proper medium to have passed thro', before I entered upon my rest.—I staid but a moment, and I have been here but a few, to satisfy me I have not managed my miseries like a wise man—and if God, for my consolation under them, had not poured forth the spirit of Shandeism into me, which will not suffer me to think two moments upon any grave subject, I would else, just now lay down and die—die—and yet, in half an hour's time, I'll lay a guinea, I shall be as merry as a monkey—and as mischievous too, and forget it all—so that this is but a copy of the present train running cross my brain.[31]

There is a strange detachment in Sterne, that he could seemingly look into his own head and see the ripples left there by experience. No wonder such sensitivity could never immerse itself in its own emotions but merely dipped in them like someone at the cold English seaside. This is the first serious premonition by Sterne of death that has survived. He found Yorkshire 'cold and churlish' and suffered from 'a thin death-doing pestiferous north-east wind,'[32] but there is no sign as yet of a real decline in his health. He seems to have suffered from melancholy that he was no more in his element in London than he was in the country. Fame had filled him up, more than he could ever have hoped for, but still he rattled. There were hollows in him, inaccessible to other people.

Elizabeth Sterne had apparently given her husband up. There is no sign that either fame or success had rubbed off on her. She was not taken to London, but stayed in Yorkshire unable to escape the reports of Sterne's antics in London. When he returned in 1761, she seems to have told him frankly that she hoped he would be off again, and farther afield, even 'to lead a bear round Europe'. So that, although illness eventually encouraged Sterne to go to France, the idea of such a trip may have been implanted by his wife's coolness.

Sterne spent the summer working hard. Apart from the two new volumes of *Tristram Shandy*, he embarked on his last pro-longed bout of preaching. To enhance such performances, he instigated a rearrangement of the pews in Coxwold church in order to 'give a better Sound a better light', and to make sure that every member of the congregation 'will all face the Parson alike'.[33]

The great excitement of the year was the coronation of the new king. This was celebrated all over the country, but the festivities at Coxwold were out of proportion to the size of the village: some three thousand people were present; Sterne preached an extempore sermon and provided an ox to be roasted in the street and distributed amongst the spectators; barrels of ale were available and 'Ringing of Bells Squibs and Crackers Tarr Barrills and Bonefires, &c and a Ball in the Evening Concluded the Joyfull Day.'[34]

Sterne's daughter, Lydia, now nearly sixteen, must have enjoyed such revels. She had a pony from the proceeds of *Tristram* just as the family had bought a chaise for riding in to call on Lord Fauconberg. Sterne presented an idyllic picture of that summer with Lydia copying out his manuscript while his wife knitted and listened. But in fact, Sterne was preparing to abandon his family to another Yorkshire winter. And since a trip to the continent would necessarily be longer than his visits to the London season, he set about finding a curate for Coxwold. He chose James Kilner and agreed to pay him £30 a year for the service. Marmaduke Callis remained in charge at Sutton and Stillington, although in the autumn of 1761 Sterne sought out the proper licences for Callis's appointment, a procedure he had neglected for two years.

What provision did Sterne make for his wife and daughter? Shortly before his departure for France, in January 1762, he spoke of bringing his wife and daughter over to join him – 'else my stay could not be so long'. But he also contemplated staying in France 'a year or two'.[35] Without a definite date, Mrs. Sterne perhaps feared that she would be marooned. This anxiety may have prompted her letter to Mrs. Montagu in about November 1761. Mrs. Montagu had entertained Sterne and it is likely that she encouraged him to see France since he left what amounted to his will with her before setting out. Elizabeth Sterne's letter is vibrant with complaint and with rural neglect:

Cou'd Mrs. Montagu think this the way to make a bad husband better, she might indeed have found a better, which I have often urg'd, though to little purpose, namely some little mark of kindness or regard to me as a kins-woman ... surely never poor girl who had done no one thing to merit such neglect was ever so cast off by her Relations as I have been. I writ three posts ago to inform Mrs. Montagu of the sorrow her indifferation had brought upon me, and beg'd she wou'd do all that was in her power to undo the mischief, though I can't for my soul see which way, and must expect to the last hour of my life to be reproach'd by Mr. Sterne as the blaster of his fortunes ... I beg you will give me one gleam of comfort by answering this directly. Mr Sterne is on the wing for London, and we remove to York at the same time, so that I fear thy letter will not arrive before me.[36]

Mrs. Montagu was well aware of failings in both the Sternes but she undoubtedly found the husband more entertaining. A few years later she told her sister how Elizabeth Sterne 'was always taking frump at somebody and for ever in quarrels and prabbles'.[37] This autumn she welcomed Sterne in London and took him and Mrs. Vesey along to Reynolds's studio so that Sterne might amuse the elderly Lord Bath as he sat for his portrait. How near he was to becoming the hirable jester of polite society.*

Volumes V and VI of *Tristram Shandy* were published on 21 December, but not by Dodsley. We do not know what caused the breach between publisher and author. A second edition of Volumes III and IV had not been as prompt as the repeat of the first volumes and, in view of the poor reviews, Dodsley may have had a large enough part of it left on his hands to eat into the profit on the first edition. He may have begun to regret his initial generosity towards Sterne. Alternatively, Sterne perhaps hoped to change his luck with a change of publisher. In October, he had personally advertised the coming volumes in the London papers without naming a publisher. Such an omission brought offers from Thomas Becket, who was in business off the Strand with P. A. Dehondt, a Dutchman. Becket had neither the list nor the assurance of the Dodsleys. He was an ill-tempered man, prone to drink, but he stood by Sterne until his death, undoubtedly profiting from the Yorkshireman's books, but equally taking care and trouble over him and his difficult life.

The reception of the two latest volumes was more encouraging. Warburton thought they were much closer to the quality of the first two and the self-contained story of Le Fever was widely admired, being reprinted in several newspapers.

But Sterne was more occupied with his final preparations for travel. On 28 December he prepared a memorandum, 'In Case I should die abroad'. As well as explaining that there were sermons at Coxwold, York and London, Sterne estimated that the sale of his estate would bring £1,800. He instructed his wife to invest this and the proceeds from Volumes V and VI, and to seek Garrick's help in the matter. It is a methodical and detailed letter, as if he hardly trusted his wife's acumen.[38] Above all, he urged her not to let Lydia marry unless she had taken care to see that she would herself be provided for after marriage. He also wondered whether his wife might like to give something to

---

* Sterne must have been aware of this tendency. In *A Sentimental Journey*, the Comte de Bissy asks whether Yorick is a jester: 'I answered, Indeed I did jest—but was not paid for it—'twas entirely at my own expence.' (*SJ*, Vol. II, The Passport, Versailles.)

his sister, Catherine. Was she still in London? Had Sterne met her? Could he not give her something himself?

For all the size of his estate, he seems to have been out of pocket at the moment of departure, for almost his last action of the year was to beg his good friend Garrick for a loan of £20 – to have gone abroad without it, he explained, would have been 'less ... than a prudent man ought'.[39]

1762

There were moments when Sterne believed he had gone to France for his health, others when he hoped to show Europe one of its greatest literary inventors or to look into the better ordering of affairs in France. But if we judge the intention by what he found in the country, then he had no other desire except to look into the variety of thought and feeling. Rather than notice the large political events or the intellectual turmoil of France, Yorick is struck by the grand metaphor of a Parisian barber. He concludes that, in France, 'the grandeur is *more* in the *word*; and *less* in the *thing*', and adds, 'I think I can see the precise and distinguishing marks of national characters more in these nonsensical *minutiae*, than in the most important matters of state.'[1]

It is with *A Sentimental Journey* that the difference between Sterne's life and art is most obvious. Both Sterne and Yorick had visited France, but Yorick's journey is the more important for man because of the way it manages to be an exploration not of terrain or foreigners but of an impossible Utopia of imaginative sensibility. Sterne boasted that he kept his eyes and heart open so as to register whatever human emotions he encountered. But we should remember that he set out as an invalid. And, like an invalid, he kept to himself, hardly understanding what he saw but sufficiently soothed by motion, change and the reckless accumulation of his imagination. He may have carried his own fantasy with him, as indifferent to onlookers as Harpo Marx. When Yorick first arrived in Calais he very quickly shut himself up in an idle chaise so as to put down a definition of himself as a traveller. In a moment, the vehicle was trembling with the agitation of this writing as if it had caught the occupant's fever.

'I am very ill,' wrote Sterne to Lady Dacre on 1 January
1762, 'having broke a vessel in my lungs.'[2] He attributed this
crisis to the strain of hard writing and preaching in the summer
before. In the dedication to Volumes V and VI, to Lord
Spencer, he had called them the best he could do 'with such bad
health as I have', just as he had ended Volume IV with the
promise to be back 'unless this vile cough kills me in the mean-
time'. 'I believe I shall try if the south of France will not be of
service to me,' he told Lady Dacre, and had 'great hopes of its
efficacy'.[3]

Yet France and England were still at war. On 2 January,
Lady Mary Wortley Montagu thought 'The Peace seems to be
more distant than ever.'[4] The peace preliminaries were not, in
fact, signed until 3 November 1762, and yet Sterne, in company,
took ship from Dover in January 1762, sailed over to Calais and
was made as welcome there as Yorick. Passports were necessary,
and it seems that Pitt helped Sterne in England and Choiseul in
France. It was certainly a civilized war that allowed the warring
parties to share their celebrities.

In France, Sterne was welcomed for being English and a
member of the victorious race. We have only to read Rousseau's
Confessions to see how far French failure was interpreted by
many Frenchmen as an omen of radical change. He noted an
accelerating collapse of government: 'the incredible disorder in
the public finances; the perpetual disagreements in the administration, until then conducted by two or three ministers at
open feud, who in injuring one another were ruining the whole
Kingdom; the general discontent of the common people and of
every other class'.[5] Disaster had been averted, Rousseau
believed, only because power had fallen to Choiseul. Sterne not
only coincided with a fashion for the English but probably
arrived as the first notable visitor after several lean years. Here
again, luck aided him. He had chanced upon a vacant season in
London in 1760 and now came to Paris with extra novelties to
reinforce his own. No wonder then that his reception in Paris
was very like that in London.

Sterne embarked with George Pitt and his secretary Richard
Phelps, friends of Henry Egerton, son of the bishop of Hereford,
with whom he had spent some time before leaving. Phelps

wrote to Egerton that Sterne was already 'better than when he left Town' and Sterne admitted to being, 'much mended. . . . Goodness! What shall I be in the balsamic air of Languedoc . . .' They moved on to Dover and his improvement was maintained with the prospect of travel: 'I am ten, nay 15 per Cent better.' He sent his thanks and kindest respects to the Egertons for the way they had treated him and assured them, 'Don't think . . . I am in a lowly frame of vile Spirits—I am so troublesome to Phelps by the Extravagance of my good Spirits, by which I turn all things in the house, upside down—'6

He arrived in Paris on about 16 January, delighted to discover 'Tristram was almost as much known here as in London.'7 That was a sanguine estimate. *Tristram Shandy* had not yet been translated and Phelps guessed that there were not five people in Paris who had a copy, and no one who understood the book. 'They know however that Tristram is a great Genius in his own Country, and he would very probably be so in this, if he would but learn to speak before he attempts talking.'8

Even Sterne admitted that he hardly knew what he was saying or what was being said to him. He may have had 'a fortnight's dinners and suppers upon my hands',9 but his head was not stilled. He thought he spoke French 'fast and fluent, but incorrect both in accent and phrase; but the French tell me I speak it most surprisingly well for the time.'10 But if that sometimes made him comic, he was confident that 'The French love such a nonsensical fellow as I am, & I have found little difficulties in getting into some of the best Circles; & am moving on with ten times the rapidity I ever moved before . . .'11

Sterne's performance in Paris must sometimes have wandered into farce and been a thorough test of a defeated nation's respect for literary fame among their opponents. This clergyman's outrageousness, for all that it entertained Paris, would have seemed weirdly inconsequential to circles conspiring towards a genuine revolution in social and intellectual attitudes. At least one young Frenchman, Jean Baptiste Suard, pursued Sterne, intent on noting the behaviour of this novel specimen. Suard was a serious young man: enough to have chosen prison for a brief period rather than inform on a friend, and to be embarked on a supplement to that immense work, *Clarissa*

Harlowe. He was very intrigued by the variety of Sterne's character:

Ce qui lui persuadait le plus que tout était vrai dans cet anglais, original même pour les Anglais, c'est qu'il était toujours et partout le même, jamais déterminé par des projets, et toujours emporté par des impressions; dans nos théâtres, dans nos salons, sur nos ponts, toujours un peu à la merci des objets et des personnes, toujours prêt à être amoureux ou pieux, bouffon ou sublime.[12]

But Suard nevertheless expected a properly considerate explanation from Sterne of the ingredients of his genius. It is easy to imagine Sterne eyeing so diligent an interviewer: it is the Reynolds face again. The ingredients? Above all, he replied, '*imagination, sensibilité*' – 'cette flamme immortelle qui nourrit la vie et la dévore'; secondly, daily reading of the Old and New Testaments; and thirdly, the study of John Locke.[13]

It was this paragon who sat down to dinner on 4 June (the King's birthday) at the table of Lord Tavistock. Sterne did not realize that he was sitting next to Louis Dutens and asked his neighbour if he knew a man called Dutens. 'Intimately', was the answer. The assembly laughed and Sterne took this as a sign that Dutens was a notorious oddity. 'Is not he rather a strange fellow?' he asked Dutens, who agreed wholeheartedly. Whereupon Sterne embarked on a lengthy description of this Dutens, extravagantly inventive. This amused everyone and, supposedly, it was only when Dutens had left that the masquerade was explained to Sterne. Dutens' account of the incident has a chastened Sterne, afraid that high spirits might have given offence and even wondering whether Dutens would demand satisfaction.[14] But as with so many Sterne stories, it is open to various interpretations. Perhaps Sterne truly blundered, thereby convincing Frenchmen of his strangeness. On the other hand, suppose he guessed that his companion was Dutens and merely thought to be playful?

Flexibility invades every interpretation of Sterne. And for all his rapid motion in Paris, it was agitation of the surface alone. He met everyone in the city, just as he had in London. And as in London, hardly an acquaintance stuck: the Prince of Conti, Michel-Étienne Lepeletier, the comte de Choiseul, baron

d'Holbach, the comte de Bissy, baron de Bagge, Buffon and
Diderot – a stream of footnotes, the names invariably mangled
in Sterne's letters. They called him 'ce Chevalier Shandy' and
he Shandied 'it away fifty times more than I was ever wont'.[15]
His French was uncertain, his emotion spilling over as improved
health seemed to presage a renewed imaginative potency. Soon
he was saying so many things that distorted reports drifted
back to him: 'I do a thousand things which cut no figure, *but in
the doing*—and as in London, I have the honour of having done
and said a thousand things I never did or dream'd of—and yet
I dream abundantly . . .'[16]

Here is Sterne's self-mystification, pouring from him as
profusely as the coloured smoke from a stage genie's lamp.
There is, indeed, hardly a single verifiable fact about Sterne in
Paris. Instead, we have a jumble of names and impressions in his
letters, a host of stories told by onlookers and that rose-coloured
view that Sterne cast over all his surroundings. He met the
comte de Bissy who was at that moment reading *Tristram
Shandy*; the comte immediately invited the author to make use
of a private way through his own rooms to see the Duke of
Orleans' paintings.

That odd incident was magnified into an entire sequence in
A Sentimental Journey in which Yorick applies to Bissy for a
passport (the emphasis on this suggests that in France, at least,
the passport was important enough to give Sterne some
anxiety). The two men talk of various things, including women.
Bissy is persuaded that Yorick has 'not come to spy the nakedness of the land', but what about ladies in the same condition?
Yorick, however, 'cannot bear the shock of the least indecent
insinuation; in the sportability of chit-chat I have often en-
deavoured to conquer it'. He insists that he would look only into
'the *nakedness* of their hearts'.

Bissy leaves Yorick for a moment and, rather than attempt
to fathom this action, Yorick dips into a volume of Shakespeare
and is 'transported . . . instantly'. There then follows a reflection of extraordinary frankness from Yorick/Sterne on his
instinct for taking flight from unhappiness, failure and boredom
in fantasy. Cut off from the mundane contacts of small talk,
Sterne used a foreign land to discover the most satisfying ways

into his own revery. For anyone who might doubt the modern flavour of Sterne's writing, compare this passage with some of the twentieth-century reports of excursions along narcotic highways:

Sweet pliability of man's spirit, that can at once surrender itself to illusions, which cheat expectation and sorrow of their weary moments!—long—long since had ye number'd out my days, had I not trod so great a part of them upon this enchanted ground: when my way is too rough for my feet, or too steep for my strength, I get off it, to some smooth velvet path which fancy has scattered over with rose-buds of delights; and having taken a few turns in it, come back strengthen'd and refresh'd.[17]

Occasionally Sterne guessed that his physical health must have improved for him to be enjoying himself so much. 'I have got a colour into my face now,' he wrote to his wife, 'though I came with no more than there is in a dishclout.'[18] He was entertained by reports from London that he had died* and sympathized with Lord Fauconberg for the 'dismal foggy winter in Town'[19] and with his wife for the 'terrible snows in Yorkshire'.[20] Paris had been frosty, but Sterne was sure it had saved him. Had he remained in London he 'had certainly been six weeks ago in my grave'. The air in Paris had obscure Shandean benefits, being 'clear always & Elastick'.[21]

On arriving in Paris, he realized, he had been so ill that doctors advised him against going farther south. But by April he had arranged to rent a little house with a large garden in Toulouse so that he might spend 'one winter free from coughs & colds'. Such a measure was all the more necessary because his daughter had been ill that winter with 'this vile Asthma of hers, which these last 3 winters has been growing worse & worse, & that unless something more than bare Medecines can be done for her, she will be lost'.[22] Was Sterne so sure of his own good nature that he could persuade himself that he had come to France to test the climate for Lydia?

One by one, Sterne ticked off the sights of the town. He had

---

* On 12 February 1762, the *Public Advertiser* had reported Sterne's death in Paris. On 8 March, Sterne wrote to Egerton: 'I find by the last english papers here, I am once more alive, & now tis high time to write to You or never – Strange! that a man should be so inconsistent!' (Arthur Cash, *TLS*, 8 April 1965.)

fallen in with the twelve-year-old Charles James Fox, who was
being escorted about Europe by George Macartney, and went
with Fox to see Clairon, the star actress of the Comédie Française, in *Iphigenie en Tauride*, by de la Touche. She was 'extremely
great' he told Garrick, 'would to God you had one or two like
her.'[23] He had also seen Clairon's rival, Marie-Francoise
Dumesnil, and thought her 'in some places, still greater'. But
the French theatre had a preponderance of tragedies and Sterne
complained that 'they have nothing here, which gives the nerves
so smart a blow, as those great characters in the hands of G!'[24]
So recently in London and a known friend of the English
actor, Sterne must have been frequently consulted about
Garrick's performances. He was even offered a play in the hope
that he might recommend it to Garrick. But he was not impressed by this piece: 'It has too much sentiment in it, (at
least for me) the speeches too long, and savour too much of
preaching—this may be a second reason, it is not to my taste—
'Tis all love, love, love, throughout, without much separation in
the character; so I fear it would not do for your stage . . .'[25] It
is interesting to see Sterne disapproving of a work for exactly
those qualities that are sometimes attributed to him, and all the
more fascinating in that the play in question was by Diderot.
Not that Sterne's theatrical instinct was at fault: the Comédie
Française had in fact turned down the play in 1757, and
when it was eventually produced, in 1771, it proved to be a
failure.*

Clearly Sterne felt an association between preaching and the
theatre, and his condemnation of 'preaching' style makes the
question of his own pulpit performance all the more intriguing.
While in Paris he had been three mornings in a row to hear
Père Clement preach and thought 'his manner, more than
theatrical, and greater, both in his action and delivery, than
Madame Clairon'.[26] Clement was a theologian, confessor and
leading funeral orator who was preacher to King Stanislaus I of
Poland. Sterne was particularly interested in the stage management of Clement's performance and may have been given ideas
for further rearrangement of the pews at Coxwold:

* The play, *Le Fils naturel*, was not accepted by Garrick, but Dodsley published it
in 1767 as *Dorval*.

his pulpit, oblong, with three seats in it, into which he occasionally casts himself; goes on, then rises, by a gradation of four steps, each of which he profits by, as his discourse inclines him: in short, 'tis a stage, and the variety of his tones would make you imagine there were no less than five or six actors on it together.[27]

The Duke of Orleans had employed Carmontelle to paint Sterne's portrait in water-colour. It is a minor picture compared with the Reynolds portrait, but Carmontelle's taste for profile poses is not without interest. Sterne is leaning against the back of a chair, his right foot caught in the act of some nervous flexing. The right hand is cupped as if weighing dice, loose change or the prospect of touching some delicacy. The head leans forward on top of his fashionable coat and shirt. The nose is large and pointed, the single eye in profile like a snake's and the mouth tight shut. The skin is so tightly drawn about the skull that the wig seems more than usually unnatural. He makes a wizened, frail dandy and resembles an old man made gay by cosmetics.

The Paris society that Sterne described was almost Utopian. 'What makes these men truly entertaining & desirable,' he explained to Egerton, 'is, that they have the art, notwithstanding their Wits, of living together without biting or scratching— an infinitude of gaity & civility reigns among them—& w^t is no small art, Every man leaves the Room wth better Opinion of his own Talents than when he enterd.'[28]

There were, however, contrary views of the benefits of the society of the *philosophes*. Horace Walpole, who observed their meetings in 1765, held a far more jaundiced opinion:

The French affect philosophy, literature, and free-thinking—the first never did, and never will possess me; of the two others I have long been tired. Freethinking is for one's self, surely not for society; besides, one has settled one's way of thinking, or knows it cannot be settled; and for others I do not see why there is not as much bigotry in attempting conversions from any religion as to it.[29]

For all that he was received by the leading members of the Enlightenment, Sterne hardly seems to have encountered their ideas. We have only to read Hume's careful account of all the leading *philosophes* to realize how totally Sterne omits the talk and seriousness of Paris. Walpole put on English affront to see a company talking without restraint on religious matters in the presence of servants. Was Sterne perhaps all the more appealing to some Frenchmen because of the apparent discredit he did to the Church? There are hints that Sterne hardly knew what sort of company he was mixing in. Jean-Baptiste Tollot,* a friend of Hall-Stevenson's, reported an optimism in Sterne that might be mindless: 'Cela me fait envier quelques fois les heureuses dispositions de notre ami Mr Sterne; tous les objets sont couleur de rose pour cet heureux mortel . . .'[30] And Richard Phelps, who had by now moved on to Turin, gave some hint of the injudiciousness of Sterne's behaviour:

> Tristram is an Author, and as such, tenacious of the privilege which all great Authors claim of being the best Judges of their own Merit. We ventur'd to give him some little Advice during our stay at Paris, which I believe would do him no harm if practis'd in other Meridians as well as those of France: Tristram receiv'd it as an Author . . .[31]

It may have been the intellectual atmosphere of Paris, or more likely the effects of illness, but we can see tears gradually overtaking Sterne. On the night of 16 March 1762 there had been a fire in which the Foire Saint-Germain had been destroyed so that many of the tradesmen who had inhabited it were ruined. Sterne described in a letter to his wife how their misfortune had affected him: '*Oh! ces moments de malheur sont terribles*, said my barber to me, as he was shaving me this morning; and the good-natured fellow uttered it with so moving an accent, that I could have found in my heart to have cried over the perishable and uncertain tenure of every good in this life.'[32]

That is the first serious evocation of sentimental tears in Sterne's correspondence, just as the story of Le Fever in Volume VI of *Tristram Shandy* is the first substantial anecdote of pathetic appeal in his fiction. Death is a presence in Sterne's life from 1761 onwards, and I think it is reasonable to suppose that from that time he was conscious of the seriousness of his illness.

---

* Tollot (1698–1773), a writer and traveller, who had a few years previously taken Hall-Stevenson from Geneva to Toulouse.

Sterne, painted in Paris by Carmontelle, 1762

Shandy Hall, Coxwold, Sterne's old home now restored by the Laurence Sterne Trust

Byland Abbey, two miles to the north-east of Coxwold

From then until his death, his neurotic sympathy for the idea of things, people and situations intensified, and a sort of manic weeping was never far away. He wrote to Garrick in April: 'I laugh 'till I cry, and in the same tender moments *cry 'till I laugh.* I Shandy it more than ever, and verily do believe, that by mere Shandeism sublimated by a laughter-loving people, I fence as much against infirmities, as I do by the benefit of air and climate.'[33]

Even while he was seeking passports for his wife and daughter from Choiseul, Sterne suffered another serious attack: 'a *defluxion Poitrine* as the french Physicians call it—it is generally fatal to weak Lungs, so that I have lost in ten days all I have gain'd since I came here—& from a relaxation of my lungs have lost my voice entirely, that twill be much if I ever quite recover it'.[34] He was now determined to go to Toulouse and wrote several anxious letters to his wife with instructions for travelling to Paris.

Distance and his own weakness seem to have made his wife more endearing than she had ever been in Yorkshire. He begged Mrs. Sterne and Lydia 'to take special care of heating your blood in travelling and come *tout doucement*, when you find the heat too much'.[35] Don't leave your baggage behind the post-chaise. Have you enough money? 'I imagine you are convinced of the necessity of bringing three hundred pounds in your pocket.'[36] 'See that they do not give you a bad vehicle, when a better is in the yard, but you will look sharp—drink small Rhenish to keep you cool, (that is if you like it). Live well and deny yourselves nothing your hearts wish. So God in heav'n prosper and go along with you—'[37]

But Sterne combined an obsessive need to remind his wife of everything she was to pack with a sunny picture of the delightful journey they would all make to Toulouse. These letters are remarkable for the way they show Sterne fussing over reality – the needs of his wife's journey – and at the same time idealizing a journey and a destination that he planned for himself. He could so enjoy the idea of travel that he hardly needed to experience it:

H

I wish, when you come here, in case the weather is too hot to travel, you could think it pleasant to go to the Spaw for four or six weeks, where we should live for half the money we should spend at Paris—after that we should take the sweetest season of the vintage to go to the south of France . . .[38]

Bring your silver coffee-pot, 'twill serve both to give water, lemonade, and orjead—to say nothing of coffee and chocolate, which, by the bye, is both cheap and good at Toulouse, like other things—I had like to have forgot a most necessary thing, there are no copper tea-kettles to be had in France, and we shall find such a thing the most comfortable utensil in the house—buy a good strong one, which will hold two quarts—a dish of tea will be of comfort to us in our journey south—I have a bronze tea-pot, which we will carry also, as China cannot be brought over from England, we must make up a villainous party-coloured tea equipage to regale ourselves, and our English friends whilst we are at Toulouse—[39]

Elizabeth and Lydia Sterne arrived in Paris early in July. The weather by now was 'as hot as *Nebuchadnezzar's oven*'[40] and Lydia did 'nothing but look out of the window, and complain of the torment of being frizled'.[41] Sterne declared himself pleased to see his daughter again – 'I wish she may ever remain a child of nature—I hate children of art.'[42]

Sterne already had a coach for their trip south. He had bought it from Thomas Thornhill, a fellow-Yorkshireman, and arranged for his wife and daughter to collect it at Calais. It was a novel improvement on the two-seated chaise with a false bottom to accommodate a third person. 'You will be in raptures with your chariot,'[43] Sterne assured his family. And in due course, about the middle of July, the three of them set off. It was already enterprising for the members of a family to travel separately to the capital of a country at war with their own. Now they proposed taking to the open road, and thence to live in a provincial town. And who were these people? – an asthmatic daughter, an obdurate mother and a professional scatterbrain. It sounds like the beginning of a short story.

Partie de Campagne

'Now I think it very much amiss,' argued Tristram, excusing himself from the methodical notes of a travel writer, '—that a man cannot go quietly through a town, and let it alone, when it does not meddle with him, but that he must be turning about and drawing his pen at every kennel he crosses over ...'[1] Sterne himself gave no offence on this score. Few travellers can have been as willing to turn a blind eye to the sights of strange lands. He passed so discreetly through France and settled so unobtrusively, first in Toulouse and then in Montpellier, that his biography almost lies idle for eighteen months. Although it is sometimes said that, from his appearance in London in March 1760 until his death, Sterne never stepped off a tread-mill of fame and excitement, he declined in provincial France into a torpor as frustrating as anything he had known in York-shire. Eventually, he was compelled to extract himself from that stagnation by returning to Paris and England. Although he had set off from Paris with the assurance to Becket that 'I am very hard at Work and when I am got down to my house at Toulouse in the South of France you will soon see ab^t What',[2] he wrote hardly a word there. He had moved into another world, as suddenly as he had appeared upon the London literary scene. When he re-emerged from the French provinces, and thought to employ his time there, he did not recollect actual experiences but passages from imaginary travels in which journey and novelty were the medicines for the ill-health that had suppos-edly prompted his own trip.

But Sterne's spirits were not unallayed when he set out for Toulouse. In May, he had heard from Becket that only 2,827 sets of Volumes V and VI of *Tristram Shandy* had been sold out of the 4,000 printed. It was the first time he had not reprinted by the end of the spring season. As for the journey itself, it was more arduous than a day-dream excursion, the accidents more intractable. The summer was hot, the roads dusty and Sterne's spluttering French may not have impressed the inhabitants of the French countryside. Soon after his arrival in Toulouse, he confessed to Hall-Stevenson that 'The humour is over for France, and Frenchmen',[3] and thought how delightful it would be to spend a month at Crazy Castle.

They had come to Toulouse 'by way of Lyons, Montpellier, &c. to shorten, I trow, our sufferings'.[4] But it is typical of Sterne that he barely mentions the details of the journey, the views, the people and customs encountered. We have only to compare Sterne's vacant itinerary with the compendium of irritations, grumbles and complaints suffered by Smollett a year later on much the same route to see how unobservant Sterne was of actuality. He later criticized Smollett for his perpetual complaint, but for anyone interested in the reality of provincial travel Smollett is crammed with detail. Sterne spoke of his journey in his fiction and there he has given himself all the properly lit charm and ghostly comfort of a Hollywood cowboy swaying to and fro on a rocking horse in front of an unwinding projection of landscape.

Only in one letter, to Robert Foley, his Paris banker, does Sterne admit the afflictions of his journey:

> In our journey we suffered so much from the heats, it gives me pain to remember it—I never saw a cloud from Paris to Nismes half as broad as a twenty-four sols piece.—Good God! we were toasted, roasted, grill'd, stew'd and carbonaded on one side or other all the way—and being all done enough (*assez cuits*) in the day, we were eat up at night by bugs, and other unswept out vermin, the legal inhabitants (if length of possession gives right) of every inn we lay at.—Can you conceive a worse accident than that in such a journey, in the hottest day and hour of it, four miles from either tree or shrub which could cast a shade of the size of one of Eve's fig leaves—that we should break a hind wheel into ten thousand pieces, and be obliged in consequence to sit five hours on a gravelly road, without one drop of water or possibility of getting any—[5]

An actual three-week plod to Toulouse proved so contrary to

the rhapsodic expectations that Sterne had entertained in Paris that he gave up the account. This neglect is worth emphasizing. Within the next year Sterne was to find himself short of money and of material for his fiction. An author of his reputation could surely have relied on an audience for an account of travels and of life in the south of France. But Sterne preferred not to explore documentary and, to excuse himself from this, he remarked ironically on the glibness with which travel writers made themselves into authorities:

> No;—I cannot stop a moment to give you the character of the people—their genius—their manners—their customs—their laws—their religion—their government—their manufactures—their commerce—their finances, with all the resources and hidden springs which sustain them: qualified as I may be, by spending three days and two nights amongst them . . .[6]

But such diffidence reveals more about Sterne than about travel writing. The vogue for descriptive accounts of travels was itself indicative of English curiosity and of the confidence that a sensible man could indeed comprehend and convey valuable information about a country simply by passing through it. Defoe in England and Smollett in France are equally instructive in their elaborate descriptions and in their faith in their own reliability.

Sterne had not reported Yorkshire, York or London, why should he be more able to give a clear account of France? It is his need to re-invent everything he sees, to subordinate it to the dominating throb of his own reactions, that denies him the solace of ever feeling at home. Thus when, with some desperation, Sterne proposed to occupy Volume VII of *Tristram Shandy* with an account of a journey through France, it was only ostensibly like the one he had made. Emotionally, it removed all the stains and bruises of that sweating, slow progress. *A Sentimental Journey* for Sterne was not just the haphazard ranging of a benign and flirtatious eye, but the absorption of the author in all the bland warmth of day-dream. For all that it was a method that produced some of Sterne's finest writing, it was also a means to seal him off completely from actuality.

Sterne's fancy was to present Tristram's speed through

France as a gay escape from death. But the dying usually travel with more reserve; only imaginary invalids have the strength left to hurry. Was Sterne's mysterious disease one that could be frightened away by its victim's impersonation of invalidism? And as for vehicles, Tristram knows that 'When the precipitancy of a man's wishes hurries on his ideas ninety times faster than the vehicle he rides in—woe be to truth! and woe be to the vehicle and its tackling (let 'em be made of what stuff you will) upon which he breathes forth the disappointment of his soul!'[7]

Tristram's post-chaise disintegrates – 'What's wrong now?— Diable!—a rope's broke!—a knot has slipt!—a staple's drawn! —a bolt's to whittle!—a tag, a rag, a jag, a strap, a buckle, or a buckle's tongue, want altering.'[8] Sterne is so far away from the inconvenience that he can make Tristram 'never chaff, but take the good and the bad as they fall in my road'.[9] Thus Tristram occupies his waiting and his boredom with the story of the Abbess of Andouillets (which only shows that Sterne's dirty stories, for all that they may have delighted the gatherings at Skelton Castle, are neither short nor dirty enough), with the visit of the Shandy brothers to the abbey of St. Germain at Auxerre and with Sterne's frustrated search at Lyons for the tomb of Amandus and Amanda, legendary lovers who survived cruel separation and met again long years afterwards only 'to fly into each other's arms, and both drop down dead for joy'. Such a black comedy was guaranteed to appeal to Tristram:

> I walk'd with all imaginable joy towards the place—when I saw the gate which intercepted the tomb, my heart glowed within me—
> —Tender and faithful spirits! cried I, addressing myself to *Amandus* and *Amanda*—long—long have I tarried to drop this tear upon your tomb—I come—I come—
> When I came—there was no tomb to drop it upon.[10]

Sterne's tears were secured by long strings and could be retrieved after use. Not that those tears were fraudulent; but no weeping eye was ever clearer. And when Tristram is attracted to converse with an ass – 'there is a patient endurance of sufferings, wrote so unaffectedly in his looks and carriage, which pleads so mightily for him, that it always disarms me'[11] – he manages both to play upon the anthropomorphic soulfulness of the Disney in us all and still watch the balance of his own feelings:

> ... thou hast not a friend perhaps in all this world, that will give thee a macaroon.—In saying this, I pull'd out a paper of 'em, which I had just purchased, and gave him one—and at this moment that I am telling it, my heart smites me, that there was more of pleasantry in the conceit, of seeing *how* an ass would eat a macaroon—than of benevolence in giving him one, which presided in the act.[12]

Is this honesty, self-exposure or even self-destruction? Whatever our answer, it is clearly insufficient to accuse Sterne of mindless escape into revery. Thus he alludes in passing to one essential condition for the free-ranging charm of a sentimental journey: Tristram, his father and uncle are travelling without Mrs. Shandy. She has remained at home knitting worsted breeches, 'to keep things right during the expedition' and to give full play to her husband's 'systems and opiniatry—they were of so odd, so mixed and tragicomical a contexture'.[13]

The remains of Tristram's journey, from Lyons through Montpellier to Toulouse, may be just the fulfilment of those diversions Sterne's wife and daughter dissuaded him from. At Lyons, for instance, Tristram gives up his coach and plans to sail down the Rhone to Avignon. This was a usual practice. But travellers who had arranged a journey by land still had to pay the stage money for the coach route. Such duplication may have deterred Sterne and one need only sample Tristram's rhapsody upon the river trip to suspect that it was one Sterne never experienced himself:

> With what velocity, continued I, clapping my two hands together, shall I fly down the rapid *Rhone*, with the Vivares on my right-hand, and Dauphiny on my left, scarce seeing the ancient cities of Vienne, *Valence*, and *Vivieres*. What a flame will it rekindle in the lamp, to snatch a blushing grape from the *Hermitage* and *Côte rôtie*, as I shoot by the foot of them? and what a fresh spring in the blood! to behold upon the banks advancing and retiring, the castles of romance, whence courteous knights have whilome rescued the distress'd—and see vertiginous, the rocks, the mountains, the cataracts, and all the hurry which Nature is in with all her great works about her—[14]

Carried away by this stream of imaginary consciousness, Sterne relaxes under the pleasant sun (only the real one burns) and congratulates himself on giving Death the slip. He plans now to take a mule and 'traverse the rich plains of *Languedoc* upon his back, as slowly as foot could fall'.[15] This is very near to the slow clip-clop of Yorick through his village. It is a strange Ruritanian donkey-ride Sterne imagines across a plain that could only be located in a man's mind:

—by stopping and talking to every soul I met who was not in a full trot—joining all parties before me—waiting for every soul behind—hailing all those who were coming through cross roads—arresting all kinds of beggars, pilgrims, fiddlers, fryars—not passing by a woman in a mulberry-tree without commending her legs, and tempting her into conversation with a pinch of snuff—In short, by seizing every handle, of what size or shape soever, which chance held out to me in this journey—[16]

This is as encouraging as a travel agent and in Montpellier Tristram meets 'a sunburnt daughter of Labour' who might have stepped down from a travel poster. She is complete in every detail, even down to the slit in her petticoat that catches in the corner of every other sentence.

Viva la joia! was in her lips—*Viva la joia!* was in her eyes. A transient spark of amity shot across the space betwixt us . . . why could not a man sit down in the lap of content here—and dance, and sing, and say his prayers, and go to heaven with this nut brown maid? Capriciously did she bend her head on one side, and dance up insiduous—[17]

The brothel of the mind is infinitely accommodating and he does not need actual satisfaction from this 'desert island' girl. In a moment, "tis time to dance off' by way of Narbonne and Carcassonne, all the way to Toulouse.

Sterne had hired a town house in Toulouse 'well furnish'd, and elegant beyond any thing I look'd for'. It had a courtyard and a garden 'laid out in serpentine walks'. As for its interior, there was 'a good *salle à manger* above stairs joining to the very great *salle à compagnie* as large as the Baron D'Holbach's; three handsome bed-chambers with dressing rooms to them—below stairs two very good rooms for myself, one to study in, the other to see company.—I have moreover cellars round the court, and all other offices.'[18] In addition, he rented a country property, two miles outside Toulouse, in the grounds of which was a summer house.

It seemed an ideal arrangement – on the threshold, at least. For the two houses, Sterne had to pay only £30 a year, and 'all things are cheap in proportion.'[19] His amenable landlord had agreed to look after the garden. They had a good cook, 'a decent *femme de chambre*, and a good looking *laquais*'.[20] It was a cheap place: Mrs. Sterne could keep 'an excellent good house, with *soupe, boulli, roti*—&c. &c. for two hundred and fifty pounds a year'.[21] But she irked her husband by being 'against all schemes of additional expenses'. With good reason, for they had very little income now from Sterne's books. In March 1763 he heard from Becket that only another 182 sets of Volumes V and VI had been sold in the last ten months:[22] to remove the author from the market was to kill demand. But he was writing nothing new at Toulouse.

There was English company in the town, but he wrote to Hall-Stevenson that he was 'as much out of the road of all intelligence here as at the Cape of Good Hope'.[23] Lydia's French was improving and she was 'hard at it with musick, dancing'.[24] The thought that her family was settled again may have allowed her to forget her asthma. But her father seemed less robust than when he had been in training to escape Death. Soon after their arrival in Toulouse Sterne had fallen ill with 'an epidemic vile fever which killed hundreds about me'.[25] And although Toulouse was a leading resort of consumptives, Sterne had acquired a poor opinion of the doctors there – 'the errantest charlatans in Europe, or the most ignorant of all pretending fools'. He had ignored their opinions and 'recommended my affairs entirely to Dame Nature'. That, he said, had made him 'stout and foolish again as a happy man can wish to be'.[26]

But plump contentment was no part for Sterne to play. Toulouse was good enough but 'not to my taste'. And the French had let him down until he was left with only their *ennui*, 'the eternal platitude of the French characters—little variety, no originality in it at all . . . for they are very civil—

but civility itself, in that uniform, wearies and bodders one to death—If I do not mind, I shall grow most stupid and sententious—'.[27]

It should be explained that Sterne slipped into *ennui* at a time when Toulouse was undergoing serious commotion. Whereas, in England, religious differences were being muffled, in France there was fierce antipathy between Catholic and Protestant. In Paris, Sterne had been interested in the growing feeling against the Jesuits. The Society had been critically embarrassed by French defeats in the Seven Years War. In particular, their mission in Martinique had been bankrupted. When creditors obtained a judgement against the Society, its leaders appealed to the Paris parliament. This action only exposed the Society to a further attack, headed by Choiseul and Mme de Pompadour. The struggle had begun while Sterne was in Paris, and by the time he reached Toulouse the Jesuits had been banned from all political activity. In Toulouse itself, there had occurred a notable atrocity. A young Catholic, Marc-Antoine Calas, had committed suicide, but suspicions in the city had fallen upon his Protestant father, Jean. Calas *père* was broken on the wheel, in March 1762, only months before Sterne's arrival, and tortured to death. The rest of his family had been persecuted and the widow fled to Switzerland where Voltaire took up her case, eventually with success. Toulouse suffered a spate of executions and recrimination, a rehearsal for terror.

It was a cold winter, but at Christmas the English colony took heart with amateur dramatics. They planned a production of *The provok'd husband; or a journey to London,* by Vanbrugh and Colley Cibber, which Sterne thought of adapting to a journey to Toulouse. He spoke of 'a happy society living all together like Brothers & Sisters'.[28] But he was worried at having 'no more than half a dozen Guineas in his pocket—& a thousand Miles from home—& in a Country where he can as soon raise the Devil, as a six Livre piece to go to market with'.[29] He was writing regularly to Foley in Paris asking for advances and wondering why cheques were so slow in reaching him. Becket sent only bleak reports about the sale of *Tristram Shandy*: 'You tell me you scarse sell any of them'[30] mourned Sterne.

Soon after Christmas, Sterne became involved as the bedside companion to a young English invalid who was dying at Toulouse. This was George Oswald, the son of Richard Oswald, a prosperous Scottish merchant with interests in Jamaica and Virginia. Sterne may have been especially drawn to the young man's plight because he was a fellow-consumptive. Oswald had come from Italy and sought medical treatment on the way at Montpellier. For a month he had followed the advice of a 'Mr. F—'only to decline still further. At last he confronted the doctor: 'I take your prescriptions punctually; but, instead of being the better for them, I have now not an hour's remission from the fever in the four-and-twenty.' The doctor is supposed not to have been surprised. Such deterioration was, he said, predictable in the sharp air of Montpellier. Oswald was appalled by this cynicism: 'Then you are a sordid villain for allowing me to stay here till my constitution is irretrievable.'[31] With that, he set out for Toulouse.

There, he was treated by the Professor of Physic at Toulouse University and attended by men from two Churches; Sterne himself and a Catholic priest, who, 'notwithstanding' his Popishness, won Sterne's admiration for 'the goodness of his disposition'.[32] Sterne insisted on a full diagnosis from the professor at Toulouse and reported the gloomy prognosis to John Mill, the agent for the Oswald family in London.

Within a week of the prognosis, on 2 March, Sterne reported the death of young Oswald to Mill: at eleven o'clock the previous night in Sterne's arms. Before the young man died he had asked Sterne for an honest estimate of his chances and Sterne had found it a 'dismal task':

He received the news in such a manner as would put Philosophy, with all its cant, to the blush. 'God's will be done, my good friend,' said he, without any emotion but that of religion; and taking hold of my hand, he added that he was more grateful for this last act of friendship and thank'd me more for it than for all the others he had received . . .[33]

The physical exhaustion of sitting up with Oswald for four nights and the emotional demands made by his death 'brought on a spitting of blood (tho' slight) with a fever'[34] in Sterne himself. This cannot have been helped by the difficulties of tying up Oswald's affairs. Indeed, Sterne wrote to Mill of having snatched the dead man's effects 'out of the hands of villainy and extortion', and of fights with 'a brace of fiery ecclesiasticks'[35] in efforts to have Oswald properly buried.

But perhaps the most significant part of the story was Sterne's presence at the post-mortem on Oswald. The young man had insisted on this in advance because he had once been shot in the area of the lungs and wished to establish whether or not his consumption derived from that wound. The professor of anatomy at Toulouse performed the operation, but it is likely that no one watched as keenly as Sterne. Here was a man well aware of his own consumption observing the full accomplishment of the disease. The uncovered lungs were 'full of abscesses—the right lobe almost entirely scirrhous and both of 'em adhering to the pleura to the greatest degree that the physician and surgeon had ever seen, so that 'twas a miracle he had lived at all these last 3 months'.[36]

This session round the anatomist's table may have been Sterne's most penetrating experience in Toulouse, the more so for the odd congruence between Oswald's wound and the fact that Sterne believed his own father had been irrevocably damaged by the wound incurred at Gibraltar. In this case at Toulouse, the surgeon exonerated the earlier bullet, but the similar circumstances must have enforced the drama of those ravaged lungs for Sterne.

It is worth noting that his account of the autopsy is sober and exact, very far from the palpitating account of Le Fever's death. And yet in the same letter in which Sterne described the operation, he dropped hints about his heroic defence of Oswald's scant effects and looked forward to 'some evening's chitchat'[37] with Mill when he could convey details of the affair too shocking to be committed to paper.

Sterne's tone to Mill was that of an equal, eager to acquire a new friend, particularly one in the City. But when Sterne wrote directly to Richard Oswald, as he had promised the dying son he would, he was much more circumspect and commonplace in his condolence. Indeed, far from the lively, touching and precise account he had given Mill, Sterne treated the bereaved father to the sort of homily that any vicar would need to have off pat. Here is the voice of pious formality and the proof that Sterne was able to make use of it:

> But He, my dear Sir, who loved him more than father or mother or the tenderest of his friends, has thought fit to order things otherwise. His will be done. It is the only consolation under the many heartfelt losses of this kind we are smit with in this turbulent passage, and devoutly do I pray to Him who directs all our events that you may bear up against this and recover the wound, if possible, without a scar . . .*[38]

Resuming his own passage, Sterne proposed in the spring of 1763 to move on to Bagnères de Bigorre, a spa eighty miles away in the foothills of the Pyrenees, 'where I expect much health and much amusement from the concourse of adventurers from all corners of the earth'.[39] He might even spend the next winter in Italy – 'but this is a sketch only, for in all things I am governed by circumstances.' By June, just as he was setting out for Bagnères, he contemplated venturing into Spain, 'which is enough for a fertile brain to write a volume upon'.[40] Already, though, he had thoughts of going back to England. Only dread of the English winter kept him in France.

Bagnères proved a disappointment, and the nearness to Spain only permitted 'the Thiness of the pyrenean Air' to bring on 'continual breaches of Vessels in my Lungs, & with them all the Tribe of evils insident to a pulmonary Consumption'.[41] They had therefore packed up again and travelled across the south of France to such an extent that Sterne marvelled that they had not been arrested as spies. They seem to have tried to find lodgings at both Aix and Marseilles before settling on the very centre of the consumptive trade, Montpellier.

Now that the peace was agreed on, there was an increasing number of English visitors, both sick and strong, to France. At Montpellier, Sterne encountered William Hewett, an occasional member of the Skelton companionhood and an eccentric to rival Sterne himself. The French were quickly adapting their

---

* When her own father had died and she was scouting for funds, Lydia Sterne tried to locate Richard Oswald and a Mills (*sic*), believing 'they were both extreamly intimate with my poor Father.' (*Letters*, Lydia Sterne to Thomas Becket, 6 October 1768, p. 442.)

fashions to suit the English. Smollett, who passed through Montpellier only a couple of months after Sterne arrived there, had noticed the reason for the high prices that had driven the Sternes back and forth:

This imposition is owing to the concourse of English who come hither, and, like simple birds of passage, allow themselves to be plucked by the people of the country, who know their weak side, and make their attacks accordingly. They affect to believe that all the travellers of our country are grand signeurs, immensely rich, and incredibly generous; and we are silly enough to encourage this opinion by submitting quietly to the most ridiculous extortion, as well as by committing acts of the most absurd extravagance. This folly of the English, together with a concourse of people from different quarters, who come hither for the re-establishment of their health, has rendered Montpellier one of the dearest places in the south of France.[42]

Sterne undoubtedly met Smollett in Montpellier. It was from there that Smollett reported the story of young Oswald, as told to him by 'Mrs. St—e'. As everywhere else abroad, the English courted one another and Smollett mentioned being visited by four or five English families, 'among whom I could pass the winter very agreeably, if the state of my health and other reasons did not call me away'.[43] Smollett was heading for Italy, conducting his family across Europe with a critical eye on the countryside. In *A Sentimental Journey*, Sterne referred to Smollett as 'the learned SMELFUNGUS' who 'set out with the spleen and jaundice,* and every object he passed by was discoloured or distorted—He wrote an account of them, but 'twas nothing but the account of his miserable feelings.'[44] Smollett did complain, but always in terms that persuade one of honest dislike or disapproval. He also frequently praised what he saw. In the vicinity of Nîmes, for instance, he thought the Pont du Garde 'so unaffectedly elegant, so simple, and majestic, that I will defy the most phlegmatic and stupid spectator to behold it without admiration'.[45] As for the amphitheatre there, 'it is ravishingly beautiful. The whole world cannot parallel it.'[46] Sterne seems

---

* Smollett had chronic rheumatism and may have been soured by an untreated ulcer. Equally, Sterne perhaps hissed at Smollett because of the Scot's association with the *Critical Review*.

to have noticed neither; he may have been too busy stopping himself from becoming sententious.

He had reason for disenchantment: his health had not improved; he had relegated himself to the provinces; his family life was no more rewarding; he had idled away the time; he was short of money. Sterne had found Smollett's view of French prices correct. He had even had to haggle with Oswald's doctor over the fee and decided that the defeated French thought the English made of money. There are few more revealing items in Sterne's letters than one from Montpellier, on 24 November 1763, to John Mill, that recent but unmet acquaintance to whom he had offered himself as a friend to make up for the loss of Oswald:

My dear Sir, will you be so kind to me as to lend me fifty pounds till I get to England or rather give me leave to draw upon You to the extent of that Summ, in case I should find it needful upon winding up my bottoms on leaving this Country: now it seems a little para-doxical, when I have so many friends and wellwishers I live with as Brothers, I should rather take this Liberty with a friend whose face I never yet saw—but the truth, upon running ove[r] the List over in my mind, I found not one, I could take such a Liberty with, wth less pain of heart—which is all the apology I will make.[47]

Early in January 1764 Sterne fell ill again and 'suffered in this scuffle with death terribly'.[48] His wife and daughter had taken a crucial decision not to go back with him to England. He told Foley, 'We all live the longer—at least the happier—for having things our own way.'[49] It was, in truth, a broken family. No matter how difficult a woman Elizabeth Sterne was, who can doubt that Sterne's own detachment from real people was the essential cause of failure?

'I shall be in high spirits, and every step I take that brings me nearer England, will I think help to set this poor frame to rights.'[50] So he anticipated on 1 February, just as in 1762 he had looked forward to Toulouse. But the south of France had only proved his shortcomings. Henceforward that 'poor frame' had only itself and its own dreams. On the coach back to Paris he may have pulled down the blinds and tried to sleep. He spoke to neither donkeys nor nutbrown maids.

1764

Sterne was probably back in Paris by the end of February. He joined Jean-Baptiste Tollot, Thomas and George Thornhill in the Hotel d'Entragues near the Luxembourg Palace and planned to leave for London with them about the middle of April. But renewed society delayed Sterne and he was not to reach London until the end of May.

Noticeably, Sterne passed his second stay in Paris in the company of fellow-countrymen. France was now crowded out with Englishmen and Sterne could not expect the attention he had enjoyed in 1762. When the notorious go into semi-retirement they must equip themselves with extra tricks before they can make their return.

Sterne could hardly compete with Wilkes and Hume. Hume had come to Paris as secretary to the Earl of Hertford, the new Ambassador, and was frankly staggered by his reception. He had agreed to the French post reluctantly, thinking that the experience might deflect him from the resignation to failure that he had taught himself. Between 1754 and 1762 he had published his *History of England*, and this, rather more than his philosophical works, ensured him a far greater reputation in France than he had had in England. A year later, Horace Walpole was amazed that 'Mr. Hume is fashion itself, although his French is almost as unintelligible as his English.'[1] Hume's Scottish accent was so broad that strangeness may have accounted for his adulation too. Such unintelligible distinction very quickly became a model for imitation. Hume was told by Sterne that this Parisian reception was, like his own of 1760, a vogue that 'lasted only one winter'.[2]

When Hertford arrived in Paris he rented the Hotel de

Lauraguais at £500 a year. He had lavishly equipped and furnished these premises as befitted an embassy so that, according to Sterne, 'It occupied the curiosity, formed the amusement, and gave a subject of conversation to the polite circles of Paris, for a fortnight at least.'[3] The embassy contained a chapel and whom should Hertford ask to preach the first sermon there but Sterne. The request came to Sterne while he 'was playing a sober game of Whist with the *Thornhills*'.[4] When he came to choose a text for the sermon, he could not resist that capriciousness he thought so playful and amusing. An 'unlucky kind of fit seized me', he explained afterwards, 'and a very unlucky text did come into my head'.[5]

The sermon Sterne chose to initiate the splendid new embassy was based on the second book of Kings, Chapter XX – 'And Hezekiah said unto the Prophet, I have shewn them my vessels of gold, and my vessels of silver, and my wives and my concubines, and my boxes of ointment, and whatever I have in my house, have I shewn unto them: and the Prophet said unto Hezekiah, thou hast done very foolishly.'*[6]

One can imagine the anticipatory grin on Sterne's face as he announced this daring text to the celebrated congregation. How startling a beginning. But the sermon itself is one of the most skilled and searching in Sterne's collection. Sterne's equivocation, so perfectly illustrated by the spuriously sensational introduction to a conventionally excellent sermon, is further explored in the content of the sermon. As is so typical of Sterne, he does not pursue his text – that would have required a stamina for wit of which he was not capable – but immediately declares that 'it will be necessary to enlarge upon the whole story,—the reflections which will arise out of it, as we go along, may help us.'[7] Hezekiah thus becomes the corpse for a remarkable essay of psychological dissection. His contradictory feelings are offered to the listener as being universal:

We are a strange compound; and something foreign from what charity would suspect, so eternally twists itself into what we do, that not only in momentous concerns, where interest lists under it all the

---

* This is the passage as quoted by Sterne. The Bible is in fact more economical, but Sterne had noted that failing before.

powers of disguise,—but even in the most indifferent of our actions— not worth a fallacy—by force of habit, we continue it: so that whatever a man is about,—observe him,—he stands armed inside and out with two motives; an ostensible one for the world,—and another which he reserves for his own private use;—this, you may say, the world has no concern with: it might have been so; but by obtruding the wrong motive upon the world, and stealing from it a character, instead of winning one;—we give it a right, and a temptation along with it, to inquire into the affair.[8]

It is worth emphasizing that this is one of the last sermons Sterne ever preached. Later in the year, in October, he told the Archbishop of York that he had to give up preaching because of physical weakness. But to read further into the Paris sermon is to wonder whether Sterne had not also come to a crisis of identity. Apply these words to Sterne himself – and Sterne was in the habit of applying everything to himself – and we can see an admission of his own phantom that Sterne allowed himself in no other form of writing. For a moment, at least, melancholy becomes seriousness:

Is it that the principles of religion want strength, or that the real passion for what is good and worthy will not carry us high enough— GOD! thou knowest they carry us too high—we want not *to be*,—but *to seem*—

Look out of your door,—take notice of that man: see what disquieting, intriguing, and shifting, he is content to go through, merely to be thought a man of plain dealing:—three grains of honesty would save him all this trouble—alas! he has them not.—

Behold a second, under a show of piety hiding the impurities of a debauched life:—he is just entering the house of GOD:—would he was more pure—or less pious:—but then he could not gain his point.

Observe a third going on almost in the same track, with what an inflexible sanctity of deportment he sustains himself as he advances: every line in his face writes abstinence;—every stride looks like a check upon his desires: see, I beseech you, how he is cloaked up with sermons, prayers, and sacraments; and so bemuffled with the externals of religion, that he has not a hand to spare for a worldly purpose;—he has armour at least—Why does he put it on? Is there no serving GOD without all this? Must the garb of religion be extended so wide to the danger of its rending?[9]

Whatever the rest of the congregation thought of this, Hume

may have recognized method's knife cutting away at motion itself. At dinner afterwards, Hume and Sterne had 'a little pleasant sparring. . . . *David* was disposed to make a little merry with the *Parson*; and, in return, the Parson was equally disposed to make a little mirth with the *Infidel*; we laughed at one another, and the company laughed with us both.'[10] Later in the year, Sterne found it necessary to deny reports that he and Hume had had a serious dispute. Neither was truly quarrelsome, but if Hume teased it may be that he had seen further into Sterne's hollow than anyone else. Sterne passed the affair off with that inflexible cheerfulness of deportment he could assume: 'I should be most exceedingly surprized to hear that *David* ever had an unpleasant contention with any man; —and if I should be made to believe that such an event had happened, nothing would persuade me that his opponent was not in the wrong: for, in my life, did I never meet with a being of a more placid and gentle nature; and it is this amiable turn of his character, that has given more consequence and force to his scepticism, than all the arguments of his sophistry.'[11]

But if Hume could outmanœuvre Sterne in philosophical argument, there were Parisian situations in which Sterne would have been the more at ease. Hume, for instance, was greatly embarrassed by a game of charades with some fashionable ladies. Mme. d'Epinay reported that Hume was playing a sultan, sat between two beautiful 'slaves'. When they pretended to be unwilling to be loved, Hume was forced to woo them, with this resource: 'he looked at them fixedly, smote the pit of his stomach and his knees several times, and could find nothing to say but, "Well, young ladies; well, there you are, then! Well, there you are. There you are, then?"'[12] Sterne might not have been so deliberate in assuring himself that the beauties were actually at his fingertips.*

Hume was in Paris in an official capacity, but John Wilkes

---

* There should be no doubt that Hume disapproved of Sterne. In 1773, he wrote to William Strahan: 'For as to any Englishman, that Nation is so sunk in Stupidity and Barbarism and Faction that you may as well think of Lapland for an Author. The best Book, that has been writ by any Englishman these thirty Years . . . is *Tristram Shandy*, bad as it is. A remark which may astonish you; but which you will find true on Reflection.' (*Letters of David Hume to William Strahan* [Oxford, 1888], ed. G. Birkbeck Hill, 30 January 1773, p. 256.)

had fled there from the prospect of imprisonment. Wilkes, M.P. for Aylesbury, had attacked Bute and George III for the conciliatory terms of the Peace of Paris, which had returned to France her losses in the West Indies. The instrument of attack was *The North Briton*, a paper founded by Wilkes and Charles Churchill. No. 45 of *The North Briton*, published on St George's Day, 1763, included a witty and insulting tirade against the king's speech from the throne. A general warrant was issued, not naming Wilkes, and he was put in the Tower.

It was a confrontation that anticipated so much of modern history. Wilkes was roguish, immensely sarcastic, licentious and charming. He had forced a stupid and brutal response from the king and his ministers on an issue that was genuine for all that Wilkes had contrived it. He was, also, a brilliant journalist and publicist, as if realizing that justice was inseparable from control of public opinion. Wilkes was another upstart: the son of a distiller, he had married an heiress and cast her off. To perfect the picture, he was ferociously ugly, with a cross-eyed leer and a head that looked squashed.

During his stay in the Tower, Wilkes suffered the indignities of political prisoners that have since become traditional. His house was searched and his papers confiscated. But on 6 May Wilkes was cleared of the charges, released and acclaimed by the London crowd. This support only stimulated Wilkes. He next successfully sued the Secretary of State for false arrest.

Wilkes was by now the hero, not only of the mob, but of a substantial part of the urban, commercial middle class. He was anathema to the king and the establishment, who made every effort to have Wilkes deprived of his seat in Parliament. An obscene poem, 'An Essay on Women', was discovered to discredit him. He was expelled from the Commons and charged with printing the poem. An attempt was made on his life and he was seriously injured in a duel provoked by opponents. At this moment, in December 1763, he had chosen to slip away to Paris.

He and Sterne must have made a good couple in Paris. 'Sterne and I often meet, and talk of you,' Wilkes wrote to Charles Churchill. '—We have an odd party for to-night at Hope's, two lively, young, handsome actresses, Hope and his mistress—Ah! poor Mrˢ Wilkes!!!'[13] Sterne did not boast of being in Wilkes's company. Indeed, in the eyes of the high society Sterne had so lately performed for, to be seen with Wilkes was a most damaging circumstance. The young Viscount Palmerston, for instance, who happened to cross Wilkes's path in Paris in 1763, had to assure his friends in London that there had been no significance in the meeting. He received this reply from Lady Charlotte Burgoyne: 'You have perfectly cleared yourself with me in regard to having an intimacy with, or friendship for, Mr. W. Indeed, I was persuaded before I had it under your hand, that you could have no connection with so vile a man . . .'[14]

Sterne seems to have had no reservations about keeping Wilkes company, but he does not appear to have been interested in the implications of the Wilkes case. The two men were both extremists, but hardly in touch with one another. For all his aptitude for playing the scoundrel, Wilkes had unearthed an issue of central importance and held to it like a terrier. Sterne, from Wilkes's point of view, may have looked like a lap-dog half asleep with speculation. Perhaps those actresses moved Sterne more than Wilkes or liberty, for in May he was writing to Hall-Stevenson explaining his delay in 'this city of seductions':

I have been for eight weeks smitten with the tenderest passion that ever tender wight underwent. I wish, dear cosin, thou couldest concieve (perhaps thou can'st without my wishing it) how deliciously I canter'd away with it the first month, two up, two down, always upon my hânches along the streets from my hôtel to hers, at first, once—then twice, then three times a day, till at length I was within an ace of setting up my hobby horse in her stable for good an all. I might as well considering how the enemies of the Lord have blasphemed thereupon; the last three weeks we were every hour upon the doleful ditty of parting—and thou mayest concieve, dear cosin, how it alter'd my gaite and air—for I went and came like any louden'd carl, and did nothing but mix tears, and *Jouer des sentiments* with her from sun-rising even to the setting of the same . . .[15]

A 'doleful ditty of parting' invariably gave way to physical symptoms in Sterne, and as soon as this *amour* had left for the south of France, he 'fell ill, and broke a vessel in my lungs and half bled to death'.[16] But the creature of such fragile vessels could nevertheless write to his daughter, who was now in Montauban with Mrs. Sterne, advising her 'to make no friendships with the French-women—not that I think ill of them all, but sometimes women of the best principles are the most *insinuating*'.[17]

But Sterne was philosophical. As for bleeding half to death, 'Voila mon Histoire!' he cried. And when it came to leaving Paris, he was filled with a memory as enchanted and idyllically vague as Hemingway recalling the good simple life there* – 'we have lived (shag rag and bobtail), all of us, a most jolly nonsensical life of it.'[18]

His return to London was announced in the newspapers early in June. But it now had little more value than to snuff the persistent rumours that Sterne had actually died on the continent. It was the end of the London season and Sterne seems to have encountered very few of his old acquaintances. He sat briefly for another portrait by Reynolds and was entertained by Lord Ligonier, the eighty-four-year-old commander-in-chief. Had he bothered to call on his publisher, Becket would have had depressing news of the current sales of *Tristram Shandy*. Sterne chose therefore to be mysteriously busy and assured Mrs. Montagu that that was his reason for not wearying her knocker. He was already planning the next season, when he might appear to better advantage:

I am going down to write a world of Nonsense—if possible like a man of *Sense*—but there is the *Rub*. Would Apollo, or the fates, or any body else, had planted me within a League of Mrs Mountague this Summer, I could have taken my horse & gone & fetch'd Wit & Wisdome as I wanted them—as for nonsense—I am pretty well provided myself both by nature & Travel. Unless you are suffocated w^h Insense, Y^r Divinityship, next winter will you be so merciful as to recieve a Scruple or two from my hands on Sundays & Saint Days—

* The comparison with Hemingway does not stop there. The lady reader invented in *Tristram Shandy* as a stooge for the author reappears a little implausibly as a newcomer at the Plaza dos Toros in *Death in the Afternoon*. Uncle Toby and Jake Barnes in *The Sun Also Rises* share a wound 'in the place'. More fundamentally, both writers habitually weaved their own lives into their fiction and worked very hard to form and nourish their own reputations. Just like Rousseau and Sterne in the eighteenth century, so Hemingway and Mailer in this have explored the confessional boast and exploited their fictional selves out of an egotism that amounts to idealism.

in the mean time like the Publican, I must be content to worship afar off.[19]

On his return to Coxwold, he had again to answer to his archbishop's visitational return. Robert Drummond had become archbishop in October 1761 on the death of Gilbert. He was a man 'of sound sense, liberality, and goodness of heart' and he had given permission for Sterne to go to France within a few months of coming to York. Thus he may have looked with special interest on Sterne's account of how he conducted Church business at Coxwold.

The return of 1743 shows Coxwold having some 170 families and over 300 communicants. But by 1764, there are 158 families and 245 communicants.[20] Church attendance may have declined in Sterne's absence, but the figures are probably a sign of the slow diminution of rural population that accompanied the industrial concentration in south-west Yorkshire. In the 1764 return Sterne admitted that he had a residing curate, 'and always shall have one, as I fear I shall never be in a condition to do duty myself—The Curates Name is Kilner. he has served the Cure two Years and a half—By some mistakes or other, either on his side or mine, some thing has ever prevented his obtaining Priest's Orders—He shall offer himself to your Grace, the next Ordination. I allow him thirty pounds a year.'[21]

James Kilner is a sad shadow in Sterne's career. He had been engaged as assistant curate to Coxwold in 1761 so hurriedly that the appointment had not been properly confirmed. In May 1762, Sterne had written to Drummond from Paris backing Kilner's candidacy for the priesthood, although confessing that he had very little personal knowledge of him: 'he came extreamly well recommended as a scholar, & a moral Man to me, from the Clergyman he last assisted; & by all I have heard from time to time of his Behaviour in the discharge of his Duty in the Parish of Coxwould, since he has given neither the Parishoners or myself cause to complain.'[22]

But Kilner himself was not happy about taking orders. He could hardly afford the journey that would be involved and wrote to Drummond that, 'Licensing might embarass me, as my Ability is yet but weakish.'[23] In 1763 Kilner had plucked up courage, but a letter of endorsement from Sterne had come too late. Thus, in 1764, Sterne found himself with a curate of two and a half years' service but no qualifications. Such a discrepancy had to be mended and Sterne testified in August, along with three other clerics, that for the past three years Kilner had 'lived piously, soberly, honestly'.

Kilner appears to have been so humble that this verdict was probably true. But it was still expedience for Sterne to attest to it and Drummond seems to have made some mild query of evidence. Sterne answered Drummond with the unconcern of a man who has made his name elsewhere: 'I know [not] whether I did do right or wrong, in signing the testimonial of Mr Kilner ... but I believed your Grace's good temper would give the only good interpretation it could admit of.'[24] Sterne then praised Kilner's morals, character and scholarship but could not prevent himself adding a damning little portrait that was both ungenerous and so contrary to his own queried reference that it indicates a disorientation in Sterne ready to relinquish everything for sake of a remark: 'I believe him a good Scholar also— I do not say, a graceful one—for his bodily presence is mean; & were he [to] stand for Ordination before a popish bishop— The poor fellow would be disabled by a Canon in a moment.'[25]

This encomium was sufficient and Kilner was duly ordained on 4 November so that Sterne could spend the winter in London with a clear conscience. Nor was Sterne's other curate, Marmaduke Callis, happy, as judged from the 1764 return. He was in charge of Sutton and Stillington for £32 a year, 'only'. Callis regretted that 'As for Catechising ye Children, I shou'd be very diligent in, but I am sorry to say it, very few will wait upon me.'[26]

Thus Sterne had two curates doing his work. He was not even able to preach. 'I am foretold by the best physicians both in france & here,' he told Drummond, 'that 'twil be fatal to me to preach.'[27] But he was not immediately prepared to write a little *Tristram* to furnish the needs of his wife and daughter in France. In July he set off 'to sojourn a week at Harrowgate', and in August he was at York for the races. There he fell in with Sarah Tuting, a girl of excellent stock, being the daughter of a racegoer and the sister of the author of the *Sporting Calendar*. Miss Tuting was bound for Italy and in the same letter that he gave instructions to his banker for paying Mrs. Sterne her allowance, Sterne asked Robert Foley to give what aid and advice he could to the racing lady. And he paid a flattering farewell to Miss Tuting herself (he was always most moved by partings): 'God be with you! in this long journey may no thorn grow near the path you tread; and when you lie down, may your pillow, gentle Sally, be soft as your own breast.'[28]

We do not know about Miss Tuting's breast, but, more used to horses, she may have thought Sterne a curious man. His letter to her is a deliberate attempt to be 'the most sentimental Letter that ever the hand of true gallantry traced out'.[29] But most of the tracing seems to be performed on the writer's soul, and the picture Sterne draws of the lady's sadness at parting may fit his own frame rather better: 'for if you hunger and thirst like a kindly Soul with too warm an impatience after those You have left behind—You will languish away the little fragment which is left of you to a shadow.'[30]

Nor did Sterne spend too much time watching the lady go. Early in September, he wrote to Hall-Stevenson on the progress of *Tristram Shandy*. 'I go on, not rapidly, but well enough with my uncle Toby's amours—There is no sitting, and cudgeling ones brains whilst the sun shines bright—'twill be all over in six or seven weeks, and there are dismal months enow after to endure suffocation by a brimstone fire-side.'[31] Rather than puzzle out his book, 'I do not think a week or ten days playing the good fellow . . . at Scarborough so abominable a thing . . . I am going to leave a few poor sheep here in the wilderness for fourteen days—and from pride and naughtiness of heart to go see what is doing at Scarborough.'[32]

Hall-Stevenson could not be enticed; he was too busy with his alum mines near Skelton. But Sterne spent at least fourteen days on the coast and 'received marvellous strength'.[33] While there, he had enjoyed the company of Lord Granby and the Earl of Shelburne. By the end of September, he had returned to his 'Philosophical Hut to finish Tristram, which I calculate will be ready for the world about Christmas'.[34]

He had had further requests for funds from Montauban and

asked Foley to forward £50 in advance of earnings from
Becket in the coming winter. Foley was somewhat alarmed to
hear from his agent in Montauban that the Sternes were
separated for life. Naturally he did not want to advance money
to a wife whose husband had given her up. Sterne anxiously
corrected this rumour – 'for in a year or two she proposes (and
indeed I expect it with impatience from her) to rejoin me'[35]–
and hoped that this might not make a bad impression in
Montauban. The separation was certainly unusual and the
parties involved may not have properly understood it themselves. Whatever the case, the need to send money regularly to
his family was to recur in Sterne's life and to put some strain on
the goodwill of his bankers.

As he was writing Volume VIII, Sterne threw in a cry of
financial complaint: 'Is it not enough that thou art in debt,
and that thou hast ten cart-loads of thy fifth and sixth volumes
still—still unsold, and art almost at thy wit's ends, how to get
them off thy hands.'[36] He had no other solution than to hope the
future would devour the past. By November, he was looking
forward to the publication of Volumes VII and VIII, and told
Foley, 'You will read as odd a Tour thro' france, as ever was
projected or executed by traveller or travell Writer, since the
world began.'[37] The winter in Coxwold only encouraged him to
set out for London. There was the boring business of enclosing
Stillington Common and 'a couple of romping girls'[38] staying
with Fauconberg that he had to entertain. There may have
been a further crisis in Sterne's health for in Volume VIII of
Tristram Shandy he confessed that he was still 'tormented with
the vile asthma' and that only 'two months ago' the sight of a
cardinal making water like a chorister had caused him to break
a vessel in his lungs from which he lost two quarts of blood.[39]

Even so, he saw no reason why he should not visit Paris again
next year, and even Italy, and looked forward to the winter
season in London: 'there I shall spend every winter of my life,
in the same lap of contentment, where I enjoy myself now—and
wherever I go—we must bring three parts in four of the treat
along with us—In short we must be happy within—and then
few things without us make much difference—This is my
Shandean philosophy.'[40]

1765

Volumes VII and VIII of *Tristram Shandy* were published on 23 January 1765. Sterne claimed that they sold well enough to give him 'a lucrative winter's campaign'[1] in London, but many found the introduction of a version of Sterne's own travels a laborious delay. The return to the Shandy household in Volume VIII was widely welcomed and Sterne was asked to abandon caprice in favour of touching revelations of Uncle Toby's life. *The Monthly Review* adopted parody as its response to these new volumes and composed a conversation between the Reviewer and Mr. Shandy. At the end of the review, Shandy mentions two further volumes and the Reviewer throws up his hands:

Ah, Mr. Shandy, your *ninth* and *tenth*! that's talking of things at a great distance! Better take a friend's advice. Stop where you are. The Public, if I guess right, will have *had enough*, by the time they get to the end of your eighth volume. . . . I am inclined to think that, all this while, you have not sufficiently cultivated your best talents. . . . Suppose you were to strike out a new plan? Give us none but amiable or worthy, or exemplary characters; or, if you will, to enliven the drama, throw in the *innocently humorous*. . . . Paint Nature in her loveliest dress – her native simplicity. Draw natural scenes, and interesting situations – In fine, Mr. Shandy, do, for surely you can, excite our passions to *laudable* purposes – awake our affections, engage our hearts – arouze, transport, refine, improve us. Let morality, let the cultivation of virtue be your aim – let wit, humour, elegance and pathos be the means; and the grateful applause of mankind will be your reward.[2]

Perhaps this advice encouraged Sterne and Becket to assemble two more volumes of Sermons. By March, Sterne foresaw the Sermons, complete with 'a prancing list of *de toute la noblesse*'[3] subscribing to them and likely to earn him £300 as well as the sale of the copyright. The money may have been a pressing consideration; not only were his wife and daughter in constant need of funds, but he hoped to visit Italy himself the following winter. Even so, he told Garrick that the money meant very little to him: 'I shall be rich in spite of myself: but I scorn you must know, in the high *ton* I take at present, to pocket all this trash.'[4]

But so casual an attitude was not likely to impress Garrick. The actor was now in Paris at the end of a continental holiday taken in the hope that absence would rekindle demand in London theatre audiences. He would have been all the more soured with Sterne's assumed indifference to the contents of his pockets by the thought of that £20 he had loaned to Sterne late in 1761 and which had never been repaid. The debt had remained in his mind. In April 1764 he had written to George Colman hoping that 'Becket has stood my friend in regard to what he ought to have received for me some time ago . . . pray hint this to him, but let him not be ungentle with Sterne.'[5]

Garrick's hint to Sterne now may have had to be a little firmer. But it did wonders with the debtor's memory, persuading him that he had recalled the sum a bare ten minutes after posting the previous letter to Garrick.

My heart smote me; & I sent to recall it—but fail'd. You are sadly to blame, Shandy! for this; quoth I, Leaning with my head on my hand, as I recriminated upon my false delicasy in the affair—Garricks nerves (if he has any left) are as fine and delicately spun, as thy own—his Sentiments as honest & friendly—thou knowest, Shandy, that he loves thee—why wilt thou hazard him a moment's pain? Puppy! Fool, Coxcomb, Jack Asse &c &c—& so I ballanced the acc^t to y^r favour.[6]

But even a letter so remorseful in the beginning could, in the space of a paragraph's fulsome praise of Garrick and his wife, reassemble itself by the end:

adieu!—I love you dearly—and Y^r Lady better.—not hobbi-horsically—but most sentimentally & affectionately.
for I am Y^{rs} (that is, if you never say another word ab^t this scoundrel 20 p^{ds})[7]

These high spirits came from Bath, where Sterne was 'playing the devil'.[8] It was natural for a famous invalid to visit this spa, and Sterne was probably encouraged by Mrs. Montagu, whose sister, Mrs. Sarah Scott, lived at Bath. Mrs. Montagu was amused and pleased to hear how gaily Sterne behaved with the ladies at Bath, for she had directed him there as much as an entertainment for the inhabitants as for the benefit to his constitution. A Mrs. Cutts had caught Sterne's alert eye, even to the extent that he believed under different circumstances they might have been made for each other. Mrs. Montagu took a patronizing attitude towards her country cousin and the way fame had made a fool of him. Praise, she thought, had turned his head 'so that he realy believes his book to be the finest thing the age has produced'.[9] Although she spoke of him with some affection, believing 'he was designed for virtue, the softness of his temper and the levity of his understanding has exposed him to follies',[10] she no longer kept open house to Sterne. She told her sister that she was now ashamed to talk for long to the author of 'a tawdry book'. Sterne may even have worked her knocker in vain: 'He has since called at my door, but I am obliged to reserve many mornings for business or quiet.'[11]

Sterne remained in Bath hardly more than a fortnight, but it was enough to stir up the town. It seems that while there he had teased a party of Irish ladies, including the 'charming widow *Moor*, where, if I had not a piece of legal meadow of my own, I should rejoice to batten the rest of my days'.[12] But Sterne had not seen his 'legal meadow' for more than a year and, in the company of ladies, he may have played with the idea that she no longer existed, that their separation was indeed lasting. The little news of his family would only have confirmed Sterne's opinion of his wife. Mrs. Montagu had heard that Elizabeth Sterne had encountered old enemies in France, 'Miss Townshend and Capt. Orme, and instead of quietly avoiding them she entered into violent quarrels till she c^d not live in the place.'[13]

By the time Sterne returned to London, a letter pursued him from a lady in Bath 'to enquire whether Tristram Shandy is a married Man or no'.[14] It was a ticklish question: was Tristram married? was it Tristram or Sterne who owed Garrick money? Sterne dilated upon the lady's question, and in reply made love by letter, not to the lady, but to the lascivious doubt she had introduced:

If T. Shandy had but one single spark of galant[r]y-fire in any one apartment of his whole Tenement, so kind a tap at the dore would have call'd it all forth to have enquired What gentle Dame it was that stood without—good God! is it You M^rs F—! what a fire have You lighted up! tis enough to set the whole house in a flame[15]

Sterne also told the lady that he was forty-four (he was fifty-one) and that there was 'not an ounce & a half of carnality about me'.[16] But the impressionable flames quickly spread and by 23 April Sterne was complaining sawnily to Lady Anne Warkworth, 'what a dishclout of a soul hast thou made of me.'[17] It is remarkable that the same household article that, in 1762, had resembled his wasted complexion should now stand for his romantic passions. Lady Warkworth was a fitting object for them. Still only nineteen, she was the daughter of Bute and the grand-daughter of Lady Mary Wortley Montagu, who had always recognized Anne as the beauty of the family. Lady Anne had married Lord Warkworth in July 1764 and had attended the York races in August of that year where she may have met the famous author.

From a coffee house in Mount Street, Sterne wrote to Lady Anne, admitting 'I feel myself drawn into a vortex, that has turned my brain upside downwards', and claiming to know nothing but that he loved her, 'perhaps foolishly'.[18] In later life, Lady Anne was to reveal a taste for amorous intrigue and she may have enjoyed a cool flirtation with so overheated a man. Alternatively, perhaps she only had to exist for Sterne to concoct agonies of suspense for himself:

Why would you tell me you would be glad to see me?—Does it give you pleasure to make me more unhappy—or does it add to your triumph, that your eyes and lips have turned a man into a fool, whom the rest of the town is courting as a wit?—I am a fool—the weakest, the most ductile, the most tender fool, that ever woman tried the weakness of—and the most unsettled in my purposes and resolutions of recovering my right mind.[19]

Even returned to York, Sterne could write to her pronouncing himself 'shandy-headed'. But, that far apart, the attraction died away. Sterne had fire enough to contend with in York-shire. On 1 and 2 August the vicarage at Sutton was burned down. Sterne attributed the disaster to 'the carelessness of my curate's wife'.[20] Certainly it was an odd accident, and may have owed something to the disenchantment of Marmaduke Callis. On the first day, the vicarage had caught fire at one end and been 'extinguished without much damage'. The embers were guarded all night against a fresh fire and next day 'every thing was thought to be safe.' But in the afternoon, the vicarage caught fire at the other end and 'the whole building was consum'd.'[21] Sterne realized that he would have to rebuild it, but it was a restoration that he neglected and which remained to torment his family.

Apart from that worry, he had the new volumes of Sermons on his mind. He had talked of them in March, and, in July, anticipated their being published in September. But, in fact, Volumes III and IV of the Sermons did not appear until 22 January 1766, by which time Sterne was in Italy. The delay may be explained by the fact that he needed the summer to compose some new sermons or to touch up some old ones. He speaks of 'sitting in my summer house',[22] his head full of sermons.

For diversions, he had the pleasure of receiving a fine silver ink stand from Lord Spencer.* He had also to consider a proposal that Lydia had received in France. She was seventeen – only a little younger than Lady Warkworth – and had been approached by 'a French gentleman of fortune', older than Sterne himself. This man had written to the father inquiring about the fortune Lydia could expect. Sterne answered in a jocular fashion that shows an unexpected aversion to elderly fondness for young ladies:

My answer was 'Sir, I shall give her ten thousand pounds the day of marriage—my calculation is as follows—she is not eighteen, you are sixty-two—there goes five thousand pounds—then Sir, you at least think her not ugly—she has many accomplishments, speaks

* John Spencer (1734–83) was the great-grandson of the Duke of Marlborough. Sterne had dedicated Volumes V and VI of *Tristram Shandy* to Spencer and the story of Le Fever to Spencer's wife.

Italian, French, plays upon the guittar, and as I fear you play upon no instrument whatever, I think you will be happy to take her at my terms, for here finishes the account of the ten thousand pounds'—I do not suppose but he will take this as I mean, that is—a flat refusal.[23]

Other fathers might have left less room for doubt, or even thought it sensible to visit the daughter and confront the suitor. But Sterne was set on nine or ten months in Italy before calling on his family on the way home. His health now preoccupied him. In September he went to York for 'the most violent spitting of blood that ever mortal man experienced',[24] rather than risk dying on the road. He planned to begin his journey by the end of September, pausing only briefly in London since 'L'hyvere a Londres ne vaut pas rien, pour les poumones—a cause d'humiditè et la fumè dont l'aire est chargèe.'[25]

He was in London early in October buying a new wig for his appearance in Paris. Sterne informed Foley at this time that Becket had £600 that he and his wife could draw upon when necessary. In five days Sterne was in Paris. Again, he stayed only a few days. In that time he encountered both Wilkes and Samuel Foote. Horace Walpole, too, was in Paris, but he despaired of the available English company: 'You will think it odd that I should want to laugh, when Wilkes, Sterne, and Foote are here; but the first does not make me laugh, the second never could, and for the third, I choose to pay five shillings when I have a mind he should divert me.'[26] Wilkes had been abroad too long, waiting for the political climate in England to become more welcoming. There is a hint that he and Sterne quarrelled at this time. John Horne Tooke,* who met Sterne at Lyons on his way to the Alps, wrote to Wilkes: 'Is there any cause of coldness between you and Sterne? He speaks very handsomely of you, when it is absolutely necessary to speak at all; but not with that *warmth and enthusiasm*, that I expect from every one that knows you.'[27] Perhaps Wilkes had lost patience with an outsider who was still able to cross the channel at will.

* Tooke (1736–1812), like Churchill, was a lapsed cleric. An argumentative materialist, in 1765 he had published a pamphlet, 'The Petition of an Englishman', in defence of Wilkes.

Two views of the bust of
Sterne by Nollekens, 1766

Sterne and Death, by Thomas Patch, 1766

By 7 November Sterne was in Beau Pont Voisin, held up 'by the sudden swelling of two pitiful rivulets from the snows melting on the Alps'. He described himself languishing 'in this state of vexatious captivity',[28] as if eager to encounter the mountains. Passing over the Alps at this time was a strenuous and exciting exercise, but Sterne offers no account of it. Eight days later we find him in Turin, again marooned by floods on the road to Milan. Sterne spoke simply of 'many difficulties'[29] on the way. Passing from Savoy into Italy there was a steep climb of three miles, six miles along the plain at over six thousand feet and then a more gradual descent of six miles. Much depended on the season. Viscount Palmerston, who made the journey in October 1763, 'found the passage quite free from any snow and, the weather being very fine, were rather troubled with heat than cold'.[30] But at the end of winter, the snow could be treacherous. Samuel Sharp* wondered in 1766 'at the composure with which we travelled so many miles on the edges of so many precipices, having often on one hand, monstrous impending rocks, threatening to fall on our heads every moment; and, on the other, a boisterous torrent'.[31]

Sharp is the second travel writer Sterne lampooned in *A Sentimental Journey* as Mundungus, who 'made the whole tour . . . without one generous connection or pleasurable anecdote to tell of; but he had travell'd straight on looking neither to his right hand or his left, lest Love or Pity should seduce him out of his road'.[32] But to travel brimming with love and pity served in Sterne's case to omit all details of the actual journey and it is the painstaking, if more mundane, Sharp who gives this description of crossing the Alps:

Both going and returning, when you arrive at the foot of the hill, your coach, or chaise, is taken to pieces, and carried upon mules to the other side, and you yourself are transported by two men, on a common straw elbow chair, without any feet to it, fixed upon two poles, like a sedan chair, with a swinging foot-board to prop up your feet; but, though it be the work of two men only to carry you, six, and sometimes eight, attend, in order to relieve one another. The

---

* Sharp (?1700–1778) had been a surgeon at Guy's Hospital. He resigned from this position in 1757 on account of his asthma and travelled in search of better health.

I

whole way that you ride in this manner being fourteen or fifteen miles, when the person carried is corpulent, it is necessary to employ ten porters. Though I have described the rise of both the hills to be extremely craggy, yet the chairmen, from long use, become so habituated to the footing, that, like goats, they seldom make a false step . . .[33]

Sharp thought Turin 'more regular and handsome than any other [town] in *Italy*, and would be a delightful abode, were a man well recommended and introduced into the best company'.[34] The delay there allowed Sterne to find his way in and out of a dozen houses, to be presented to King Charles Emmanuel of Sardinia and to find a travelling companion, Sir James Macdonald. Macdonald was only twenty-three but in 1763 he had delighted Paris society and had come to Turin from a meeting with Voltaire at Geneva. 'He is . . . a very extraordinary young man for variety of learning,' wrote Horace Walpole. 'He is rather too wise for his age, and too fond of showing it.'[35] He may have been all the more agreeable a companion for his ability to mimic Hume.

After 'a joyous fortnight'[36] in Turin, Sterne and Macdonald passed slowly across the plain of Lombardy, through Milan, Piacenza, Parma and Bologna before crossing the Apennines to Florence. Sterne was enchanted by the journey – 'Weather as delicious, as a kindly April in England'.[37] Vagueness may have made an easier journey than the meticulous eye of Sharp who was sure that, until experienced, it was not possible to 'imagine half the disagreeableness that *Italian* beds, *Italian* cooks, *Italian* post-horses, *Italian* postilions, and *Italian* nastiness, offer to an Englishman'.[38]

It was while in Milan that Sterne collided with the Marchesa Fagnini. In reality, it may only have been the momentary indecision of two people in a narrow space. But Sterne magnified the incident in *A Sentimental Journey* until it epitomized exactly the fervent diagnosis of his own feelings that he lived for. When Sterne travelled it was not to see the wonders of the world, works of art, waterfalls and monuments, nor even local customs and the faces of native people, but to brush against a lady's arm and in that instant to identify ecstasies and mysteries enough to occupy a vacant life:

I was going one evening to Martini's concert at Milan, and was just entering the door of the hall, when the Marquesina di F*** was coming out in a sort of a hurry—she was almost upon me before I saw her; so I gave a spring to one side to let her pass—She had done the same, and on the same side too; so we ran our heads together: she instantly got to the other side to get out: I was just as unfortunate as she had been; for I had sprung to that side, and opposed her passage again—We both flew together to the other side, and then back—and so on—it was ridiculous; we both blush'd intolerably; so I did at last the thing I should have done at first—I stood stock still, and the Marquesina had no more difficulty. I had no power to go into the room, till I had made her so much reparation as to wait and follow her with my eye to the end of the passage—She look'd back twice, and walk'd along it rather side-ways, as if she would make room for any one coming up stairs to pass her—No, said I—that's a vile translation: the Marquesina has a right to the best apology I can make her; and that opening is left for me to do it in—so I ran and begg'd pardon for the embarrassment I had given her, saying it was my intention to have made her way. She answered, she was guided by the same intention towards me—so we reciprocally thank'd each other. She was at the top of the stairs; and seeing no *chichesbee* near her, I begg'd to hand her to her coach—so we went down the stairs, stopping at every third step to talk of the concert and the adventure—Upon my word, Madame, said I when I had handed her in, I made six different efforts to let you go out—And I made six efforts, replied she, to let you enter—I wish to heaven you would make a seventh, said I—With all my heart, said she, making room—Life is too short to be long about the forms of it—so I instantly stepp'd in, and she carried me home with her—And what became of the concert, St Cecilia, who, I suppose, was at it, knows more than I.

I will only add, that the connection which arose out of that translation, gave me more pleasure than any one I had the honour to make in Italy.[39]

1766

Sterne conducted himself through the splendours of Italy with all possible speed. He allowed three days for Florence, less to see the city and its museums than to dine with Sir Horace Mann, the British envoy and plenipotentiary, and with Thomas Patch, the artist, who was living with Mann. Then, he planned a fortnight in which he could 'tread the Vatican, and be introduced to all the Saints in the Pantheon'.[1] So determined a hurry argues against the extremity of his health, and yet it was the prospect of winter mildness in Naples that led him on.

Samuel Sharp was so impressed by the winter climate of Naples that he was prepared to recommend any London asthmatic like himself jumping there immediately. 'You see no damps on their stair-cases, nor on the walls of their chambers; their iron does not rust as with us, nay, the paintings on the outside of buildings in fresco, remain for years,'[2] he reported. Sterne was delighted by the warmth and dryness. At the turn of this year Naples had had unusually severe weather; Sharp had spoken of thunder and lightning. But by February, according to Sterne, 'the sun has been as hot as we could bear it.'[3] He hoped to have added ten years to his life and found 'new principles of health in me, which I have been long a stranger to'.[4] It is unlikely that his flesh bore out the dreams, but he was soon optimistic enough to see himself 'growing fat, sleek'.[5]

Macdonald, however, did not respond as well to Naples. He was suffering from 'a long and most cruel fit of the rheumatism'[6] that must have prevented him from sightseeing. In fact, he had little longer to live, for he died at Frascati on 26 July 1766. But Sterne had found a new, more vigorous companion in Henry Errington, a Northumbrian, some twenty-five years younger than himself. Errington and Sterne had met three years before and joined forces again as Sterne passed through Rome.

'We have a jolly carnival of it,' Sterne said of Naples, 'nothing but operas—punchinellos—festinos and masquerades'.[7] These entertainments attracted Sterne's attention more than a minor eruption of Vesuvius that took place in February. Naples appears to have been a haven of rowdy informality, diversion and low taste such as might have appealed to Sterne. Sharp was dismayed that the Neapolitans used the Opera simply as a rendezvous and liked to 'laugh and talk through the whole performance, without any restraint; and, it may be imagined, that an assembly of so many hundreds conversing together so loudly, must entirely cover the voices of the singers'.[8] As for the theatre, 'the principal entertainments seem to arise from double entendres and blunders, mistaking one word for another, and even from dirty actions, such as spitting or blowing the nose in each others faces; just as we see still practised in *England* by *Merry Andrews*.'[9]

The best English company could be relied upon every evening at the house of William Hamilton, who had been appointed envoy and plenipotentiary at Naples in 1764.* The English visitors gathered there whenever they had nothing better to do, played cards and billiards or put on an amateur concert. Otherwise, they might be invited to the Prince and the Princess Francavilla's. They sometimes gave three balls a week for as many as eight hundred people. Sterne wrote to Hall-Stevenson that he was invited to such an assembly, 'which is to be superb'.[10] Miss Tuting was in Naples and she may have been able to plump Sterne's spirit a little more with her gratitude.

But the travelling English were seldom relaxed. Even when the winter weather was so exceptionally warm, they could not stop themselves noticing that it encouraged flies. Samuel Sharp believed that every Englishman abroad would really have preferred to be at home and that he only made the tour 'as a kind of apprenticeship for qualifying'.[11] One can picture the English visitors caught in dwindling conversations over the inscrutability of weather in this account of Sharp's: 'I have heard

---

* Hamilton (1730–1803) was, of course, the future husband of Nelson's Emma.

some of the *English* assert such a day to be as cold as any day he ever felt in *England*, but then I have heard another declare that same day to be as warm as our first of May; so little can we depend upon one another, and so violently affected are we, generally, by our different feelings for the present moment.'[12]

Sterne was probably sufficiently untypical an Englishman to be amused by the gravity of his countrymen on holiday. His complaints against Smollett and Sharp, for all that he was so sketchy a reporter of foreign countries himself, may represent irritation with English manners abroad. He advised himself in *A Sentimental Journey* that '*an Englishman does not travel to see Englishmen.*'[13] When he had left Naples, he wrote an English thank you letter to Hamilton and his wife, 'for the many civilities and attentions paid me by you both ... which upon looking back upon at this distance, I estimate higher, and feel the pleasure I partook of more sensibly, than I did w^n I was actually enjoying them'.[14] As always, recollection or anticipation easily surpassed an event itself.

Curtis has noted[15] that, whatever his enjoyment of Naples, Sterne was prepared to sacrifice his opinion for a striking remark. At d'Holbach's house, he confessed to the abbé Galiani, 'Il vaut mieux mourir à Paris que vivre à Naples.'[16] Travelling, whether through countries, people or ideas, permitted Sterne an overriding flexibility whereby opinions could be altered to suit circumstances. But such compromise would not have come so easily to a man seriously touched by experience. It meant that Sterne could never persuade himself, either of joy or of sadness. Consequently, he passed through walls, sights and social gatherings like a ghost – thrilling anyone who thought he saw him, but incapable of being touched himself.

Sterne and Errington made their way to Rome about the middle of March to be in time for Holy Week. They travelled by way of Monte Cassino, where they were 'rec^d and treated like Sovereign Princes'. But Sterne also claimed to have had a grotesque accident, as violent but insubstantial as the punishments devised for the cat in Tom and Jerry cartoons: 'a Dromedary of a beast fell upon me in full Gallop, and by rolling over me crushed me as flat as a Pankake.'[17]

The damage cannot have been too great for it was while at

Rome that Sterne sat for the sculptor Joseph Nollekens. Nollekens was not yet thirty and had had his first success with a bust
of Garrick, made in Rome in 1763. His marble bust of Sterne is
remarkably good* and speaks very well of the improvement in
the writer's health at Naples. It is a lean head still – so lean that
its Roman hairstyle makes Sterne seem fit for the part of Cassius
– but suggesting more strength and calm than the Reynolds
portrait would lead one to believe. The mouth is wide and level,
as if it could be amusing without being foolish. The nose is very
large but the jaw is firm and controlled. Compared with the
Reynolds portrait, Nollekens's bust shows much more sense,
patience and kindness. Only in profile does the vast angle of
nose hint at the buffoonery in the man.

From Rome, Sterne had hoped to accompany Errington
back to England by way of Venice, Vienna, Berlin, Hanover
and Holland. He had even written to Hall-Stevenson asking for
letters to be forwarded to Venice. But this excursion failed,
probably because of the death of the wife of the English ambassador at the Imperial Court. Thus Sterne was left without dis-
traction from his original intention of calling on his wife and
daughter in France.

At the height of his fame Sterne had boasted that a letter
addressed to Tristram Shandy from anywhere in Europe would
be sure to find him. But for Sterne to trace a wandering wife
and daughter was no easy matter. 'Never man has been such a
wild goose chase after a wife as I have been,'[18] he complained. He found her at last near Dijon, having failed in five
or six other towns. In view of the difficulty, it was hardly
surprising that Mrs. Sterne asked to be left in France a little
longer.

Sterne perhaps needed no fierce persuading, and he was able
to enjoy a brief holiday with his family. It was 'a delicious part
of the world' in May, with 'most celestial weather'. They lay all
day long on the grass, 'inspired twice a day with the best
Burgundy that grows upon the mountains'. Lydia's progress was

* Nollekens, himself, was particularly pleased with it, 'even to his second childhood, and often mentioned a picture which Dance had made of him leaning upon
Sterne's head'. It may have had an added sentimental value in that Nollekens
employed a hollow cast of the bust for smuggling silk and lace from Rome to
England. (J.T. Smith, *Nollekens and his Times* [London, 1920 edn] Vol. I, pp. 8, 13.)

a great satisfaction to her father.* Earlier that winter, both she
and her mother had been ill with the ague, but now Sterne
found Lydia 'greatly improved in every thing I wish'd her'.[19]
Sterne was stimulated to be playful and when Miss Trist, a lady
in the same company, was interrupted in writing a letter to her
mother, Sterne could not resist filling up the empty paper, his
pen quickly passing from flattery to romance:

Miss Triste having gone out of the room (but upon what occasion
God knows) Tristram Shandy has thought meet to profit by her
absence and the temptation this void has laid in his way, of sending
his best respects to the mother, not altogether for the sake of the
daughter (for that wd. be uncivil), but in testimony of his esteem for
Mrs Triste and her worthy character, and at the same in Homage to
the Graces of her fair offspring, which appear so lovely in the eyes of
Tristram Shandy, that 'tis well for the fair Goddesse that he is under
a slight pre-engagement—indeed 'tis only marriage.[20]

Sterne interpreted this practical joke as part of a renewed
urge to take up the pen; he wrote to Hall-Stevenson suspecting
that he would die with it in his hand, though not for ten years.
But Mrs. Sterne was anxious about her husband's health and
'most melancholy on that account'.[21]

He made his way by Paris, Calais, London and York back to
Coxwold. He was detained from writing at first by 'a thousand
nothings, or worse than nothings'[22] and was prepared to suffer
further delay at the York races or, if it appealed to Hall-
Stevenson, in a trip to Scarborough.

It is interesting to wonder exactly when Sterne commenced
Volume IX of *Tristram Shandy* because of a curious and touching
letter he received late in July. It came from Ignatius Sancho, a
Negro born on a slave-ship and subsequently employed as butler
to the Duke of Montague. 'I am one of those people whom the
illiberal and vulgar call a Nee-gur', wrote Sancho, and added
that his chief pleasure was reading, particularly philanthropic
works. '. . . how much do I owe you good Sir,' he wrote to
Sterne, 'for that soul pleasing Character of your amiable uncle
Toby! I declare I would walk ten miles in the dog days, to shake

---

* Curtis notes that Lydia had transcribed some passages in French in
Sterne's copy of the first edition of Rousseau's *Emile*. (*Letters*, p. 188, n. 11.)

hands with the honest Corporal . . .'[23] Sancho was particularly
pleased by Sterne's sermon on 'Job's Account of the Shortness
and Troubles of Life' which referred to the bitter draught of
slavery and the many millions that were made to drink it.*
Only that sermon and *The History of Sir George Ellison*, as far as
Sancho knew, 'had a tear to spar[e] for the distresses of my poor
moorish brethren'.[24]

But Sancho was not content with these few defences and
lobbied Sterne to look into the conditions of slavery in the West
Indies and perhaps deal with the subject 'in your own manner'.
Sancho ended with an entreaty skilfully modelled on Sterne's
own style: 'dear Sir think in me, you behold the uplifted hands
of Millions of my moorish brethren—Grief (you pathetically
observe) is eloquent—figure to yourselves their attitudes—hear
their supplicatory address—humanity must comply.'[25]

Thus briefed, Sterne could not argue. He replied with enthusiasm: 'I never look *Westward* (when I am in a pensive mood at
least) but I think of the burdens which our Brothers & Sisters
are *there* carrying—& could I ease their shoulders from one
ounce of 'em, I declare I would set out this hour upon a pil-
grimage to Mecca for their sakes.'[26] It was characteristic of
Sterne to propose marching eastwards as a solution for a problem that lay to the west. And his lingering looks across the
Atlantic may have been mixed with the thought that his father
had died in Jamaica while attempting to uphold a slave empire.
But Sterne had every liberal response. What was colour? he
asked himself. 'It is by the finest tints, and most insensible
gradations, that nature descends from the fairest face about S^t
James's, to the sootiest complexion in africa: at which tint of
these, is it, that the ties of blood are to cease? and how many
shades must we descend lower still in the scale, 'ere Mercy is to
vanish with them?'[27]

Above all, Sterne was struck by the coincidence of Sancho's
letter and his own train of thought: 'for I had been writing a
tender tale of the sorrows of a friendless poor negro-girl, and my
eyes had scarse done smarting with it, when your Letter of

* Sancho remained an admirer of Sterne and in 1780 was given a cast of the
sculpted bust by Nollekens himself. (Smith, *op. cit.*, pp. 25-6.)

recommendation in behalf of so many of her brethren and sisters, came to me.'[28]

That incident occurs in Chapter VI of Volume IX. The girl in question is seen 'flapping away flies—not killing them', a sign that she had learned mercy from her own persecution. Trim asks Toby, doubtfully, 'A Negro has a soul?' 'I suppose, God would not leave him without one,' answers Toby. There is a sharper insight when Toby suggests that it is the very defence-lessness of the Negress that 'recommends her to protection—and her brethren with her; 'tis the fortune of war which has put the whip into our hands *now*—where it may be hereafter, heaven knows!'[29]

Sterne may have invented this scene before receiving Sancho's letter. But in Chapter I of Volume IX, he writes, 'here am I sitting, this 12th day of *August*, 1766, in a purple jerkin and yellow pair of slippers, without either wig or cap on.' His reply to Sancho had been dated 27 July. Thus, on balance, I think it more likely that Sterne took his cue from Sancho, just as he had claimed to have recollected his debt to Garrick. This is no dis-credit to Sterne, but it would illustrate the extraordinary flexibility in his composition, and his willingness to be led by whatever intruded on him.

At the end of August, Sterne told Becket that he planned two new volumes of *Tristram Shandy*, although a month earlier he had told a friend that there would be one volume only and that next year 'I shall begin a new work of four volumes, which when finish'd, I shall continue Tristram with fresh spirit.'[30] Early in 1767, Sterne told William Combe* that he had miscarried the tenth volume 'by the violence of a fever'.[31] Did Sterne 'end' *Tristram Shandy*, or did ending impose itself on him? By 1766 he was known for his perilous health. Thomas Patch had portrayed him in an aghast confrontation with patient Death. So tremu-lous an existence lived from day to day. Just as the plight of the Negro had earned a place in *Shandy* so Sterne may have been open to any suggestion. In which case, the opinion of his publisher could have been crucial. The critics had

---

* Combe (1741–1823) had been educated at Eton and Oxford. He first met Sterne in 1764 or 5, possibly on the continent. He cultivated Sterne's friendship and became one of the most skilled forgers of Sterneana.

recommended winding up the book. Becket perhaps insisted on it.

York races in 1766 were a week of more than usual excitement since the Duke of York patronized the meeting and its assemblies. Sterne was even persuaded to preach before the Duke: probably his last sermon.

There is no record of a fever that might have prevented Volume X except for a cryptic reference in Chapter XXIV of Volume IX to having 'lost some fourscore ounces of blood this week in a most uncritical fever which attacked me at the beginning of this chapter; so that I have still some hopes remaining, it may be more in the serous or globular parts of the blood, than in the subtile *aura* of the brain—be it which it will—an Invocation can do no hurt—and I leave the affair entirely to the *invoked*, to inspire or to inject me according as he sees good'. For all Sterne's claims of the blood he had lost at different times, this view of blood as a humour makes one suspicious of the medical accuracy of some of his diagnoses.

The illness that most occupied Sterne during the autumn of 1766 was suffered by his wife. He had heard in September that she was ill and, were she to deteriorate, 'however expensive the journey would be, I would fly to Avignon to administer consolation to both her and my poor girl.'[32] A month later, he believed his wife was 'going fast down by all accounts' and underlined a request to Foley to expedite funds with the thought that ''tis melancholy in her situation to want any aid that is in my power to give.'[33] But by the end of November he was pleased to hear that she was out of danger. She and Lydia were living at Vaucluse very comfortably with seven rooms and fishing rights, all for sixteen guineas a year.

Sterne planned to be in London by Christmas 'to ly in of another child of the Shandaick procreation'.[34] Ill or not, he may have had some intimations of the little time he had left, for Volume IX of *Tristram Shandy* contains one of those unexpected revelations that Sterne practised, as if a door on to his soul had suddenly blown open. Not that the disclosure is entirely candid. On the contrary, it is a show of frankness. He so romanticized himself that he could even speak these supposedly intimate thoughts to that imaginary mistress always waiting in some side-room of his mind:

I will not argue the matter: Time wastes too fast: every letter I trace tells me with what rapidity Life follows my pen; the days and hours of it, more precious, my dear *Jenny*! than the rubies about thy neck, are flying over our heads like light clouds of a windy day, never to return more—every thing presses on—whilst thou art twisting that lock,—see! it grows grey; and every time I kiss thy hand to bid adieu, and every absence which follows it, are preludes to that eternal separation which we are shortly to make.—[35]

1767–8

If Sterne's life up to the age of fifty-three had been a series of excursions into fantasy to evade the unsatisfactory reality of his existence, 1767 saw his most extreme journey into abstraction. In that year he came closest to escaping the constant deterioration of his body and directed all his energy to the exotic flowering of his imagination. The *Journal to Eliza* and *A Sentimental Journey*, both written in 1767, not only broke new literary ground for Sterne but indelibly marked his reputation, both as a man and as a writer. If that reputation has so often been erroneous or unjustified, it is because 1767 has been misunderstood. Few men are able to arrange their lives so that their conclusion is actually dramatic. But Sterne managed this, as if to make up for the carelessness of his birth and the inconsequence of so much of his early life. He was a man who always thought himself ill, never less than during 1767, but his eventual death, in March 1768, was clinically rather unexpected. It is almost as if his sense of the fiction of his own life recognized the unrepeatable frenzy of 1767 and expired. He had talked of and with death so many times that the moment itself may have crept up on him unnoticed.

***

Sterne travelled down to London in the first week of January 1767 in 'a terrible Hurricane of Wind & Snow'.[1] With snow up to the horses' stomachs, he needed four days to reach London. He took lodgings in Old Bond Street, the rooms in which a little over a year later he was to die.* They were in the house of the 'Hair-Bag Maker to his Majesty', Mrs. Mary Fourmantel.

---

* Curtis established that this building, demolished in 1904, was on the site now occupied by no. 48. (*TLS*, 24 March 1932.)

The reappearance of that name in Sterne's life is surely more than a coincidence. Was this woman even the mother who had accompanied Kitty Fourmantel to York in 1759? Was Kitty alive or dead? No answer to these questions. Sterne does not refer to Kitty, not even in a loving aside.

The cold in London was so great that Sterne 'could scarse lay in bed for it'.[2] And when the thaw came, the streets were dirtier than those in Coxwold. But Sterne scuttled through the slush to see Garrick's new play, *Cymon*, at the Theatre Royal. He also enjoyed a concert in Soho where he scarcely recognized Lord Fauconberg's daughter, Anne, 'she was so prudently muffled up.'[3] This was one of Theresa Cornelys's assemblies at Carlisle House. Mme. Cornelys was a Venetian impresario, the mistress of influential men and the wife of a dancer named Pompeati. For most of the 1760s she held subscription assemblies at Soho Square in which music was a prominent attraction. J.C. Bach was one of the conductors at Carlisle House and Sterne said that this was 'the best Concert I ever had the honour to be at'.[4]

At about this time, Sterne made two new friends: Commodore William James and his wife, who had a house in Gerrard Street. Sterne's attachment to this couple, though brief, seems to have been warm and again emphasizes how few of his friends were men of letters. James was something of a sailor-of-fortune. He had run away to sea as a youth and in 1747 joined the East India Company at the rank of ship's mate. Yet by 1751 he had been promoted to commodore and made commander-in-chief of the Company's fleet. He took grateful advantage of this success by hounding the pirate Angria, taking first the fortress of Severndroog, near Bombay, and then, with the aid of the young Clive, that of Gheria. This victory brought with it booty in excess of £100,000, of which James certainly had a large share.

In 1759 he returned to England, wealthy enough to buy Park Place Farm at Eltham, as well as a house in Soho. In 1765, he married Anne Goddard, and together in Gerrard Street they established an Anglo-Indian salon.

On 29 January, Volume IX of *Tristram Shandy* was published. Sterne claimed it was liked best of all the volumes in London. But the reviews hardly support this, and Sterne cannot really have hoped for much better from them. There had been enough warnings that the Shandy joke had been exhausted. *The Monthly Review* deplored the fact 'that Nature should thus capriciously have embroidered the choicest flowers of genius, on a paultry groundwork of buffoonry!'[5] and also discerned the role of jester that several individuals had already attributed to Sterne:

'The Reviewers have, at length, discovered his *real* prototype, – HARLEQUIN. Do you see the resemblance, Reader? ... the *Reverend Tristram*, does not sound half so well as *Harlequin-Shandy*; ... the PANTOMIME OF LITERATURE.'[6]

Despite his previous allegiance to playfulness, so much reproach had touched on a feeling in Sterne that wanted to be taken seriously. It is possible that *Tristram Shandy* already bored him; if not, *The Monthly Review*'s final accusation may have decided him on sincerity. Late in January he sent his collected works to a young woman he had met at the home of Commodore and Mrs. James with a comment that suggests a new commitment to genuineness: 'the Sermons came all hot from the heart —I wish that could give em any title, to be offer'd to Y^{rs}—the Others came from the head—I'm more indifferent ab^t their Reception—'[7]

The young woman was Mrs. Eliza Draper. She was twenty-two, and Sterne concluded the note to her: 'I'm half in love with You.—I ought to be *wholy so*—for I never valued, (or saw more good Qualities to value,)—or thought more of one of Y^r Sex than of You.'[8] We do not know what Eliza looked like. For all that Sterne collected paintings of her, talked of wearing a miniature of her round his neck and made her a celebrity with his attentions, none has survived with proper authentication. Sterne noticed her eyes and the 'most perfect oval' of her face but did not relish her for beauty:

You are not handsome, Eliza,* nor is yours a face that will please the tenth part of your beholders,—but are something more; for I scruple not to tell you, I never saw so intelligent, so animated, so good a countenance. . . . A something in your eyes, and voice, you possess in a degree more persuasive than any woman I ever saw,

---

* 'I saw no Rarety in Eliza,' reported Mrs. Thrale. 'She was a Woman all as another in my Eyes.' (*Thraliana, op. cit.,* p. 384.)

read, or heard of. But it is that bewitching sort of nameless excellence, that men of nice sensibility alone can be touched with.[9]

Eliza's real attraction for Sterne may have rested in the pathetic story that accompanied those tender eyes. She was a victim such as 'nice sensibility' could hardly resist. Eliza Sclater had been born in 1744 on the Malabar Coast, the daughter of an East India man. Orphaned at four, Eliza came to England to be educated at a boarding school where she seems to have suffered rather more than Sterne had done at his school. She returned to Bombay in 1757 and, when still only fourteen, married Daniel Draper, an officer in the Company. By the time she was eighteen she had had two children and enough of both her husband, a 'morose and reserved' man, and, particularly, of India. Eliza, clearly, was no fool. She regretted her poor education and her isolation in India:

– it is the case of all girls destined for India – No beings in the world are less indebted to education – None living require greater assistance from it – for the regulation of time in Eastern countries is such that every woman must naturally have a large portion of it; Leisure—this is either a blessing or a curse as our minds are disposed. The majority of us are extremely frivolous; this I grant. How should it be otherwise? We were never instructed in the importance of anything but one world point, that of getting an establishment of the luxurious kind, as soon as possible. A tolerable complexion, an easy manner, some degree of taste in the adjustment of our ornaments, some little skill in dancing a minuet and singing an air are the *summum bonum* of perfections here [India] – and these are all that mothers, aunts and governesses inculcate with some merit – into the accomplishments – the very best of us – leave Europe and commence [as] wives in the East at fourteen. Climate, custom, and immediate examples induce to indolence – this betrays us into the practice of gallantry – that poisoner of all that's amiable and good.[10]

The untaught observation of that letter may have attracted Sterne just as much as its regretful tendency to 'gallantry'. Equally, Sterne was a great conquest for an ingenue of the Empire. If without much justification, Eliza may have looked to the famous author as a tutor and sponsor. She was in London while her children went to school and her husband sailed back to Bombay. She knew Sterne for only a little more than two months before she was compelled to follow her husband back to India.

What sort of romance was it? Wright and Sclater, Eliza's biographers, doubted

any real reciprocity. Eliza admired him as a man of genius, had high respect for his understanding, and was grateful to him for the efforts he made to promote her intellectual development. But that was about all. When she set her foot on board the *Earl of Chatham* [her ship back to India] she had merely a pleasing memory of a charming intellectual companionship. Before the vessel reached Bombay even that memory had grown dim.[11]

That seems to me to miss the point of the *Journal to Eliza* and not to recognize the essential love of fantasy in Sterne. The truth is that he fell heavily in love with Eliza only when she had left him. The *Journal* is not so much a lament for a lost sweetheart as a conjuring up of impossible passion, to such an effect that it virtually exhausted Sterne. Richard Griffith, an acquaintance of Sterne's, not only noticed the element of unreality in the affair, but gives a frightening picture of its grotesqueness that adds one more Gothic character to Sterne's repertoire:

... in Truth, there was nothing in the Affair worth making a Secret of—The World, that knew of their Correspondence, knew the worst of it, which was merely a simple Folly. Any other Idea of the Matter would be more than the most abandoned Vice could render probable. To intrigue with a Vampire! To sink into the Arms of *Death alive!*[12]

Sterne's most inimitable work is also that which assisted his fullest escape from reality. Written like a diary, and probably inspired by the model of Swift's *Journal to Stella*, which was first published in 1766,* it is a work that rescues Sterne from life and enshrines him in a radiant, rococo fiction.

Eliza was additionally enchanting to Sterne's imagination

---

* Swift's intimate style was proving very infectious. For instance, Catherine Talbot wrote to Elizabeth Carter in the summer of 1766: 'I shall fancy if I write thus Journal-wise, by bits and scraps, that I am Dean Swift, and you Stella and Mrs Dingley, for we are reading those three new volumes, in which he writes to them in that style.' By March 1767, Sterne told Eliza – among other comparisons – that Swift had not loved Stella more than he did her. (*A Series of Letters between Mrs. Elizabeth Carter and Miss Catherine Talbot* [London, 1819], Vol. II, p. 337.)

because she too was unwell, although this was probably an emotional *malaise* brought about by her reluctance to return to India. In February, Eliza was so indisposed that she stayed indoors. Sterne wrote to her begging for admission: 'Remember, my dear, that a friend has the same right as a physician. The etiquettes of this town (you'll say) say otherwise.—No matter! Delicacy and propriety do not always consist in observing their frigid doctrines.'[13]

But the guardians of those frigid doctrines managed to spread news of Sterne and Eliza as far as Vaucluse where Mrs. Sterne and Lydia were the neighbours of the Abbé de Sade.* By 23 February, Sterne was writing with some irritation to Lydia: 'I do not wish to know who was the busy fool, who made your mother uneasy about Mrs. [Draper] 'tis true I have a friendship for her, but not to infatuation—I believe I have judgment enough to discern hers, and every woman's faults.'[14] Even so, in London, Sterne was boasting of Eliza. He had dined with Bathurst and talked of Eliza for 'a most sentimental afternoon' until that eighty-four-year-old voluptuary hoped he would 'live long enough to be introduced as a friend to my fair Indian disciple, and to see her eclipse all other nabobesses'.[15]

In March, Sterne still regarded Eliza with encouraging friendship, and with sympathy for all her troubles:

Thou hast been bowed down, my child, with every burden that sorrow of heart, and pain of body, could inflict upon a poor being; and still thou tellest me, thou art beginning to get ease;—thy fever gone, thy sickness, the pain in thy side vanishing also.—May every evil so vanish that thwarts Eliza's happiness, or but awakens thy fears for a moment!—Fear nothing, my dear!—Hope every thing; and the balm of this passion will shed its influence on thy health, and make thee enjoy a spring of youth and chearfulness, more than thou hast hardly yet tasted.[16]

At the same time, he assured her that her husband would 'press thee to him with more honest warmth and affection' and was glad to hear that there would be friendly companions on her

---

* de Sade (1705–78) was uncle of the man who created Justine. Was the nephew, twenty-seven in 1767, there to entertain Lydia? It seems so, for Sterne writes to his daughter of a 'truly coarse' answer the Marquis had given the Abbé. (*Letters*, 23 February 1767, p. 301.)

passage to India. He told Eliza that she 'would civilize savages' and encouraged her to speak with 'the easy carelessness of a heart that opens itself'.[17] This is far from the agonized separation of the *Journal*. But such robust sense may have done nothing for Eliza's spirits. On 9 March Sterne wrote to Lydia 'in a melancholy mood' because 'the dear friend I mentioned in my last letter is going into a decline. . . . I can never see or talk to this incomparable woman without bursting into tears.'[18] But no man ever had more mixed emotions for, although Eliza still lived, Sterne had taken the precaution of writing an epitaph for her, a copy of which he sent to Lydia. It was an odd frankness that passed this on to his family, but odder still that in the same letter he urged Lydia to persuade his wife to come home – 'for life is too short to waste in separation.'[19]

But a final separation with Eliza was now only days away and we may see the remorseless increase in her indispensability to Sterne as those days slid by. At first, he still seems to be resigned to losing her:

I probably shall never see you more; yet I flatter myself you'll sometimes think of me with pleasure; because you must be convinced I love you, and so interest myself in your rectitude, that I had rather hear of any evil befalling you, than your want of reverence for yourself. I had not power to keep this remonstrance in my breast. —It's now out; so adieu. Heaven watch over my Eliza![20]

As Mrs. Draper exchanged farewell presents with her London acquaintances, 'I think I lose both firmness and philosophy, as I figure to myself your distresses.'[21] Thus the inventive mind was at work. Eliza was already out of sight, for she had gone to Deal several days before the ship was due to sail in order to equip her cabin. But this only stimulated Sterne's anxiety: 'Oh! I grieve for your cabin.—And the fresh painting will be enough to destroy every nerve about thee. Nothing so pernicious as white lead. Take care of yourself, dear girl; and sleep not in it too soon. It will be enough to give you a stroke of an epilepsy.'[22]

In the next letter – once Eliza is safely stowed on board – Sterne raises the idea that she might 'put off all thoughts of returning to India this year'. He is sure Mr. Draper will be accommodating. What better than ship Eliza off to the south of

France where she and all the Sternes may get well together. But a few lines later Sterne tells her 'My wife cannot live long . . . and I know not the woman I should like so well for her substitute as yourself. – 'Tis true, I am ninety-five in constitution, and you but twenty-five—rather too great a disparity this!—but what I want in youth, I will make up in wit and good humour.'[23]

By the end of March, the mounting sensation of romantic loss has brought Sterne to the two conditions that made his ecstasy: illness and dream:

I have been within the verge of the gates of death.—I was ill the last time I wrote to you; and apprehensive of what would be the consequence.—My fears were but too well founded; for in ten minutes after I dispatched my letter, this poor, fine-spun frame of Yorick's gave way, and I broke a vessel in my breast, and could not stop the loss of blood till four this morning. I have filled all thy India handkerchiefs with it.—It came, I think, from my heart! I fell asleep through weakness. At six I awoke, with the bosom of my shirt steeped in tears. I dreamt I was sitting under the canopy of Indolence, and that thou camest into the room, with a shaul in thy hand, and told me, my spirit had flown to thee in the Downs, with tidings of my fate; and that you were come to administer what consolation filial affection could bestow, and to receive my parting breath and blessing.—With that you folded the shaul about my waist, and, kneeling, supplicated my attention. I awoke; but in what a frame! Oh! my God! 'But thou wilt number my tears, and put them all into thy bottle.'—Dear girl! I see thee,—thou art for ever present to my fancy.[24]

This was the last letter from Sterne before salt water divided the invalids for ever. Even so, it cheers up a little before its end. Sterne eats a good breakfast after this feverish night and tells Eliza to 'Remember, that Hope shortens all journies, by sweetening them—so sing my little stanza on the subject, with the devotion of an hymn, every morning when thou arisest, and thou wilt eat thy breakfast with more comfort for it.'[25] Eliza's ship sailed on 3 April. But Sterne had made a pact with Eliza to keep a journal for her. Although only a part of that work survives, from 12 April to 1 November 1767, the contrast it makes with Sterne's letters and actual dealings with Eliza show how far it was a journal to himself, an interior monologue that moved its writer more than any flesh and blood creature could ever do. Sterne sent the journal in batches to Eliza, but that posting involved sea voyages of such length of time that the writer could easily evade the thought that the letters would ever be read.

The *Journal* is the work of a sick man, but the sickness is not medically specific and the true fatality is less in any symptoms than in the pleasure Sterne gains in dissolving his own nervous system. For all that its language is that of self-pity, the *Journal* is not repellent. Instead, there is a unique intellectual curiosity at work as Sterne seems to participate in the unpicking of his own mind. Above all, the *Journal* is revolutionary because of the way it anticipates Romantic collapse and trauma and because of its rapturous description of disintegration. Sterne died apparently of consumption, and was treated only months beforehand for venereal disease, but the essential disability under which he lived was a morbid grasp of his own insubstantial identity. On 15 April, he wrote:

> worn out with fevers of all kinds but most, by that fever of the heart with wch I'm eternally wasting, ⟨since⟩* & shall waste till I see Eliza again—dreadful Suffering of 15 Months!—it may be more. . . . What a change, my dear Girl, hast thou made in me!—but the Truth ⟨s⟩ is, thou hast only turn'd the ⟨whole⟩ tide of my passions a new way—they flow, Eliza to thee—& ebb from every other Object in this world—& Reason tells me they do right—for my heart has rated thee at a Price, that all the world ⟨should⟩ is not rich enough to purchase thee from me, at. In a high fever all the night.[26]

The desolation increased, but morbid sensitivity carried its own rewards and Sterne admitted that he began 'to feel a pleasure in this kind of resigned Misery arising from ⟨these⟩ this Situation⟨s⟩, of heart unsupported by aught but its own tenderness'.[27] He did what he could to make the memory of Eliza real. Apart from pictures of her, he sent for maps on which he could trace her route – by Madeira to the Cape of Good Hope. But on 19 April, it was 'poor Sick-headed, sick hearted Yorick! Eliza has made a shadow of thee.' He had dined with the Jameses but had been unable to talk of Eliza without bursting into tears 'a dozen different times'.[28]

* ⟨ ⟩ indicates manuscript deletions made by Sterne.

He was attended now by doctors and, on 21 April, he 'parted with 12 Ounces of blood, in order to quiet what was left in me'.[29] The next day he was bled again but 'my arm broke loose, & ⟨lost⟩ I half bled to death in bed before I felt it.'[30] Sterne had also been taking a medicine, James's powder, from which he had caught cold, the worst injury of which, he said, 'fell, you must know, upon the worst part it could,—the most painful, & most dangerous of any in the human Body'.[31]

This is the prelude to the most grotesque comic incident in Sterne's life, and it is very much to his credit that, however ill he was, he saw the joke. Indeed, it appealed to him so much that he could not resist passing it on to Eliza and all his acquaintances: 'and now, if I have strength & Spirits to trail my pen down to the bottom of the page, I have as whimsical a Story to tell you, and as comically disastrous as ever befell one of our ⟨Shan⟩ family—Shandy's Nose—his *name*—his Sash-Window are fools to it.'[32]

Sterne called in a surgeon and physician he knew to examine him. Immediately the *Journal* discards its headlong feverishness and picks up the cross-talk patter so characteristic of the Shandy household:

—tis a venerial Case, cried my two Scientifick friends.—'tis impossible. at least to be that, replied I—for I have had no commerce whatever with the Sex—not even with my wife, added I, these 15 Years—You are xxxxx however my good friend, said the Surgeon, or there is no such Case in the world—what the Devil! said I without knowing Woman—we will not reason ab^t it, said the Physician, but you must undergo a course of Mercury,—I'll lose my life first, said I,—& trust to Nature, to Time—or at the worst—to Death,—so I put an end with some Indignation to the Conference; and determined to bear all the torments I underwent, & ten times more rather than, submit to be treated as a *Sinner*, in a point where I had acted like a *Saint*. Now as the father of mischief w^d have it, who has no pleasure like that of dishonouring the righteous—it so fell out, That from the moment I dismiss'd my Doctors—my pains began to rage with a violence not to be express'd, or supported.—every hour became more intollerable—I was got to bed—cried out & raved the whole night—& was got up so near dead, That my friends insisted upon my sending again for my Physician & Surgeon—I told them upon the word of a man of Strict honour, They were both mistaken as to my case—but tho' they had reason'd wrong—they might act right—but that sharp as my sufferings were, I felt them not so sharp as the Imputation, wch a venerial treatment of my case, laid me under—They answerd that these taints of the blood laid dormant 20 Years—but that they would not reason with me in a matter wherein I was so delicate—but Would do all the Office for wch they were call'd in—⟨&⟩ namely, to put an end to my torment, wch otherwise would put an end to me.—& so have I been compell'd. to surrender myself—& ⟨so⟩ thus Eliza is your Yorick, y^r Bramine—your friend with all his sensibilities, suffering the Chastisement of the grossest Sensualist—Is it not a most ridiculous Embarassm^t, as ever Yorick's Spirit could be involved in—[33]

Only two things need be said of this embarrassment. First, however wrong the diagnosis, the mercury cure appears to have worked. Although for several months, Sterne adhered to his consumption with Eliza, which he insisted was half his sickness, the other half seems to have responded to the mercury treatment, for all that it gave him 'terrible Cholicks. both in Stomach & Bowels'.[34] Sterne's health is always elusive; so many imaginary circumstances contributed to it. So distraught in April, he still rose to achieve the sheer gaiety of *A Sentimental Journey* in the summer and autumn of 1767, and then died the following winter.

But the most telling aspect of Sterne's pox is the way he recovers his dignity by transforming the whole affair into fiction. His account is full of those small easeful additions that polish a story but which would be unlikely in reality. In other words, the frankness is not self-destructive, but truly creative. Sterne has so fashioned his account, and so let artfulness show, that he persuades the reader to think that his pox was an invention. He achieves a genuinely funny effect from what might have been a conclusively damaging incident by the simple but brilliant device of taking us into the physicians' minds. By volunteering that 'they would not reason with me in a matter wherein I was so delicate', Sterne has entirely disarmed disapproval. It is perhaps the most accomplished trick in his life and the most illuminating instance of his need to fictionalize himself.

And as the mercury seeped through his body, Sterne imagined it reducing his reality: 'I shall be sublimated to an etherial

Substance by the time my Eliza sees me . . . but I was always transparent & a Being easy to be seen thro'.'[35] Dreams were providing Sterne with an Eliza that was exactly to his requirements. First, he would 'Idolize thee for two wakeful hours upon my pillow'[36] and then be sure to 'find thee out in my dreams; for I have been with thee almost the whole night, alternately soothing ⟨Y⟩ Thee, or telling thee my sorrows—I have rose up comforted & strengthend'.[37]

By 1 May Sterne was feeling a little better and ventured into the park. There he met 'Sheba' (probably either Mrs. Vesey or Lady Warkworth) who thought him half dead. Sterne's account of this meeting, for all that he makes it a tribute to Eliza that one old flame should have been so eclipsed by the new, conveys an extraordinary sense of a sick man staggering in the fresh air and at the sight of his past:

—I *fear* your Wife is dead, quoth Sheba—no, you don't *fear* it Sheba said I—Upon my Word Solomon! I would quarel with You, was you not so ill—If you knew the Cause of my Illness, Sheba, replied I, you w^d quarrel but the more with me—You lie, Solomon! answerd Sheba, for I know the Cause already—& am so little out of Charity with You upon it—That I give You leave to come & drink Tea with me before You leave Town—you're a good honest Creature Sheba—no! you Rascal, I am not—but I'm in Love, as much as you can be for y^r Life—I'm glad of it Sheba! said I—You Lie. said Sheba, & so canter'd away.[38]

It is all the more vivid a scene for its sense of the invalid gazing up at the imperious woman on horseback.

Later the same night Sterne went to Ranelagh and next day he relapsed, 'being able neither able to walk, stand or sit upright'.[39] By 3 May, he was wondering 'What can be the matter with me! Some thing is wrong, Eliza, in every part of me—I do not gain strength; nor have I the feelings of health returning back to me; even my best moments seem merely the efforts of my mind to get well again.'[40] Increasingly, he seemed to have given himself over to fantasy. On 7 May; 'continue poorly, my dear!—but my blood warms, every mom^t I think of our future Scenes.—so must ⟨go⟩ grow strong, upon the Idea—what shall I do upon the Reality?—O God!—'[41]

On 21 May Sterne dined with Lord and Lady Spencer and the next day he began to limp back to Coxwold, 'like a bale of cadaverous goods consigned to Pluto and company—lying in the bottom of my chaise most of the rout, upon a large pillow'.[42] He rested for two days with the Archbishop and then moved on to Coxwold. Within a few days of his arrival, he was surprised by a letter from Lydia: 'She and her Mama, are coming to pay me a Visit—but on Condition I promise not to detain them in England beyond next April—when, they purpose, by my Consent, to retire into France, & establish themselves for Life—To all which I have freely given my parole of Honour'.[43]

But Sterne was certain that this visit was 'of pure Interest—to pillage What they can from me'.[44] Mrs. Sterne and Lydia did not materialize until October but the thought of them coming was with him 'every moment of the Summer—think w^t restraint upon a Fancy that should Sport & be in all points at its ease'.[45] He believed at first that a modest settlement would satisfy his wife but eventually he was persuaded to make Mrs. Sterne an annual remittance of 300 guineas and to give Lydia £2,000, the proceeds from the sale of his estate. Sterne chose to describe this settlement to Eliza in November as a gentlemanly agreement: 'Mrs Sterne retires into france, whence she purposes not to stir, till her death—& never, has she vow'd, will give me another sorrowful or discontented hour—I have conquerd her, as I w^d every one else, by humanity & Generosity—& she leaves me, more than half in Love wth me—'[46] But, in fact, it was comprehensively businesslike, as if Elizabeth Sterne had been more worried by the imminence of her husband's death than by his philandering. Sterne may have thought he had been freed; but in truth he had been stripped and abandoned.

June began with 'pining penetrating north-east winds'.[47] Once they had abated, Sterne started *A Sentimental Journey*,[48] dreading the journey his wife threatened, but reassured by the improvement in his health. He wrote to a Cheshire friend that he had been confined for a month by illness which '*ought* to have killed me—but that I made a point of it, not to break faith with the world, and in short *would* not die, (for in some cases, I hold this affair to be an act of the will)'.[49] And as he worked in the summer warmth he willed the very presence of Eliza:

I have this week finish'd ⟨up⟩ a⟨n⟩ sweet little apartment which all the time it was doing, I flatter'd the most delicious of Ideas, in thinking I was making it for you—Tis a neat little simple elegant room, overlook'd only by the Sun—just big enough to hold a Sopha, —⟨to enable us to sit close together⟩ for us—a Table, four Chairs, a Bureau—& a Book case,—They are to be all y^{rs}, Room & all—& there Eliza! ⟨by thy leave⟩ shall I enter ten times a day to ⟨my⟩ give thee Testimonies of my Devotion—Was't thou this moment sat down ⟨it⟩, it w^d be the sweetest of earthly Tabernacles—I shall enrich it, from time to time, for thee—till ⟨I⟩ Fate lets me lead thee by the hand into it—& then it can want no Ornament.—tis a little oblong room—with a large Sash at the end—a little elegant fire-place—wth as much room ⟨around⟩ to dine around it, as in Bond street.—But in sweetness & Simplicity, & silence beyond any thing—Oh my Eliza!—I shall see thee surely Goddesse of this Temple.[50]

Sterne's thoughts of Eliza already fluctuated. Was it the mercury, the country air or the simple passage of time that made the language of the *Journal* generally less hectic? In its place there was often a gloating revery as the solitary watched over his day-dreams until they were life-like. Hardly two miles from Sterne's house in Coxwold were the extensive ruins of Byland Abbey, a twelfth-century Cistercian monastery that had fallen into decay after Thomas Cromwell's attack upon the Catholic Church in England. The ruin made an appealing sight, in a meadow beneath a steep wooded hillside (although not as impressive as the ruin of Rievaulx, only seven miles to the north-east, and well within Sterne's range). From his house, Sterne could walk across country to Byland, over Brink Hill, plucking up 'a score Bryars by the roots wch grew ⟨up⟩ near the edge of the foot way, that they might not scratch or incommode'[51] Eliza. He wrote to Eliza that he often made this 'delicious Walk of Romance . . . which I am to tread a thousand times over with You swinging upon my arm'.[52] Perhaps it was the imaginary company of Eliza on this walk that made Sterne think of Byland as 'these delicious Mansions of our long-lost Sisters',[53] and it may have been the evocation of an impossible presence by his side that persuaded Sterne to see in the ruins a ghost: a fellow-sentimentalist called Cordelia.

Sterne even claimed nocturnal visits to this spirit and 'as I lay half reclined upon her grave' talked to her about Eliza. The ghost proved so sympathetic that Sterne was sure she 'could not have been a stranger to the passion on earth'. At Sterne's description of Eliza, Cordelia 'glow'd insensibly, as sympathetic Spirits do' and promised 'that she will one night or other come in person, and in this sacred Asylum pay your Shade a sentimental Visit along with me.'[54]

The extraordinary abstraction of Sterne's mind is illustrated by a comparison of his own account of Byland with that composed by William Combe for his *Letters Supposed to have been Written by Yorick and Eliza*, published in 1779. Sterne hardly notices the real Byland. Indeed, it is as if his entire colloquy with Cordelia might have been inspired by a picture of the place, or the report of a traveller. Combe, on the other hand, who presumably wished to make his forgery as authentic as possible, seems actually to have visited Byland, notebook in hand. As a result, his account of the place is a curious mixture of the circumstantial and the emotional:

These remains are situated on the banks of a clear gliding stream; on the opposite side whereof rises a bold ridge of hills, thick with wood – and finely varied by jutting rocks and broken precipices; – and these are so very abrupt, that they not only by their magnitude, but by the shade they cast, encrease the solemnity of the place. – Many parts of the ruin are still entire; the refectory is almost perfect, and great part of the chapel has hitherto defied the power of time. – A few bunches of alders grow fantastically among the broken columns and contrast, with their verdure, the dark green ivy which clings to the walls. – But it is not all solitude and silence! – A few cottages are scattered here and there in the suburbs of this venerable pile, which has, I suppose, furnished the materials for erecting them.[55]

Although Sterne saw Cordelia at Byland, he does not mention these cottagers. Combe's account is probably accurate, just as his invented Sterne is a fair copy of the original, even if its romantic strain is more prosaic:

There I rest against a pillar till some affecting sentiment brings tears upon my cheek: – sometimes I sit me down upon a stone, and pluck up the weeds that grow about it, – then, perhaps, I lean over a neighbouring gate, and watch the gliding brook before me, and listen to its gentle murmurs; they are oftentimes in unison with my feelings.[56]

The willing reporter does his best but hardly seems capable of seeing what Sterne discovered at Byland. It is not too far-fetched an irony to imagine Combe making an excursion to the abbey in search of 'colour' while Sterne merely made the journey in his mind.

But the 'magic of a warm Mind' and actual independence began to reduce Sterne's London anguish, and mellowed him until he sounded like a contented married man. To find such nourishment in the company of ghosts may have made Sterne think the less of real wives. By the end of June, he was writing to reassure Eliza, 'Adieu my dear Wife—you are still mine—not-withstanding all the Dreams & Dreamers in the World.'[57] He spoke of expecting Eliza's return from India next year, but his seriousness became less compelling. He acknowledged that 'my Life will be little better than a dream, till we approach nearer to each other—I live scarse conscious of my existence—or as if I wanted a vital part; & could not live above a few hours.'[58] Which vital part he lacked it is for the reader to decide. It was certainly not respect for his own imagination. On 27 July he received letters from Eliza:

I instantly shut the door of my Bed-Chamber, and orderd myself to be denied—& spent the whole evening, and till dinner the next day, in reading over and over again the most interesting Acc^t—& the most endearing one, that ever tried the tenderness of man—I read & wept—and wept and read till I was blind—then grew sick, & went to bed—& in an hour calld again for the Candle—to read it once more—as for my dear Girls pains & her dangers I cannot write ab^t them—because I cannot write my feelings or express them any how to my mind—[59]

Furnishing his house in complicity with Eliza and strolling in the moonlight with her to the ruins of Byland Abbey were the best convalescence for a sentimental invalid.

On 11 August, he wrote to Hall-Stevenson saying 'I never have been so well since I left college.'[60] Sterne was sufficiently recovered, both physically and mentally, for an active summer. Just as in other years, he went to York, Scarborough, visited

Hall-Stevenson at Skelton and took the waters at Harrogate. In addition, he had funds to procure for his family, a new curate to find for Sutton and Stillington and a fresh book to write. In early August Sterne had been offered another living, in Surrey, worth £350 a year. At Scarborough, in September, he met Dr. Jemmett Browne, the bishop of Cork and Ross, who offered him further livings in Ireland.

Browne also introduced Sterne to Richard Griffith, the author of *The Triumvirate*. In the preface to that work, Griffith had made some mixed comments on Sterne's writing, calling him an 'anomalous, heteroclite genius',[61] praising his benevolence but warning against his lack of taste:

'Tis easier to make one *laugh* than *smile*; and when dullness would be witty, it lets fly bawdry, as it does something else, satisfied to raise a laugh, though it does a stink also. Loose expressions, in a woman, are a double vice, as they offend against decency, as well as virtue; but in a clergyman, they are treble; because they hurt religion also.[62]

But Sterne was eager to be amenable and asserted that, as he had read on, he 'was sensible of a strong Sympathy for *feeling* . . . and said to himself, "This Man, surely, hath no Inimicability in his Nature."'[63] Sterne came to Griffith's room every day to see what his companion was writing and when shown the Memoir of Griffith's life 'actually dropped Tears as he went on'.[64] In return, Sterne showed Griffith what he had written of *A Sentimental Journey* and described it as '*his Work of Redemption*'.[65]

Not many writers happily share work in progress, and this is an interesting glimpse of Sterne's openness. Those visits to Griffith's room when he claimed 'the Privilege of looking into my Manuscripts'[66] may also be a hint of Sterne scouting for *données* to nudge his own invention. In which case, he was eventually given tit for tat since Griffith, in 1770, published *The Posthumous Works of a Late Celebrated Genius*, supposedly in Sterne's own hand. There is no doubt of the real authorship, but Griffith had known Sterne and observed him carefully so that the *Posthumous Works* need not be discarded entirely.* Griffith at

---

* *The Posthumous Works* is generally a miserable imitation of Sterne's humour, but it is interesting for its comments on the relationship between Laurence and Jaques Sterne. It may be that Griffith was recollecting conversations with Sterne when he wrote this: 'I happened to have an uncle once, who was a minister of the gospel, but

least had no doubt how close Sterne was to the end of his tether. After Sterne's death, he wrote: 'His living for Ten Years past was a Miracle, and that he should live for Twenty Years to come, was the only *Miracle*, I fancy, that he believed in.'[67]

Flirtation gradually reasserted itself, an inescapable and exhausting passion. Even as early as June, Sterne had adapted for Eliza – complete with Cordelian chatter – a version of a letter that he had first sent to an unknown countess, without bothering to eliminate its note of sexual tease. Curtis calls this letter 'the most compromising document that remains to us in Sterne's autograph'.[68] But such severity depends on a closer involvement in the epistolary affair with Eliza than I can share. Sterne invariably behaved badly with women; it was only in his mind that he doted on them and in his fiction that he worshipped their presence. *A Sentimental Journey* comes daintily close to bad taste because of its preoccupation with flirtation. It is absurd to call that book simply charming or good-natured and not recognize the voyeuristic sensibility it indulges. It is about Sterne's realization that the idea of sex may be more potent than the achievement. Mrs. Sterne doubtless concluded that it was impossible to live with him. We, mercifully, are spared that, which makes it easier for us to enjoy the dangerous subtlety of his fiction.

While Sterne was writing *A Sentimental Journey*, whatever intimations he may have had of the future, he believed himself as well as he had been since he left Cambridge. That, surely, is only a sign of the extremes to which his nervy soul could oscillate, but it is essential to appreciate the vein of enjoyment in *A Sentimental Journey* especially since there is no good reason for attributing that cheerfulness to courage.

In September, while he waited for his wife and began to lose interest in Eliza, Sterne was pleased to reply to a mysterious Hannah who had written to him:

---

his only study was politics. He had a laudable ambition to rise in life. Religion is undoubtedly a necessary qualification for that purpose in the next world – but is not sufficient to help us forward in this.' Griffith has Sterne recount how he helped his uncle in the war of pamphlets but was denied any reward. He also suggests that Sterne composed a portrait of his uncle but was warned off such tactlessness by friends and therefore 'altered' the character to Uncle Toby! (Griffith, *Posthumous Works of a Late Celebrated Genius Deceased* (Dublin, 1770), Vol. I, pp. 9, 17-18.)

Ever since my dear H wrote me word she was mine, more than ever woman was, I have been racking my memory to inform me where it was that you and I had that affair together.—People think that I have had many, some in body, some in mind, but as I told you before, you have had me more than any woman—therefore you must have had me, H, both in mind, and in body.—Now I cannot recollect where it was, nor exactly when—it could not be the lady in Bond-street, or Grosvenor-street, or—Square, or Pall-mall.—We shall make it out, H, when we meet—I impatiently long for it—[69]

Perhaps Sterne had talked airily of so many ladies that, when one wrote to him, he was uncertain whether he had known her in body or mind. The imaginative tickle of rumour and suggestion was paramount and a week after writing to Hannah he engaged Sir William Stanhope with coy reproach:

You are perhaps the drollest being in the universe—Why do you banter me so about what I wrote to you?—Tho' I told you, every morning I jump'd into Venus's lap (meaning thereby the sea) was you to infer from that, that I leap'd into the ladies beds afterwards? —The body guides you—the mind me.[70]

He then told Stanhope of 'the most whimsical letter' he had just sent to Hannah before plunging again into his 'intimate' voice:

Enough of such nonsense—The past is over—and I can justify myself unto myself—can you do as much?—No faith!—'You can feel!' Aye so can my cat, when he hears a female caterwauling on the house top—but caterwauling disgusts me. I had rather raise a gentle flame, than have a different one raised in me.—Now, I take heav'n to witness, after all this *badinage* my heart is innocent—and the sporting of my pen is equal, just equal, to what I did in my boyish days, when I got astride of a stick, and gallop'd away—The truth is this—that my pen governs me—not me my pen.[71]

That letter is a fascinating confession, but see how Sterne still insists on obscuring its sense. He shuffles seriousness and *badinage* about so that the one is always available as a retreat from the other. Draw any conclusion from the letter and Sterne could have answered, 'Ah, there I was being playful' or, 'Oh, no, you misunderstand me. I meant that seriously.' The speed of the pen and the jumping association of thoughts are measures to conceal true revelation from the writer himself, and the alluring

sense of shared confidence has made the passage virtually
impossible to decipher. In less than ten days Sterne was able to
write again to Stanhope with a polished picture of himself that
a publisher would have been pleased to use as a blurb:

> ... my Sentimental Journey will, I dare say, convince you that my
> feelings are from the heart, and that that heart is not of the worst of
> molds—praised be God for my sensibility! Though it has often made
> me wretched, yet I would not exchange it for all the pleasures the
> grossest sensualist ever felt.[72]

Sterne spent the autumn 'hard writing'; as so often he had
preferred to take a holiday in the summer months. Lydia and
his wife arrived in York on 1 October.* His daughter seemed
to him 'affectionate, and most elegant in body, and mind', 'an
elegant accomplish'd little slut'.[73] However precise the family's
monetary negotiations had been, Sterne said that when Lydia
and her mother left for York, Sterne offered his daughter ten
guineas. But she answered, 'No, my dear papa, our expences of
coming from France may have straiten'd you—I would rather
put an hundred guineas in your pocket than take ten out of it.'[74]

Sterne had little left. *A Sentimental Journey* may have taken his
last energy. He no longer thought of Eliza returning, but tried
to fit himself for his new publication. The clerical offers of the
autumn were declined, on the grounds that his family had to
return to France. At the end of the year he jotted down a memorandum as to where his letters might be found and wrote to the
Jameses warning 'Youl see Me enter like a Ghost—so I tell you
before hand, not to be frighten'd.'[75]

London was suffering its second consecutive bad winter.
Horace Walpole noted nearly three weeks of frost and snow at
Strawberry Hill, with 'opposition-lumps of ice'[76] that would not
melt. When the thaw came it caused flooding and slush in the

---

* Rufus Putney has noted that Sterne lied to Eliza (as an excuse for neglect) by
saying that his family had arrived at the start of September. He used this deception
to illustrate Sterne's survival of emotional crisis and to prove that *A Sentimental
Journey* had been written 'in the gayest spirits' at a time when Sterne believed he
had health enough to last him ten more years. Griffith's comment makes it clear
that if that opinion was entertained by Sterne it was surely in the wishful spirit of
A Sentimental Journey and that 'sweet pliability of man's spirit, that can at once
surrender itself to illusions'. (*TLS*, 9 March 1946.)

streets. Sterne lodged again in Old Bond Street and was doubtful of visiting the Jameses in Gerrard Street because of the
moisture. There was a caution in his voice that spoke of tired-
ness. In no previous London season had Sterne been so reserved.
When he thought he mended, it was only with the notion that
'this, with all other evils and uncertainties of life, will end for the
best.'[77] Already Sterne was besieged with invitations, but they
no longer excited him. He felt 'tyed down neck and heels (twice
over) by engagements every day'[78] as if the instinct for motion
was dwindling in him. He would have been content simply to
'glide like a shadow uninvited'[79] to see his friends the Jameses
who seem to have been pestering him to find a ticket for the
Cornelys assembly, a mission which left him without a moment's
rest.

The jester was quiet. In November 1767, Sterne had confessed, 'I have long been a sentimental being. . . . The world has
imagined, because I wrote Tristram Shandy, that I was myself
more Shandean than I really ever was—'tis a good-natured
world we live in, and we are often painted in divers colours
according to the ideas each one frames in his head.'[80] Again, in
February 1768, as he waited for the publication of *A Sentimental
Journey*, he wrote sadly to an American enthusiast: 'There is so
little true feeling in the *herd* of the *world*, that I wish I could have
got an act of parliament, when the books [*Tristram Shandy*] first
appear'd, "that none but wise men should look into them". It is
too much to write books and find heads to understand them.'[81]

A Sentimental Journey was published on 27 February, when
Sterne had barely three weeks left to enjoy its success. Even
Horace Walpole thought it 'very pleasing, though too much
dilated . . . there is great good nature and strokes of delicacy'.[82]
The Monthly Review called the two volumes 'diverting, edifying,
and satirical'.[83] 'But what is the gratification of my feelings on
this occasion?' Sterne wrote to Lydia, '—the want of health
bows me down, and vanity harbours not in thy father's breast—
this vile influenza—be not alarm'd, I think I shall get the better
of it.'[84] He could not make up his mind about the state of his
health. One morning he felt 'absolutely . . . free from every
bodily distemper',[85] but a few days later 'I am ill—very ill—Yet
I feel my Existence Strongly.'[86] He began a comic Romance,

asked for jellies from Mrs. Montagu and complained of being oppressed by attentions. He assured Lydia that he would heal, but admitted 'if I escape 'twill not be for a long period.'[87]

His room was often crowded with people, though shadowy figures whose identities have not survived. There were ladies there, but who? A clergyman who called on him two days before his death met two ladies on the stairs and one more in the room with the patient: a girl called Fanny who 'withdrew to a window'. 'Had you come sooner,' said Sterne, 'you might have seen thirteen.'[88] Those, perhaps, that Sterne had encountered and forgotten in Pall Mall.

There was no hint of spring. From Arlington Street, Horace Walpole wrote to George Montagu. 'The weather is so very March, that I cannot enjoy my new holidays at Strawberry yet. I sit reading and writing close to the fire.'[89] On 15 March Sterne wrote to Mrs. James:

Your poor friend is scarce able to write—he has been at death's door this week with a pleurisy—I was bled three times on Thursday, and blister'd on Friday—The physician says I am better—God knows, for I feel myself sadly wrong, and shall, if I recover, be a long while of gaining strength.—Before I have gone thro' half this letter, I must stop to rest my weak hand above a dozen times.[90]

Sterne was astonished by a rumour reported to him by Lydia that he proposed entrusting his daughter to Eliza Draper. On the contrary, he wrote to her, he would leave her in the care of Mrs. James – 'from her you will learn to be an affectionate wife, a tender mother, and a sincere friend'. It was not a role that Lydia ever filled with any ease and her father may have had an inkling of its implausibility, for in the same letter he recommended Mrs. James's 'milk of human kindness ... which will serve to check the heat of your own temper, which you partake in a small degree of'.[91] Does the imminence of death account for this rare note of paternal frankness?

Mrs. James appears to have been closest to Sterne during his last days, and his final letter contains a touching tribute to her and confession of his faults, all the more interesting for the way it reverses the sentimental scale of values he had so often held to:

do not weep my dear Lady—your tears are too precious to shed for me—bottle them up, and may the cork never be drawn.—Dearest, kindest, gentlest, and best of women! may health, peace, and happiness prove your handmaids.—If I die, cherish the remembrance of me, and forget the follies which you so often condemn'd—which my heart, not my head betray'd me into.[92]

How would a man like Sterne die, someone who had peered so ardently into a world of phantoms, and who had perched so long on the edge of death? In the last chapter of *Tristram Shandy*, Walter had remarked sadly on the way the passion of conception 'couples and equals wise men with fools, and makes us come out of caverns and hiding-places more like satyrs and four-footed beasts than men'.[93] Removed from his family, was Sterne reminded of his father's unattended, animal-like death? He was surely respectful enough of death not to have to face it bravely. Whatever courage he had would have been needed for the remorseless attentions of his doctor. Perhaps he recollected that wavering decline he had measured out for Le Fever and even rehearsed it for himself, conjuring the brink until he began to fall:

Nature instantly ebb'd again,—the film returned to its place,—the pulse fluttered—stopp'd—went on—throb'd—stopp'd again—moved—stopp'd—shall I go on?—No.[94]

On 18 March John Crauford sat down to dinner in Clifford Street. He had met Sterne on the continent and supplied him with the basis of the story that ends *A Sentimental Journey*. His guests at dinner were several acquaintances of Sterne: the Duke of Roxburgh, the Earl of March, the Earl of Ossory, the Duke of Grafton, Garrick, Hume and James. They talked of Sterne, and Crauford sent his footman, John Macdonald, to inquire after him. Macdonald proceeded to Old Bond Street and was sent up to Sterne's room. 'I waited ten minutes; but in five he said: *"Now it is come."* He put up his hand as if to stop a blow, and died in a minute.' Macdonald went back to Clifford Street with the news and 'the gentlemen were all very sorry and lamented him very much.'[95]

Epilogue: The Few Cold Offices

In *Tristram Shandy*, Sterne had imagined for himself a private death, but with one eye open perhaps to count the attendance at his funeral. He declared that he was 'against submitting to it before my friends' and hoped 'that the Disposer of all things may so order it, that it happen not to me in my own house'. There, he foresaw, he would be worried to death by having his brow wiped by solicitous friends. He would rather settle for that abode of the naturally rootless – an inn, where 'the few cold offices I wanted, would be purchased with a few guineas, and paid me with an undisturbed, but punctual attention.'[1]

Sterne's death interested the town but hardly seems to have touched people deeply. There may have been a service in the Bond Street lodgings, or at St. George's Church, immediately south of Hanover Square. But no one who might have been present recorded such an occasion. And although the gentlemen had been very sorry to hear of Sterne's passing, only James attended the burial, along with Becket and two others.

Years later, John Croft said that Sterne's funeral was conducted 'by the late Prince of Wales's Chaplain' who then burned Sterne's 'loose papers', including 'a large Parcel of Letters of Love and Gallantry from Ladies of the first Rank and Quality.'[2] However, we know that the officious arsonist was John Botham, Sterne's brother-in-law. His parish was in Surrey and it is likely that he heard quickly of the death and hurried to Bond Street to be sure none of those papers was stolen. While there, he may have spoken the necessary words and led the 'most private' procession out to the St. George's burial ground in Paddington.

That burial ground was in open country, just beyond

Tyburn; as well as the dead of Hanover Square parish, it received the executioner's remains. The two facts together naturally gave it an unwholesome reputation, and far from public gaze the burial ground became the object of private enterprise. Less than a year before Sterne's funeral, body-snatchers had raided the burial ground and, when a mastiff was set to guard the dead, the dog too was taken.[3]

Neither widow nor daughter was there. Hall-Stevenson and Fauconberg were in Yorkshire. Garrick, Crauford, Hume and Mrs. Montagu remained indoors. It seems that neither a stone nor even a mourning page was put up over the grave – to conceal it perhaps from resurrectionists? Garrick had an epitaph ready for such a gravestone:

> Shall Pride a heap of sculptur'd marble raise,
> Some worthless, unmourn'd titled fool to praise;
> And shall we not by one poor grave-stone learn
> Where Genius, Wit, and Humour, sleep with *Sterne*?

It is hard to say why such a project was not carried out; perhaps concealment really was the plan. Or were the relatives uncertain that Sterne's corpse remained in London?

For there were rumours attending Sterne's death just as there had been at most stages of his life. Some said that, no matter the state of his lungs, Sterne had been fatally wounded by a lady's malicious wit at Reynolds's house and merely tottered back to Bond Street to die.[4] Others said that the dead body had been robbed as it lay in its lodgings. But most sensational of all was the report that Sterne's body had been stolen from the burial ground and sold to the anatomy school at a university. The most telling account of this theft was contained in Hall-Stevenson's spurious additions to *A Sentimental Journey*. When that friend published *Yorick's Sentimental Journey Continued* in 1769, he attached to it a Preface that let it be known that 'the body of Mr. Sterne, who was buried near Marybone, was taken up some time after his interment, and is supposed to have been carried to Oxford, and anatomized by an eminent surgeon of that city.'[5]

In a later edition, when the publicity value of the revelation may have been exhausted, Hall-Stevenson admitted that this story was unsubstantiated. That did not prevent many people believing it. In March 1769, the *Public Advertiser* reported the rumour of Sterne's appearance on a university dissecting table and added that, 'it seems now to be put beyond all Doubt by a Gentleman's having applied in Town to search for the Body, and it could not be found'.[6]

It is not possible to say how rapidly the story gained fleshy detail. But a final version emerged in which Sterne's body was seized only days after burial and sold to Dr. Charles Collignon, professor of anatomy at Cambridge. Collignon duly performed on the corpse and only late in the operation did scientific curiosity lift the cloth that covered the dead face. At that moment, it is said, Sterne was recognized by a bystander. Collignon is then supposed to have concealed the bones in the Cambridge collection, thus affording the opportunity for scholars to hunt for Sterne's head.[7]

That hunt has lasted until today. By November 1769 'two Brother Masons' had remedied the lack of a memorial to Sterne in the St. George's burial ground and put up a stone that contained this inscription:

> Alas! Poor Yorick.
> Near to this Place
> Lyes the Body of
> The Reverend Laurence Sterne, A.M.
> Dyed September 13th, 1768,
> Aged 53 Years.

The errors suggest how far this was an independent gesture, based on remote knowledge of Sterne himself. We can only speculate as to whether 'Near to this Place' is a discreet acknowledgement of the body-snatching theory and/or a reference to the fact that it was no longer known where exactly in that graveyard Sterne had been buried.

In 1893, a further, correcting stone was added to the first by the then owner of the old Sterne estate at Halifax. The burial ground became increasingly neglected. During the First World War, the headstones were all moved to the walls and the ground given over to allotments. In the 1930s, an American visitor found the place 'such a medley of tennis courts and other facilities for sports, stray graves, cabbages and dahlias, chrysanthemums and benches for meditative sitting in the sun, as must be seen to be believed'.[8]

But eventually progress overtook this overgrown sanctuary and the St. George's Hanover Square Burial Ground Act, 1964, cleared the way for the eventual building on the site of blocks of flats for the Utopian Housing Society. The Act offered financial assistance to anyone who could legitimately claim a body from the ground and then properly rebury it.

On Wednesday 4 June 1968, the Laurence Sterne Trust excavated in the area of the two Sterne gravestones. According to *The Times:*

Five separate skulls and assorted bones were unearthed from the grave. The top of one of the skulls had been sawn off. A Harley Street surgeon made minute measurements with calipers, and compared them with the bust of Sterne by Nollekens, which is likely to have been anatomically exact.* The measurements of the sawn-off skull, unusually small for a grown man, fitted perfectly; all the others were far too big. The portraits show Sterne as a lanky man with an extremely small head.

From a femur found beside the sawn-off skull the surgeon calculated that it came from a man 5 ft. 10 in. tall: Sterne says he was nearly 6 ft. High cheek-bones and prominent top teeth on the skull also matched Sterne.

The sawing of the skull in half indicated either a post-mortem examination or dissection by anatomists. Post-mortem examinations in the eighteenth century were extremely rare. Only two or three skulls of the 11,500 found in St. George's burial ground have been sawn. The provisional and plausible deduction is that the Cambridge anatomists were so horrified when they learnt of the eminence of the man beneath their scalpels that they hastily and secretly returned his remains to the grave from which they had been stolen.[9]

In view of the vagueness of the first gravestone and the purely speculative nature of the theory that the body was returned to

---

* That exactness is far from certain. Although Nollekens's biographer, J.T. Smith, does record him measuring George III's nose with calipers because the queen had complained that it was too broad in the bust. Smith also admits, '... in my opinion, Mr. Nollekens trusted more to the eyes, nose, and mouth, for a likeness, than to the bones of the head; and in this belief I am supported most powerfully by the mask taken from Mr. Fox after his death. In his busts of that statesman, the foreheads are low and rugged; whilst that of the mask is even, high, and prominent.' (Smith, *Nollekens and His Times*, Vol. I, p. 381.)

London, I wrote to *The Times* hoping that doubt might be left intact.[10] Kenneth Monkman, the Hon. Secretary of the Sterne Trust, replied that he was 'reasonably sure' he had the right skull and added:

We shall naturally subject our measurements and other findings to further scientific scrutiny before venturing to say finally whether we believe the skull to be Sterne's. If we have reburied the wrong one, nobody, I feel beyond reasonable doubt, would enjoy the situation more than Sterne.[11]

But by then, Mr. Monkman and the Trust had reburied that sawn-off skull in Coxwold churchyard. It is still there, with the two London headstones but, as yet, no new stone that suggests what is there or how it came to be there. Whether or not Sterne would have laughed, it seems to me that we will now never know beyond a reasonable doubt where his head lies.

***

Uncle Toby would have sat, impotent and motionless, stunned at the rawness of Sterne's removal from the world. He would have been just as harrowed by the unrestrained antics of Sterne's widow and daughter once he was dead. For it is only when Sterne dies that the women in his family suddenly begin to exist as people. His spurious zest had overpowered them while he was alive – why else had they left all the stage to him and sat on hillsides in Languedoc? The women in his fiction are, at worst, obtuse and resigned; for the most part they are pliant, alluring and witlessly sympathetic – the sort of creatures that as modest a man as Toby might have invented for his reveries. Elizabeth and Lydia Sterne were active, argumentative and independent women. Lydia even possessed some of that intense animation that her father had cultivated to keep other people at bay.

Sterne had made so many provisions for impossible futures, but throughout his illness he had omitted to make a will. He had done little more than speculate on who might care for Lydia and scrawl hurried instructions on the wrapper of his Letter Book as to which correspondents had a worthwhile stock of his originals. That arrangement he had made with his wife and daughter the previous autumn now stood for nothing. Indeed, events suggested that it had been a hollow pact involving allowances that were beyond Sterne's means.

The ladies may have anticipated the gap between Sterne's promises and resources for they wasted no time. Letters of administration were not granted to Elizabeth Sterne by the Prerogative Court of York until 4 June. But weeks before then, on 12 April, she advertised a sale of:

... All the Houshold Goods and Furniture of the late Mr. STERNE, deceased, at Coxwold, with a Cow near calving and a Parcel of Hay; also a handsome Post-Chaise with a Pair of exceeding good Horses; and a compleat set of coloured Table China ... all Persons who have any Claim upon the Estate and Effects of the said Mr. Sterne, are desired immediately to send in an Account of their Demands to Mr. Ricard, Attorney in York. Likewise all Persons who stood indebted to the said Mr Sterne, at the Time of his Decease, are desired immediately to pay the same to the said Mr. Ricard.[12]

Many observers guessed that hardship faced the Sterne ladies. The Archbishop of York wrote to Mrs. Montagu on 26 March, 'The Widow and daughter of Mr. Sterne are most distressed objects, and have a Scene of unhappiness opened to them, wch it will be difficult for the best-intentioned to prevent.'[13]

But in ten days' time Lydia was writing to Mrs. Montagu, confident that she and her mother would emerge not only intact but with £1,500 secure. Was that bravado? Was it really the case, as she announced, 'that Mr Sterne's personel estate will pay all his debts'?[14] Or is that just the inventive optimism of a girl not yet twenty who may have shared her father's method with problems – that if denied they might vanish? Certainly, a year later, she wrote to John Wilkes in a much humbler and more appealing style. She confessed to Wilkes, in an attempt to persuade him to subscribe to the posthumous publication of her father's remaining sermons, that she and her mother had in fact been left

in the most distress'd circumstances his debts amounted to el[e]ven hundred pounds – his effects when sold did not raise above four hundred – my mother nobly, engaged to pay the rest out of a little estate of 40£ per an which was all all she had in the world – she could not bear the thoughts of leaving his debts unpaid & I honour her for it – this was or rather would have been a scanty provision at least to us who have seen better days![15]

Perhaps we have a sight here of the young adult version of that girl who, eight years before, had incriminated the local theatre in romances with her schoolfriends. The onus of manœuvre certainly seems to have been upon Lydia. Just as Agnes Sterne had once sent an attractive daughter to plead her case, so Lydia may have proved a more effective mendicant than her mother. In the summer of 1768 an appeal was opened in York for the ladies although only on the condition that the proceeds would provide an annuity for Lydia. Mrs. Sterne, it was said, 'was so little loved or esteemed there would not have been a single guinea given if that condition had not been made'.[16]

It was a testing year for Lydia Sterne to come of age, with financial perils and a cantankerous mother to steer. One of their problems was the claim the new vicar of Sutton, Andrew Cheap, had upon the family for restoration of the burned vicarage. Sterne himself had successfully evaded rebuilding and in March 1768 the Archbishop of York gave his opinion that 'the Successor has a right to claim it to be done by Mr. Sterne's Executors.'[17] But the ladies contested the claim on the grounds that Sterne had not lived at Sutton at the time of the fire. Even the Archbishop was alienated by Mrs. Sterne's truculence: 'I . . . am not surprised at the absurdity of Mrs Sterne wth regard to the dilapidations at Sutton: considering the different bubbles of Vanity and levity wch have upheld her for sometime, and the silly cunning of that crooked-headed Attorney, into whose hands she hath unluckily fallen.'[18] On whatever advice, the Sternes held firm and Cheap was forced eventually to settle for £60 – 'the Widow being in indigent circumstances'. That compromise cannot have been a happy one, for the new building cost £576 13s 5d, as meticulously recorded in the Sutton parish register by the bitter Cheap.[19]

Lydia may have been more adaptable to her plight than the Archbishop could admire. He described her and her mother to Mrs. Montagu in terms that express the wish that the deprived should behave in character:

There is generally falsehood mixed wth little cunning; and as it is designed to have a subscription for them opened at York, they think it their interest to depreciate their estate. – I think they depreciate themselves, to think of a collection, wthout making it appear by a fair account how far they may want it: and I am sure, you w^{d} rather assist them, when they are returned to a sober sense of their circumstances and their character; than let your name be mentioned in the roll of ostensible benefactors; wch will only increase their vanity.[20]

As with so many of the Sterne concerns, there is a lack of firm knowledge. Was the claim of Andrew Cheap part of that £1,100? And what income did the ladies receive from the sales of *A Sentimental Journey*? The initial success of that book must have been boosted by the news of the author's death. Becket had published a second edition before the end of March, and yet another edition appeared in 1768.

In York, the appeal on behalf of the ladies was being ably conducted by a Miss Ann Moritt. It reached its climax during York race week in August. On 23 August, Sterne's library was sold at the premises of Todd & Sotheran in Stonegate for some £80. When York was crowded with wealthy visitors, mother and daughter moved into the garret of the house where they lodged. Lydia said that this was done in order that the landlord should be able to let their rooms. It may also have occurred to her that potential subscribers[21] to the appeal fund would be more moved by ladies compelled to live in an attic room. The appeal flourished and most Yorkshire worthies contributed; the final total was about £800.

Lydia was elated by the success and wrote rapturously to Mrs. Montagu, invoking the family symptom of emotion, the tear:

... how gracious, how merciful is God to us! what comfort has he sent us what friends has he rais'd us up! O may we ever retain a just sense of his mercy, and the most grateful remembrance of what we owe to our friends. indeed Madam I scarce can write for Tears when I think how peculiarly kind providence has been towards us.[22]

A little fortified, Lydia and her mother looked to gain what they could from Sterne's literary remains. As we have seen, this put them in an ambivalent position, in that they might have to exploit unsavoury family secrets to earn themselves a living. The first project was to publish three more volumes of Sterne's Sermons. There were some doubts about this venture. Sterne himself had said there were only the sweepings of his study left. But Hall-Stevenson encouraged Lydia and asserted upon his honour that Sterne had had an almost bottomless bag of sermons so that he had only to dip in his hand and take one.[23]

It was enough for Lydia and she stretched eighteen sermons through three volumes at 2s 6d each. Becket perhaps doubted the value of such a project, although most publishers would have been eager to carry anything with Sterne's name on it so soon after his death. It is more likely that the strain between him and Lydia was because of the experiments the girl made with publishing. This was her first experience of it and so she wondered whether Becket was being properly generous. Becket seems to have sought to improve his original terms. He had first offered £400 for the copyright but then made further conditions that Lydia jibbed at. She therefore wrote with youthful con- spiracy to William Strahan, another printer and bookseller:

. . . this affair of not offering them [the sermons] to anyone else must be managed with the greatest caution – for you see he says that he will not take them if offer'd elsewhere. He will be judge of the quantity and quality – & insists on a year's credit. All these points my mother and myself most earnestly desire you to consider – unless you could be pretty sure of getting us more than £400 the offering them might perhaps come to Beckett's knowledge – yet believe me, S^r we had rather anyone had them than Becket – he is a *dirty fellow*.[24]

Only a few months before writing this letter, Lydia had had her twenty-first birthday. Even her godmother, Mrs. Montagu, was alarmed at the rapid progress the girl was making and apparently wrote to Lydia querying the quality of these last sermons and warning of the mixture of wit and girlishness. Lydia's answer is reminiscent of the instability that had infected her father. She declared that one of her advantages was that of 'having spent my days with my mother who has taken great pains to form both my head, & heart',[25] hardly aware that it was that

distinction her father had worn on his sleeve. As for the accusation of pertness, she rejected it with all the cool adroitness of a
young woman confident of her tongue:

> as to inheriting my father's wit I have not the least grain in my
> composition we both thought it an unhappy turn in my father. . . . I
> am so far from being a diseuse de bons mots I think I never was
> guilty of one in my life. I am when in company extreamly diffident
> seldom give my opinion but upon the most trivial things – I am
> 'often check'd for silence but never tax'd for speech'.[26]

Diffidence had its effect. Lydia's plot served to publish the
sermons under a hasty alliance of Becket with Strahan and his
partner Thomas Cadell. They appeared on 3 June 1769 with
729 subscribers. As her father had done, Lydia came to London
for the event, although she departed from the family tradition
in bringing her mother with her.

On 25 May, Hall-Stevenson had published his tedious
continuation of *A Sentimental Journey* and Lydia eagerly pursued
her father's reputation. It was then that she visited Wilkes in
prison and he offered to write a life of Sterne with Hall-
Stevenson as a collaborator.

With that project to look forward to, Lydia and her mother
left for France. They lived first at Angoulême and adopted a
life of cultivated ease:

> Angouleme is a pretty town, the country most delightful; and from
> the principal walk there is a very fine prospect: a serpentine River
> which joins the Garonne at Bordeaux has a very good effect: trees in
> the middle of it which form little Islands where the inhabitants go
> and take the fresco – in short 'tis a most pleasing prospect – and I
> know no greater pleasure than sitting by the side of the River reading
> Milton or Shakespear to my mother – sometimes I take my Guitarr
> and sing to her. – thus do the hours slide away imperceptibly, with
> reading, writing drawing and musick.[27]

Lydia worked at the drawings Wilkes had suggested she
contribute to the collected edition of Sterne's works. But by the
autumn of 1769 that project had become a pressing necessity.
Isaac Panchaud, Sterne's old Paris banker, had gone broke and
it is probable that some of the ladies' funds were lost in his
failure.

Once more, we cannot measure the hard times Lydia owned up to. She and her mother had income from several sources, albeit small and irregular ones. Emotionally, their life in France altered completely. They now noticed only the dull, provincial company and the expensiveness of the local markets. Neither of them was well and in March 1770 Lydia spoke of retiring early after having been bled – the cure that had debilitated her father.[28]

They moved farther south, to Albi – 'but there is little society, and the little there is, is scarce worth the trouble of searching after.'[29] The ladies preferred reading and declined into ill-health. Lydia, still only twenty-three, was very thin and acknowledged: 'I partake too much of my Father's condition.'[30] Her mother now was fifty-seven and distraught, either from illness or 'the Violence of her temper':

... my mother has had two narrow escapes from Death. about two months ago, she was awakend in the night by the Barking of a turn-spit, and getting up she perceiv'd a man coming down her chimney by the means of a Rope. she allarm'd the familly and the Villain ascended the Chimney. there was found upon the Tiles a large knife which was open. and the Rope still fasten'd round the Chimney. if my poor mother had not had a light in her room she would not have seen the Rope and in all probability would have been murther'd what a mercy it was that she was awaken'd by the Barking of the Dog! – we have got all the Chimneys grated, so that no one can descend. since that alass she has had an Epileptick fit and has continued ill ever since. may God restore her health. her loss would be irreparable to me.[31]

But just as Lydia seemed likely to lose her mother, she found herself a husband. In March 1772, she wrote to Mrs. Montagu with the first news that she had had an offer, 'which tho' not advantageous, yet was far from disagreeable to me'.[32] However, her suitor's father was insisting on the French practice whereby 'my mother should give up her estate immediately.' The suitor, Jean-Baptiste-Alexandre-Anne Medalle, the son of a customs official at Albi, 'was far from displeasing to me'.[33] Lydia was harrowed by the generosity of her mother in encouraging the match:

my mother is willing almost to leave herself without bread for the advantage of her Lydia. my heart bleeds to think she should be under the necessity of reducing herself to so small a pittance: therefore my dear Mrs Montague permit me to plead for her to you. I here thrust my chair from me and write upon my knees, consider her, and her alone. and withdraw not your bounty from her whilst she lives! I ask nothing for myself but shall feel doubly on her account if you grant my humble petition.[34]

Mrs. Montagu was cool in answer. She helped the potentially impoverished Mrs. Sterne by transferring to her the annual allowance of £20 she had previously made to Lydia. As to the marriage, she was 'a perfect stranger' to the man. On the matter of Lydia's professed quandary as to how to act, Mrs. Montagu replied with the tartness of one who had many Sterne doubts to settle:

... all you give your friends is that you are going to marry a man of a different Religion, and to reduce your Mother to almost beggary, both these things you confess. You seem at the same time to declare steadfastness in Religion and Filial piety to your parent. My dear cousin the actions not the words are what shall decide the judgment of God and man.[35]

Action settled the matter. On 28 April 1772, Lydia was converted to the Catholic faith and married to Medalle. The two events took place in the private chapel of the Provost's house at Albi. On 6 August 1772, Lydia gave birth to a son, Jean-François-Laurent.[36]

Elizabeth Sterne had short joy of her grandson, for she died in Albi, at the house of a physician named Linières, on 13 January 1773.[37] She would have been fifty-eight or fifty-nine. Lydia had a second son, Jacques-François Guillaume, on 21 December 1773. Shortly after that, Medalle himself died.

It was in 1775 that Lydia Medalle returned to England to publish *Letters of the late Rev. Mr. Laurence Sterne*, along with the Memoir of his life. Despite earlier disagreements, Becket handled this book and it was published on 25 October. It carried a frontispiece of an engraving of a portrait by Benjamin West that showed Lydia, fetching in a costume that had slipped from her shoulder, protectively clasping a laurelled bust of her father. When the *Letters* were reprinted in 1776 Becket had his revenge by abandoning this frontispiece. To judge by the sly-faced handsomeness of Mrs. Medalle, it is to be regretted that we have no account of how the widow fared in London with her two infant sons in tow.

After that, nothing is known of her except that one son died in 1783 at the Benedictine school at Soreze. In his death certificate it was said that his mother was already dead. What we know of her suggests a vivacious, enterprising young woman. Perhaps she was seriously ill; perhaps, like her father, she could not tolerate idleness and withered in Albi. It is not known when or where she died, or what became of her other son. Sterne had come unofficially into the world and, within fifteen years of his own death, his immediate family line had vanished.

There is only one more person to trace: Eliza Draper. She had sailed back to India, pursued by letters, but without any alternative to resuming her unhappy married life. The Drapers moved in 1768 from Bombay to Tellicherry where Eliza seems to have enjoyed the life of a Raj lady, no doubt enhanced by the reputation she had acquired in England as the inspiration of a great writer.

News of Sterne's death concerned her, if only because she feared what might become of the letters between Sterne and herself. It is entertaining to see Eliza speculating on what action the Sterne ladies would take. She acted with a curious mixture of circumspection and tactlessness. Thus, soon after news of Sterne's death, Eliza wrote to Lydia renewing that hint of guardianship that Sterne had played with. It was a curious proposal, Eliza being only three years older than Lydia. Odder still, her offer had omitted all reference to Mrs. Sterne. Eliza made a tortuous defence of this omission – Sterne had told her so many unpleasant things about his wife that she could not talk of her; in addition, for all Eliza knew, she might now be confined because of her 'Malady'. But clearly, the provocative offer had made certain of enemies, if there had been any earlier doubt. Eliza now had to spin and plot to match the impoverished ladies:

... Miss Sterne, in her letter, tells me – *that her Father did sometimes misrepresent her mother, in order to justify his neglect of her* – I do not think highly of a Daughter, who could compliment a living Parent,

however justly at the expence of a Deceased one . . . my silence on
the subject [Mrs. Sterne], as I've hinted before, only proceeded from
a Delicacy w'ch is natural to me, when I either wish or mean, to
speak to the Affections – I have been strangely deceived in Miss
Sternes – or she never could have perverted my Sentiments so much,
as to suppose I did her an Injury, in addressing her as a kindred
Spirit, and with all the freedom, I could wish to subsist between
myself and a Sister of my Heart.[38]

Deep suspicion now joined Eliza and England, where once
lovelorn pity had held sway. She no longer had illusions about
Sterne. In life, she had been 'almost an Idolator, of His Worth';[39]
but with his death, she had seen that he was 'tainted with the
Vices of Injustice, Meanness – & Folly'.[40] The widow, she had
been assured by Sterne, was 'a Drinker, a Swearer, venal &
Unchaste'.[41] As for the daughter, Eliza had heard that she was
'rather speciously attractive than mildly amiable'.[42]

Several travellers to India from England intimated to Eliza
that the poverty of the ladies might force them to take advantage
of those letters concerning Eliza. She seems genuinely to have
feared such revelation, although there is no positive evidence
that Lydia and her mother intended to publish. Eliza arranged
with Becket that she would pay him to suppress the letters and
hand them over to Mrs. James. At the same time, she organized
collections for the ladies among the Indian gentry and even
encouraged a Colonel Campbell of Bengal to visit England with
a view to marrying Lydia. But this plan was hardly underway
when the chimneys of Albi were witnessing a more effective
intrigue.

Eliza was eager to return to England, to see her daughter who
was still at school, and perhaps to reassure herself about the
discretion of the Sternes. By now, she was also keen to escape
her husband. In January 1773, she deserted him and eloped
with a naval officer, Sir John Clark. Scandal followed and Eliza
was forced to shelter with her uncle, John Whitehill, at Masuli-
patam. She lived with him collecting evidence against her
husband so defamatory that he was dissuaded from suing for
divorce.

Late in 1774, Eliza returned to England, and to London. She
seems to have lived there in comfort and as a thirty-year-old

M

with the colourful reputation of being 'Sterne's Eliza' she must have had many visitors. The Letters from *Yorick to Eliza* had been published in 1773, without any foreword from Eliza, but hardly without her cooperation. She was courted in London by both Wilkes and William Combe. But her most serious admirer was the Abbé Raynal. He pursued her retirement to Bristol, where Eliza died on 3 August 1778. She is buried in Bristol Cathedral with a lavish monument, probably provided by Raynal. It is a much more sumptuous memorial than any her lover-by-letter ever had.

BIBLIOGRAPHY

This is a list of the main sources consulted in writing this book. Extensive Sterne bibliographies may be found in:

Wilbur L. Cross, *The Life and Times of Laurence Sterne* (see below)

Lodwick Hartley, *Laurence Sterne in the Twentieth Century* (Chapel Hill, North Carolina, 1966)

Alan B. Howes, *Yorick and the Critics: Sterne's Reputation in England, 1760–1868* (New Haven, 1958)

WORKS BY STERNE

There are two editions: *Works and Life*, ed. Wilbur L. Cross (New York, 1904) and *Works* (Oxford, 1926–7). I have used the Cross edition for the Sermons, *A Political Romance* and for *A Dream*

Plans for a new and much needed complete edition of the Works have recently been announced by the Florida University Press

The standard edition of *Tristram Shandy*, which I have used in this book, is edited by James Aiken Work (New York, 1940)

There are two good editions of *A Sentimental Journey*: one edited by Gardner D. Stout (Berkeley, California, 1967) and the other, which I have used, by Ian Jack (Oxford, 1968)

The Letters are edited by Lewis Perry Curtis (Oxford, 1935), in a volume that also contains Sterne's Memoir and the *Journal to Eliza*, both of which I have quoted from there

LIVES OF STERNE

Willard Connely, *Laurence Sterne as Yorick* (London, 1958) (which deals only with the years 1760–68)

Wilbur L. Cross, *The Life and Times of Laurence Sterne* (New York, 1909; new edn New Haven, 1925; rev. edn, 1929; reissued New York, 1967).

Lewis Perry Curtis, *The Politicks of Laurence Sterne* (London, 1929) (which deals with the 1741 election)

Percy Fitzgerald, *The Life of Laurence Sterne* (London, 1864)

Lodwick Hartley, *This Is Lorence* (Chapel Hill, North Carolina, 1943) (reissued in 1968 as *Laurence Sterne: A Biographical Essay*)

Lewis Melville, *The Life and Letters of Laurence Sterne* (London, 1911)

Margaret R.B. Shaw, *Laurence Sterne: The Making of a Humourist, 1713–62* (London, 1957)

Walter Sichel, *Sterne: A study* (London, 1910)

H.D. Traill, *Sterne* (London, 1882)

W.B.C. Watkins, 'Yorick Revisited', *Perilous Balance: The Tragic Genius of Swift, Johnson and Sterne* (Princeton, 1939), pp. 99–156

Thomas Yoseloff, *Laurence Sterne: A Fellow of Infinite Jest* (London, 1948)

WORKS ON ASPECTS OF STERNE'S LIFE

W. Baster, *An Essay on the Nature, Causes and Cure, of the Rheumatism . . . To which are added Observations on the Medical Treatment of The Rev. Mr. Sterne, During his last Illness* (London, 1776)

John Burton, *British Liberty endanger'd* (London, 1749)

Arthur H. Cash, 'Some New Sterne Letters', *TLS*, 8 April 1965

— 'Who Was Sterne's Mother?', *Notes & Queries*, May 1967, pp. 162–9

— 'The Birth of Tristram Shandy: Sterne and Dr. Burton', *Studies in the Eighteenth Century*, ed. R.F. Brissenden (Canberra, 1968)

J.W. Clay, 'The Sterne Family', *Yorkshire Archaeological Journal*, Vol. XXI, 1911, pp. 91–107

C. Collyer, 'Laurence Sterne and Yorkshire Politics: Some New Evidence', *Proceedings of the Leeds Philosophical and Literary Society*, Vol. VII, 1952, pp. 83–7

William Combe, *Second Journal to Eliza, hitherto known as Letters Supposed To Have Been Written by Yorick and Eliza . . .*, presented with an Introduction by Margaret R.B. Shaw (London, 1929)

Thomas Cox, *A Popular History of The Grammar School of Queen Elizabeth, at Heath, near Halifax* (Halifax, 1879)

John Croft, *Scrapeana*, 2nd edn (York, 1792)

— *The Whitefoord Papers*, ed. W.A.S. Hewins (Oxford, 1898)

Lewis P. Curtis, 'The First Printer of Tristram Shandy', *PMLA*, Vol. XLVII, 1932, pp. 777–89

— 'New Light on Sterne', *MLN*, Vol. LXXVI, 1961, pp. 498–501

Robert Davies, *A Memoir of The York Press* (London, 1868)

— 'A Memoir of John Burton', *Yorkshire Archaeological and Topographical Journal*, Vol. II, 1873, pp. 403–40

Dominique-Joseph Garat, *Memoires Historiques Sur La Vie de M. Suard, Sur Ses Ecrits, et Sur Le XVIIIe Siecle* (Paris, 1820), Vol. II

Richard Griffith, *A Series of Genuine Letters between Henry and Frances* (London, 1786)

— *The Posthumous Works of a Late Celebrated Genius* (Dublin, 1770)

John Hall-Stevenson, *Crazy Tales* (London, 1762)

Harlan Hamilton, *Doctor Syntax: A Silhouette of William Combe Esq* (London, 1968)

Lodwick Hartley, 'Sterne's Eugenius as Indiscreet Author: The Literary Career of John Hall-Stevenson', *PMLA*, Vol. *LXXXVI*, 1971, pp. 428–45.

James M. Kuist, 'New Light on Sterne: An Old Man's Recollections of the Young Vicar', *PMLA*, Vol. LXXX, 1965, pp. 549–53

Kenneth Monkman, 'The Bibliography of the Early Editions of *Tristram Shandy*', *Transactions of the Bibliographical Society*, March 1970, pp. 11–39

— 'Sterne, Hamlet and Yorick: Some New Material', *The Winged Skull*, ed. Arthur H. Cash and John M. Stedmond (London, 1971)

— and James Diggle, 'Some New Sterne Letters', *TLS*, 6 May 1965; 'Yorick and his Flock: A New Sterne Letter', *TLS*, 14 March 1968

S.L. Ollard and P.C. Walker, 'Archbishop Herring's Visitation Returns, 1743', *Yorkshire Archaeological Society Record Series*, Vol. LXXI (York, 1928)

Frederick A. Pottle, 'Bozzy and Yorick', *Blackwood's Magazine*, Vol. CCXVII, 1925, pp. 297–313

I.P. Pressly, *A York Miscellany* (London, 1938)

Archibald B. Shepperson, 'Yorick as Ministering Angel', *Virginia Quarterly Review*, Vol. XXX, 1954, pp. 54–66

Robert Stearne, *The Royal Regiment of Foot of Ireland. Journal of Robert Stearne (1685–1717)* (MS. Hove public library and National Army Museum)

Ralph Straus, *Robert Dodsley* (London, 1910)

Todd & Sotheran, *A Facsimile Reproduction of a Unique Catalogue of Laurence Sterne's Library*, with a Preface by Charles Whibley (London, 1930)

Earl R. Wasserman, 'Unedited Letters by Sterne, Hume, and Rousseau', *MLN*, Vol. LXVI, 1951, pp. 73–80.

Arnold Wright and William Lutley Sclater, *Sterne's Eliza: Some Account of her Life in India: with her Letters written between 1757 and 1774* (London, 1922)

COMMENTARIES ON STERNE

A. Alvarez, 'Introduction', *A Sentimental Journey*, Penguin edn (Harmondsworth, 1967)

Walter Bagehot, *Collected Works*, ed. Norman St John-Stevas (London, 1965), Vol. II, pp. 278–312

Theodore Baird, 'The Time-Scheme of *Tristram Shandy* and a Source', *PMLA*, Vol. LI, 1936, pp. 803–20

Wayne Booth, 'Did Sterne Complete Tristram Shandy?', *Modern Philology*, Vol. XLVIII, 1951, pp. 172–83

— *The Rhetoric of Fiction* (Chicago, 1961), pp. 221–40, 430–32

R.F. Brissenden, 'Sterne and Painting', *Of Books and Humankind*, ed. John Butt (London, 1964), pp. 93–108

Arthur H. Cash, 'The Lockean Psychology of *Tristram Shandy*', *ELH*, Vol. XXII, 1955, pp. 125–35

— 'The Sermon in Tristram Shandy', *ELH*, Vol. XXI, 1961, pp. 395–417

— 'Sterne's Comedy of Moral Sentiments: A Revaluation of the Journey', *Dissertation Abstracts*, Vol. XXII, 1962, pp. 4013–14

— and John M. Stedmond (eds.), *The Winged Skull* (London, 1971)

Ernest N. Dilworth, *The Unsentimental Journey of Laurence Sterne* (New York, 1948)

John Ferriar, *Illustrations of Sterne* (London, 1798; 2nd edn, 1812)

Henri Fluchere, *Laurence Sterne: From Tristram to Yorick: An Interpretation of Tristram Shandy*, trans. Barbara Bray (London, 1965) (an abridged edn of book first published Paris, 1961)

Alice Green Fredman, *Diderot and Sterne* (New York, 1955)

Northrop Frye, *Anatomy of Criticism: Four Essays* (Princeton, 1957), pp. 303–8

Graham Greene, 'Fielding and Sterne', *Collected Essays* (London, 1969), pp. 83–94

Lansing van der Heyden Hammond, *Laurence Sterne's 'Sermons of Mr Yorick'* (New Haven, 1948)

Edwin Muir, 'Laurence Sterne', *Essays on Literature and Society* (London, 1949), pp. 49–56

V.S. Pritchett, 'Tristram Shandy', *Books in General* (London, 1953), pp. 173–8

Peter Quennell, 'Sterne', *Four Portraits: Boswell, Gibbon, Sterne, Wilkes* (London, 1945), pp. 139–94

Herbert Read, 'Sterne', *The Sense of Glory: Essays in Criticism* (Cambridge, 1929), pp. 123–51

Christopher Ricks, 'Introduction', *Tristram Shandy*, Penguin edn (Harmondsworth, 1967)

George Saintsbury, *Prefaces and Essays* (London, 1933), pp. 130–93

John Traugott, *Tristram Shandy's World: Sterne's Philosophical Rhetoric* (Berkeley and Los Angeles, 1954)

Virginia Woolf, 'Sterne', 'Sterne's Ghost' and 'Eliza and Sterne', *Collected Essays*, ed. Leonard Woolf (London, 1967), Vol. III, pp. 86–104

NOTES

ABBREVIATIONS: *TS* – Tristram Shandy, *SJ* – Sentimental Journey,
JE – Journal to Eliza, LS – Laurence Sterne

PROLOGUE: TOUCHED BY STERNE (pp. 1–29)

1. *SJ*, Vol. II, The Passport, Versailles.
2. *TS*, Vol. I, motto (from Epictetus).
3. *SJ*, Vol. II, Maria, Moulines.
4. *Boswell's Life of Johnson*, ed. G.B. Hill, rev. L.F. Powell (Oxford, 1934), Vol. II, p. 449.
5. Vicesimus Knox, 'On Modern Criticism', *Winter Evening* (London, 1790), Vol. II, p. 159.
6. *Works of Coleridge* (New York, 1884), Vol. IV, p. 281.
7. Thackeray, 'Sterne and Goldsmith', *English Humourists* (London, 1853), p. 284.
8. Graham Greene (1969), p. 89.
9. F.R. Leavis, *The Great Tradition* (London, 1948), p. 2.
10. Berkeley, *Treatise Concerning the Principles of Human Knowledge*, Everyman edn (London, 1910), p. 114.
11. Hume, *Treatise of Human Nature*, Penguin edn (Harmondsworth, 1969), Book I, Part IV, VI, p. 300.
12. *Letters, JE*, 9 July 1767, p. 377.
13. *TS*, Vol. III, Ch. XVIII.
14. *ibid.*, Vol. V, Ch. VII.
15. *ibid.*, Vol. IV, Ch. XVII.
16. *Letters, JE*, 16 April 1767, p. 323.
17. John Macdonald, *Memoirs of an Eighteenth-Century Footman*, ed. John Beresford (London, 1927), pp. 91–2.
18. *SJ*, Vol. I, In the Street, Calais.
19. *ibid.*, The Remise Door, Calais.
20. *ibid.*
21. *ibid.*, The Pulse, Paris.
22. *ibid.*, The Gloves, Paris.
23. *TS*, Vol. I, Ch. XXIII.
24. *ibid.*, Vol. III, Ch. XXXVIII.
25. *ibid.*, Vol. I, Ch. XIX.
26. *ibid.*, Vol. III, Ch. IX.
27. *ibid.*, Vol II, Ch. XIX.
28. *ibid.*, Vol. I, Ch. II.
29. *ibid.*, Vol. VII, Ch. XXX.
30. *ibid.*, Vol. V, Ch. VI.
31. *ibid.*, Vol. I, Ch. XXII.
32. *ibid.*, Ch. XI.
33. *ibid.*, Vol. III, Ch. XX.
34. *ibid.*, Vol. I, Ch. II.
35. *Letters*, LS to My Witty Widow, Mrs F., 3 August 1760, p. 120.
36. *TS*, Vol. III, Ch. XVI.
37. *ibid.*, Vol. VI, Ch. II.
38. *ibid.*, Vol. II, Ch. XIX.
39. *ibid.*, Vol. IV, Ch. XVII.
40. *ibid.*, Vol. III, Ch. XXIX.

41. *ibid.*, Vol. IV, Ch. II.
42. *ibid.*, Vol. I, Ch. X.
43. *SJ*, Vol. I, Nampont, The Postillion.
44. *TS*, Vol. V, Ch. I.
45. *ibid.*, Vol. VII, Ch. I.
46. *ibid.*, Ch. II.
47. *Letters*, LS to David Garrick, 27 January 1760, p. 87.
48. *TS*, Vol. II, Ch. XI.
49. *ibid.*, Vol. VI, Ch. VI.
50. *ibid.*, Vol. VIII, Ch. II.
51. *ibid.*, Vol. I, Ch. XXV.
52. *Letters*, LS to John Hall-Stevenson, June 1761, p. 139.
53. *TS*, Vol. III, Ch. XXVIII.
54. *Crazy Tales*, pp. 17–18.
55. *TS*, Vol. VII, Ch. XXXIII.
56. *ibid.*, Vol. IV, Ch. XIII.
57. *Letters*, Lydia Sterne to John Hall-Stevenson, 13 February 1770, p. 453.
58. *ibid.*, Lydia Sterne to Mrs. Montagu, 5 April 1768, p. 434.
59. *ibid.*
60. *ibid.*, Lydia Sterne to John Wilkes, 22 July 1769, p. 451.
61. *Memoirs of Mrs. Hannah More*, ed. W. Roberts (London, 1834), Vol. I, p. 67.
62. Cross, p. 523.
63. *Letters*, Memoir, p. 5.

'WHEN THEY BEGOT ME' (pp. 33–44)

1. Cross, p. 2.
2. Arthur Gray and Frederick Brittain, *A History of Jesus College Cambridge* (London, 1960), p. 77.
3. J.W. Clay (1911), p. 92.
4. *ibid*, p. 97.
5. *Letters*, p. 5, n. 1.
6. *TS*, Vol. VI, Ch. XXXII.
7. Clay, *op. cit*, p. 98.
8. Richard Cannon, *Historical Record of the Thirty-Fourth ...* (London, 1844), p. 16.
9. George Farquhar, *The Recruiting Officer* (1706), Act III, Sc. I.
10. Major R.E. Scouller, *The Armies of Queen Anne* (Oxford, 1966), p. 89.
11. *ibid.*, p. 126.
12. *The Life and Adventures of Matthew Bishop* (1744), quoted by Scouller, *op. cit.*, p. 152, n. 4.
13. PRO, Ind. 5431, p. 149.
14. Cannon, *op. cit.*, p. 17.
15. *ibid.*
16. *ibid.*
17. Byron, *Works, Letters and Journals*, ed. Prothero, Vol. II, p. 359.
18. *Letters*, Memoir, p. 1.
19. Cannon, *op. cit.*, p. 19.
20. PRO, Treas. Cal. IV, p. 603; Scouller, *op. cit.*, p. 246.
21. Cannon, *op. cit.*, p. 19.
22. PRO, W.O. 26/15, p. 31.
23. Frank O'Connor, *Leinster, Munster & Connaught* (London, n.d.), p. 136.
24. *Correspondence of Jonathan Swift*, ed. Harold Williams (London, 1965), Vol. IV, p. 34.
25. Albert Carré, *L'Influence des Huguenots Français en Irlande aux XVIIᵉ et XVIIIᵉ Siècles* (Paris, 1937), p. 55.
26. *Letters*, LS to Jaques Sterne, 5 April 1751, p. 35.
27. William Burke, *History of Clonmel* (Clonmel, 1907), p. 125.
28. Arthur Cash (1967), pp. 162–9.
29. *TS*, Vol. I, Ch. I.

'HEY-GO-MAD' (pp. 45–58)

1. PRO, W.O. 26/15, p. 31.
2. *Letters*, Memoir, p. 1.
3. *ibid.*
4. *ibid.*, pp. 1–2.
5. *The Life of Mr Thomas Gent* (London, 1832), p. 158.
6. *Letters*, Memoir, p. 2.
7. *Correspondence of Jonathan Swift*, Vol. I, p. 178.
8. Lady Mary Wortley Montagu, *Complete Letters*, ed. Robert Halsband (London, 1967), Vol. I, p. 189.
9. *Letters*, Memoir, p. 2.
10. PRO, W.O. 5/23, pp. 96, 166.
11. *Letters*, Memoir, p. 2.
12. *ibid.*
13. PRO, Ind. 5431, p. 148; W.O. 25/2979; Ind., 5433, p. 28; 5435, p. 6.
14. *Letters*, Memoir, p. 2.
15. Irish Genealogical Office, 275, Cape XV, Betham, p. 208.
16. *Letters*, Memoir, p. 2.
17. *Diary of Ralph Thoresby*, ed. Joseph Hunter (London, 1830), Vol. II, p. 15.
18. Scott, *Biographical Memoirs* 'Edinburgh, 1834), p. 275n.
19. *Letters*, Memoir, p. 2.
20. *ibid.*, pp. 2–3.
21. *Journal of Robert Stearne* (*1685–1717*), MS., pp. 28–9 and passim.
22. *ibid.*, p. 36.
23. *ibid.*, p. 33.
24. *TS*, Vol. VI, Ch. XXXII.
25. *Journal of Robert Stearne, op. cit.*, p. 131.
26. Theodore Baird (1936), pp. 803–20.
27. *Journal of Robert Stearne, op. cit.*
28. *Letters*, Memoir, p. 3.
29. *Dublin Literary Repository*, January 1814, p. 233.
30. Samuel Smiles, *The Huguenots, their Settlements, Churches, & Industries in England and Ireland* (London, 1867), p. 368 and n.
31. V.S. Pritchett, 'Tristram Shandy', *Books in General* (London, 1953), p. 177.
32. G.B. Shaw, *John Bull's Other Island* (1904), Act I.

'A BOY OF GENIUS'? (pp. 59–68)

1. *Letters*, LS to John Hall-Stevenson, 28 July 1761, p. 142.
2. *ibid.*, Memoir, p. 3.
3. *ibid.*
4. *ibid.*, pp. 3–4.
5. Fielding, *Tom Jones* (1749), Book 3, Ch. 5.
6. *ibid.*, Ch. 2.
7. Thomas Cox (1879), p. 3.
8. Locke, *On Education* (1693).
9. Berkeley, *op. cit.*, Introduction, p. 94.
10. *TS*, Vol. V, Ch. XLIII.
11. John Traugott (1954), p. 26.
12. *TS*, Vol. V, Ch. XLIII.
13. *ibid.*
14. *Thraliana, The Diary of Mrs. Hester Lynch Thrale*, ed. Katherine Balderston (Oxford, 1951), Vol. I, pp. 23–4.
15. Baird, *op. cit.*, p. 804.
16. *ibid.*
17. Wayne C. Booth (1951), p. 183.
18. *TS*, Vol. IX, Ch. XXIV.
19. Booth, *op. cit.*, p. 183.
20. *TS*, Vol. V, Ch. VII.
21. Traugott, *op. cit.*, p. 7.
22. *TS*, Vol. V, Ch. I.
23. *ibid.*, Vol. VIII, Ch. V.

THE STORY OF ROGER STERNE, CONCLUDED
(pp. 69–73)

1. Cannon, *op. cit.*, pp. 22, 81.
2. Captain Sayer, *The History of Gibraltar* (London, 1862), p. 212.
3. *Letters*, Memoir, p. 3.
4. PRO, C.O. 137/19, p. 25.
5. W.J. Gardner, *A History of Jamaica* (London, 1873), p. 165.
6. PRO, C.O. 137/19, p. 25.
7. *ibid.*, p. 26.
8. *ibid.*, 137/53, pp. 328–9.
9. *Letters*, Memoir, p. 3.
10. *ibid.*
11. Thackeray, *Henry Esmond* (1852), Book III, Ch. I.
12. *ibid.*, Ch. V.
13. *ibid.*, Book II, Ch. IX.
14. *TS*, Vol. VI, Ch. XXXII.

'IN SUCH A GLOOM' (pp. 74–81)

1. Defoe, *A Tour Through the Whole Island of Great Britain*, Everyman edn (London, 1962), Vol. II, pp. 197, 198.
2. Clay, *op. cit.*, p. 100.
3. *ibid.*
4. *Letters*, LS to Jaques Sterne, 5 April 1751, p. 34.
5. *ibid.*, p. 35.
6. *ibid.*, pp. 39–40.
7. Gibbon, *Memoirs of My Life*, ed. George A. Bonnand (London, 1966), p. 48.
8. *Letters of Thomas Gray*, ed. Duncan Tovey (London, 1900), Vol. I, p. 4.
9. *The Diary of a Country Parson: Rev. James Woodforde*, 1758–81
ed. John Beresford (London, 1924), pp. 18–19.
10. Gray and Brittain, *op. cit.*, p. 103.
11. G. M. Trevelyan *English Social History* (London, 1942; 1967 edn) p. 381.
12. Gibbon, *op. cit.*, p. 54.
13. Christopher Wordsworth, *Scholae Academicae* (Cambridge, 1877), pp. 129–32.
14. *Crazy Tales*, p. 17
15. BM, Add. MS. 35640, f. 406, quoted in D.A. Winstanley, *Unreformed Cambridge* (Cambridge, 1935), pp. 210–11.
16. BM, Add. Ch. 16158.
17. *ibid.*, 16160.

PART TWO: 'IN A BYE CORNER...' 1738–59 (pp. 85–167)

1. *TS*, Vols I and II (2nd edn, 1760), dedication.
2. *Letters*, LS to ?, summer 1759, p. 76.
3. Pope, 'The Happy Life of a Country Parson', lines 17–20, *Poetical Works*, ed. Herbert Davis (London, 1966), p. 238.
4. *Gentleman's Magazine*, Vol. XXX, May 1760, pp. 317–18.
5. Charles Churchill, *The Author* (1763), line 352.
6. Keats to George and Georgiana Keats, 14 February 1819, *Letters of John Keats*, selected and ed. Robert Gittings (Oxford, 1970), p. 214.
7. William Warburton, *Letters to and from Doddridge* (London, 1811), p. 202.
8. Jane Austen, *Pride and Prejudice* (1813), Ch. XIII.
9. Francis Drake, *Eboracum: or the*

History and Antiquities of the City of York (1736), pp. 239–40.

10. Defoe, *op. cit.*, Vol. II, p. 234.

11. *ibid.*, pp. 230–31.

12. *Memoirs of a Royal Chaplain, 1729–1763; The Correspondence of Edmund Pyle*, ed. Albert Hartshorne (London, 1905), p. 74.

13. *ibid.*, p. 76.

14. BM, Add. MS., 32719, ff. 251–2; *Letters*, pp. 425–6.

15. *ibid.*, 32729, ff. 299–300; *Letters*, p. 428.

16. Warburton to Ralph Allen, *Surtees Society*, Vol. 124, *North Country Diaries*, Vol. II, pp. 195–6.

17. Robert Davies (1868), p. 255.

18. *Pyle, op. cit.*, p. 168.

19. Richardson, *Pamela* (1740), Letter XIX.

20. Ian Watt, *The Rise of the Novel* (London, 1957; 1963 edn), p. 154.

21. *TS*, Vol. I, Ch. XI.

22. LS to Rev. Dealtry, 20 November 1739, see L.P. Curtis (1961), pp. 498–501.

23. *Letters*, Memoir, p. 4.

24. *ibid.*, LS to Elizabeth Lumley, ?1739/40, p. 18.

25. *ibid.*, pp. 10–11; see also *JE*, 16 and 19 April 1767, pp. 323–5.

26. *ibid.*, pp. 12–15.

27. *ibid.*, Memoir, p. 4.

28. *The Whitefoord Papers*, p. 226.

29. Emily J. Climenson, *Elizabeth Montagu, The Queen of the Blue-Stockings, Her Correspondence from 1720 to 1761* (London, 1906), Vol. I, p. 73.

30. *ibid.*, p. 55.

31. *ibid.*, p. 74.

32. *Whiteford Papers*, p. 226.

33. Johnson, *Dictionary*.

34. *York Courant*, 13 October 1741.

35. *York Gazetteer*, 15 December 1741.

36. *Letters*, Memoir, p. 4.

37. *York Courant*, 29 September 1741.

38. *ibid.*, 20 October 1741.

39. *ibid.*, 8 December 1741.

40. *ibid.*, 27 October 1741.

41. *ibid.*, 3 November 1741.

42. *ibid.*, 10 November 1741.

43. *ibid.*

44. *ibid.*, 15 December 1741.

45. Gent, *op. cit.*, p. 194.

46. *York Courant*, 1 January 1742.

47. *TS*, Vol. I, Ch. XII.

48. *York Courant*, 27 July 1742.

49. *Whitefoord Papers*, pp. 225–6.

50. *York Courant*, 27 November 1744.

51. *ibid.*, 4 December 1744.

52. *ibid.*

53. *Letters*, LS to Jaques Sterne, 5 April 1751, p. 41.

54. *ibid.*, p. 36.

55. Sutton on the Forest, parish records.

56. *Letters*, p. 36.

57. *ibid.*

58. *ibid.*

59. *ibid.*

60. *ibid.*, p. 37.

61. *ibid.*, Memoir, p. 4.

62. *ibid.*, p. 37.

63. *ibid.*, p. 35.

64. James M. Kuist (1965), p. 549.

65. *Letters*, p. 37.

66. *ibid.*, pp. 37–8.

67. *ibid.*, p. 39.

68. *Monthly Repository of Theology and General Literature*, Vol. 3, 1808, p. 12.

69. *Whitefoord Papers*, p. 230.

70. *Letters*, p. 33.

71. *Letters*, LS to John Blake, 30 September 1758, p. 61.

72. *TS*, Vol. I, Ch. XVIII.

73. *ibid.*, Vol. V, Ch. V.

74. *ibid.*, Vol. I, Ch. III.

75. *ibid.*, Vol. VI, Ch. XX.

76. *ibid.*, Vol. I, Ch. I.

77. *ibid.*, Ch. XVII.

78. W. Henderson, *Folklore of the Northern Counties* (London, 1879), p. 15.

79. Sutton and Stillington, parish records.

80. Clay, *op. cit.*, p. 102.

81. *Scrapeana*, p. 25.

82. *TS*, Vol. II, Ch. IX.

83. John Burton (1749), pp. 15–16.

84. *ibid.*, p. 6.

85. *ibid.*, p. 19.

86. *York Courant*, 2 July 1745.

87. M. Dorothy George, *English Political Caricature to 1792* (Oxford, 1960), p. 96.

88. *York Courant*, 29 October 1745.

89. Cross, p. 79.

90. Burton, p. 25.

91. *ibid.*, p. 28.

92. *Letters*, Jaques Sterne to Lord Irwin, 7 December 1745, p. 424.

93. *ibid.*, LS to Theophilus Garencieres, ?1751, p. 44.

94. *ibid.*, p. 45.

95. *ibid.*, LS to the Earl of Shelburne, ?21 May 1767, p. 343.

96. *Whitefoord Papers*, p. 226.

97. Kuist, p. 549.

98. *Scrapeana*, p. 22.

99. *TS*, Vol. IX, Ch. I.

100. *Letters*, LS to John Hall-Stevenson, June 1761, p. 140.

101. *ibid.*, LS to John Blake, 29 July 1758, pp. 56–7.

102. *ibid.*, September 1758, p. 59.

103. *ibid.*, 7 July 1758, p. 54.

104. *Whitefoord Papers*, p. 234.

105. *Mrs. Montagu, 'Queen of the Blues', Her Letters and Friendships from 1762 to 1800*, ed. Reginald Blunt (London, 1923), Vol. I, p. 188.

106. *Letters*, LS to John Hall-Stevenson, December 1760, p. 124.

107. *ibid.*, Mrs. Sterne to Mrs. Montagu, 9 March 1753, pp. 430–31.

108. Kenneth Monkman and James Diggle (1968), p. 276.

109. *ibid.*

110. *ibid.*

111. Elizabeth Sterne to John Blake (MS. letter in the possession of Kenneth Monkman).

112. *Letters*, LS to John Blake, ?July 1758, p. 55.

113. *ibid.*, ?August 1758, p. 57.

114. *ibid.*, 17 December 1758, p. 66.

115. *ibid.*, 30 September 1758, p. 61.

116. *Whitefoord Papers*, pp. 234–5.

117. Fielding, *Joseph Andrews* (1742), Book II, Ch. XIV.

118. Sutton, parish records.

119. *Whitefoord Papers*, p. 226.

120. J.H. Plumb, *England in the Eighteenth Century* (Harmondsworth, 1950), p. 82.

121. *Private Acts of Parliament*, 29 Georg II, *c.* 10.

122. *TS*, Vol. IV, Ch. XXXI.

123. *Letters*, LS to Sir William Stanhope, 19 September 1767, p. 394.

124. *ibid.*, LS to John Blake, 17 December 1758, p. 66.

125. *ibid.*, LS to Bishop of Gloucester, 19 June 1760, p. 116.

126. John Burnett, *A History of the Cost of Living* (Harmondsworth, 1969), pp. 128–38.

127. Kuist, p. 550.

128. *Letters*, LS to Rev. Robert Brown, 9 September 1760, p. 122.

129. *TS*, Vol. IX, Ch. XXXI.

130. *Diary of a Country Parson, op. cit.*, p. 102.

131. Drake, *op. cit.*, p. 242.

132. *Letters*, LS to John Hall-Stevenson, 12 August 1762, p. 180.

133. David Magarshack, *Chekhov* (London, 1952), pp. 80–81.

134. George Orwell to F.J. Warburg, 16 May 1949, *Collected Essays, Journalism and Letters*, eds. Sonia Orwell and Ian Angus (1970 edn), Vol. IV, pp. 562–3.

135. Drake, *op. cit.*, p. 227.

136. Joseph Spence, *Observations, Anecdotes and Characters of Books and Men*, ed. James M. Osborn (Oxford, 1966), Vol. I, p. 439.

137. *Letters*, LS to John Blake, 30 September 1758, p. 61.

138. *ibid.*, December 1758, p. 64.

139. *TS*, Vol. I, Ch. XXI.

140. J.S. Fletcher, *A Picturesque History of Yorkshire* (London, 1899), Vol. I, p. 221.

141. *Whiteford Papers*, pp. 230–31.

142. *Letters*, LS *et al.* to the Overseers of Highways for Clifton, 13 June 1757, p. 48.

143. *ibid.*, LS to John Blake, December 1758, p. 65.

144. *Crazy Tales*, p. 3.

145. *ibid.*, p. 2.

146. *Whiteford Papers*, p. 229.

147. William Hutton, *A Trip to Coatham* (London, 1810), p. 151.

148. *Crazy Tales*, p. 5.

149. Cross, p. 130.

150. *Crazy Tales*, p. 4.

151. *Letters*, LS to John Hall-Stevenson, 17 December 1766, p. 290.

152. *ibid.*, 12 August 1762, p. 181.

153. *County Magazine*, November 1786, p. 170.

154. *Whiteford Papers*, p. 231.

155. R.F. Brissenden (1964), p. 107.

156. *SJ*, Vol. II, The Temptation, Paris.

157. *ibid.*

158. *ibid.*

159. *TS*, Vol. II, Ch. XVII.

160. *Letters*, LS to Richard Berenger, ?8 March 1760, p. 99.

161. 1743 Visitational Returns (Borthwick Institute, MS. no. 66).

162. S.L. Ollard and P.C. Walker (1928), pp. i–xxiv.

163. *Boswell for the Defence*, 21 March 1772, eds William K. Wimsatt Jr and Frederick A. Pottle (London, 1960), p. 49.

164. George B. Hill, *Johnsonian Miscellanies* (New York, 1897), Vol. II, p. 429.

165. *Joseph Andrews*, Book II, Ch. II.

166. Bagehot (1965), Vol. II, pp. 296–7.

167. Kuist, p. 550.

168. Lansing van der Heyden Hammond (1948), p. 102.

169. Frank Baker, *William Grimshaw 1708–1763* (London, 1963), p. 51.

170. *ibid.*, p. 112.

171. *TS*, Vol. II, Ch. XVII.

172. Joyce Hemlow, *The History of Fanny Burney* (Oxford, 1958), p. 19.

173. *Letters of Thomas Gray, op. cit.*, Vol. II, p. 147.

174. *Monthly Review*, May 1760, p. 422.

175. See *York Courant*, 4 March 1760.

176. Bagehot, *op. cit.*, p. 283.
177. H.D. Traill (1882), p. 56.
178. *Whitefoord Papers*, p. 231.
179. Kuist, pp. 549–50.
180. *Letters of Thomas Gray, op. cit.*, p. 148.
181. *York Courant*, 27 November 1739.
182. *Letters*, LS to George Whatley, 25 March 1761, p. 134.
183. *TS*, Vol. IV, Ch. XXVI.
184. *Works*, Sermons, Vol. I, p. xlviii.
185. *ibid.*
186. *ibid.*, p. 320.
187. *ibid.*, pp. 320–21.
188. *ibid.*, p. 329.
189. *ibid.*
190. *ibid.*, p. 322.
191. *ibid.*, p. 17.
192. *ibid.*, p. 13.
193. *ibid.*, pp. 67–8.
194. *ibid.*, Letters, Vol. II, p. 269.
195. *ibid.*, p. 278.
196. *ibid.*, p. 279.
197. *ibid.*
198. *TS*, Vol. I, Ch. X.
199. *ibid.*, Ch. XI.
200. *ibid.*, Ch. X.
201. *ibid.*, Ch. XII.
202. *Works*, Sermons, Vol. I, p. 319.
203. *TS*, Vol. I, Ch. X.
204. *Whitefoord Papers*, p. 231.
205. *The Letters of Horace Walpole*, ed. Mrs. Paget Toynbee (Oxford, 1904), Vol. IV, p. 314.
206. *Letters*, LS to Mrs. F., 19 November 1759, p. 84.
207. *ibid.*, p. 148, n. 7.
208. *Works*, Letters, Vol. II, p. 235.
209. *ibid.*
210. *ibid.*, p. 246.

211. *ibid.*, p. 249.
212. *ibid.*, p. 30, letter dated 15 April 1760, as copied out on fly-leaves of a first edition copy of Vols. I and II of Sterne's Sermons.
213. *Boswell's Life of Johnson*, Vol. II, p. 174.
214. *Letters of Lady Mary Wortley Montagu*, Vol. III, p. 90.
215. Johnson, *The Rambler*, no. 4, 31 March 1750.
216. *ibid.*
217. *ibid.*, *The Idler*, no. 59, 2 June 1759.
218. *ibid.*, *Rasselas* (1759), Ch. XLVII.
219. *ibid.*, Ch. XVIII.
220. Kuist, p. 550.
221. *Whitefoord Papers*, p. 229.
222. *TS*, Vol. I, Ch. XVIII.
223. *ibid.*
224. *Letters*, LS to Robert Dodsley, 23 May 1759, pp. 74–5.
225. *ibid.*, LS to —, summer 1759, pp. 75–6.
226. *ibid.*, p. 76.
227. *ibid.*, LS to Robert Dodsley, October 1759, p. 80.
228. *ibid.*, p. 81.
229. John W. Harvey, 'A Lost Link with Laurence Sterne', *Yorkshire Archaeological Journal*, Vol. XLII, 1966, pp. 103–7.
230. *European Magazine*, March 1792, p. 170.
231. *Letters*, LS to Mrs. F., 19 November 1759, p. 84.
232. *ibid.*, LS to Catherine Fourmantel, 1759, p. 82.
233. *ibid.*, LS to David Garrick (via Catherine Fourmantel), 1 January 1760, p. 85.
234. *TS*, Vol. I, Ch. XIV.

PART THREE: 'TRISTRAM IS THE FASHION...'

1760 (pp. 171–89)

1. *Letters*, letter book version of letter to —, summer 1759, pp. 79–80.
2. *ibid.*, LS to Catherine Fourmantel, 1759, p. 83.
3. *ibid.*, enclosure to Fourmantel for Garrick, 1 January 1760, p. 85.
4. *ibid.*, p. 86.
5. *Monthly Review*, December 1759, p. 562.
6. *ibid.*, p. 568.
7. *ibid.*, p. 571.
8. *Letters*, LS to David Garrick, 27 January 1760, p. 86.
9. *ibid.*, pp. 86–7.
10. *York Courant*, 4 March 1760.
11. *Whitefoord Papers*, p. 227.
12. *ibid.*
13. *ibid.*, pp. 227–8.
14. Edmund Gosse, *Life of Gray* (London, 1882), p. 105.
15. *Letters*, LS to Catherine Fourmantel, 8 March 1760, p. 97.
16. *ibid.*, LS to Richard Berenger, 8 March 1760, pp. 99–100.
17. *Whitefoord Papers*, pp. 231–2.
18. *Letters*, LS to Catherine Fourmantel, 8 March 1760, p. 96.
19. *ibid.*, 16–22 March 1760, p. 102.
20. Spence, *op. cit.*, Vol. I, p. 217.
21. *Letters*, LS to David Garrick, 6 March 1760, p. 93.
22. Warburton to Garrick, 7 March 1760, *Private Correspondence of David Garrick* (London, 1831), Vol. I, p. 115.
23. *Letters from the Reverend Dr. Warburton to the Hon. Charles Yorke* (London, 1812), p. 89.
24. *Boswell's Life of Johnson, op. cit.*, Vol. II, p. 222.

25. *Letters of Thomas Gray, op. cit.*, Vol. II, p. 137.
26. *Letters of Horace Walpole*, Vol. IV, p. 369.
27. *Letters*, LS to Eliza Draper, March 1767, p. 305.
28. Frederick A. Pottle (1925), p. 308.
29. *TS*, Vol. VII, Ch. XXXIII.
30. *The London Chronicle*, 3–6 May 1760; *Works*, Letters, Vol. I, p. 34.
31. *ibid.*, p. 46.
32. *Letters*, LS to Stephen Croft, ?1 May 1760, p. 107.
33. *The Clock-Maker's Outcry against Tristram Shandy* (London, 1760).
34. *Gentleman's Magazine*, Vol. XXX, 1760, p. 243.
35. *Letters*, LS to Catherine Fourmantel, 1 April 1760, p. 104.
36. *ibid.*, April 1760, pp. 105–6.
37. *ibid.*, May 1760, pp. 108–9.
38. *ibid.*, p. 109.
39. *Public Ledger*, 17 September 1760.
40. *Whitefoord Papers*, p. 224.
41. *Letters*, LS to 'My Witty Widow, Mrs F', 3 August 1760, p. 120.
42. *ibid.*
43. *ibid.*, LS to Rev. Robert Brown, 9 September 1760, p. 122.
44. *ibid.*, Warburton to LS, 15 June 1760, p. 113.
45. *ibid.*, LS to Warburton, 19 June 1760, p. 115.
46. *ibid.*, p. 116.
47. *TS*, Vol. III, Ch. II.
48. *ibid.*, Vol. IV, Ch. VII.
49. *ibid.*, Vol. III, Ch. IV.
50. *ibid.*, Vol. IV, Ch. XXXII.

1761 (190–201)

1. *Letters*, LS to John Hall-Stevenson, December 1760, p. 124.
2. *ibid.*, Warburton to LS, 15 June 1760, p. 113.
3. *ibid.*, LS to Warburton, 19 June 1760, p. 115.
4. *ibid.*
5. *York Courant*, 7 October 1760.
6. *Letters*, LS to Stephen Croft, 25 December 1760, p. 126.
7. *ibid.*
8. *ibid.*, LS to Stephen Croft, 17 February 1761, pp. 129–30.
9. *London Magazine*, January 1761.
10. *Monthly Review*, February 1761, p. 103.
11. *Critical Review*, April 1761, p. 314.
12. *Letters of Horace Walpole*, Vol. V, p. 32.
13. *Correspondence of Richard Hurd and William Mason* (Cambridge, 1932), p. 53.
14. Thomas Newton to John Dealtry, 26 February 1761, see Curtis (1961), p. 501.
15. Samuel Richardson to Bishop Hildesley, 1761, *Correspondence*, Vol. V, p. 146.
16. *ibid.*
17. *Letters*, LS to Stephen Croft, January 1761, p. 128.
18. Jonas Dennis, *A Key to the Regalia* (London, 1820), pp. 102–3n.
19. *Letters*, LS to Stephen Croft, 25 December 1760, p. 126.
20. *ibid.*
21. *Political Journal of George Bubb Dodington*, eds. John Carswell and L. A. Dralle (Oxford, 1965), 4 October 1760, p. 392.
22. *Letters*, LS to Stephen Croft, 17 February 1761, p. 129.
23. *ibid.*
24. *ibid.*, 17 March 1761, p. 132.
25. *Mrs. Montagu, 'Queen of the Blues'*, *op. cit.*, Vol. I, p. 188.
26. *Letters*, LS to Mrs. Vesey, 20 June 1761, p. 137.
27. *ibid.*, p. 138.
28. *ibid.*
29. *Mrs. Montagu, 'Queen of the Blues'*, *op. cit.*, Vol. I, p. 187.
30. *Lloyd's Evening Post*, 1–4 May 1761, p. 419.
31. *Letters*, LS to John Hall-Stevenson, June 1761, p. 139.
32. *ibid.*
33. Hist. MSS. Commission, *Report on MSS. in Various Collections* (London, 1903), Vol. II, p. 188.
34. *ibid.*, p. 189.
35. *Letters*, LS to Lady D—, 1 January 1762, p. 150.
36. Climenson, *op. cit.*, Vol. II, pp. 176–7.
37. *Mrs. Montagu, 'Queen of the Blues'*, *op. cit.*, Vol. I, p. 188.
38. *Letters*, LS to Mrs. Sterne, 28 December 1761, pp. 146–8.
39. *ibid.*, LS to David Garrick, 24 December 1761, p. 146.

1762 (pp. 202–212).

1. *SJ*, Vol. I, The Wig, Paris.
2. *Letters*, LS to Lady D—, 1 January 1762, p. 150.
3. *ibid.*
4. *Letters of Lady Mary Wortley Montagu*, Vol. III, p. 285.
5. Rousseau, *The Confessions* (1781) (Harmondsworth, 1955), Book XI, 1761, p. 522.
6. Arthur Cash (1965).
7. *Letters*, LS to David Garrick, 31 January 1762, p. 151.
8. Cash (1965).
9. *Letters*, LS to Garrick, 31 January 1761, p. 151.
10. *ibid.*, LS to Elizabeth Sterne, 17 March 1762, p. 155.
11. Cash (1965).

12. Dominique-Joseph Garat (1820),Vol. II, p. 148.

13. *ibid.*, p. 149.

14. Louis Dutens, *Memoirs of a Traveller* (London, 1806), Vol. II, p. 148.

15. *Letters*, LS to David Garrick, 19 March 1762, p. 157.

16. *ibid.*

17. *SJ*, Vol. II, The Passport, Versailles.

18. *Letters*, LS to Elizabeth Sterne, 17 March 1762, p. 155.

19. *ibid.*, LS to Lord Fauconberg, 10 April 1762, p. 159.

20. *ibid.*, LS to Elizabeth Sterne, 17 March 1762, p. 155.

21. *ibid.*, LS to Lord Fauconberg, 10 April 1762, p. 159.

22. *ibid.*, p. 160.

23. *ibid.*, LS to David Garrick, 31 January 1762, p. 152.

24. *ibid.*, 19 March 1762, p. 157.

25. *ibid.*, 19 April 1762, p. 162.

26. *ibid.*, LS to Elizabeth Sterne, 17 March 1762, p. 154.

27. *ibid.*, p. 155.

28. Cash (1965).

29. *The Letters of Horace Walpole*, Vol. VI, p. 301.

30. J.-B. Tollot to John Hall-Stevenson, 4 April 1762, *Seven Letters written by Sterne and his Friends* (London, 1844), p. 22.

31. Cash (1965).

32. *Letters*, LS to Elizabeth Sterne, 17 March 1762, p. 154.

33. *ibid.*, LS to David Garrick, 19 April 1762, p. 163.

34. *ibid.*, LS to Robert Drummond, 10 May 1762, p. 164.

35. *ibid.*, LS to Elizabeth Sterne, 31 May 1762, p. 171.

36. *ibid.*, 7 June 1762, p. 172.

37. *ibid.*, 16 May 1762, p. 170.

38. *ibid.*, 14 June 1762, p. 174.

39. *ibid.*, 17 June 1762, p. 176.

40. *ibid.*, LS to John Hall-Stevenson, 12 August 1762, p. 180.

41. *ibid.*, LS to Lady D—, 9 July 1762, p. 179.

42. *ibid.*

43. *ibid.*, LS to Elizabeth Sterne, 7 June 1762, p. 172.

Partie de Campagne (pp. 213–25)

1. *TS*, Vol. VII, Ch. IV.

2. *Letters*, LS to Thomas Becket, 16 May 1762, p. 169.

3. *ibid.*, LS to John Hall-Stevenson, 12 August 1762, p. 181.

4. *ibid.*

5. *ibid.*, LS to Robert Foley, 14 August 1762, pp. 182–3.

6. *TS*, Vol. VII, Ch. XIX.

7. *ibid.*, Ch. VIII.

8. *ibid.*

9. *ibid.*

10. *ibid.*, Ch. XL.

11. *ibid.*, Ch. XXXII.

12. *ibid.*

13. *ibid.*, Ch. XXVII.

14. *ibid.*, Ch. XXIX.

15. *ibid.*, Ch. XLII.

16. *ibid.*, Ch. XLIII.

17. *ibid.*

18. *Letters*, LS to Robert Foley, 14 August 1762, p. 183.

19. *ibid.*

20. *ibid.*, LS to John Hall-Stevenson, 12 August 1762, p. 181.

21. *ibid.*, 19 October 1762, p. 187.

22. *ibid.*, p. 192 n. 3.

23. *ibid.*, LS to John Hall-Stevenson, 19 October 1762, p. 186.

24. *ibid.*

25. *ibid.*, p. 185.

26. *ibid.*, pp. 185–6.

27. *ibid.*, p. 186.

28. *ibid.*, LS to Robert Foley, 8 December 1762, p. 190.

29. *ibid.*, p. 189.

30. *ibid.*, LS to Thomas Becket, 12 March 1763, p. 191.
31. Smollett, *Works, Travels through France and Italy* (London, 1900), p. 128.
32. LS to John Mill, 2 March 1763, see Archibald B. Shepperson (1954), pp. 57–8.
33. LS to John Mill, 5 March 1763, Shepperson, p. 60.
34. *ibid.*, 2 March 1763, Shepperson, p. 57.
35. *ibid.*, 5 March 1763, Shepperson, p. 60.
36. *ibid.*
37. *ibid.*
38. LS to Richard Oswald, 18 March 1763, Shepperson, *op. cit.*, p. 63.
39. *Letters*, LS to Robert Foley, 18 April 1763, p. 193.
40. *ibid.*, 12 June 1763, p. 198.
41. *ibid.*, LS to John Mill, 24 November 1763, p. 205.
42. Smollett, *op. cit.*, pp. 113–14.
43. *ibid.*, pp. 114–15.
44. *SJ*, Vol. I, In the Street, Calais.
45. Smollett, *op. cit.*, p. 106.
46. *ibid.*, p. 112.
47. *Letters*, LS to John Mill, 24 November 1763, p. 204.
48. *ibid.*, LS to Robert Foley, 5 January 1764, p. 208.
49. *ibid.*, 20 January 1764, p. 209.
50. *ibid.*, LS to Mrs. F., 1 February 1764, p. 211.

1764 (pp. 226–36)
1. *The Letters of Horace Walpole*, Vol. VI, p. 298.
2. J.Y.T. Greig, *David Hume* (London, 1931), p. 304.
3. *Letters*, LS to William Combe, July 1764, p. 219.
4. *ibid.*

5. *ibid.*
6. *ibid.*
7. *Works*, Sermons, Vol. I, p. 270.
8. *ibid.*, p. 277.
9. *ibid.*, pp. 278–9.
10. *Letters*, LS to William Combe, July 1764, p. 218.
11. *ibid.*
12. *Memoires et Correspondance de Mme d'Epinay* (Paris, 1817), Vol. III, p. 284.
13. BM, Add. MSS. 30878, f. 44.
14. Brian Connell, *Portrait of a Whig Peer* (London, 1957), p. 43.
15. *Letters*, LS to John Hall-Stevenson, 19 May 1764, p. 213.
16. *ibid.*
17. *ibid.*, LS to Lydia Sterne, 15 May 1764, p. 212.
18. *ibid.*, LS to John Hall-Stevenson, 19 May 1764, pp. 213, 214.
19. *ibid.*, LS to Mrs. Montagu, June 1764, p. 216.
20. *Archbishop Drummond's Visitational Returns, 1764* (Borthwick Institute, MS. no. 63)
21. *ibid.*
22. *Letters*, LS to Robert Drummond, 10 May 1762, p. 164.
23. Kilner to Robert Drummond, 6 September 1762, Bishopthorpe MSS, Bundle 5, no. 320.
24. *Letters*, LS to Robert Drummond, 30 October 1764, p. 229.
25. *ibid.*
26. *Drummond, op. cit.*
27. *Letters*, LS to Robert Drummond, 30 October 1764, p. 229.
28. *ibid.*, LS to Sarah Tuting, 27 August 1764, pp. 223–4.
29. *ibid.*, p. 224.
30. *ibid.*
31. *ibid.*, LS to John Hall-Stevenson, 4 September 1764, p. 225.
32. *ibid.*

33. *ibid.*, 27 September 1764, p. 226.

34. *ibid.*, LS to Robert Foley, 29 September 1764, p. 228.

35. *ibid.*

36. *TS*, Vol. VIII, Ch. VI.

37. *Letters*, LS to Robert Foley, 11 November 1764, p. 231.

38. *ibid.*, LS to John Hall-Stevenson, 13 November 1764, p. 233.

39. *TS*, Vol. VIII, Ch. VI.

40. *Letters*, LS to Robert Foley, 16 November 1764, p. 234.

1765 (pp. 237–45).

1. *Letters*, LS to David Garrick, 16 March 1765, p. 235.

2. *Monthly Review*, Vol. XXXII, 1765, pp. 138–9.

3. *Letters*, LS to Garrick, 16 March 1765, p. 235.

4. *ibid.*

5. R.B. Peake, *Memoirs of the Colman Family* (London, 1841), Vol. I, pp. 101–2.

6. *Letters*, LS to Garrick, 6 April 1765, p. 236.

7. *ibid.*, p. 237.

8. *ibid.*

9. Mrs. Montagu, '*Queen of the Blues*', *op. cit.*, Vol. I, p. 188.

10. *ibid.*

11. *ibid.*, p. 189.

12. *Letters*, LS to William Combe, 11 June 1765, p. 250.

13. Mrs. Montagu, '*Queen of the Blues*', *op. cit.*, Vol. I, p. 189.

14. *Letters*, LS to Mrs. F., April 1765, p. 240.

15. *ibid.*

16. *ibid.*, p. 241.

17. *ibid.*, LS to Lady Warkworth, 23 April 1765, p. 242.

18. *ibid.*, p. 243.

19. *ibid.*, pp. 242–3.

20. *ibid.*, LS to John Wodehouse, 23 August 1765, p. 256.

21. *York Courant*, 6 August 1765; *London Chronicle*, 8–10 August 1765.

22. *Letters*, LS to Wodehouse, 23 August 1765, p. 256.

23. *ibid.*

24. *ibid.*, 20 September 1765, p. 258.

25. *ibid.*, LS to Thomas Hesilrige, 5 July 1765, p. 253.

26. *Letters of Horace Walpole*, Vol. VI, p. 333.

27. Alexander Stephens, *Memoirs of John Horne Tooke* (London, 1813), Vol. I, p. 77.

28. *Letters*, LS to Isaac Panchaud, 7 November 1765, p. 262.

29. *ibid.*, 15 November 1765, p. 263.

30. Connell, *op. cit.*, p. 43.

31. Samuel Sharp, *Letters from Italy* (London, 1767), p. 289.

32. *SJ*, Vol. I, In the Street, Calais.

33. Sharp, *op. cit.*, p. 290.

34. *ibid.*, p. 279.

35. *Letters of Horace Walpole*, Vol. VI, pp. 305–6.

36. *Letters*, LS to Isaac Panchaud, 28 November 1765, p. 265.

37. *ibid.*, 18 December 1765, p. 266.

38. Sharp, *op. cit.*, p. 43.

39. *SJ*, Vol. I, The Translation, Paris.

1766 (pp. 246–54)

1. *Letters*, LS to Isaac Panchaud, 18 December 1765, p. 266.

2. Sharp, *op. cit.*, p. 168.

3. *Letters*, LS to John Hall-Stevenson, 5 February 1766, p. 269.

4. *ibid.*, LS to Lydia Sterne, 3 February 1766, p. 267.

5. *ibid.*, LS to Hall-Stevenson, 5 February 1766, p. 269.

6. *ibid.*, LS to Panchaud, 14 February 1766, p. 272.

7. *ibid.*, LS to Hall-Stevenson, 5 February 1766, p. 269.

8. Sharp, *op. cit.*, p. 78.

9. *ibid.*, p. 96.

10. *Letters*, LS to Hall-Stevenson, 5 February 1766, p. 269.

11. Sharp, *op. cit.*, p. 172.

12. *ibid.*, p. 168.

13. *SJ*, Vol. I, Preface, In the Desobligeant.

14. *Letters*, LS to Hon. William Hamilton, 17 March 1766, p. 273.

15. *ibid.*, p. 268, n. 4.

16. Ferdinando Galiani, *Correspondance* (Paris, 1881), Vol. II, p. 328.

17. *Letters*, LS to Hamilton, 17 March 1766, p. 273.

18. *ibid.*, LS to Hall-Stevenson, 24 May 1766, p. 277.

19. *ibid.*

20. *ibid.*, LS to Miss Trist, 24 May 1766, p. 276.

21. *ibid.*, LS to Hall-Stevenson, 24 May 1766, p. 277.

22. *ibid.*, 15 July 1766, p. 281.

23. *ibid.*, Ignatius Sancho to LS, 21 July 1766, p. 282.

24. *ibid.*

25. *ibid.*, p. 283.

26. *ibid.*, LS to Sancho, 27 July 1766, p. 286.

27. *ibid.*

28. *ibid.*, pp. 285–6.

29. *TS*, Vol. IX, Ch. VI.

30. *Letters*, LS to Edward Stanley, 23 July 1766, p. 284.

31. *ibid.*, LS to William Combe, 7–9 January 1767, p. 294.

32. *ibid.*, LS to Panchaud, 21 September 1766, p. 288.

33. *ibid.*, LS to Robert Foley, 25 October 1766, p. 289.

34. *ibid.*, LS to Panchaud, 25 November 1766, p. 290.

35. *TS*, Vol. IX, Ch. VIII.

1767–8 (pp. 255–77)

1. *Letters*, LS to Lord Fauconberg, 6 January 1767, p. 292.

2. *ibid.*, 9 January 1767, p. 295.

3. *ibid.*, 16 January 1767, pp. 296–7.

4. *ibid.*, p. 296.

5. *Monthly Review*, Vol. XXXVI, 1767, p. 102.

6. *ibid.*, p. 93.

7. *Letters*, LS to Eliza Draper, January 1767, p. 298.

8. *ibid.*

9. *ibid.*, March 1767, pp. 312–13.

10. Arnold Wright and William Lutley Sclater (1922), p. 12.

11. *ibid.*, p. 58.

12. *A Series of Genuine Letters, between Henry and Frances* (1786), Vol. V, pp. 199–200.

13. *Letters*, LS to Eliza Draper, February 1767, p. 299.

14. *ibid.*, LS to Lydia Sterne, 23 February 1767, p. 301.

15. *ibid.*, LS to Eliza Draper, March 1767, pp. 304, 305.

16. *ibid.*, p. 305.

17. *ibid.*, p. 306.

18. *ibid.*, LS to Lydia Sterne, 9 March 1767, pp. 307–8.

19. *ibid.*, p. 307.

20. *ibid.*, LS to Eliza Draper, March 1767, pp. 309–10.

21. *ibid.*, p. 310.

22. *ibid.*, pp. 315–16.

23. *ibid.*, pp. 317, 319.

24. *ibid.*, 30 March 1767, p. 320.

25. *ibid.*, p. 321.

26. *ibid.*, *JE*, 15 April 1767, p. 323.

27. *ibid.*, 17 April 1767, p. 324.

28. *ibid.*, 19 April 1767, pp. 324–5.
29. *ibid.*, 21 April 1767, p. 326.
30. *ibid.*, 22 April 1767, p. 326.
31. *ibid.*, 24 April 1767, p. 329.
32. *ibid.*
33. *ibid.*, pp. 329–30.
34. *ibid.*, 31 May 1767, p. 347.
35. *ibid.*, 26 April 1767, p. 332.
36. *ibid.*, 27 April 1767, p. 334.
37. *ibid.*, 28 April 1767, p. 334.
38. *ibid.*, 1 May 1767, p. 335.
39. *ibid.*, 2 May 1767, p. 336.
40. *ibid.*, 3 May 1767, p. 337.
41. *ibid.*, 7 May 1767, p. 338.
42. *ibid.*, LS to John Hall-Stevenson, 25 May 1767, p. 346.
43. *ibid.*, *JE*, 2 June 1767, p. 347.
44. *ibid.*
45. *ibid.*, 3 June 1767, p. 350.
46. *ibid.*, 1 November 1767, p. 399.
47. Earl R. Wasserman (1951), LS to Richard Davenport, 9 June 1767, p. 74.
48. *ibid.*
49. *ibid.*
50. *ibid.*, *JE*, 7 June 1767, p. 352.
51. *ibid.*, 12 June 1767, p. 356.
52. *ibid.*
53. *ibid.*, LS to Countess******/ Eliza Draper, 18 June 1767, p. 360.
54. *ibid.*
55. William Combe, *Letters Supposed to have been Written by Yorick to Eliza*, in 'Laurence Sterne', *Second Journal to Eliza* (London, 1929), ed. Margaret R.B. Shaw, p. 27.
56. *ibid.*
57. *Letters*, *JE*, 28 June 1767, p. 366.
58. *ibid.*, 9 July 1767, p. 377.
59. *ibid.*, 27 July 1767, p. 381.
60. *ibid.*, LS to Hall-Stevenson, 11 August 1767, p. 390.
61. *The Triumvirate* (London, 1764), Vol. I, p. xiv.
62. *ibid.*, p. xvi.
63. *A Series of Genuine Letters between Henry and Frances*, Vol. V, p. 83.
64. *ibid.*, p. 87.
65. *ibid.*, p. 83.
66. *ibid.*, p. 87.
67. *ibid.*, p. 199.
68. *Letters*, p. 362.
69. *ibid.*, LS to Hannah, 12 September 1767, p. 393.
70. *ibid.*, LS to Sir William Stanhope, 19 September 1767, p. 394.
71. *ibid.*
72. *ibid.*, LS to Stanhope, 27 September 1767, pp. 395–6.
73. *ibid.*, LS to Mr. and Mrs. James, 3 October 1767, p. 398.
74. *ibid.*, LS to A. L—e, 7 December 1767, p. 407.
75. *ibid.*, LS to Mr. and Mrs. James, 28 December 1767, p. 409.
76. *Letters of Horace Walpole*, Vol. VII, p. 157.
77. *Letters*, LS to Mr. and Mrs. James, 3 January 1768, p. 409.
78. *ibid.*, 18 February 1768, p. 414.
79. *ibid.*, 3 January 1768, p. 409.
80. *ibid.*, LS to Earl of —, 28 November 1767, pp. 402–3.
81. *ibid.*, LS to Dr. John Eustace, 9 February 1768, p. 411.
82. *Letters of Horace Walpole*, Vol. VII, p. 175.
83. *Monthly Review*, Vol. XXXVIII, 1768, p. 174.
84. *Letters*, LS to Lydia Sterne, March 1768, p. 417.
85. *ibid.*, LS to Mrs. Montagu, February 1768, p. 414.
86. *ibid.*, March 1768, p. 416.
87. *ibid.*, LS to Lydia Sterne, March 1768, p. 417.

88. *Monthly Repository of Theology and General Literature*, Vol. III, 1808, p. 12.

89. *Letters of Horace Walpole*, Vol. VII, p. 175.

90. *Letters*, LS to Mrs. James, 15 March 1768, p. 418.

91. *ibid.*, LS to Lydia Sterne, March 1768, p. 417.

92. *ibid.*, LS to Mrs. James, 15 March 1768, p. 419.

93. *TS*, Vol. IX, Ch. XXXIII.

94. *ibid.*, Vol VI, Ch. X.

95. Macdonald, *op. cit.*, pp. 91–2.

EPILOGUE: THE FEW COLD OFFICES (pp. 278–92)

1. *TS*, Vol. VII, Ch. XII.

2. *Whitefoord Papers*, p. 230.

3. *St James's Chronicle*, 24–6 November 1767.

4. James Northcote, *Memoirs of Sir Joshua Reynolds* (London, 1818), Vol. I, p. 105.

5. John Hall-Stevenson, *Yorick's Sentimental Journey Continued* (London, 1769), Preface.

6. *Public Advertiser*, 24 March 1769.

7. Alexander Macalister, *History of the Study of Anatomy in Cambridge* (Cambridge, 1891), pp. 22–3.

8. Dorothy Tyler, 'A Lodging in the Bayswater Road', *Atlantic Monthly*, Vol. CLV, 1935, p. 322.

9. *The Times*, 4 June 1968.

10. *ibid.*, 8 June 1968.

11. *ibid.*, 16 June 1968.

12. *York Courant*, 12 April 1768.

13. *Letters*, p. 433.

14. *ibid.*, p. 435.

15. *ibid.*, p. 448.

16. *ibid.*, p. 439.

17. *ibid.*, p. 433.

18. *ibid.*, p. 436.

19. Sutton, parish records.

20. *Letters*, pp. 436–7.

21. *ibid.*, p. 438.

22. *ibid.*, pp. 437–8.

23. *ibid.*, p. 443.

24. *ibid.*, p. 447.

25. *ibid.*, p. 446.

26. *ibid.*

27. *ibid.*, p. 450.

28. *ibid.*, p. 454.

29. *ibid.*, p. 455.

30. *ibid.*, p. 456.

31. *ibid.*

32. *ibid.*

33. *ibid.*, p. 457.

34. *ibid.*

35. *ibid.*, p. 458.

36. *Inventaire-Sommaire des Archives Communales d'Albi* (Paris, 1869), ed. Emile Jolibois, p. 49.

37. *ibid.*

38. *Letters*, pp. 463–4.

39. *ibid.*, p. 460.

40. *ibid.*, p. 464.

41. *ibid.*, p. 459.

42. *ibid.*, p. 461.

INDEX